MAKE AMERICA GREAT AGAIN BASEBALL CAP
SIGNED AND INSCRIBED “HORNY” BY STORMY DANIELS

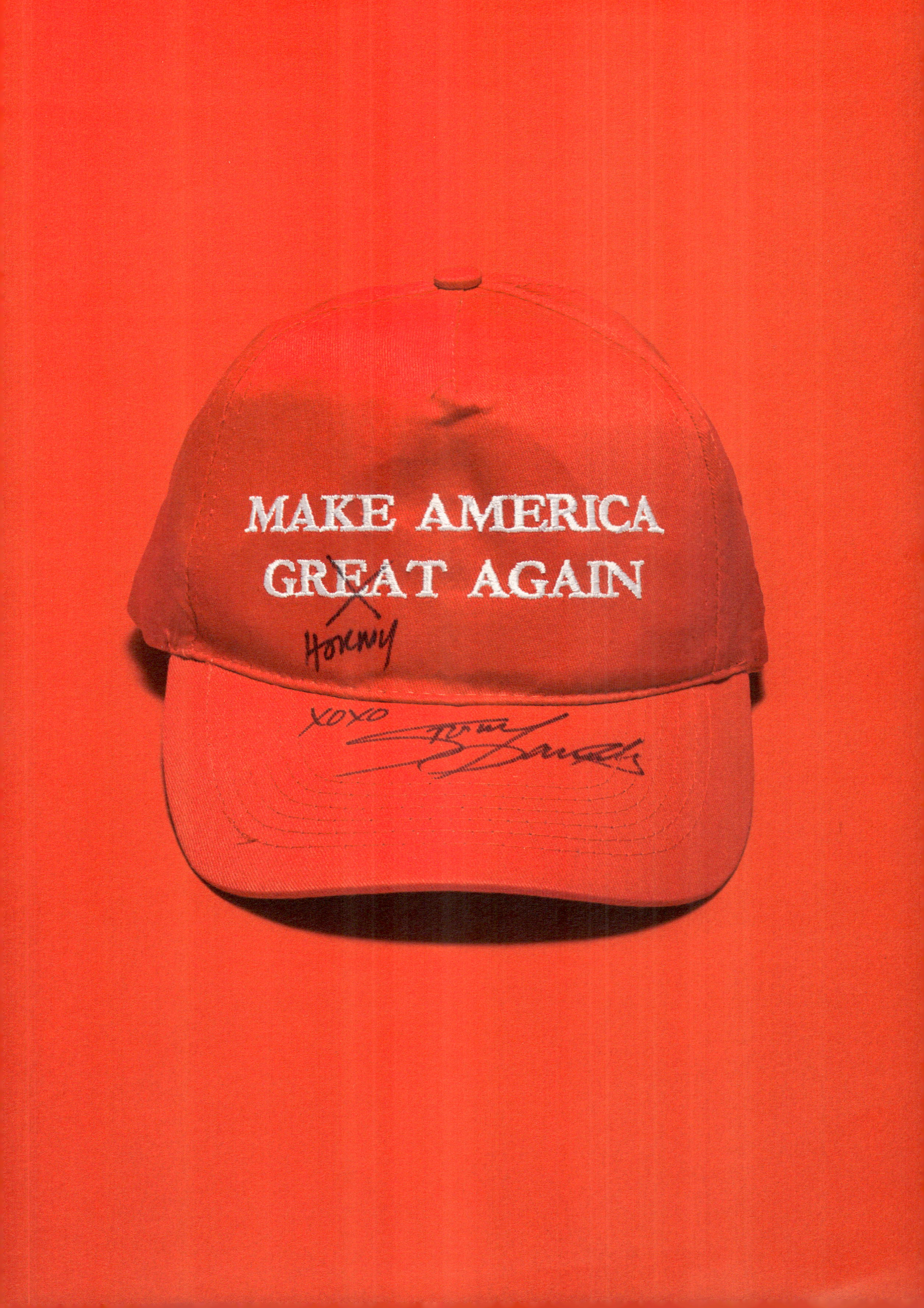

MAKE AMERICA GREAT AGAIN CAMOUFLAGE BASEBALL CAP

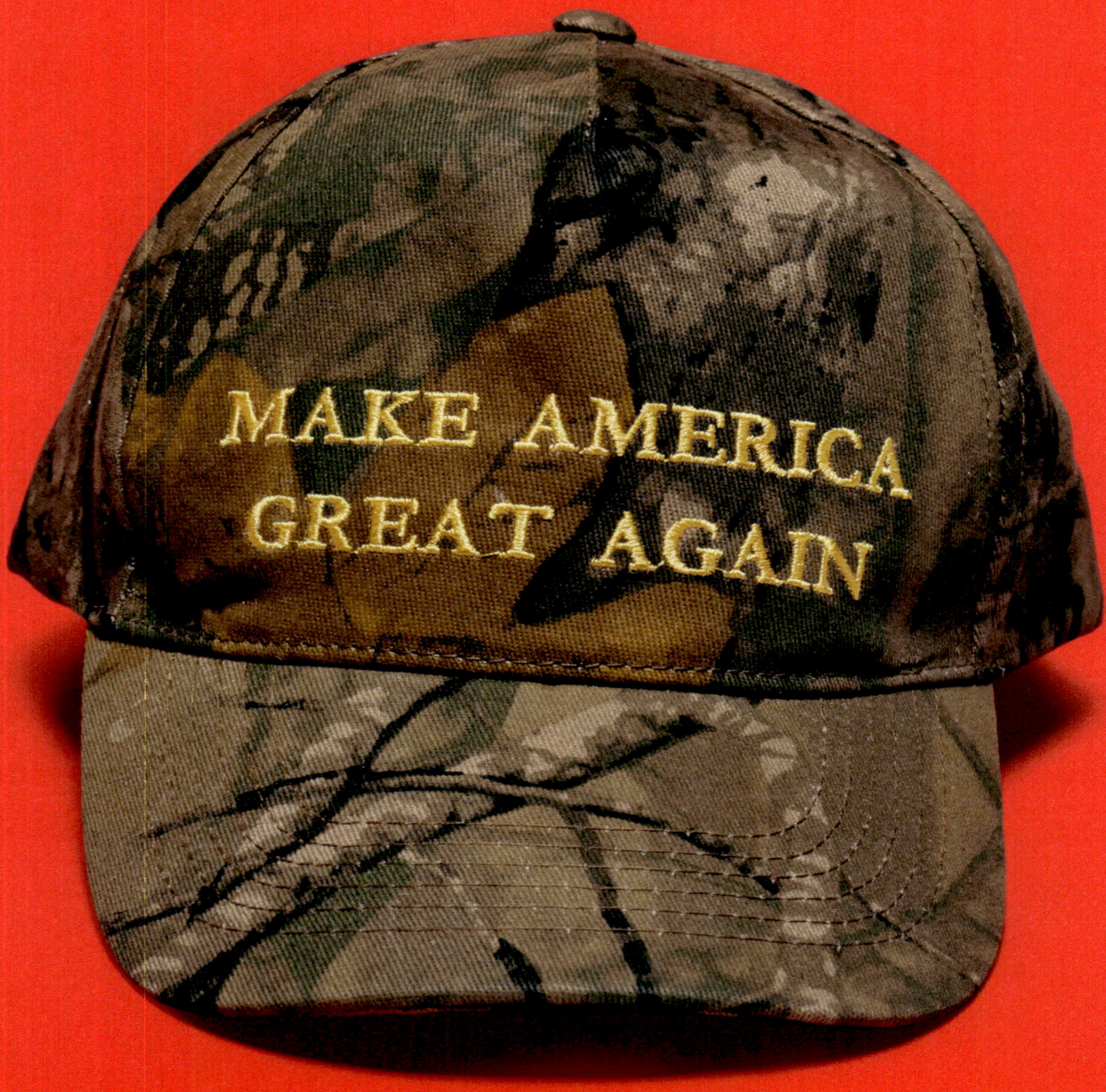

SIGNED PHOTOGRAPH OF DONALD TRUMP AT MILITARY ACADEMY, 1964

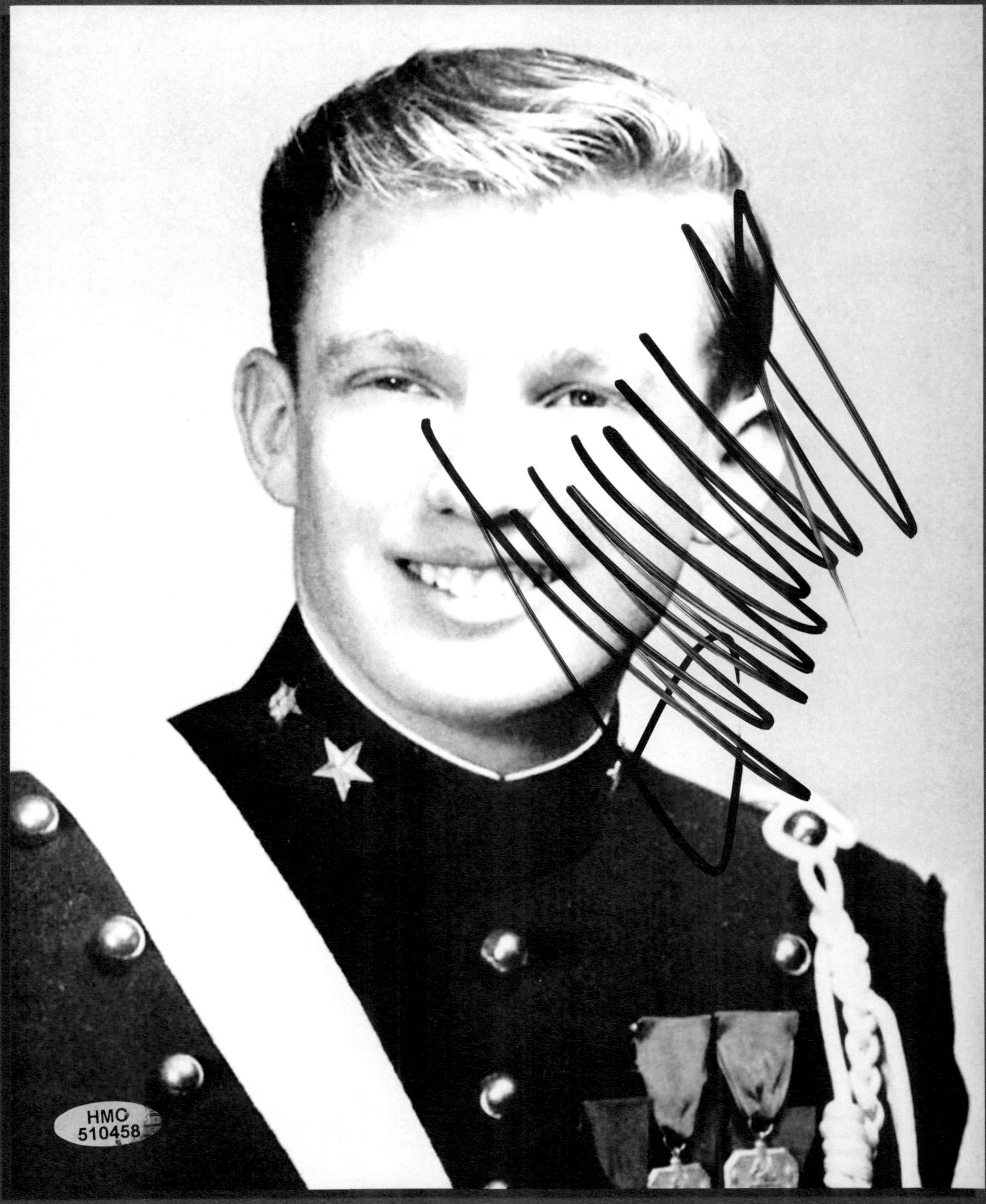

VOTE TRUMP CAMPAIGN CARD, 2016
SIGNED DONALD TRUMP

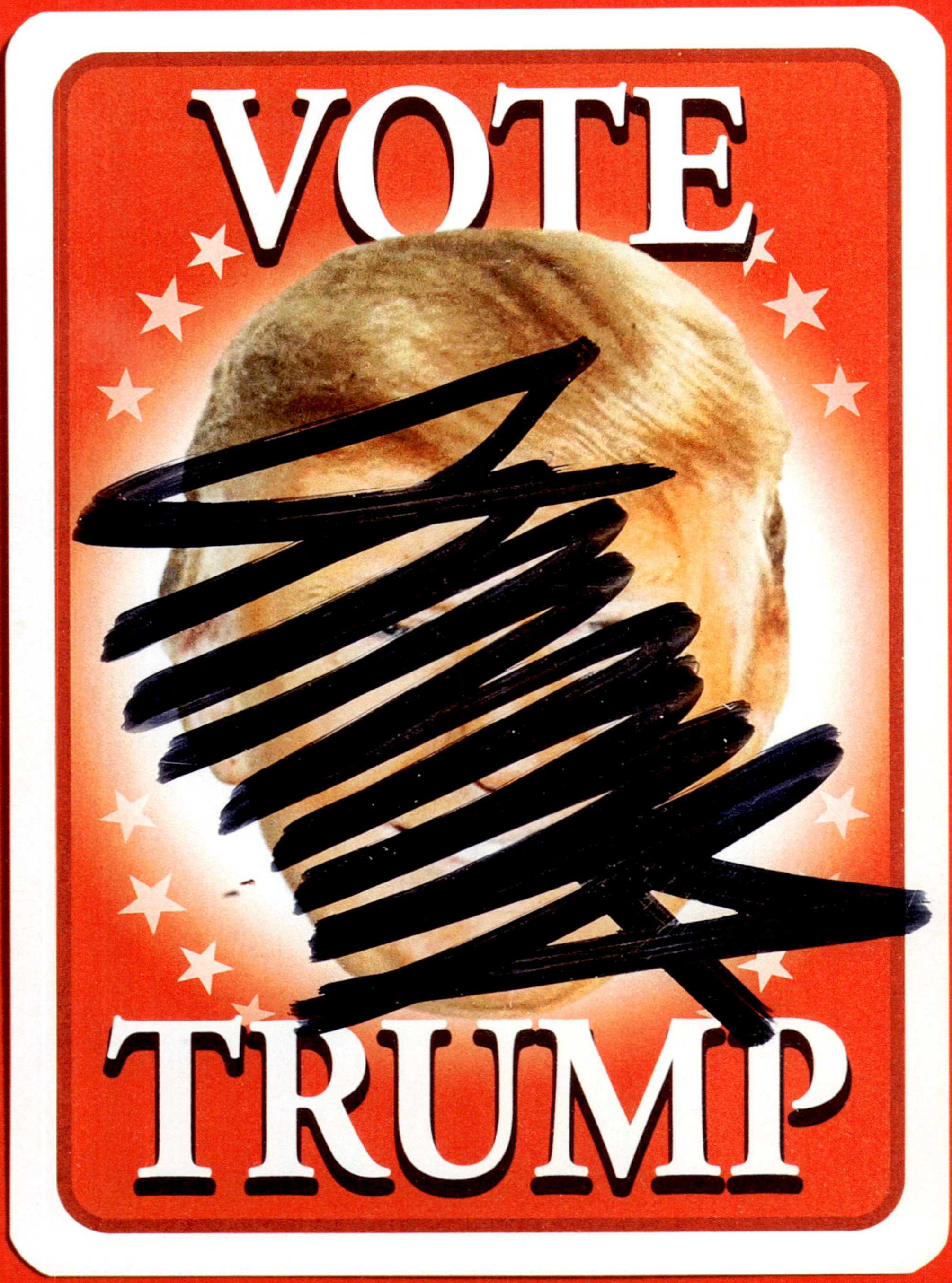

THE GAME: ALL THINGS TRUMP

ANDRES SERRANO

EDITED BY
BECKY HAGHPANAH-SHIRWAN &
STEPHEN STAPLETON

Booth-Clibborn Editions

a/political

DONALD TRUMP LIBERTY GOLD COIN, 2017

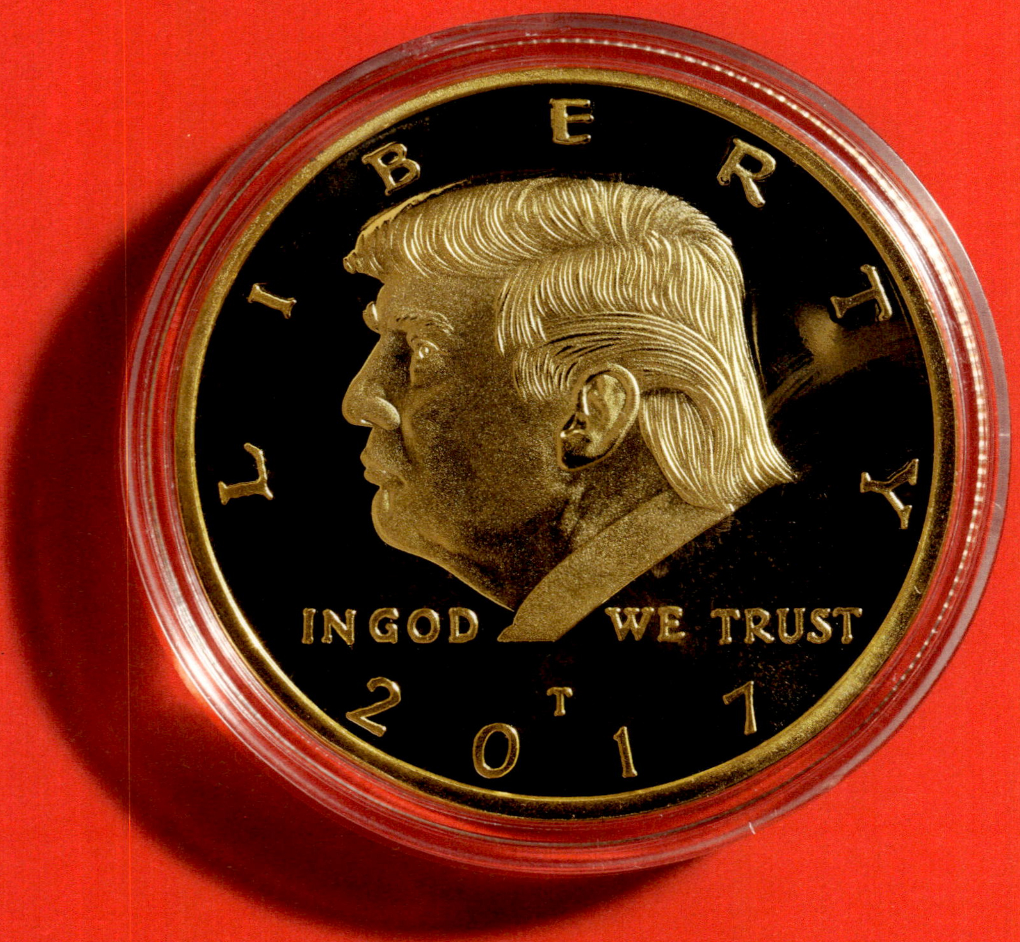

PUTTING THE 45TH PRESIDENT OF
THE UNITED STATES OF AMERICA IN HIS
FRAME, ANDRES SERRANO PRESENTS
A LANDSCAPE OF A COMPLICATED AMERICA
AND A PHENOMENON OF OUR TIME.

THE GAME: ALL THINGS TRUMP IS AN
A/POLITICAL PROJECT FIRST PRESENTED
IN APRIL 2019 AT ARTX – A FORMER
ICONIC NIGHTCLUB IN MANHATTAN'S
MEATPACKING DISTRICT. IT FEATURED
OVER 1,000 TRUMP-SIGNED AND BRANDED
OBJECTS, ALONGSIDE A SOUNDTRACK
OF CLASSIC ROCK AND POP SONGS.
A TV COMMERCIAL DIRECTED BY
SERRANO RAN DURING PRIME TIME
ON CNN, HANNITY ON FOX NEWS AND
THE RACHEL MADDOW SHOW ON MSNBC.

THE COLLECTION CONTINUES TO EVOLVE.

A/POLITICAL EXPLORES RADICAL KNOWLEDGE
THROUGH THE PRINCIPLE OF CULTURAL TERROR,
PLATFORMING VOICES THAT UNDERMINE
THE DOMINANT NARRATIVES OF OUR TIME.
THE COLLECTIVE COLLABORATES WITH ARTISTS
AND AGITATORS TO PRODUCE PROJECTS PREVIOUSLY
THOUGHT UNREALIZABLE DUE TO THEIR
SUBJECT MATTER, SCALE AND COMPLEXITY.

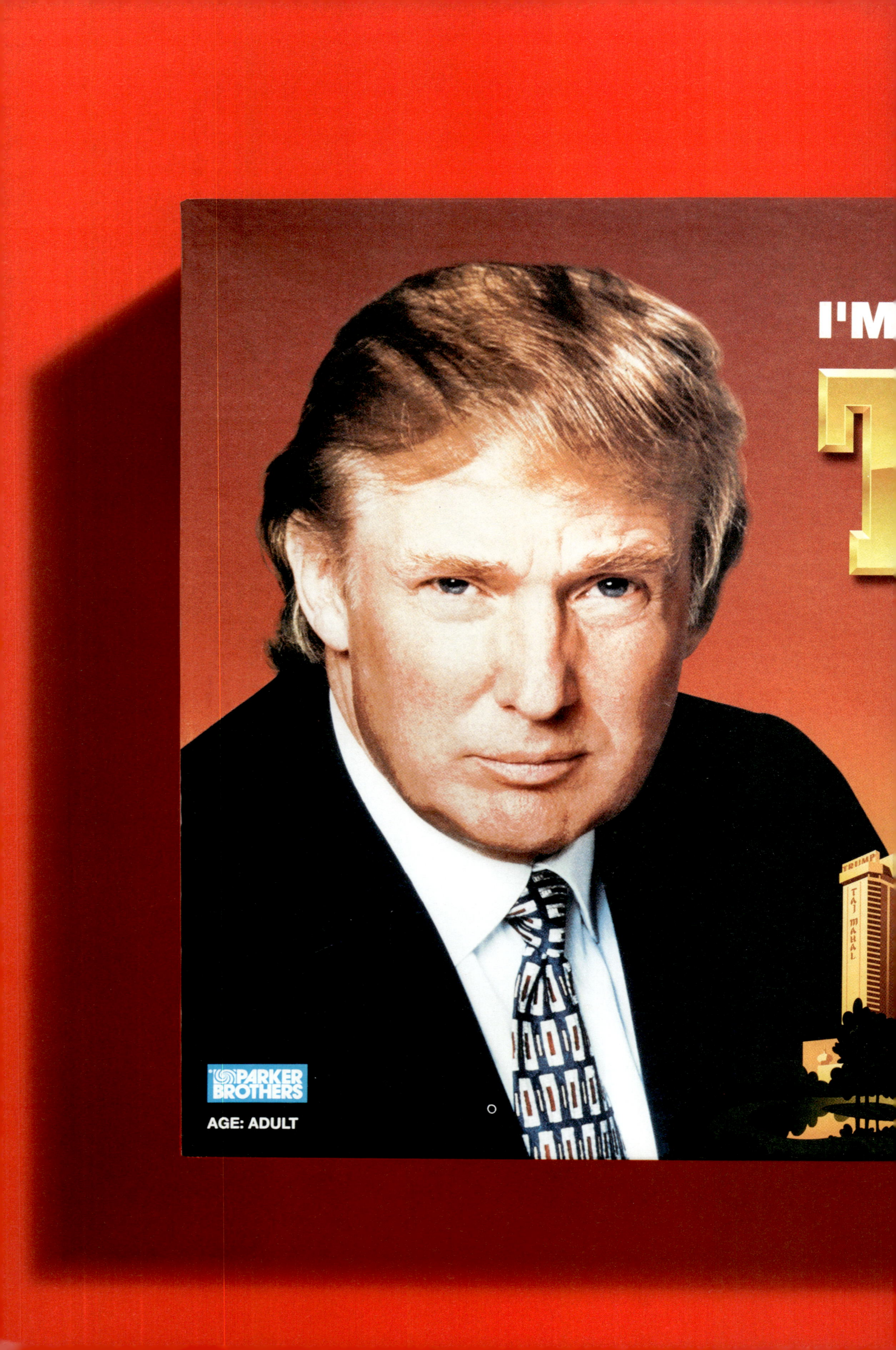
I'M
TRUMP
TAJ MAHAL
PARKER BROTHERS
AGE: ADULT

TRUMP: THE GAME
REISSUED PARKER BROTHERS BOARD GAME, 2004

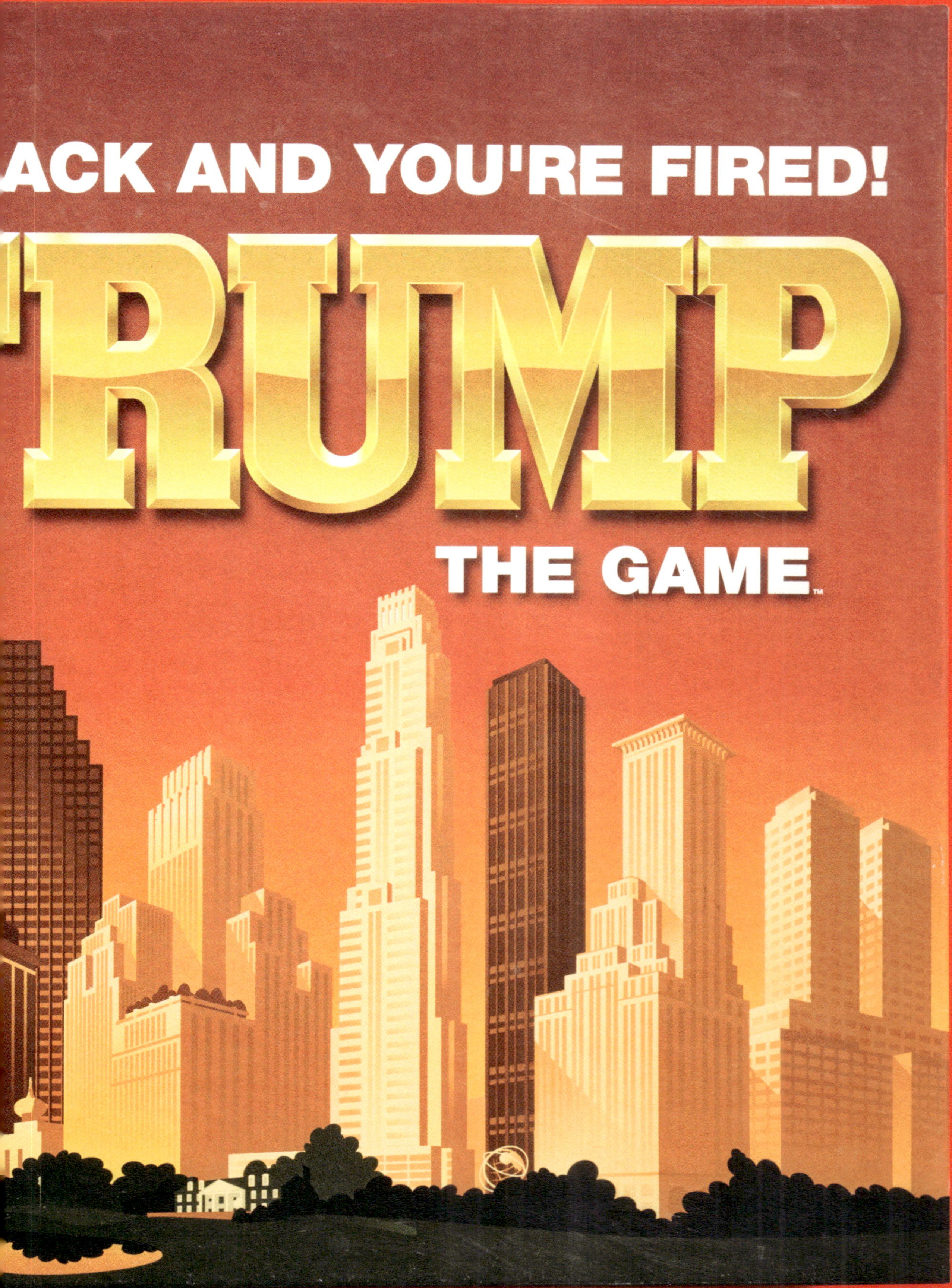

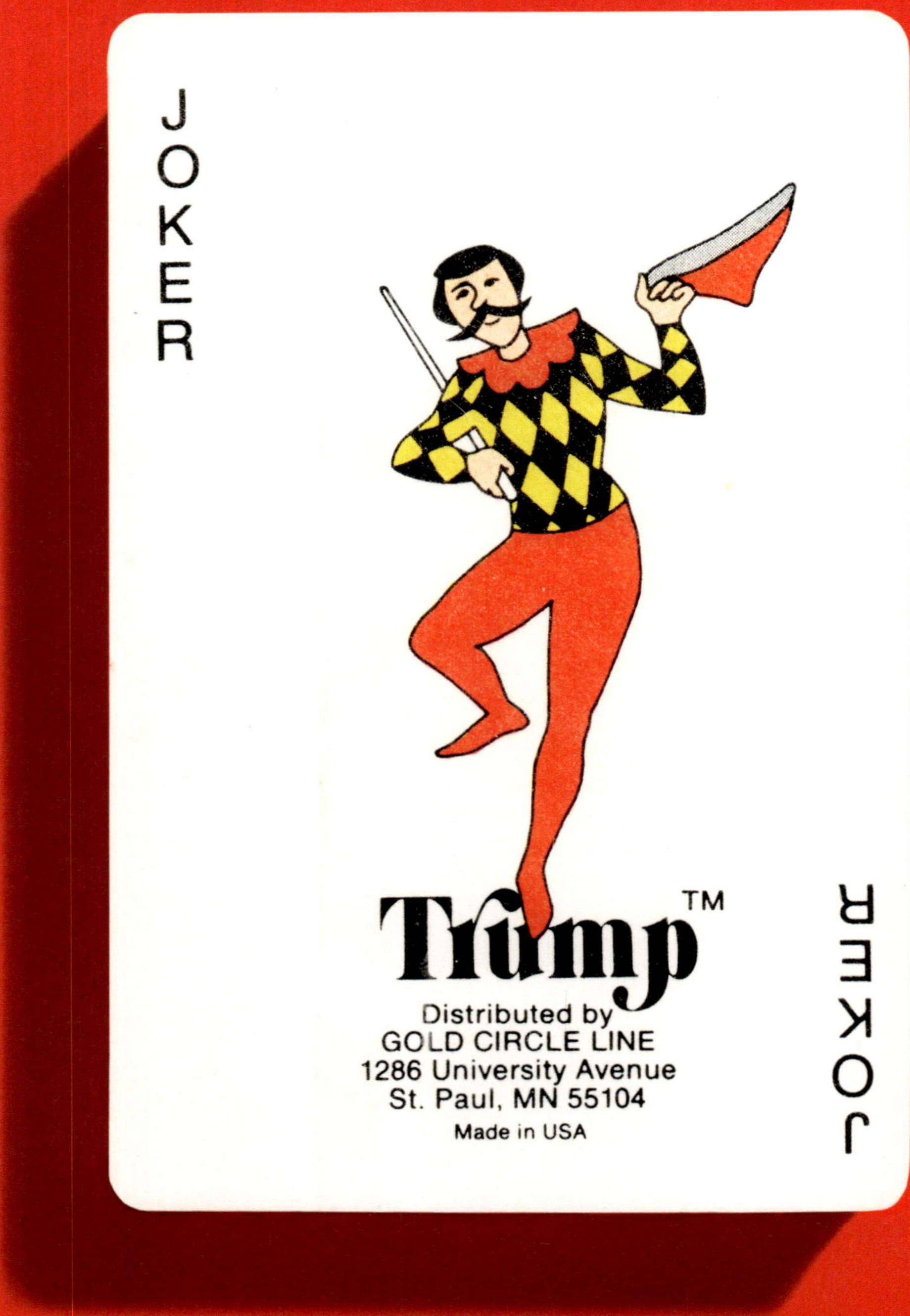
JOKER
Trump™
Distributed by
GOLD CIRCLE LINE
1286 University Avenue
St. Paul, MN 55104
Made in USA
JOKER

THE GAME: ALL THINGS TRUMP

ANDRES SERRANO

"ART IS ALL A MATTER OF PERSONALITY." —MARCEL DUCHAMP

MY WORK IS OFTEN ABOUT THE BIG PICTURE: LIFE, DEATH, SEX, RELIGION, RACE. IN APRIL 2018, I LOOKED AROUND ME AND REALIZED THE BIG PICTURE WAS DONALD TRUMP.

SO I EMBARKED ON CREATING A HUGE INSTALLATION OF MORE THAN 1,000 OBJECTS ALL BEARING THE NAME TRUMP: THINGS MADE FOR DONALD TRUMP, HIS BRAND, HIS HOTELS, HIS CASINOS AND HIS EMPIRE DATING FROM THE 1980S TO THE PRESENT. AMONG THE OBJECTS

I ACQUIRED WERE SUCH TRUMP CLASSICS AS TRUMP STEAKS, TRUMP VODKA, TRUMP SHUTTLE ITEMS, TRUMP SNAPPLE, TRUMP ICE WATER, TRUMP COCA-COLA, TRUMP TEA, A DEODORANT CALLED SUCCESS BY TRUMP, AS WELL AS DONALD TRUMP'S 1989 BOARD GAME, THE GAME. ACCOMPANYING THE PICTURE OF TRUMP ON THE BOX OF THE GAME IS A QUOTE:

"IT'S NOT WHETHER YOU WIN OR LOSE, IT'S WHETHER YOU WIN."

THERE IS ALSO A TRUMP UNIVERSITY DIPLOMA (MUCH DISCUSSED BUT RARELY SEEN) AND A MELANIA AND DONALD TRUMP SOUVENIR WEDDING CAKE FROM 2005, TAKEN HOME BY ONE OF 350 GUESTS WHO INCLUDED, AMONG OTHERS, RUDY GIULIANI, HEIDI KLUM,

P. DIDDY, SIMON COWELL, SENATOR HILLARY CLINTON AND PRESIDENT BILL CLINTON.

THE TWO BIGGEST OBJECTS IN THE GAME: ALL THINGS TRUMP ARE THE PICTURE I TOOK OF DONALD TRUMP IN 2004, FOR MY "AMERICA" SERIES AND THE EGO SIGN FROM THE TRUMP TAJ MAHAL IN ATLANTIC CITY. THE TRUMP PORTRAIT WAS ONE OF MORE THAN 100 I DID OF PEOPLE FROM ALL WALKS OF LIFE THAT EMBODIED MY PICTURE OF AMERICA. IT MEASURES OVER EIGHT FEET TALL. THE EGO SIGN IS AN ELEGANT ROTATING SCULPTURE NEARLY 11 FEET TALL THAT ONCE GREETED VISITORS AT THE TAJ MAHAL CASINO'S EGO LOUNGE.

INCLUDED IN THE EXHIBITION ARE DOZENS OF MAGAZINES,

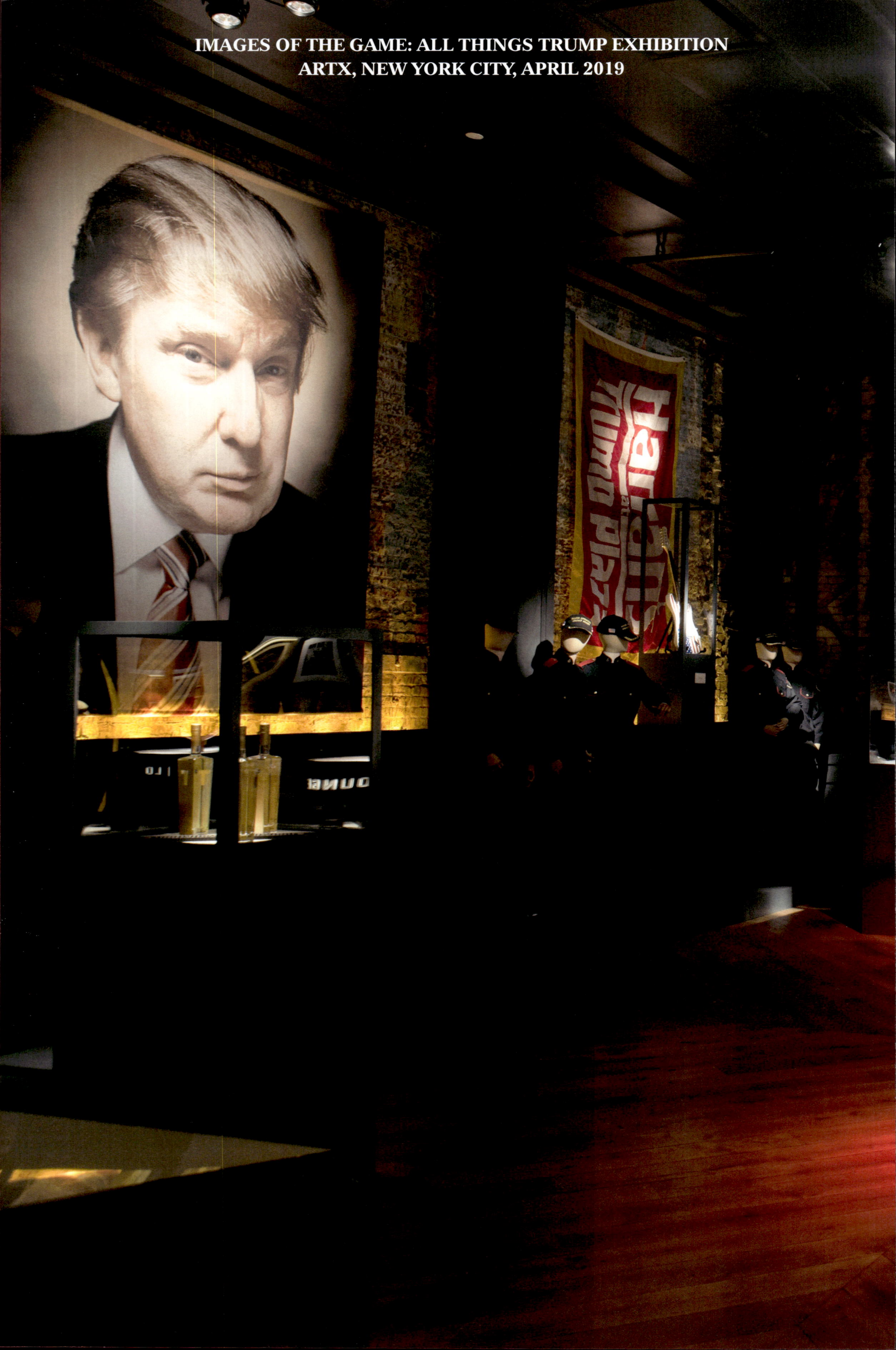

IMAGES OF THE GAME: ALL THINGS TRUMP EXHIBITION
ARTX, NEW YORK CITY, APRIL 2019

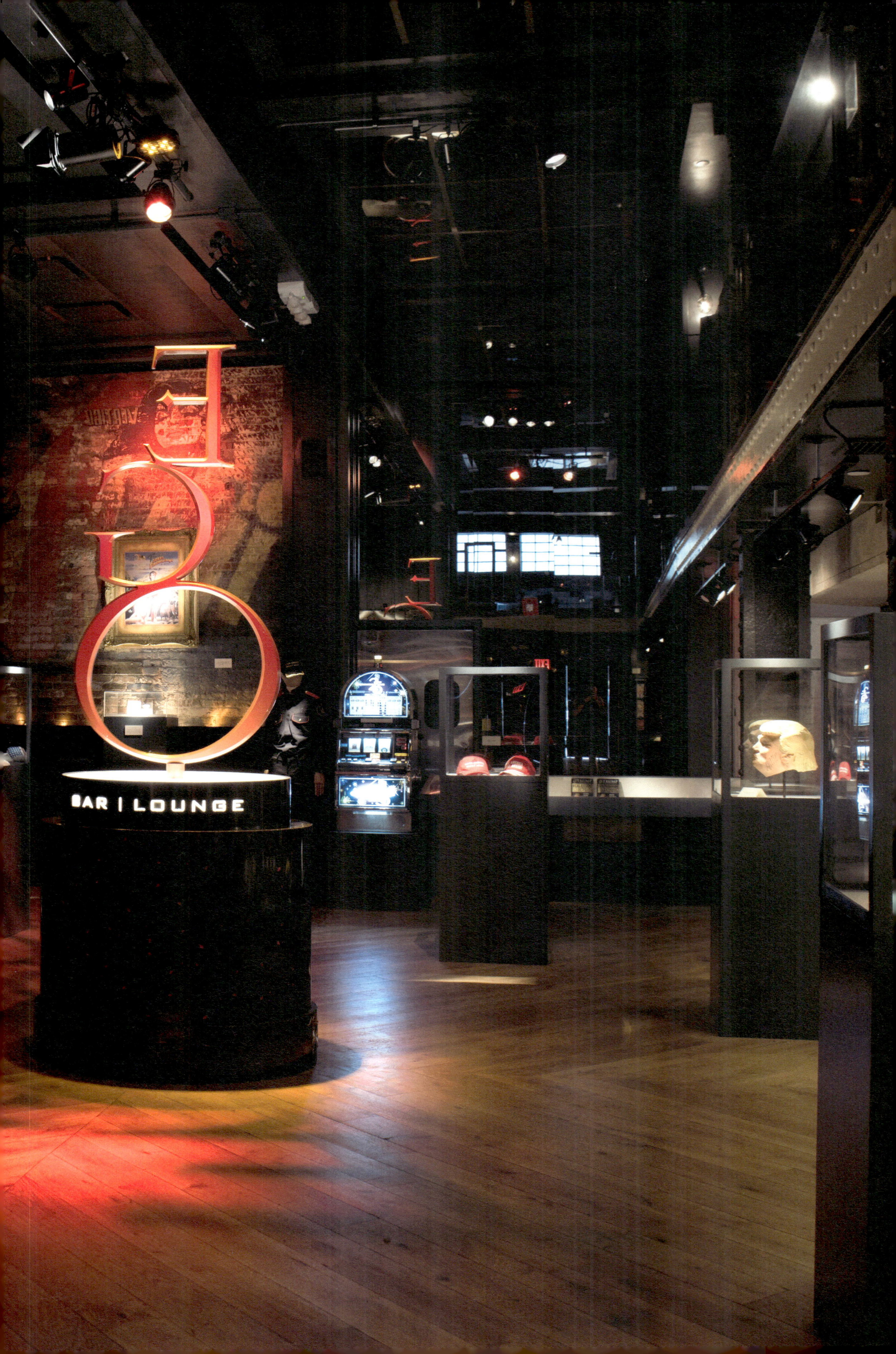
BAR | LOUNGE

PHOTOGRAPHS AND OBJECTS SIGNED BY DONALD TRUMP. TRUMP IS A MASTER AT SIGNING HIS NAME, PARTICULARLY OVER HIS FACE, LIKE AN ARTIST WHO QUICKLY ASSESSES HOW TO MAKE AN IMPRESSION.

NOT SURPRISINGLY, SOME OF THE MAGAZINES ARE CRITICAL OF TRUMP, WITH COVERS THAT READ "HATER IN CHIEF," "KING ME," "TRUMP VS. THE CONSTITUTION," AND "THE MIND OF DONALD TRUMP," SHOWING THAT DONALD TRUMP WILL TAKE BAD HEADLINES OVER NO HEADLINES. HIS FANCIFUL SIGNATURES BEAR WITNESS TO BOLD ASSERTIONS THAT SAY, "I'M BIGGER THAN THIS."

IF TRUMP WERE A SHAKESPEAREAN CHARACTER, IT WOULD BE HARD

TO SAY WHICH ONE. THE BARD WOULD HAVE TO INVENT HIM. A MAN OF THE PEOPLE IS NEVER A MAN OF THE PEOPLE. IF HE WERE, HE'D BE ONE OF THEM. NOTHING MORE.

FOR SOME, DONALD TRUMP IS THE GREAT WHITE HOPE, THE NIETZSCHEAN SUPERMAN THEY PRAYED FOR. BASED ON ALL WE KNOW ABOUT DONALD TRUMP, WE SHOULD HAVE SEEN IT COMING. DONALD TRUMP HAS ALWAYS BEEN AN OPEN BOOK. THOSE WHO DIDN'T SEE HIM COMING WEREN'T LOOKING.

HE DID NOT WRITE THE BOOK ON NARCISSISM; HE PERFECTED IT. HE DIDN'T NEED TO READ MACHIAVELLI TO BECOME MACHIAVELLIAN BECAUSE DONALD TRUMP DOESN'T READ BOOKS; HE READS PEOPLE.

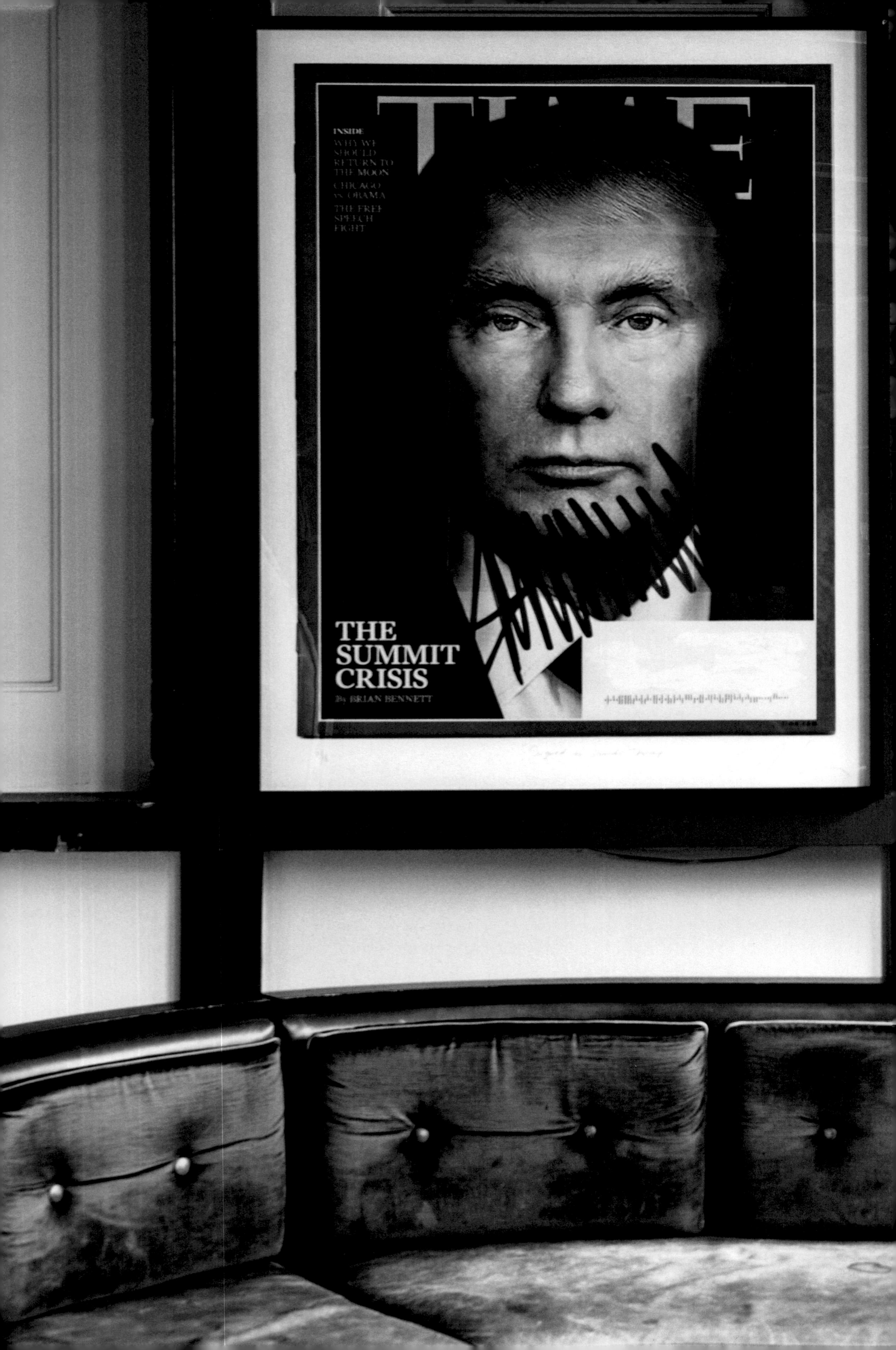
TIME
INSIDE
WHY WE SHOULD RETURN TO THE MOON
CHICAGO vs OBAMA
THE FREE SPEECH FIGHT
THE SUMMIT CRISIS
By BRIAN BENNETT

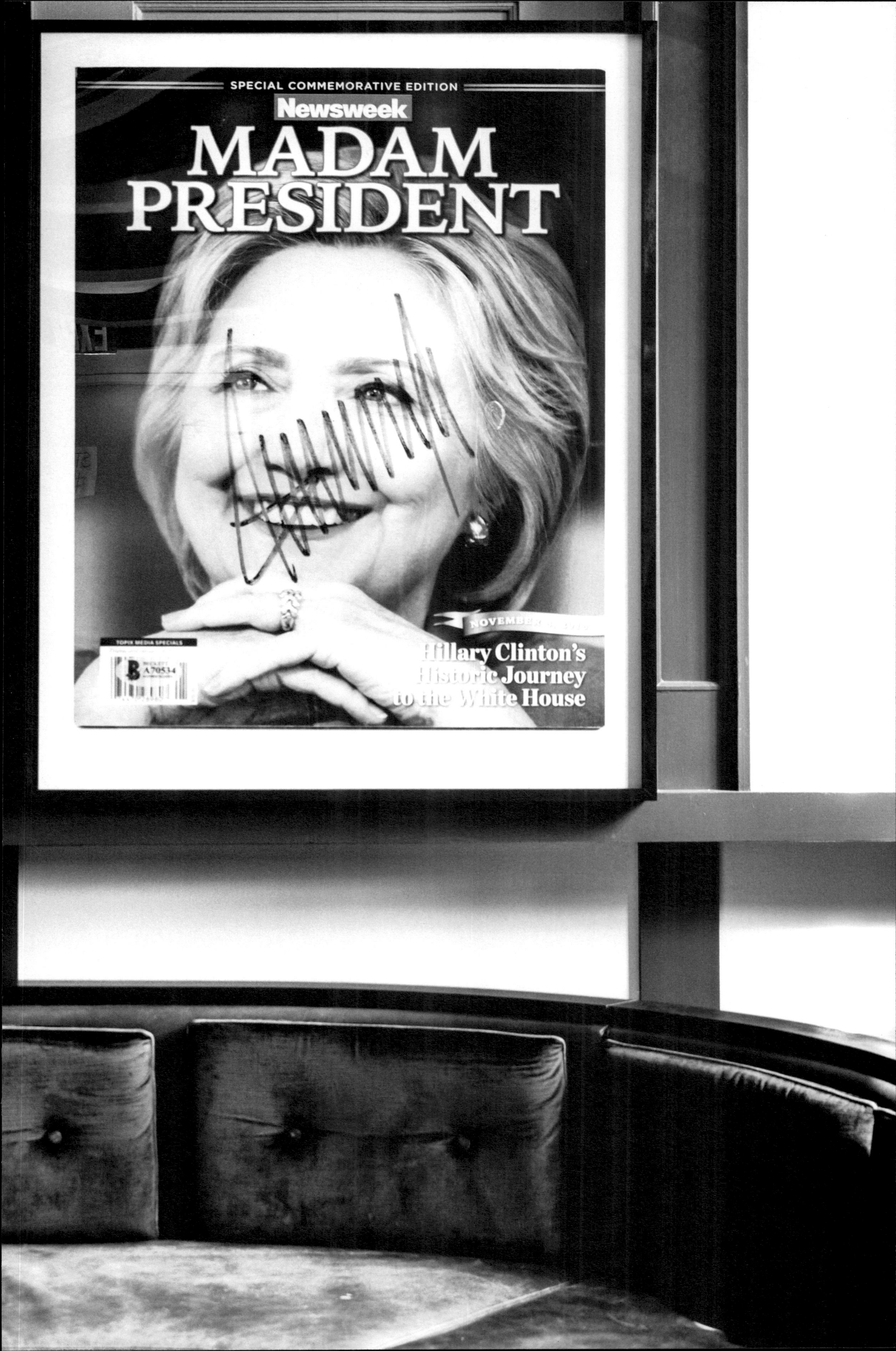
SPECIAL COMMEMORATIVE EDITION
Newsweek
MADAM PRESIDENT
Hillary Clinton's Historic Journey to the White House

THE SECRET OF BEING **TRUMP** IS TO ALWAYS BE RIGHT. WITHOUT GRASPING THIS FUNDAMENTAL TRUTH, ANY ATTEMPT TO UNDERSTAND **TRUMP** IS POINTLESS, ANY SYSTEM OF BELIEF IS USELESS. FOR DONALD **TRUMP** DOES NOT ARGUE WITH LOGIC; HE ARGUES WITH CONFIDENCE.

DONALD **TRUMP** IS ALL THINGS TO ALL PEOPLE. HE'S THE RORSCHACH TEST THAT LIVES UP TO OUR EXPECTATIONS.

THE **TRUMP**IAN UNIVERSE THAT DONALD **TRUMP** ONCE CREATED FOR HIMSELF, HE HAS NOW CREATED FOR US, PROVING THAT DONALD **TRUMP** DOES NOT LIVE IN OUR WORLD. WE LIVE IN HIS.

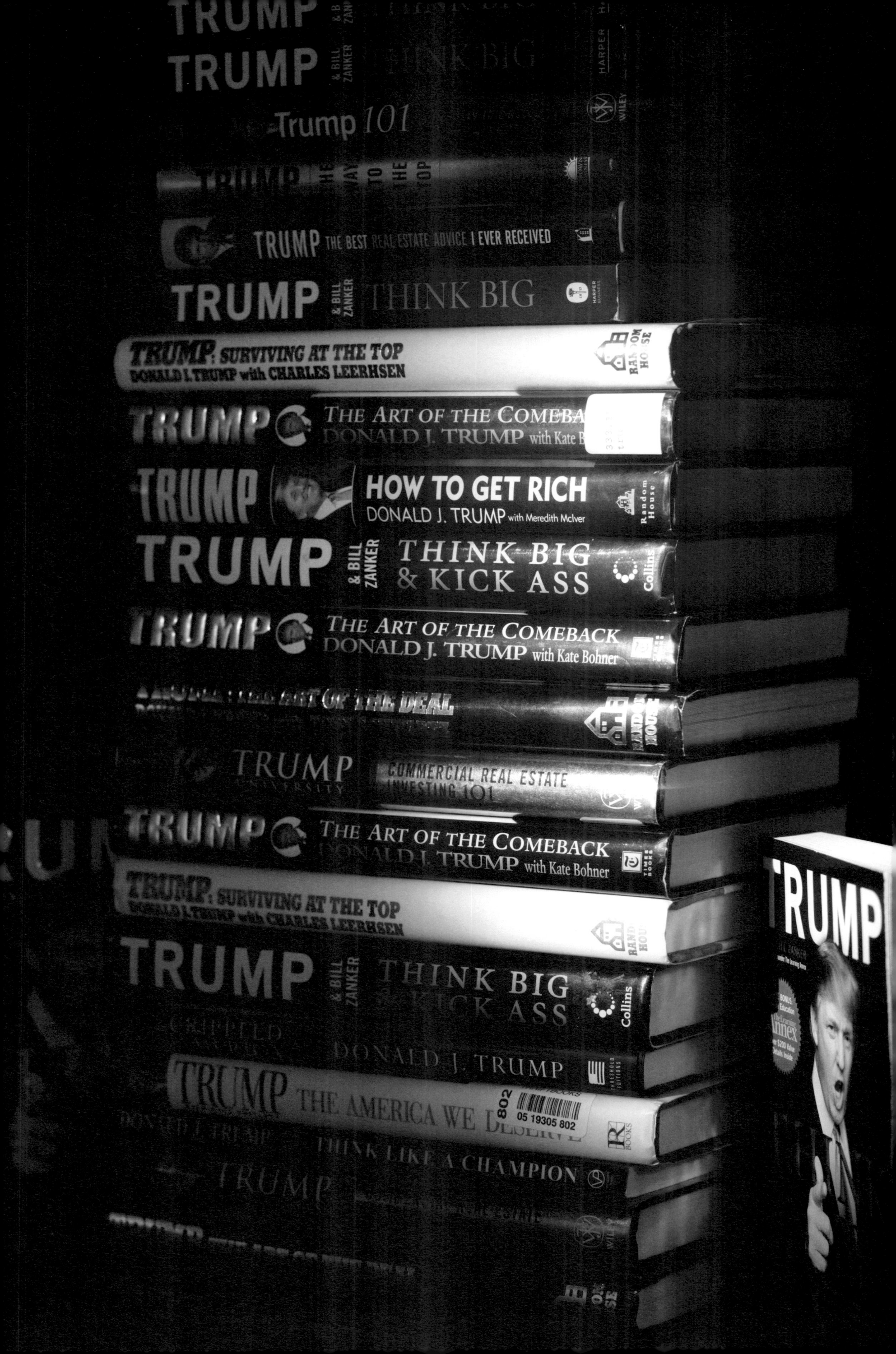
TRUMP
TRUMP & BILL ZANKER THINK BIG HARPER
Trump 101 WILEY
TRUMP THE WAY TO THE TOP
TRUMP THE BEST REAL ESTATE ADVICE I EVER RECEIVED
TRUMP & BILL ZANKER THINK BIG HARPER BUSINESS
TRUMP: SURVIVING AT THE TOP
DONALD J. TRUMP with CHARLES LEERHSEN
RANDOM HOUSE
TRUMP THE ART OF THE COMEBA
DONALD J. TRUMP with Kate B
TRUMP HOW TO GET RICH
DONALD J. TRUMP with Meredith McIver
Random House
TRUMP & BILL ZANKER THINK BIG & KICK ASS
Collins
TRUMP THE ART OF THE COMEBACK
DONALD J. TRUMP with Kate Bohner
THE ART OF THE DEAL
RANDOM HOUSE
TRUMP UNIVERSITY COMMERCIAL REAL ESTATE INVESTING 101
TRUMP THE ART OF THE COMEBACK
DONALD J. TRUMP with Kate Bohner
TIMES BOOKS
TRUMP: SURVIVING AT THE TOP
DONALD J. TRUMP with CHARLES LEERHSEN
TRUMP & BILL ZANKER THINK BIG & KICK ASS
Collins
DONALD J. TRUMP
THRESHOLD EDITIONS
TRUMP THE AMERICA WE DESERVE
BOOKS
THINK LIKE A CHAMPION
TRUMP
WILEY
TRUMP

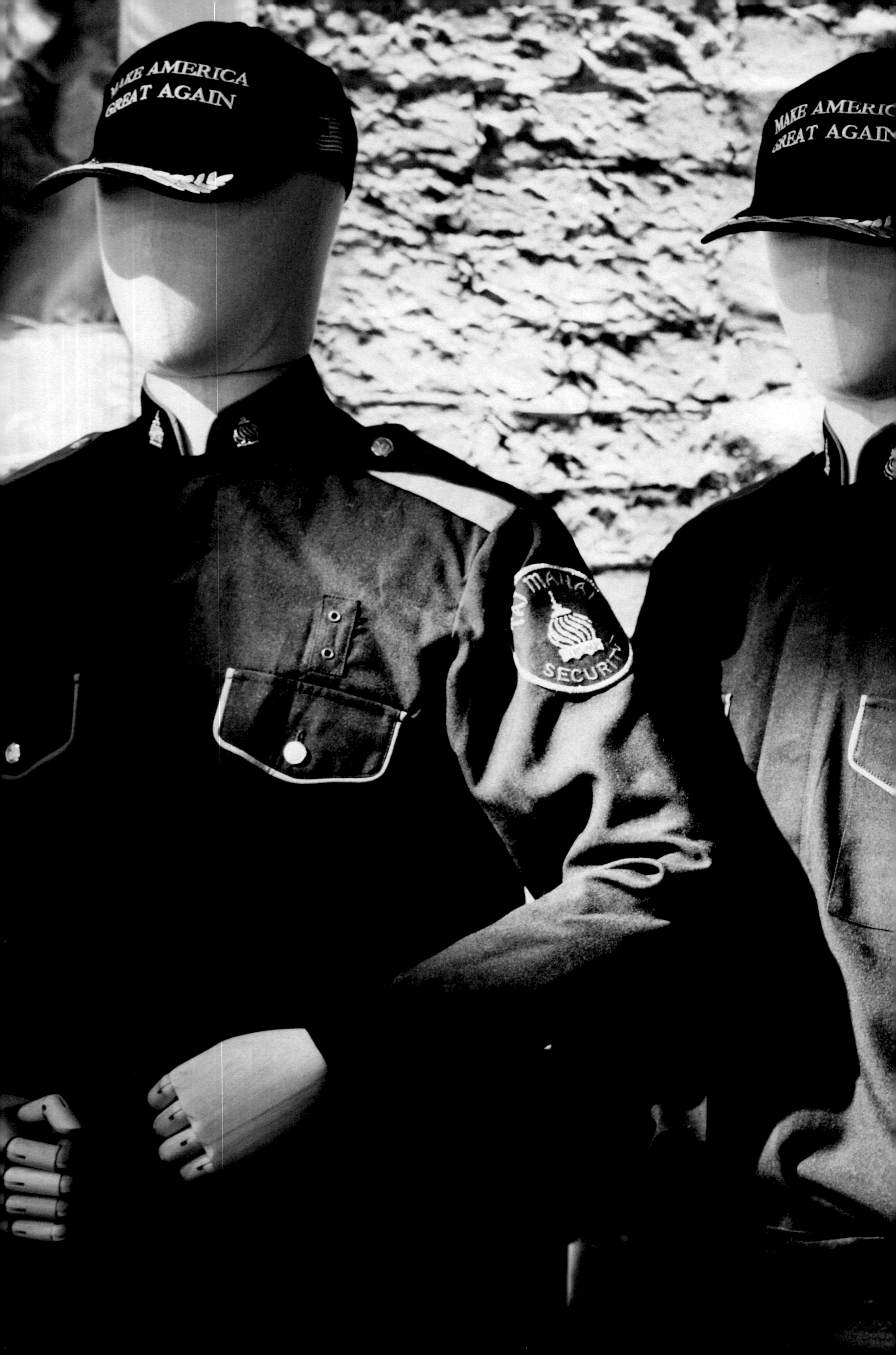
MAKE AMERICA
GREAT AGAIN

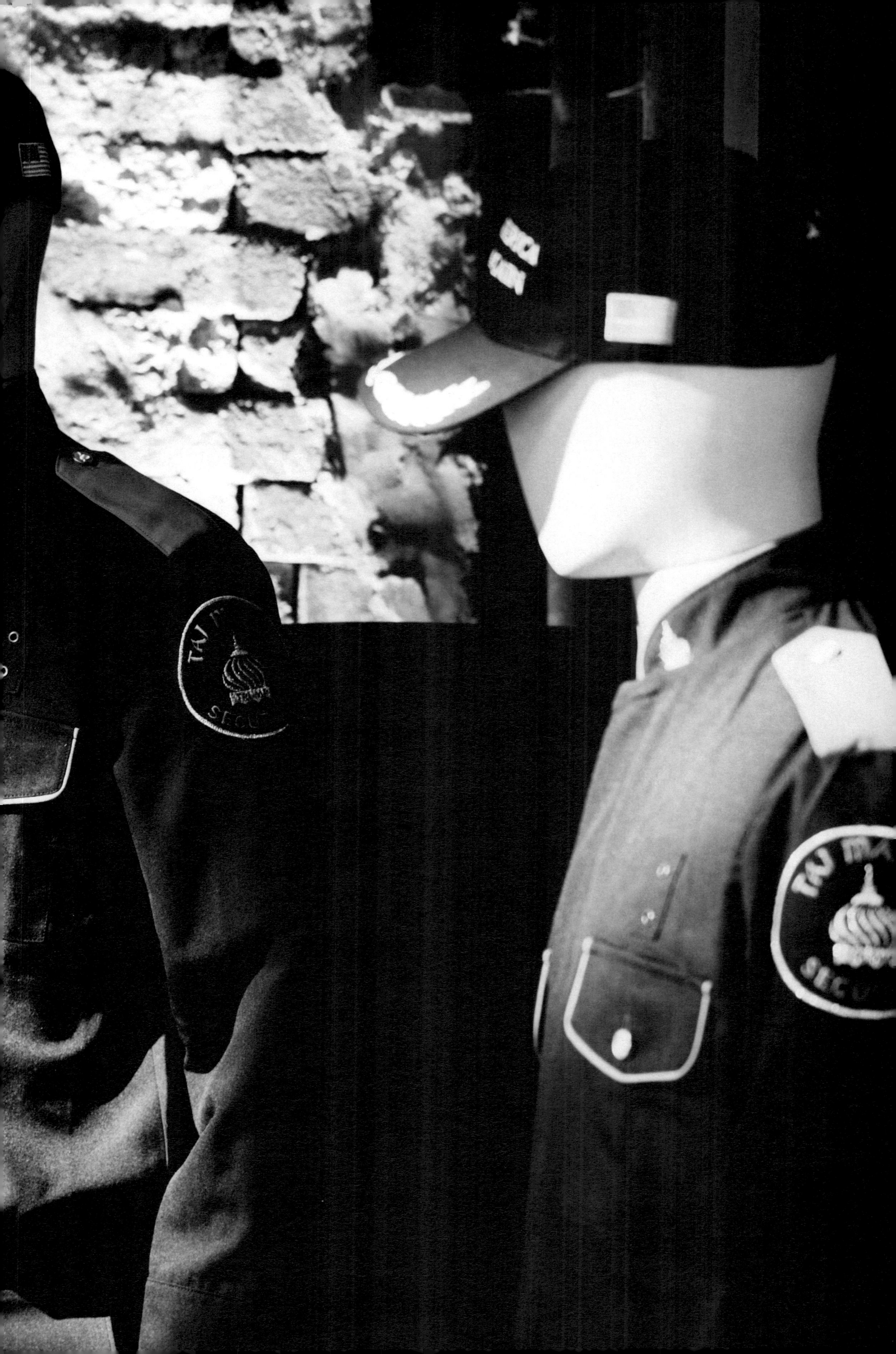

MAKE AMERICA GREAT AGAIN BASEBALL CAP
SIGNED DONALD TRUMP

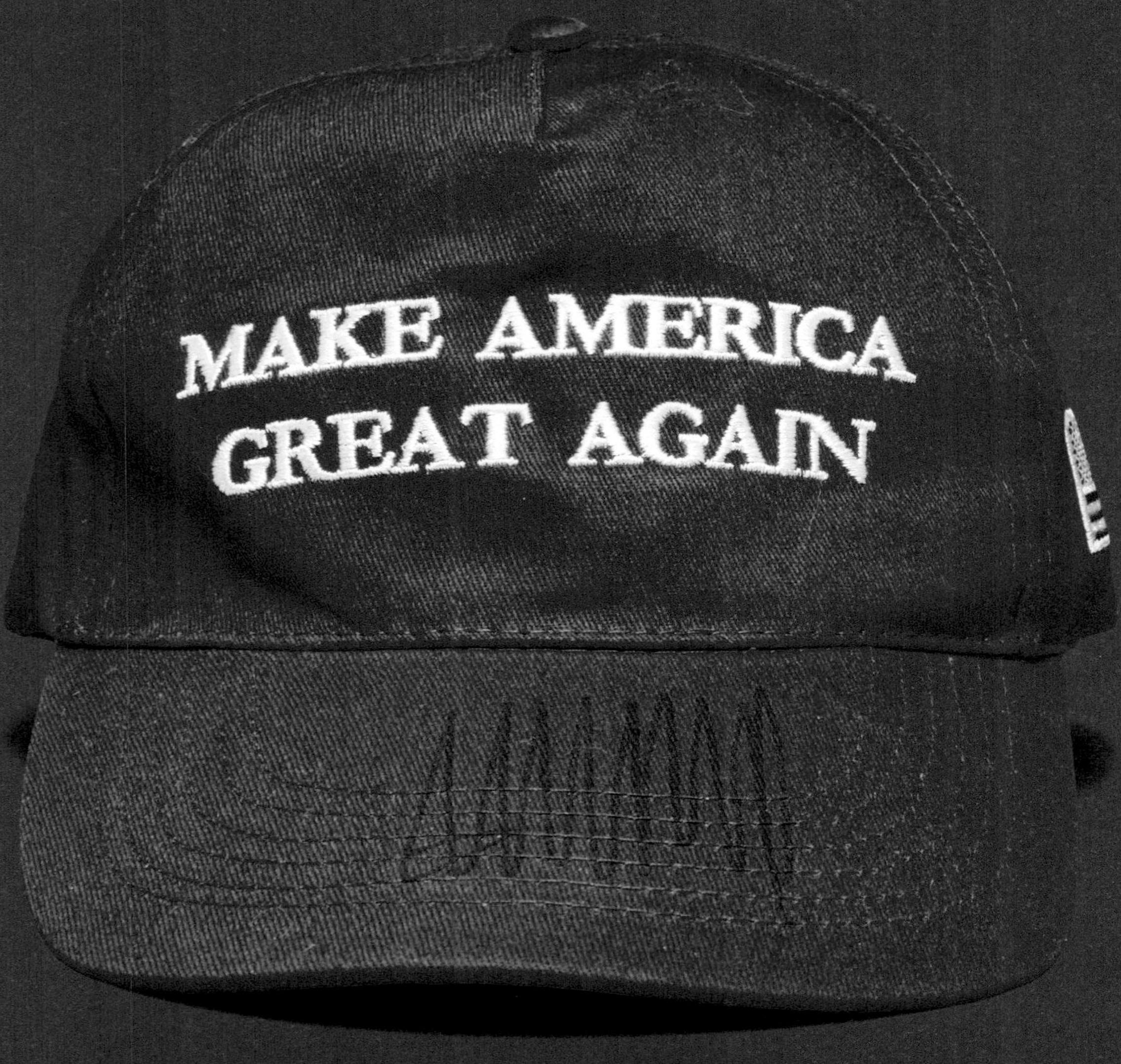

FOR DECADES, WE ALL ATE TRUMP UP. ARTIST ANDRES SERRANO ASKS, "WHY?"

JERRY SALTZ

AT THE DARK HEART OF ANDRES SERRANO'S THE GAME: ALL THINGS TRUMP IS WHAT I CONSIDER THE AMERICAN SWASTIKA: A RED HAT WITH TRUMP'S NATIVIST SLOGAN, "MAKE AMERICA GREAT AGAIN." BY THAT, I DON'T MEAN THAT THE HAT REPRESENTS NAZISM, BUT THAT MAGA IS THE CLOSEST THIS COUNTRY HAS COME TO CREATING A SYMBOL, GRAPHIC EMBLEM, OR VISUAL REPRESENTATION THAT RADIATES ITS MESSAGE WITH SUCH RORSCHACH POWER — THAT SERVES

AS A VISUAL EXPLICATION OF AN IDEOLOGY AND ONE MAN: TRUMPISM AND TRUMP.

BUT THE SHOW THAT SPAWNED THIS BOOK WAS MUCH BIGGER THAN THAT ONE HAT. SERRANO'S LARGE, TWO-FLOOR MUSEOLOGICAL INSTALLATION IN A WEST VILLAGE GALLERY/CLUB FEATURED OVER 1,000 TRUMP-RELATED OBJECTS AND PRODUCTS BOUGHT ON EBAY BY THE ARTIST (AT A COST OF $200,000). ITEMS WERE DISPLAYED IN CASES, ON BASES, AND BEHIND GLASS, ALL CAREFULLY LABELED. IT LOOKED LIKE A TRUMP JUNK SHOP. AMONG THE MANY OBJECTS WITH HIS VISAGE, SIGNATURE, OR NAME (OR HIS FAMILY'S AND FELLOW CON MEN AND CON WOMEN) ARE ITEMS SPOUTING PORN-Y HEADLINES, BRANDED RESORT SOUVENIRS,

SPONSORSHIP LOGOS, MEMENTOS OF HIS FAILED BUSINESSES AND GOLF COURSES, FORECLOSURE NOTICES HE TOOK OUT ON OTHERS AND THAT WERE TAKEN OUT ON HIM, AND EVIDENCE OF THE NEVER-ENDING COVERAGE BY HIS MOST IMPORTANT 30-YEAR ENABLER: THE PRESS. SEE THE NUMEROUS NEW YORK POST COVERS FEATURING RACY STORIES ABOUT TRUMP'S DIVORCES AND BAD BUSINESS DEALS. SEE THE POST'S "BEST SEX I EVER HAD" ISSUE — SUPPOSEDLY A QUOTE FROM HIS SOON-TO-BE SECOND WIFE, MARLA MAPLES, THAT TURNED OUT TO HAVE BEEN PHONED IN BY TRUMP HIMSELF MASQUERADING AS A TRUMP ORGANIZATION SPOKESPERSON NAMED "JOHN BARRON." (THE REPORTER RECORDED IT. TRUMP DENIED IT WAS HIM. THIS IS ONE

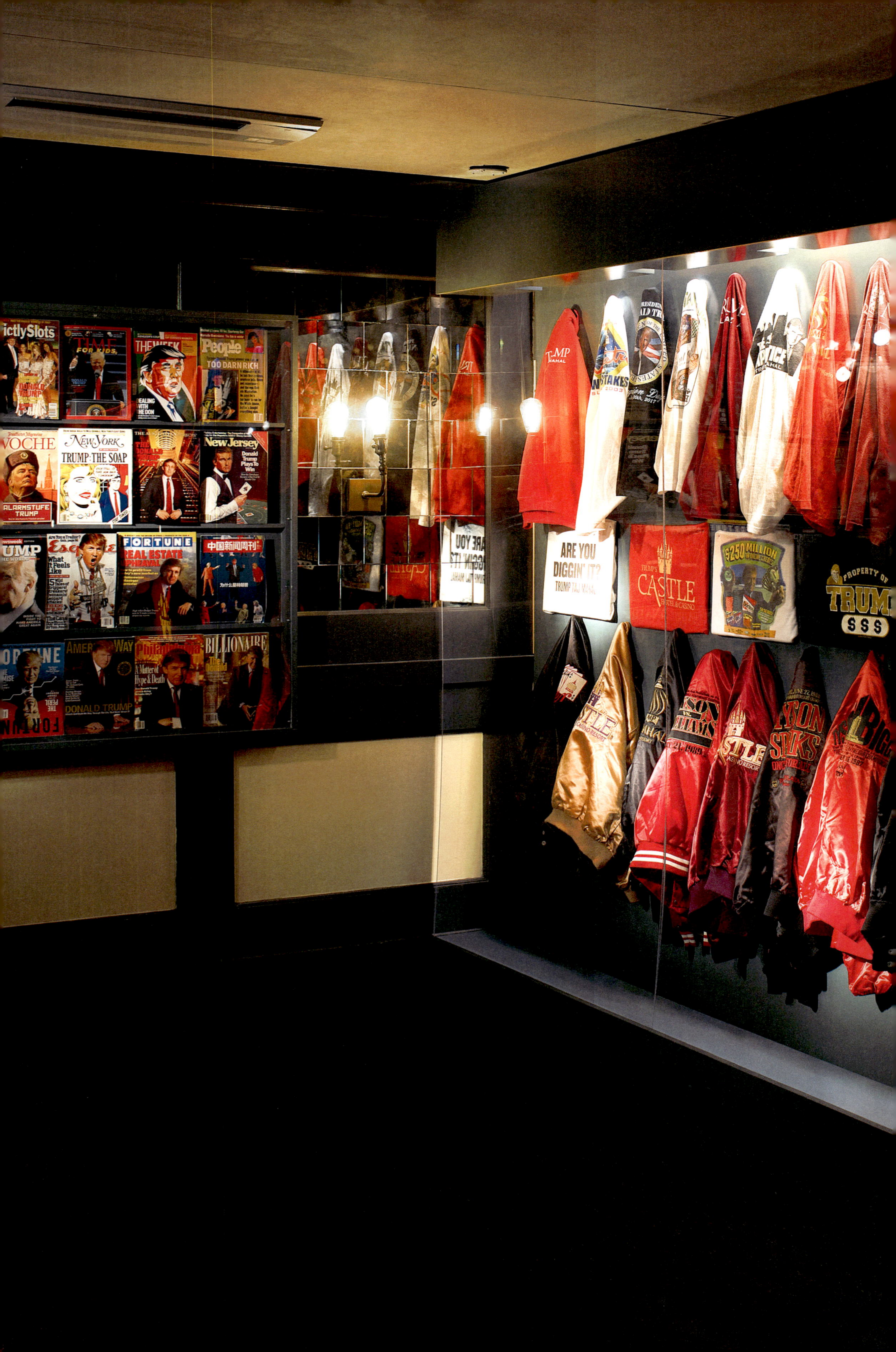
TIME FOR KIDS
THE WEEK
People
TOO DARN RICH
NEW YORK
TRUMP: THE SOAP
New Jersey
Donald Trump Plays To Win
ALARMSTUFE TRUMP
FORTUNE
REAL ESTATE UPHEAVAL
中国新闻周刊
Philadelphia
A Matter of Hype & Death
DONALD TRUMP
BILLIONAIRE
ARE YOU DIGGIN' IT?
TRUMP TAJ MAHAL
CASTLE
HOTEL & CASINO
$250 MILLION
PROPERTY OF
$ $ $

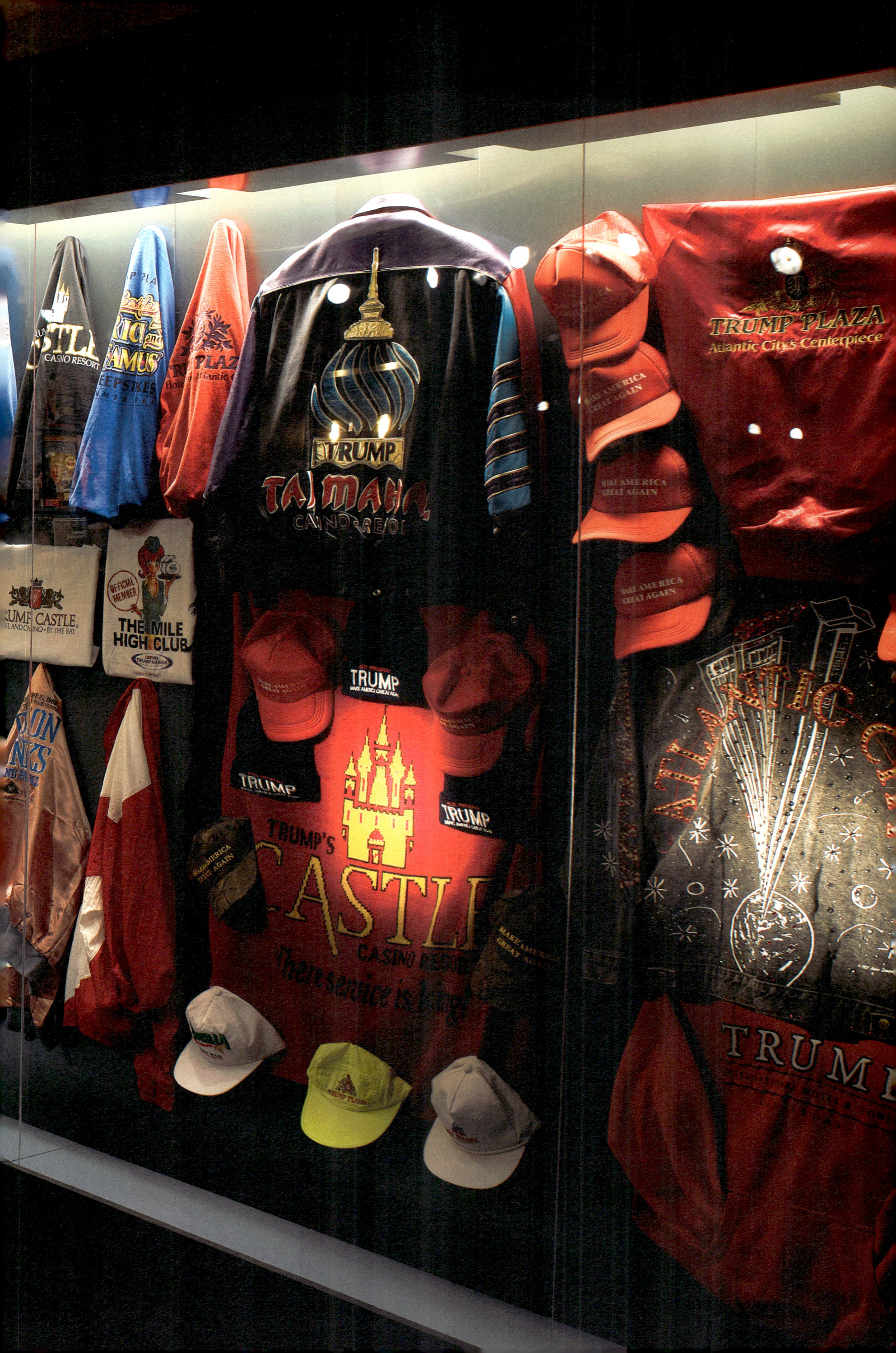

TRUMP PLAZA
Atlantic City's Centerpiece
TRUMP
MAKE AMERICA GREAT AGAIN
OFFICIAL MEMBER
THE MILE HIGH CLUB
TRUMP
TRUMP'S
CASTLE
CASINO RESORT
TRUMP

SICK FUCK.) SEE HIS FACE ON THE COVERS OF TIME, NEWSWEEK, SPY, TV GUIDE, PEOPLE, GQ, FORTUNE, PALM SPRINGS LIFE, THE NATIONAL ENQUIRER, AND MANY OTHERS, NOT TO MENTION THE ENDLESS PROMOTION BY TELEVISION NETWORKS. HAVING TAKEN IT ALL IN, I FIND IT HARD TO FEEL THAT THE COLLECTION MERELY TELLS THE STORY OF ONE MAN, NO MATTER HOW FLAMBOYANTLY FAME-CRAZY, TASTELESS, RUTHLESS, AND FULL OF ENTITLEMENT AND RAGE. IT IS A PORTRAIT OF US, AMERICA.

SERRANO HAS SAID, “I WANTED TO PAINT A PORTRAIT OF DONALD TRUMP USING HIS OWN BRUSHES… EVER SINCE THE ’80S, DONALD TRUMP HAS BEEN ASSOCIATING HIMSELF WITH A PARTICULAR VISION OF AMERICAN SUCCESS … THAT PAINTS

HIM AS ALL-AMERICAN." TO THIS END, SERRANO PURCHASED TRUMP-RELATED ITEMS FOR SEVEN HOURS A DAY SINCE APRIL 7, 2018. "I MAKE ART ABOUT VERY BASIC THINGS," HE SAYS. "LIFE, DEATH, SEX, RELIGION, EXCREMENT ... IT'S ONLY NATURAL THAT IT'S NOW TRUMP." TO ANYONE OFFENDED THAT SERRANO'S "PORTRAIT" IS NOT AN OBVIOUS PIECE OF ANTI-TRUMP AGITPROP, THE ARTIST SAYS, "I'VE SEEN A LOT OF ARTWORK THAT'S ANTI-TRUMP, AND FRANKLY IT'S NOT GOOD." HE'S RIGHT.

THE GAME IS MUCH MORE INTERESTING. IT ISN'T ABOUT CHAINSAW POLITICS AND PROPAGANDA. INSTEAD, IT EMPLOYED THE MOST POLARIZING FIGURE IN THE WESTERN WORLD — PERHAPS IN AMERICAN HISTORY — TO CREATE TWO DIFFERENT EXHIBITIONS IN ONE.

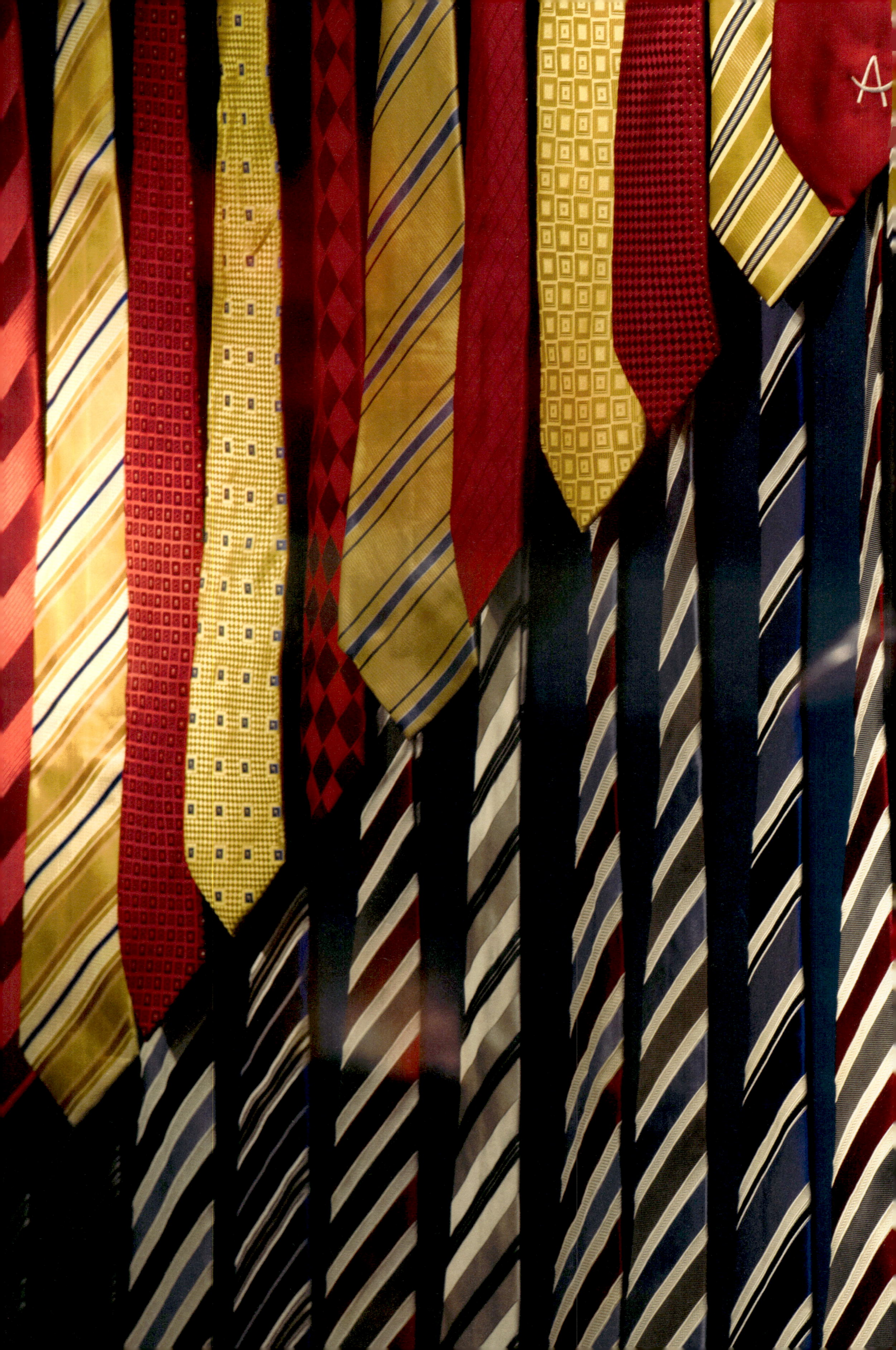

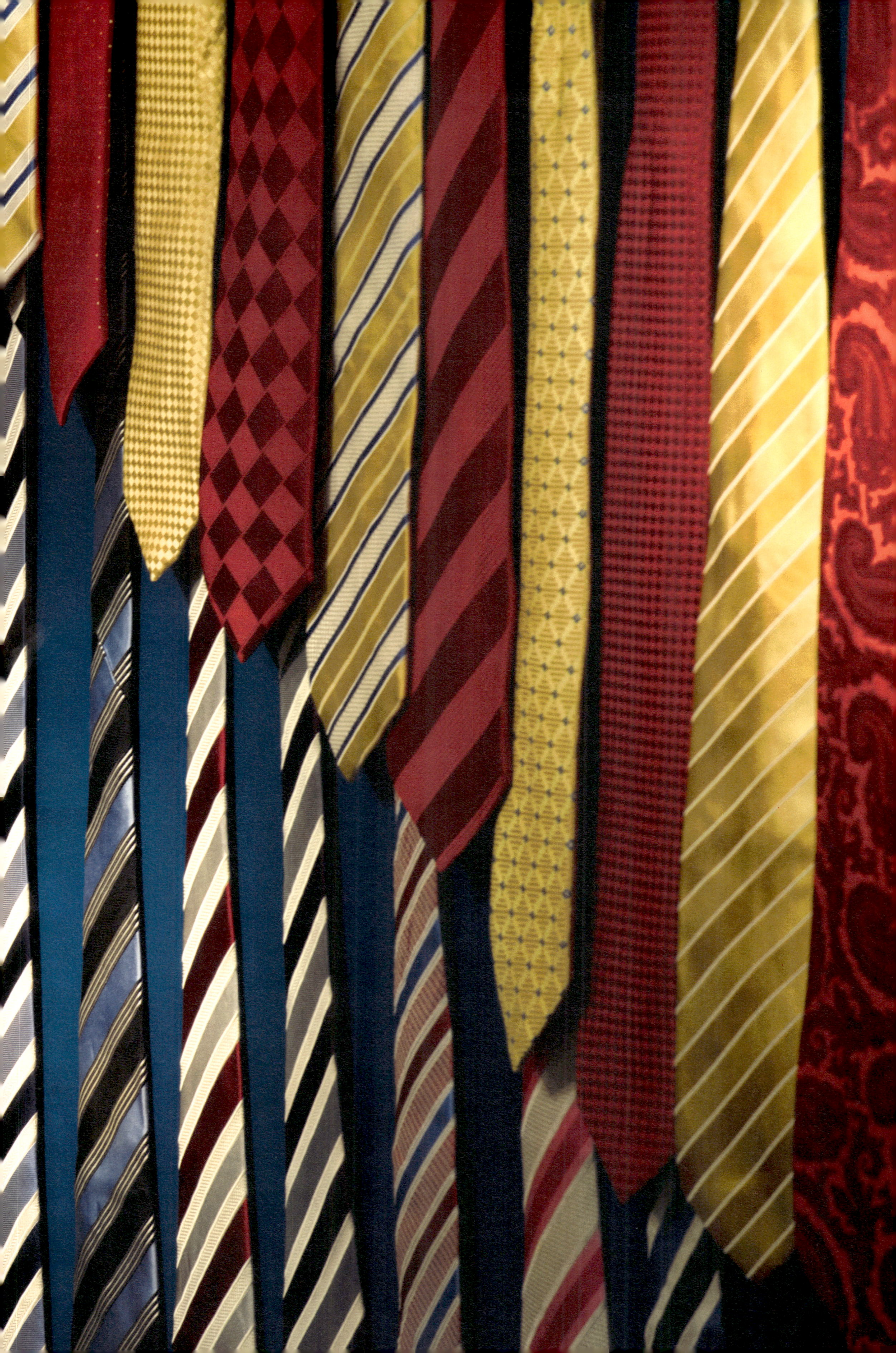

TRUMP SUPPORTERS, HAPPY-TALKING FOX NEWS CONSPIRACY THEORISTS, VICHY REPUBLICANS IN CONGRESS, WEALTHY BENEFICIARIES OF RECENT REPUBLICAN TAX BREAKS, AND THE RED-MEAT BASE WILL LOOK AT THIS BOOK, AND SAY, "THIS IS WHO WE ARE! ISN'T IT GREAT?" THE REMAINING (APPROXIMATELY 60%) OF THIS COUNTRY, INCLUDING THOSE OF US WHO SEE ALL THINGS MAGA AS REPRESENTING AMERICA AS A FAILED STATE RUN BY MINORITY RULE RESULTING IN A REIGN OF DOMESTIC TERROR THAT TRAFFICS IN MALICIOUS VICIOUSNESS, SPECTACLE, GRAFT, XENOPHOBIA, NATIONALISM AT ITS MOST DANGEROUS, AND COMMON SCUMBAGGERY, WILL LOOK AT THIS BOOK AND SAY, "THIS IS WHO WE ARE! THIS IS TRAGIC."

EGO SIGN
11FT ROTATING LOGO FROM THE EGO BAR & LOUNGE
AT TRUMP TAJ MAHAL CASINO IN ATLANTIC CITY

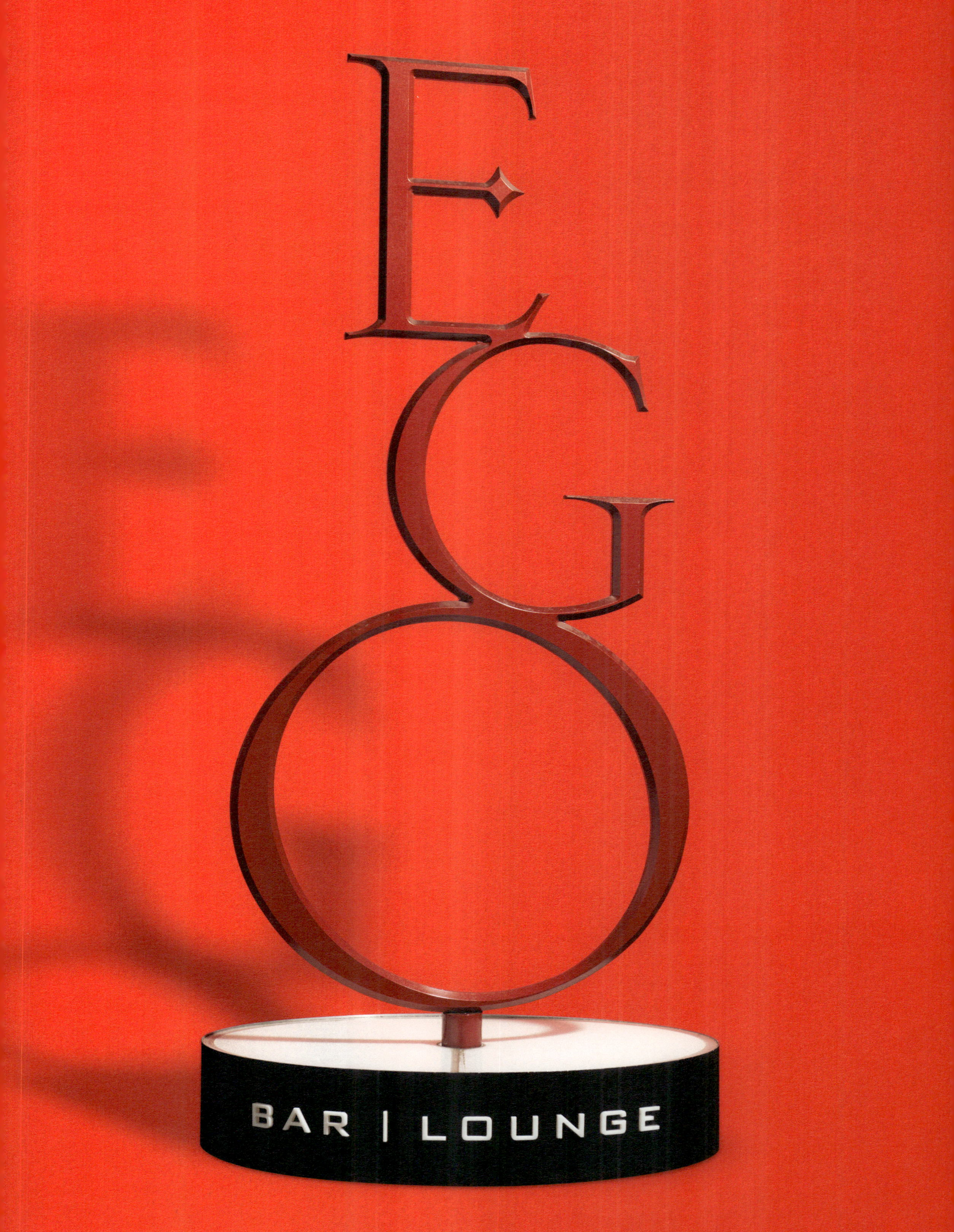

BY "US," SERRANO MEANS AMERICA'S 40-YEAR FASCINATION WITH AND FIXATION ON THIS BRASH, BOMBASTIC, OBVIOUSLY UNSCRUPULOUS, AND BRUTAL SELF-BRANDED AVATAR OF AMERICAN CELEBRITY AND SUCCESS. TO FEED THE FIRES, HE MADE HIMSELF FOREVER AVAILABLE TO THE PRESS, AND THE PRESS FED ON HIM. IN TURN, HE FED ON IT AND OUR INABILITY TO EVER LOOK AWAY — HAPPY TO CAST HIM AS "OUR" CARTOON MODERN P. T. BARNUM OF UNLEASHED AMERICAN ID, AMBITION, BLUSTER, AND SHOWBOATING. OVER THAT TIME, TRUMP BECAME INEXORABLY ENTWINED WITH AMERICA'S NATIONAL CONSCIOUSNESS AND GREW STRONGER. AND MORE VISIBLE, BECOMING A TV STAR.

BY THE TIME HE RODE DOWN THE ESCALATOR OF TRUMP TOWER AND BEFORE BEGINNING HIS THINLY VEILED WHITE-NATIONALIST IMMIGRANT-HATING CAMPAIGN, HE HAD 100% NAME RECOGNITION. INDEED, FOR THAT NEXT YEAR, NO ONE COULD LOOK AWAY WHEN THIS CELEBRITY HOT DOG WAS ON TV, POMPOUS BUT TOTALLY COMFORTABLE IN HIMSELF, SPOUTING WHATEVER HE NEEDED TO SAY TO WOO THE RUBES. WHEN HE FIRST ANNOUNCED HIS CANDIDACY, MANY PROGRESSIVES SAW TRUMP'S BLUSTERING RAGE AS A PATH TO A 50-STATE PRESIDENTIAL VICTORY AND THE FINAL ELIMINATION OF REPUBLICAN CONSERVATISM AS IT HAD EVOLVED IN THE 21ST CENTURY. OUR OLD RACIST UNCLE TRUMP AT THE END OF THE AMERICAN BAR WOULD

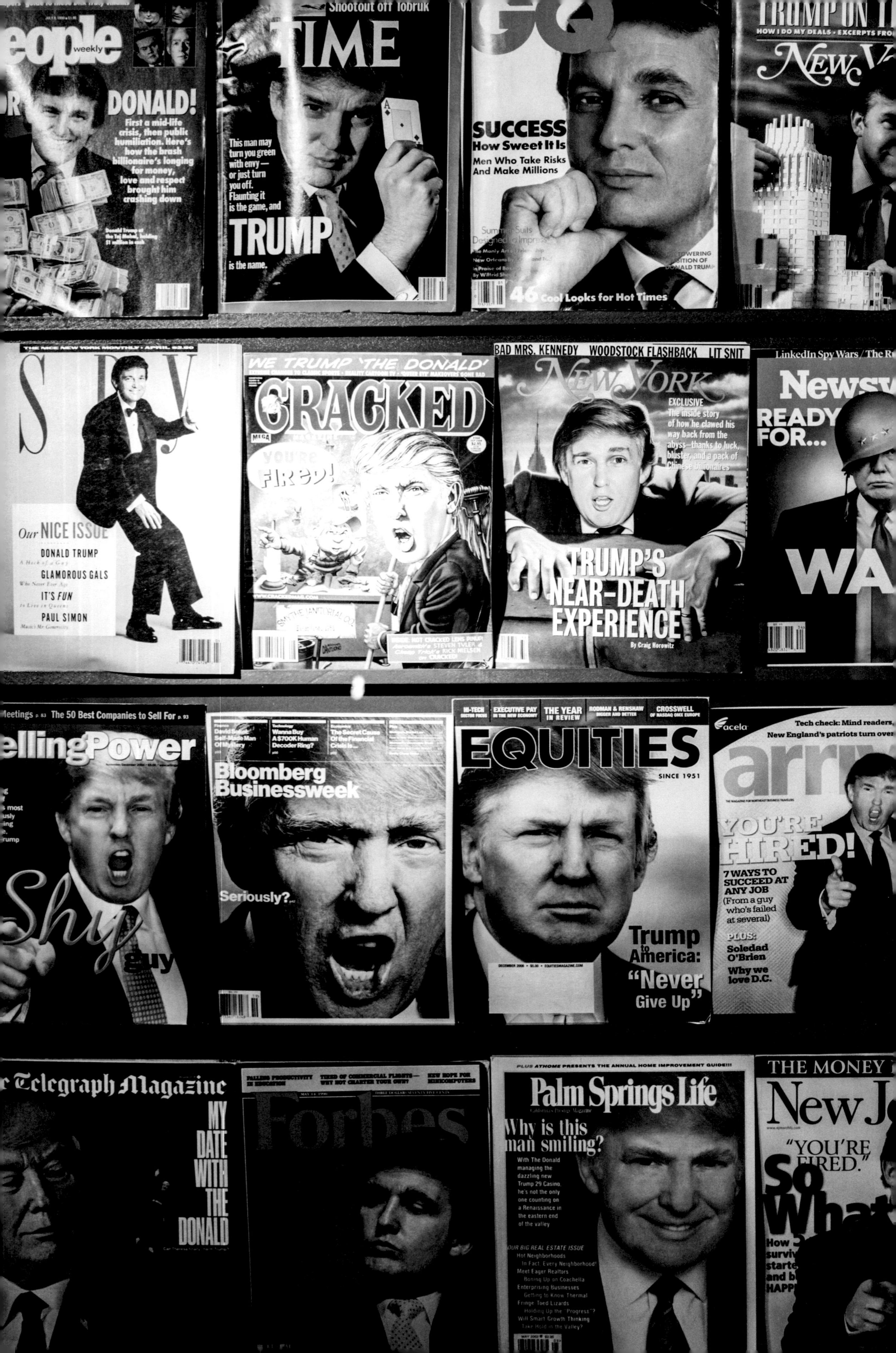

people weekly
DONALD!
First a mid-life crisis, then public humiliation. Here's how the brash billionaire's longing for money, love and respect brought him crashing down
Shootout off Tobruk
TIME
This man may turn you green with envy — or just turn you off. Flaunting it is the game, and
TRUMP
is the name.
GQ
SUCCESS
How Sweet It Is
Men Who Take Risks And Make Millions
46 Cool Looks for Hot Times
TRUMP ON TI
HOW I DO MY DEALS • EXCERPTS FRO
New Y
THE NICE NEW YORK MONTHLY • APRIL $2.50
SPY
Our NICE ISSUE
DONALD TRUMP
GLAMOROUS GALS
IT'S FUN
PAUL SIMON
WE TRUMP 'THE DONALD'
CRACKED
YOU'RE FIRED!
BAD MRS. KENNEDY
WOODSTOCK FLASHBACK
LIT SNIT
New York
EXCLUSIVE
The inside story of how he clawed his way back from the abyss—thanks to luck, bluster, and a pack of Chinese billionaires
TRUMP'S NEAR-DEATH EXPERIENCE
By Craig Horowitz
LinkedIn Spy Wars / The R
Newsw
READY FOR...
WA
The 50 Best Companies to Sell For
ellingPower
Shy guy
Bloomberg Businessweek
Seriously?
HI-TECH
EXECUTIVE PAY
THE YEAR IN REVIEW
RODMAN & RENSHAW
CROSSWELL
EQUITIES
SINCE 1951
Trump to America: "Never Give Up"
Tech check: Mind readers,
New England's patriots turn over
arr
YOU'RE HIRED!
7 WAYS TO SUCCEED AT ANY JOB
(From a guy who's failed at several)
PLUS:
Soledad O'Brien
Why we love D.C.
Telegraph Magazine
MY DATE WITH THE DONALD
Forbes
PLUS ATHOME PRESENTS THE ANNUAL HOME IMPROVEMENT GUIDE!!!
Palm Springs Life
Why is this man smiling?
With The Donald managing the dazzling new Trump 29 Casino, he's not the only one counting on a Renaissance in the eastern end of the valley
OUR BIG REAL ESTATE ISSUE
THE MONEY
New J
"YOU'RE FIRED."
So What

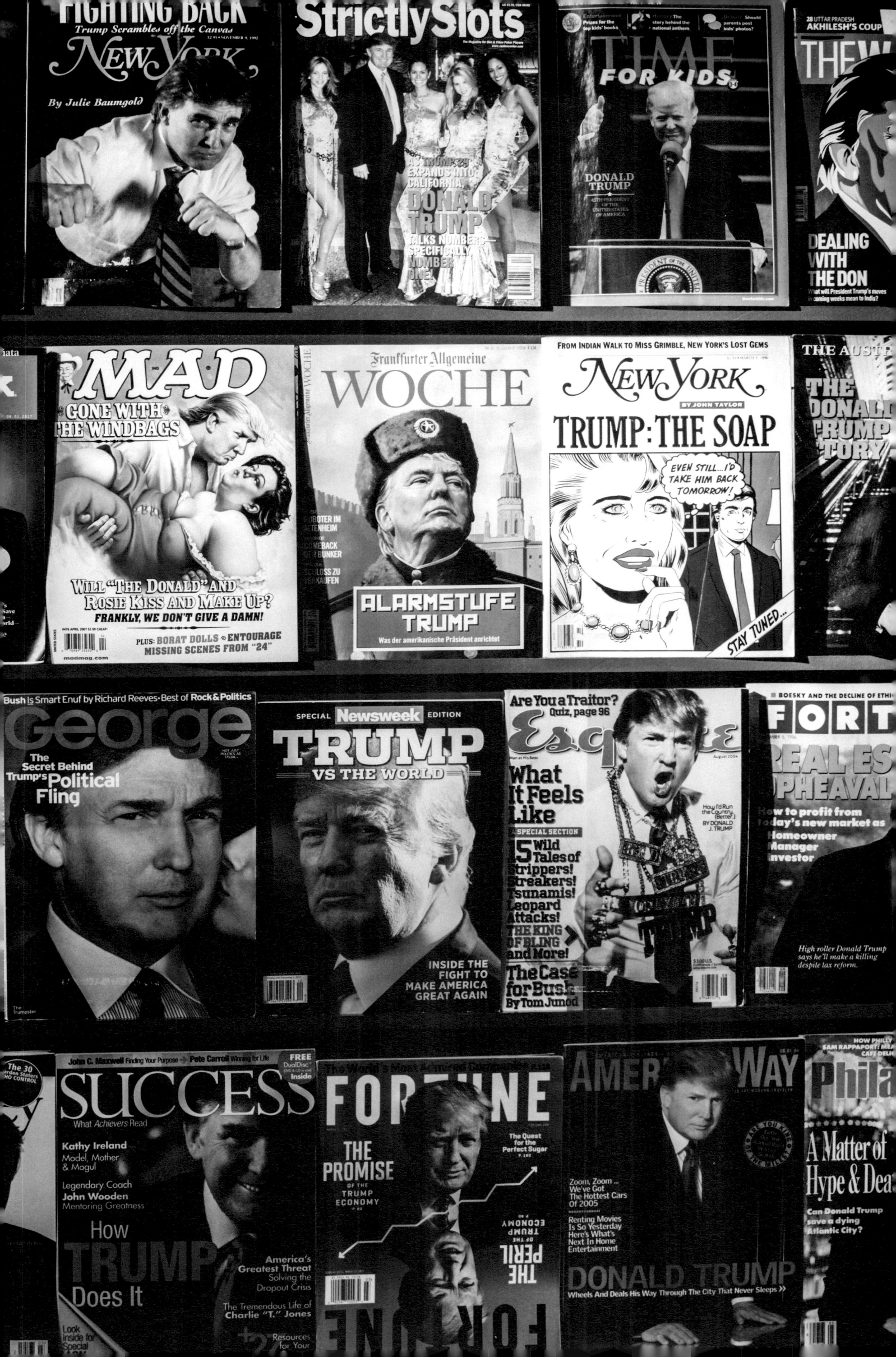
FIGHTING BACK
Trump Scrambles off the Canvas
NEW YORK
By Julie Baumgold
Strictly Slots
DONALD TRUMP
TALKS NUMBERS—SPECIFICALLY NUMBER ONE.
TIME FOR KIDS
DONALD TRUMP
AKHILESH'S COUP
DEALING WITH THE DON
MAD
GONE WITH THE WINDBAGS
WILL "THE DONALD" AND ROSIE KISS AND MAKE UP?
FRANKLY, WE DON'T GIVE A DAMN!
PLUS: BORAT DOLLS • ENTOURAGE MISSING SCENES FROM "24"
madmag.com
Frankfurter Allgemeine
WOCHE
ALARMSTUFE TRUMP
Was der amerikanische Präsident anrichtet
FROM INDIAN WALK TO MISS GRIMBLE, NEW YORK'S LOST GEMS
NEW YORK
BY JOHN TAYLOR
TRUMP: THE SOAP
EVEN STILL...I'D TAKE HIM BACK TOMORROW!
STAY TUNED...
Bush Is Smart Enuf by Richard Reeves • Best of Rock & Politics
George
The Secret Behind Trump's Political Fling
SPECIAL Newsweek EDITION
TRUMP
VS THE WORLD
INSIDE THE FIGHT TO MAKE AMERICA GREAT AGAIN
Are You a Traitor? Quiz, page 96
Esquire
What It Feels Like
15 Wild Tales of Strippers! Streakers! Tsunamis! Leopard Attacks!
THE KING OF BLING and More!
The Case for Bush By Tom Junod
How I'd Run the Country. (Better.) BY DONALD J. TRUMP
BOESKY AND THE DECLINE OF ETHICS
FORT
REAL ESTATE UPHEAVAL
How to profit from today's new market as Homeowner Manager Investor
High roller Donald Trump says he'll make a killing despite tax reform.
John C. Maxwell Finding Your Purpose • Pete Carroll Winning for Life
FREE DualDisc Inside
SUCCESS
What Achievers Read
Kathy Ireland Model, Mother & Mogul
Legendary Coach John Wooden Mentoring Greatness
How TRUMP Does It
America's Greatest Threat Solving the Dropout Crisis
The Tremendous Life of Charlie "T." Jones
FORTUNE
THE PROMISE OF THE TRUMP ECONOMY
The Quest for the Perfect Sugar
THE PERIL OF THE TRUMP ECONOMY
AMERICAN WAY
Zoom, Zoom ... We've Got The Hottest Cars Of 2005
Renting Movies Is So Yesterday Here's What's Next In Home Entertainment
DONALD TRUMP
Wheels And Deals His Way Through The City That Never Sleeps
A Matter of Hype & Deal
Can Donald Trump save a dying Atlantic City?

LOSE SO DECISIVELY THAT THE LONG ARC OF JUSTICE WOULD FINALLY CUT THE HEAD OFF THIS PART OF THE LONG AMERICAN NIGHT. WE COULD FINALLY GO HIGH WHEN THEY WENT LOW.

OF COURSE, AS SOON AS THE GAME OPENED, OUR ONLINE KNEE-JERK OUTRAGE CULTURE KICKED IN. SERRANO WAS TAKEN BEHIND THE DIGITAL WOODSHED, AS PROGRESSIVES CHARGED HIM WITH "GLORIFYING THIS MONSTER," "GIVING HIM ATTENTION," "ADDING POWER TO THIS AWFUL MAN," AND ACTING AS "TRUMP PROPAGANDIST." PERHAPS, HAD ALL THIS BEEN DISPLAYED AT TRUMP CAMPAIGN STOPS (OFTEN IT IS) AND IN FOX NEWS GREENROOMS, PARROTED BY JERRY FALWELL AND THE EVANGELICAL RIGHT. BUT COME ON! THIS INSTALLATION WAS BY ONE

OF THE MOST VISIBLE ARTISTS OF COLOR IN THE LAST 30 YEARS AND DISPLAYED IN A QUASI ART GALLERY NEAR CHELSEA. I'M ALL FOR BEING INTOLERANT OF INTOLERANCE, UNLEASHING OUR ANGER AND NEVER NEGOTIATING WITH HIS BASE, WHICH THINKS THAT THE COUNTRY IS BEING TAKEN OVER BY BROWN PEOPLE, THAT EVERYONE IS OUT TO GET THEM AND LIVING ON THE DOLE (MANY TRUMPISTS RECEIVE MANY SORTS OF GOVERNMENT ASSISTANCE), WHILE TAKING THEIR WHITE PRIVILEGES AWAY. IT SEEMS DISINGENUOUS TO EXPRESS DISMAY THAT AN ARTIST IS TRYING TO DOCUMENT THIS LONG RISE AND THE CONSIDERABLE COMPLICITY NECESSARY FOR IT TO HAVE GROWN INTO THIS MALIGNANCY AND NATIONAL EMERGENCY.

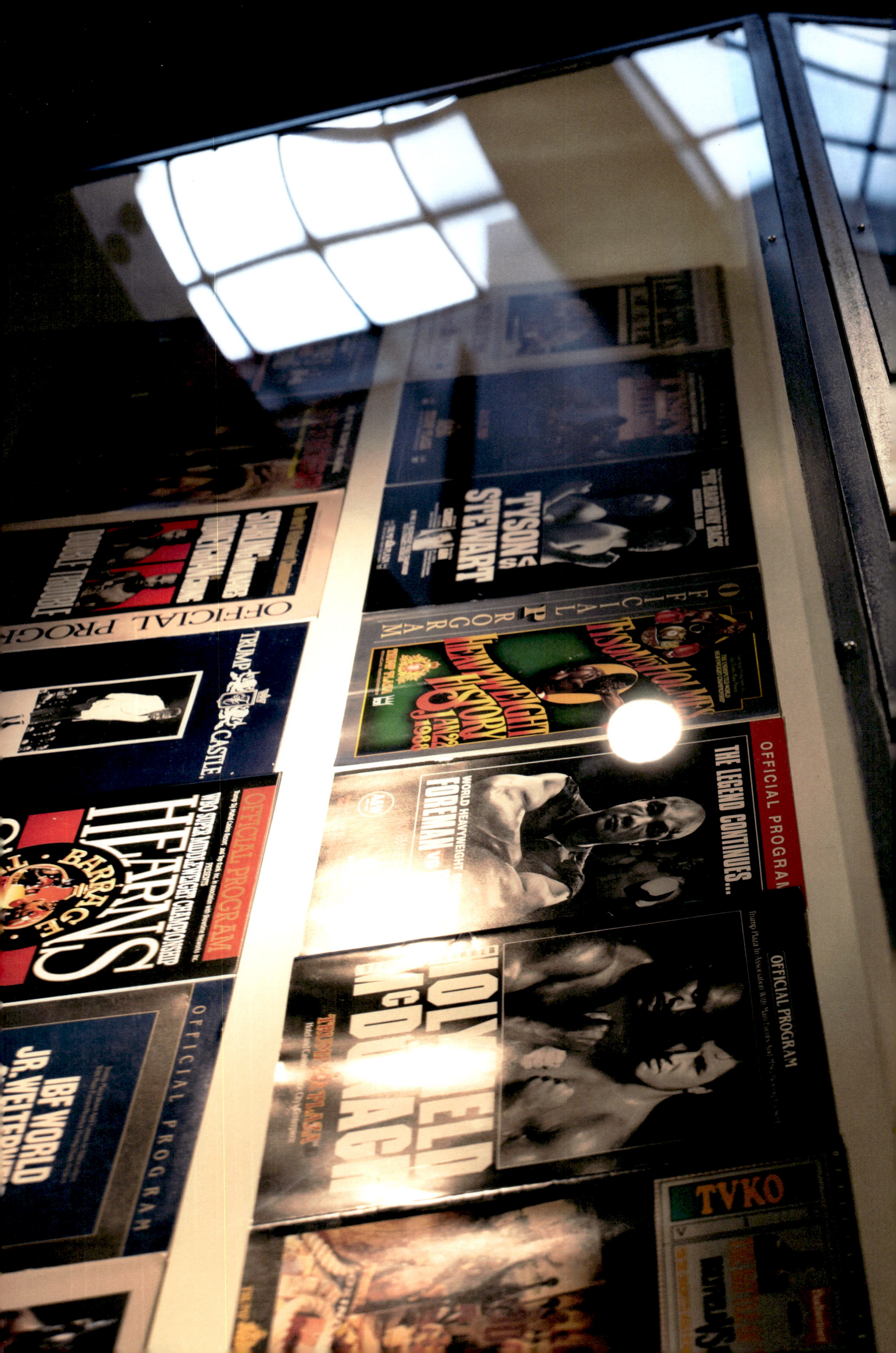
TYSON vs STEWART
OFFICIAL PROGRAM
HEAVYWEIGHT HISTORY
JAN 22 1988
TRUMP CASTLE
OFFICIAL PROGRAM
HEARNS
BARRAGE
WBO SUPER MIDDLEWEIGHT CHAMPIONSHIP
OFFICIAL PROGRAM
THE LEGEND CONTINUES...
WORLD HEAVYWEIGHT
FOREMAN vs
OFFICIAL PROGRAM
TRUMP PLAZA
OFFICIAL PROGRAM
IBF WORLD
TVKO

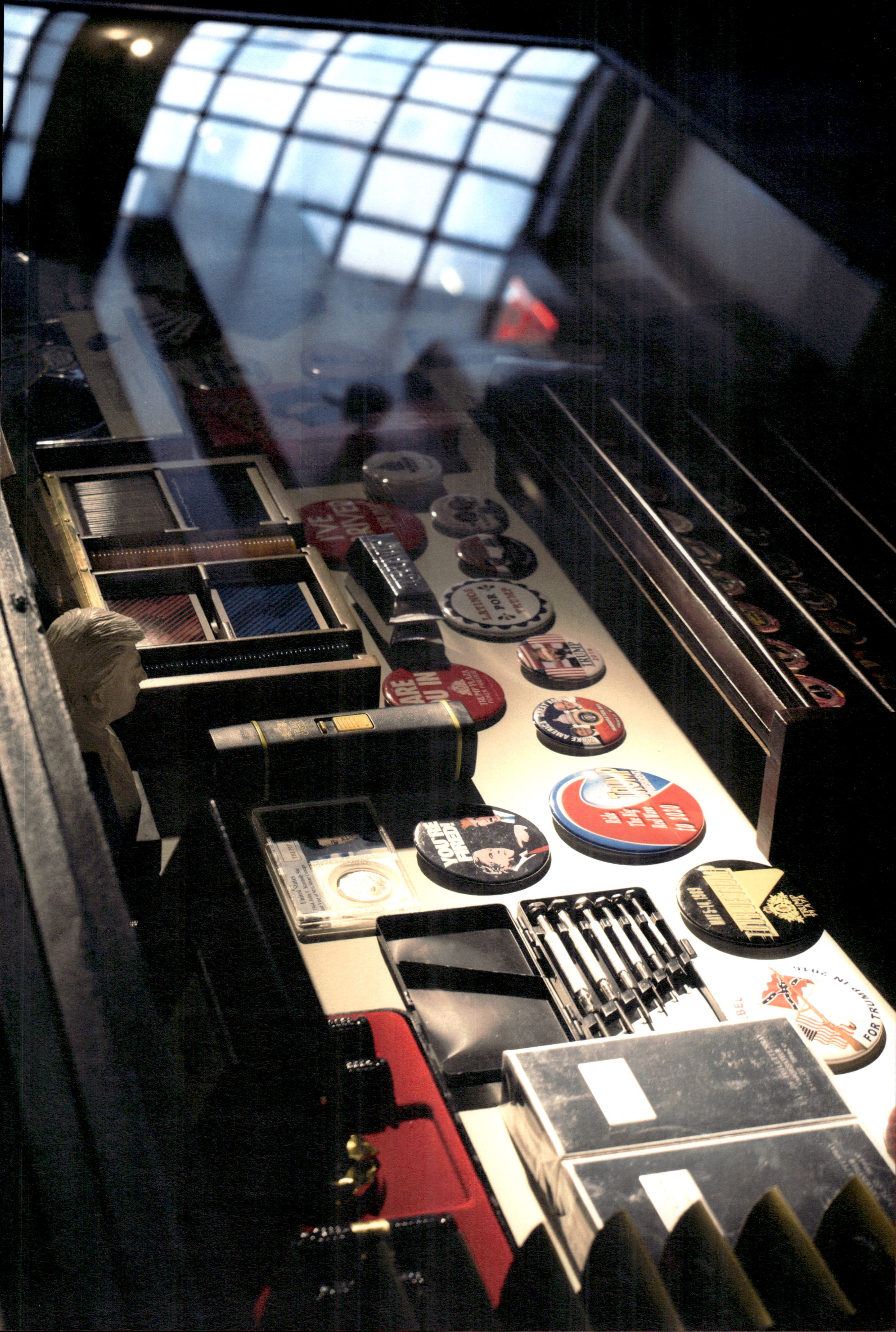
LATINOS FOR TRUMP
YOU'RE FIRED!

PLUS SERRANO HAS EARNED OUR TRUST. HE IS NO STRANGER TO CULTURE WARS. HE WAS THERE AT GROUND ZERO ON MAY 1, 1989, WHEN A CATALOGUE WITH HIS ICONIC PHOTOGRAPH "PISS CHRIST" WAS TORN UP ON THE FLOOR OF THE U.S. SENATE. SOON THEREAFTER, GAY PHOTOGRAPHER ROBERT MAPPLETHORPE WAS DENOUNCED IN CONGRESS FOR HIS MAN IN A POLYESTER SUIT, A PHOTOGRAPH OF A BLACK MAN WITH A LONG PENIS. IN 1999, ATTACK DOG RUDY GIULIANI WENT AFTER THE WORK OF YET ANOTHER ARTIST OF COLOR, CHRIS OFILI'S "THE HOLY VIRGIN MARY," A DEPICTION OF MARY AS BLACK. THIS HATE HAS BEEN VISIBLY HERE AND NURTURED FOR A LONG TIME.

AND YET, ON VIEW HERE IS SOMETHING A BIT DIFFERENT:

NOT OUT-AND-OUT HATE, BUT A REAL EXAMPLE OF WHAT THE BANALITY OF BANALITY AND THE BANALITY OF EVIL LOOK LIKE. SEE TRUMP-SIGNED GOLF BAGS, AMERICAN-FLAG BOXING GLOVES, POSTERS OF HIM AS BETSY ROSS SEWING AN AMERICAN FLAG, MAGA HATS AND JACKETS, "HILLARY FOR PRISON" NOVELTY BILLS, AND TRUMP: THE GAME — THE BOARD GAME'S MOTTO IS: "IT'S NOT WHETHER YOU WIN OR LOSE; ITS WHETHER YOU WIN." THERE'S A PIECE OF HIS AND MELANIA'S 2005 GOLDEN-FLAKED WEDDING CAKE, A TRUMP DESIGNER TIE COLLECTION, SLOT-MACHINES, SOAP, CUFF LINKS, BODY LOTION, BOOKS HE SUPPOSEDLY WROTE, HAIRSPRAY, BEER MUGS, MISS AMERICA PARAPHERNALIA, AND BUNCHES OF STUFF FROM THE FAILED TRUMP SHUTTLE.

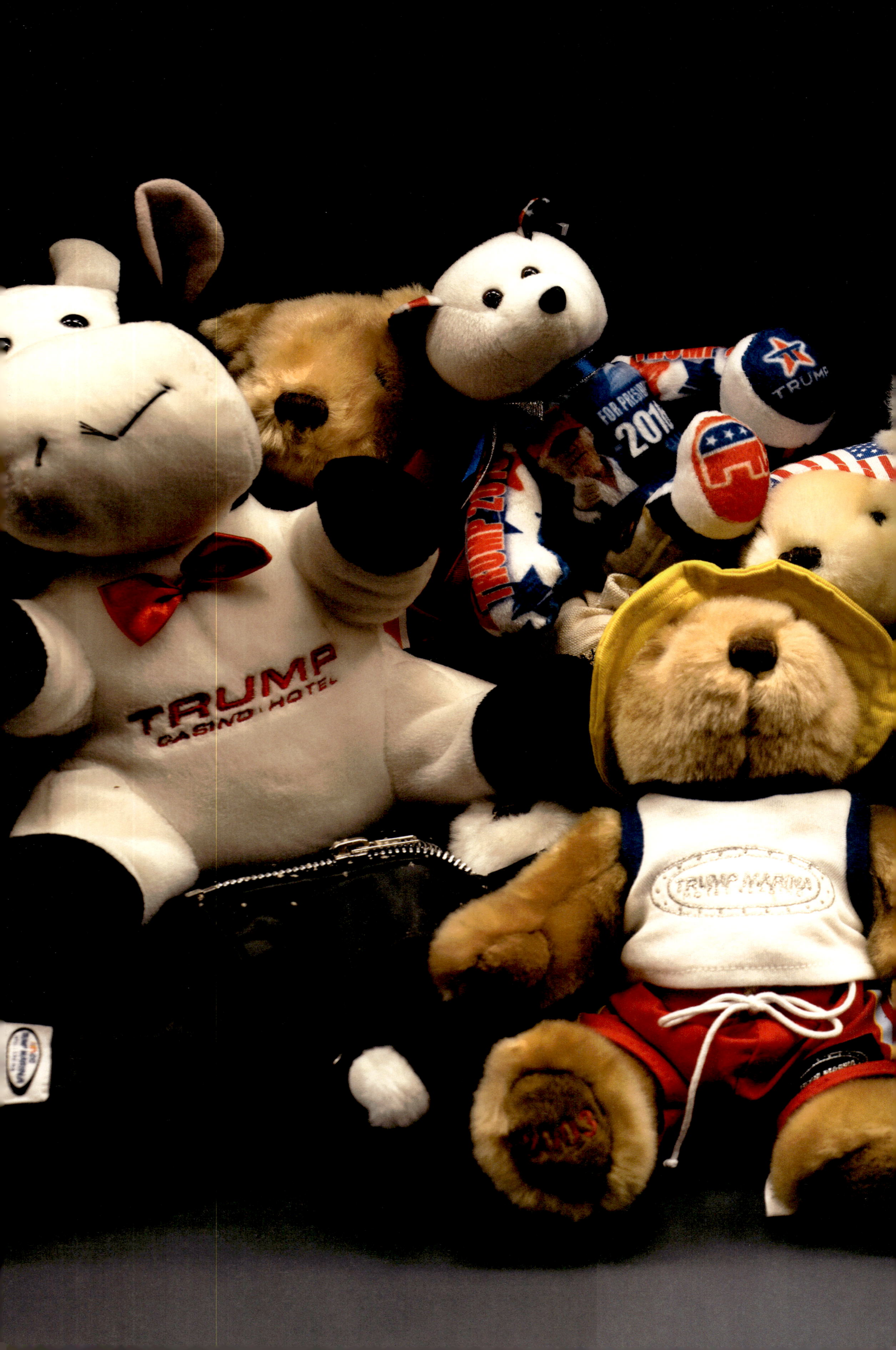
TRUMP
CASINO HOTEL
TRUMP
TRUMP MARINA

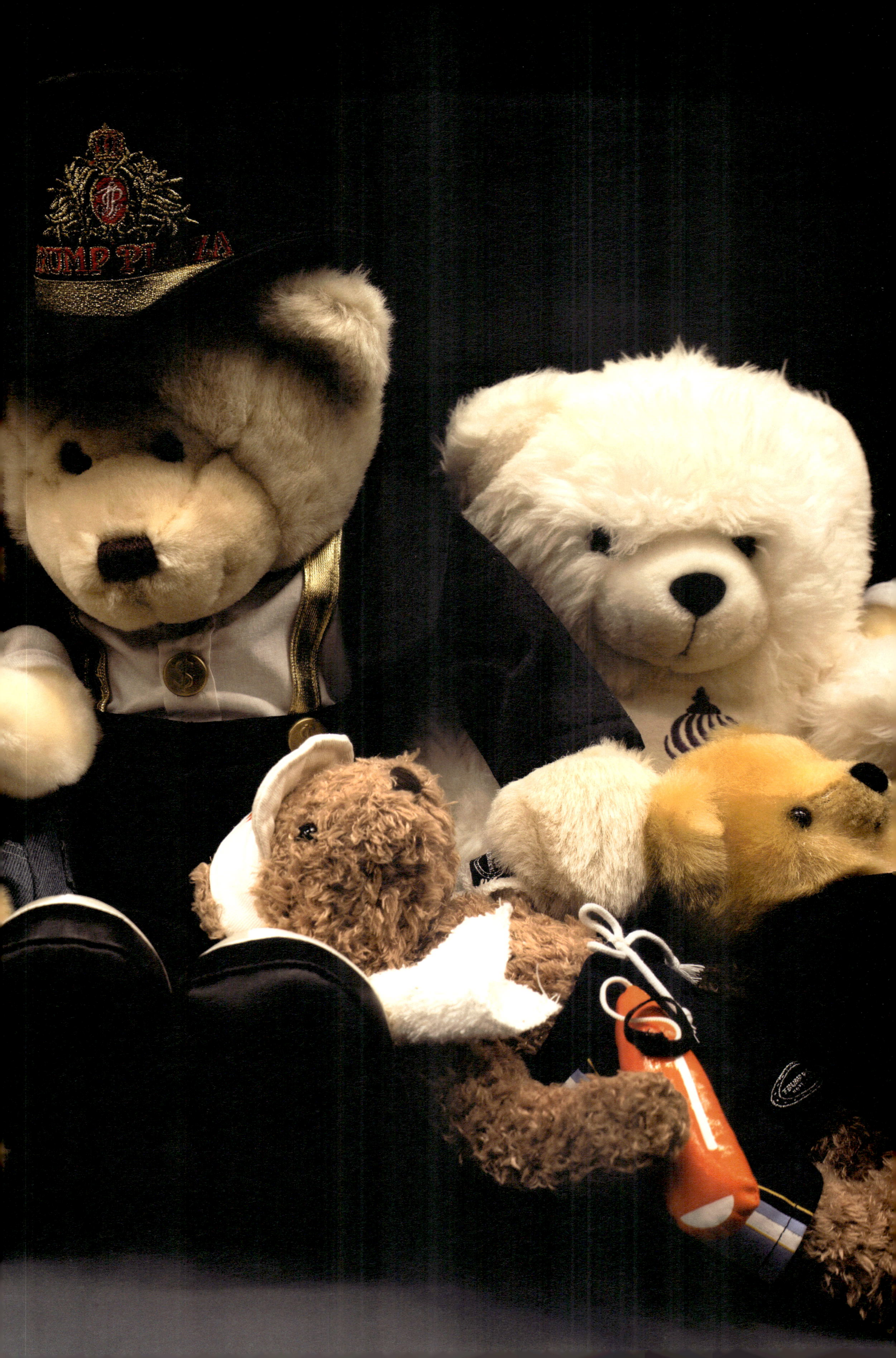

ALSO HERE ARE SIGNED PICTURES OF ALL OF HIS WIVES, IVANKA, KELLYANNE CONWAY, AND THE OTHER PATSIES AND HUSTLERS. WE LOVED THIS SHIT, ATE IT UP — EVEN AS WE HATED IT AND MOCKED IT. WE THOUGHT WE COULD ENJOY THE PLEASURE OF HIS CRASSNESS AND STILL REMAIN SUPERIOR, ALOFT AND ALOOF, SAFE FROM WHAT HE REPRESENTED. BUT IN ENJOYING IT, WE EMPOWERED HIM.

OF COURSE, SERRANO'S NOBLE PROJECT IS ONLY A PICTURE OF THE SURFACE OF WHAT THIS PYRAMID-OF-BULLSHIT, TRILLION-DOLLAR-DEFICITS, "NASCENT TOTALITARIANISM BY A BIRTHER WHO ACCUSED BARACK OBAMA OF BEING A KENYAN-BORN SLEEPER" CANDIDATE LOOKED LIKE BEFORE IT BECAME MAGA MADNESS. THE GAME IS NOT

AN ACTUAL "PORTRAIT." IT DOESN'T GIVE US TRUMP AGED, BLOATED, SURROUNDED BY REPUBLICAN HENCHMEN AND HENCHWOMEN, CHAMPIONED BY PERHAPS THE WORST IMMIGRANT IN AMERICAN HISTORY, RUPERT MURDOCH. (MY IMMIGRATION POLICY WOULD BE DEPORT JUST ONE FAMILY: THE MURDOCHS — I SURMISE AMERICA WOULD BEGIN TO HEAL BEFORE LONG.) THE GAME CAN'T GIVE US THE MAN WHO SUPPORTED AN ACCUSED CHILD MOLESTER FOR THE U.S. SENATE, CALLED FASCISTS "GOOD PEOPLE," WAS ACCUSED BY 23 (!) WOMEN OF SEXUAL ASSAULT OR HARASSMENT, AND LIED ABOUT PAYING OFF A PORN STAR AFTER SLEEPING WITH HER WHILE HIS WIFE WAS AT HOME WITH A NEWBORN INFANT. THE MEANNESS ISN'T HERE OR THE TERRIBLE JUDGMENT AND DANGER. SADLY, MISSING FROM THIS

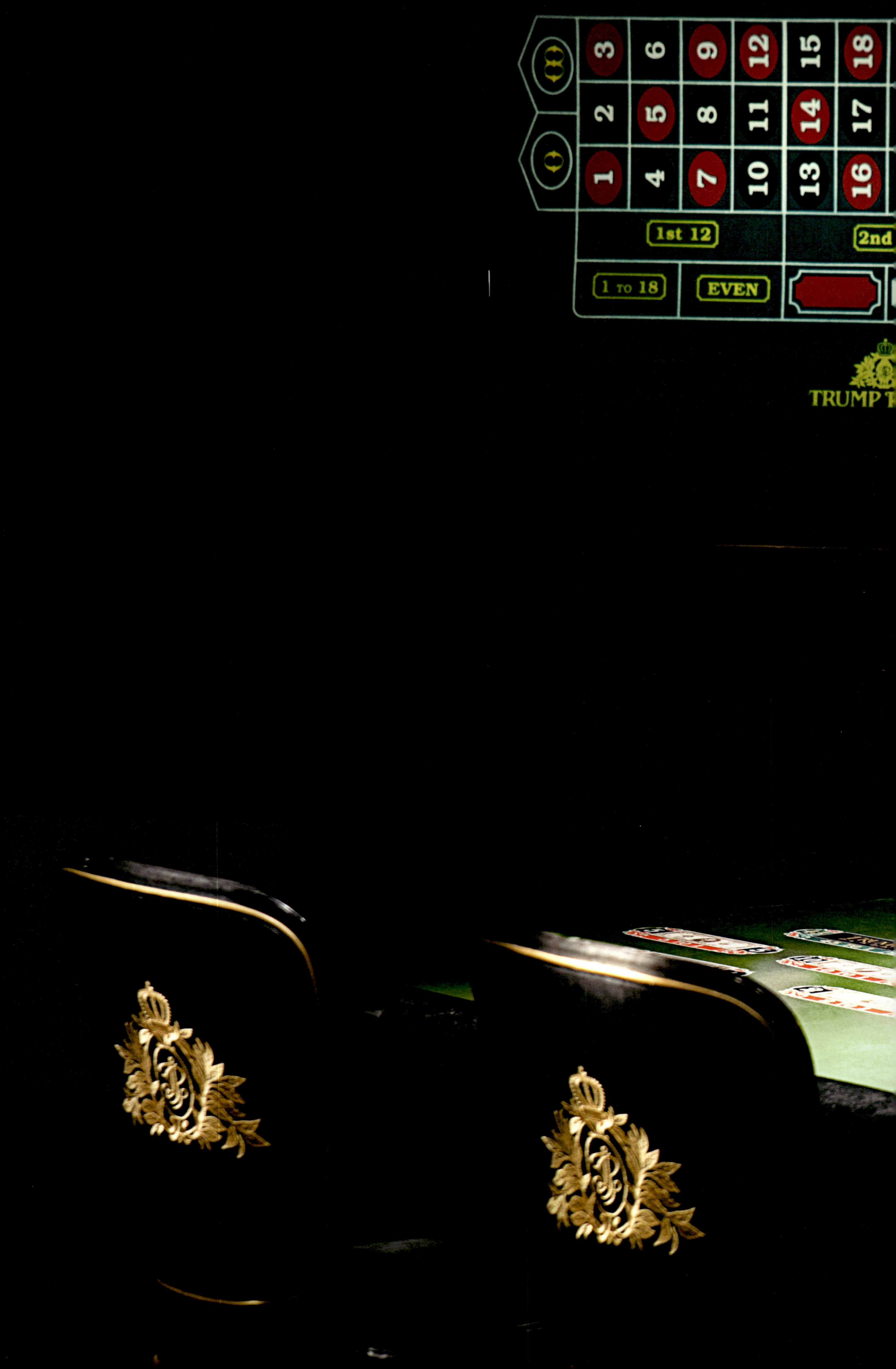
1st 12
2nd
1 TO 18
EVEN

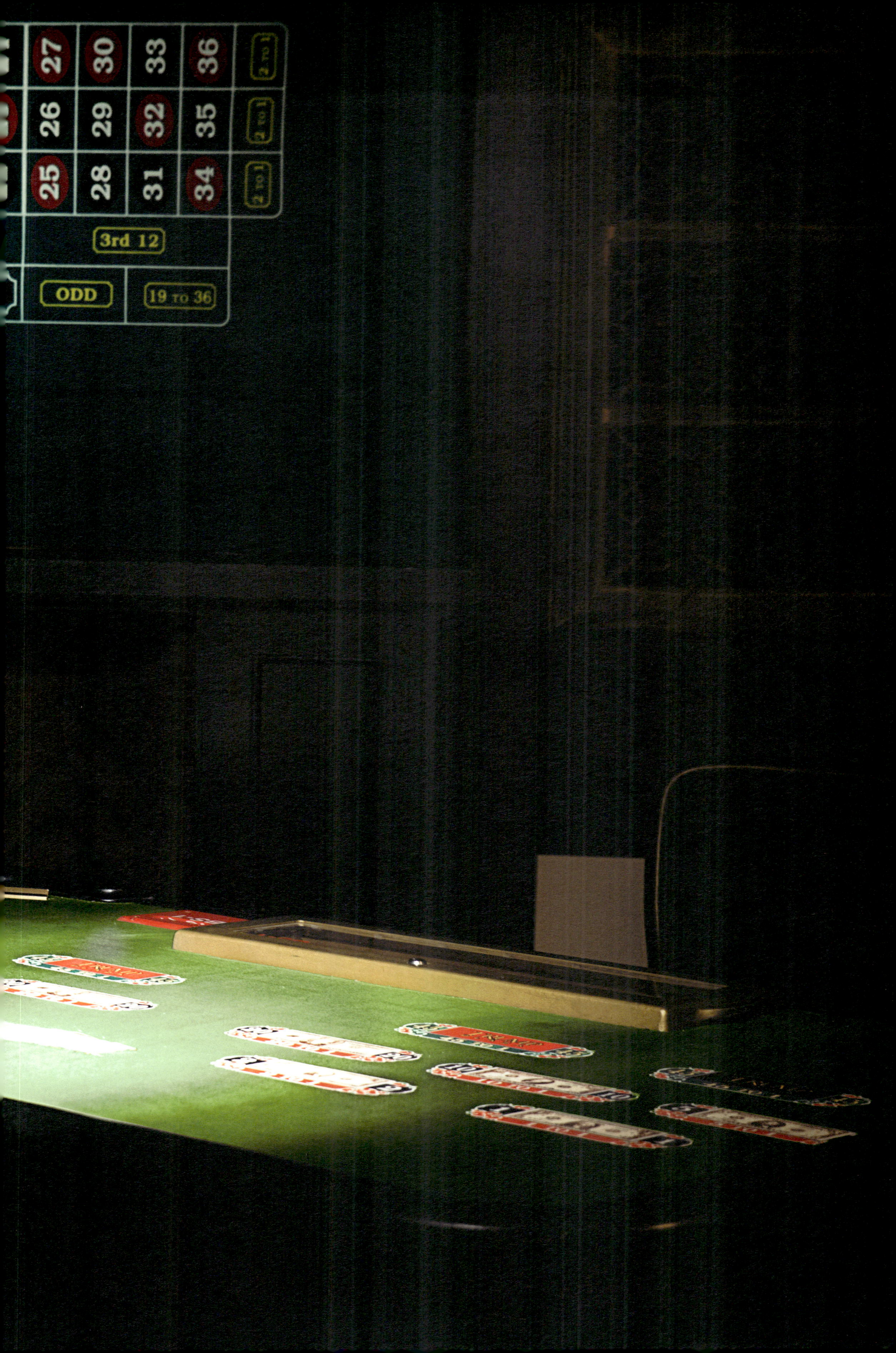
27
30
33
36
2 TO 1
26
29
32
35
2 TO 1
25
28
31
34
2 TO 1
3rd 12
ODD
19 TO 36

UNDERTAKING (THE SMITHSONIAN SHOULD PURCHASE THE WHOLE THING) ARE THE CRAZY FULL-PAGE ADS TRUMP TOOK OUT IN ALL THE NEW YORK NEWSPAPERS ON MAY 1, 1989 — AS FATE WOULD HAVE IT, THE SAME DAY SERRANO'S "PISS CHRIST" WAS DESTROYED AND SERRANO WAS MADE INTO A BLACK DEVIL OF THE REPUBLICANS. TRUMP'S AD CALLED FOR THE RETURN OF THE DEATH PENALTY TO KILL "THE CENTRAL PARK FIVE." THESE WERE FOUR BLACK BOYS AND ONE HISPANIC WHO WERE ACCUSED OF, AND LATER ACQUITTED OF, THE BRUTAL RAPE OF A WHITE FEMALE JOGGER. BARING THE FANGS OF WHO HE WAS AND IS, THAT MAY, TRUMP TOLD LARRY KING, "I HATE THESE PEOPLE, AND LET'S ALL HATE THESE PEOPLE, BECAUSE MAYBE HATE IS WHAT WE NEED IF WE'RE GONNA GET SOMETHING DONE."

DAILY NEWS, MAY 1, 1989
DONALD TRUMP TOOK OUT FULL-PAGE ADVERTS IN FOUR OF NEW YORK'S MAIN NEWSPAPERS, CALLING FOR THE DEATH PENALTY, AFTER FIVE YOUNG AFRICAN-AMERICAN AND LATINO BOYS WERE ACCUSED OF AN ATTACK ON A JOGGER IN CENTRAL PARK. WRONGLY CONVICTED, "THE CENTRAL PARK FIVE" WERE EXONERATED IN 2002, EVENTUALLY RECEIVING AROUND $40 MILLION IN COMPENSATION

BRING BACK THE DEATH PENALTY.

BRING BACK OUR POLICE!

What has happened to our City over the past ten years? What has happened to law and order, to the neighborhood cop we all trusted to safeguard our homes and families, the cop who had the power under the law to help us in times of danger, keep us safe from those who would prey on innocent lives to fulfill some distorted inner need. What has happened to the respect for authority, the fear of retribution by the courts, society and the police for those who break the law, who wantonly trespass on the rights of others? What has happened is the complete breakdown of life as we knew it.

Many New York families — White, Black, Hispanic and Asian — have had to give up the pleasure of a leisurely stroll inthe Park at dusk, the Saturday visit to the playground with their families, the bike ride at dawn, or just sitting on their stoops — given them up as hostages to a world ruled by the law of the streets, as roving bands of wild criminals roam our neighborhoods, **dispensing their own vicious brand of twisted hatred on whomever they encounter. At what point did we cross the line from the fine and noble pursuit of** genuine civil liberties to the reckless and dangerously permissive atmosphere which allows criminals of every age to beat and rape a helpless woman and then laugh at her family's anguish? And why do they laugh? They laugh because they know that soon, very soon, they will be returned to the streets to rape and maim and kill once again — and yet face no great personal risk to themselves.

Mayor Koch has stated that hate and rancor should be removed from our hearts. I do not think so. I want to hate these muggers and murderers. They should be forced to suffer and, when they kill, they should be executed for their crimes. They must serve as examples so that others will think long and hard before committing a crime or an act of violence. Yes, Mayor Koch, I want to hate these murderers and I always will. I am not looking to psychoanalyze or understand them, I am looking to punish them. If the punishment is strong, the attacks on innocent people will stop. I recently watched a newscast trying to explain the "anger in these young men". I no longer want to understand their anger. I want them to understand our anger. I want them to be afraid.

How can our great society tolerate the continued brutalization of its citizens by crazed misfits? Criminals must be told that their CIVIL LIBERTIES END WHEN AN ATTACK ON OUR SAFETY BEGINS!

When I was young, I sat in a diner with my father and witnessed two young bullies cursing and threatening a very frightened waitress. Two cops rushed in, lifted up the thugs and threw them out the door, warning them never to cause trouble again. I miss the feeling of security New York's finest once gave to the citizens of this City.

Let our politicians give back our police department's power to keep us safe. Unshackle them from the constant chant of "police brutality" which every petty criminal hurls immediately at an officer who has just risked his or her life to save another's. We must cease our continuous pandering to the criminal population of this City. Give New York back to the citizens who have earned the right to be New Yorkers. Send a message loud and clear to those who would murder our citizens and terrorize New York—
BRING BACK THE DEATH PENALTY
AND BRING BACK OUR POLICE!

Donald J. Trump

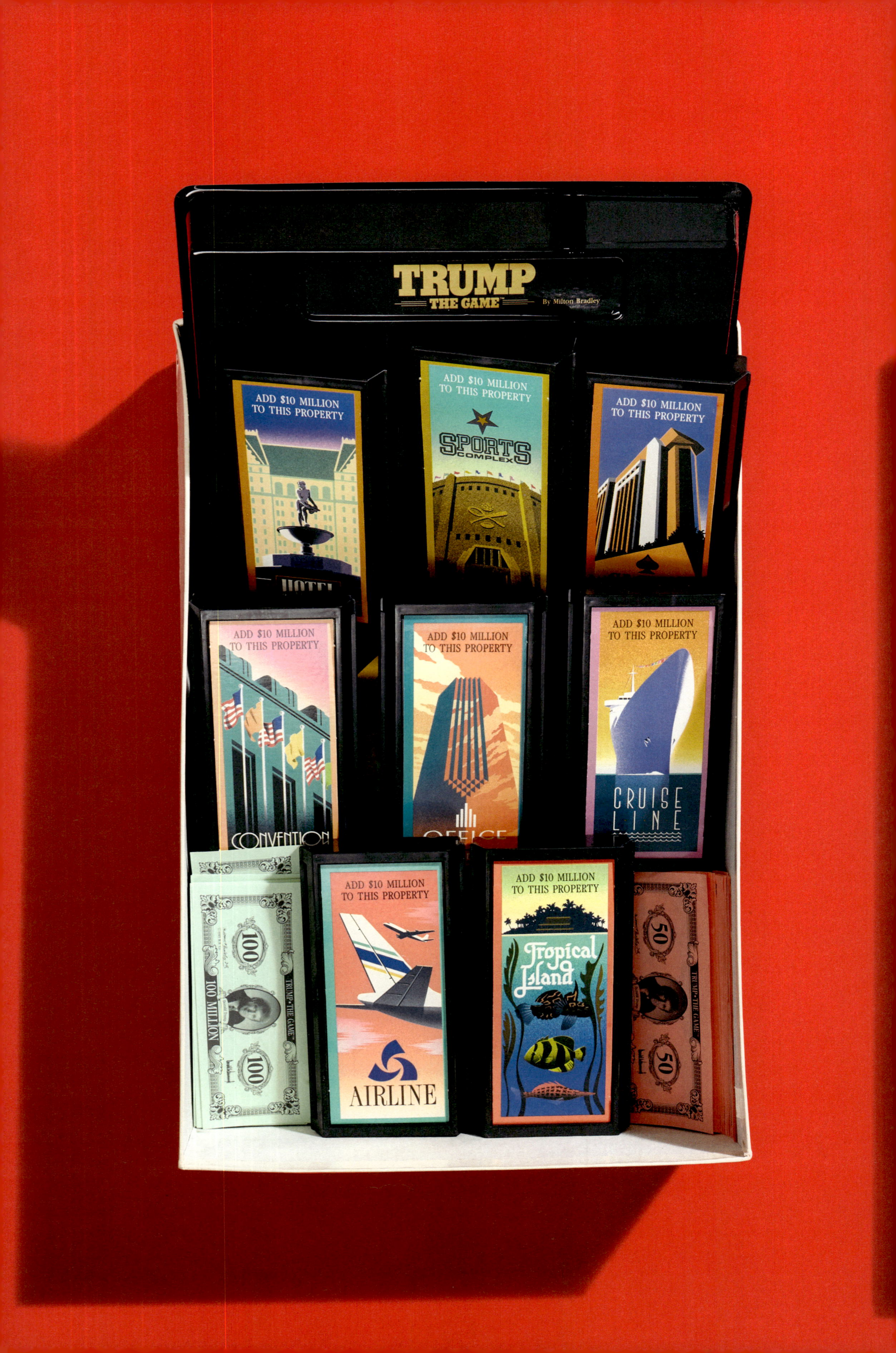
TRUMP
THE GAME
By Milton Bradley
ADD $10 MILLION TO THIS PROPERTY
SPORTS COMPLEX
CRUISE LINE
CONVENTION
AIRLINE
Tropical Island
100 MILLION
TRUMP · THE GAME

TRUMP: THE GAME
ORIGINAL MILTON BRADLEY BOARD GAME, 1989

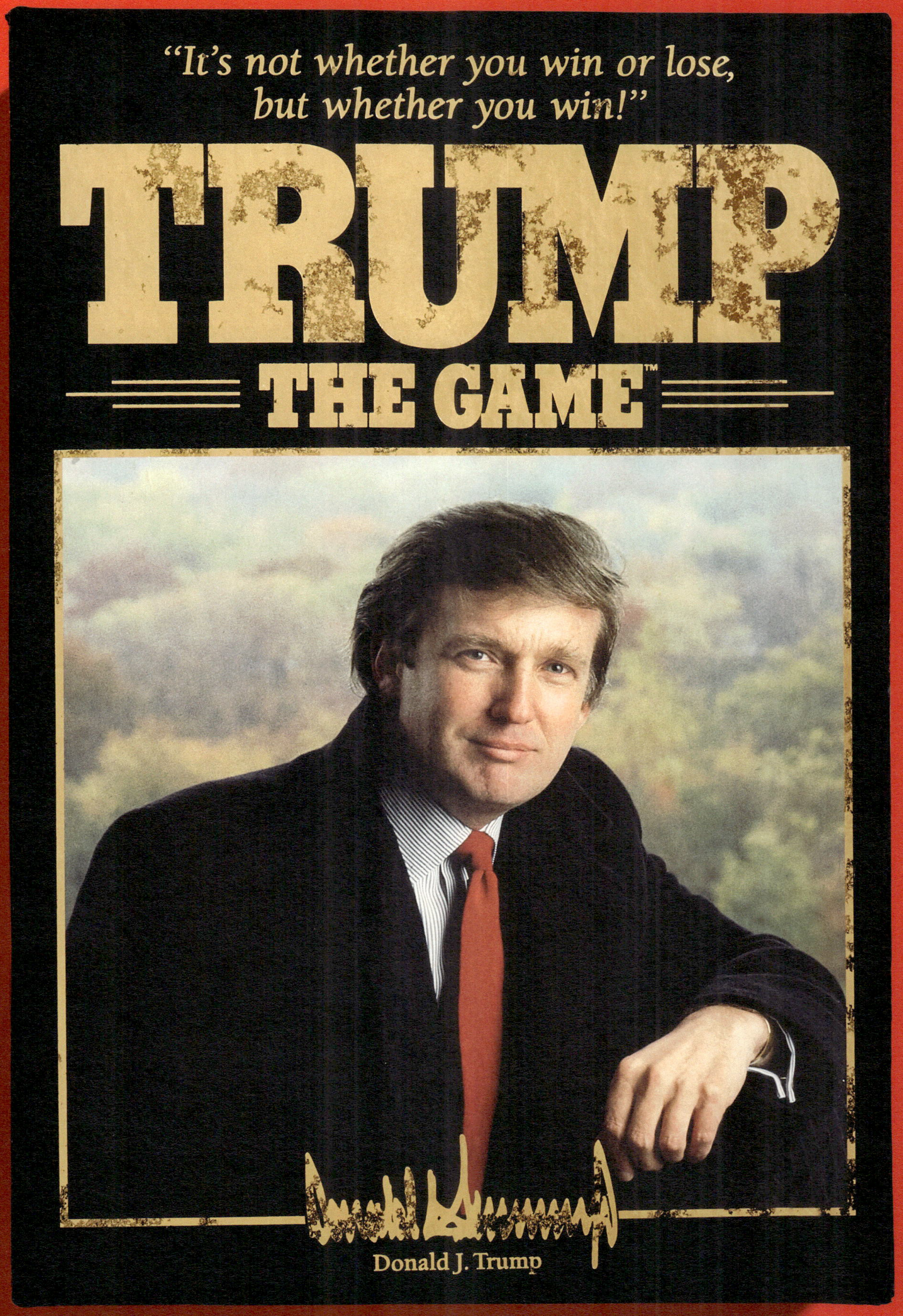

NEWSWEEK MAGAZINE, NOVEMBER 8, 2016
125,000 COPIES WERE PRINTED, DISTRIBUTED AND RECALLED
SIGNED DONALD TRUMP

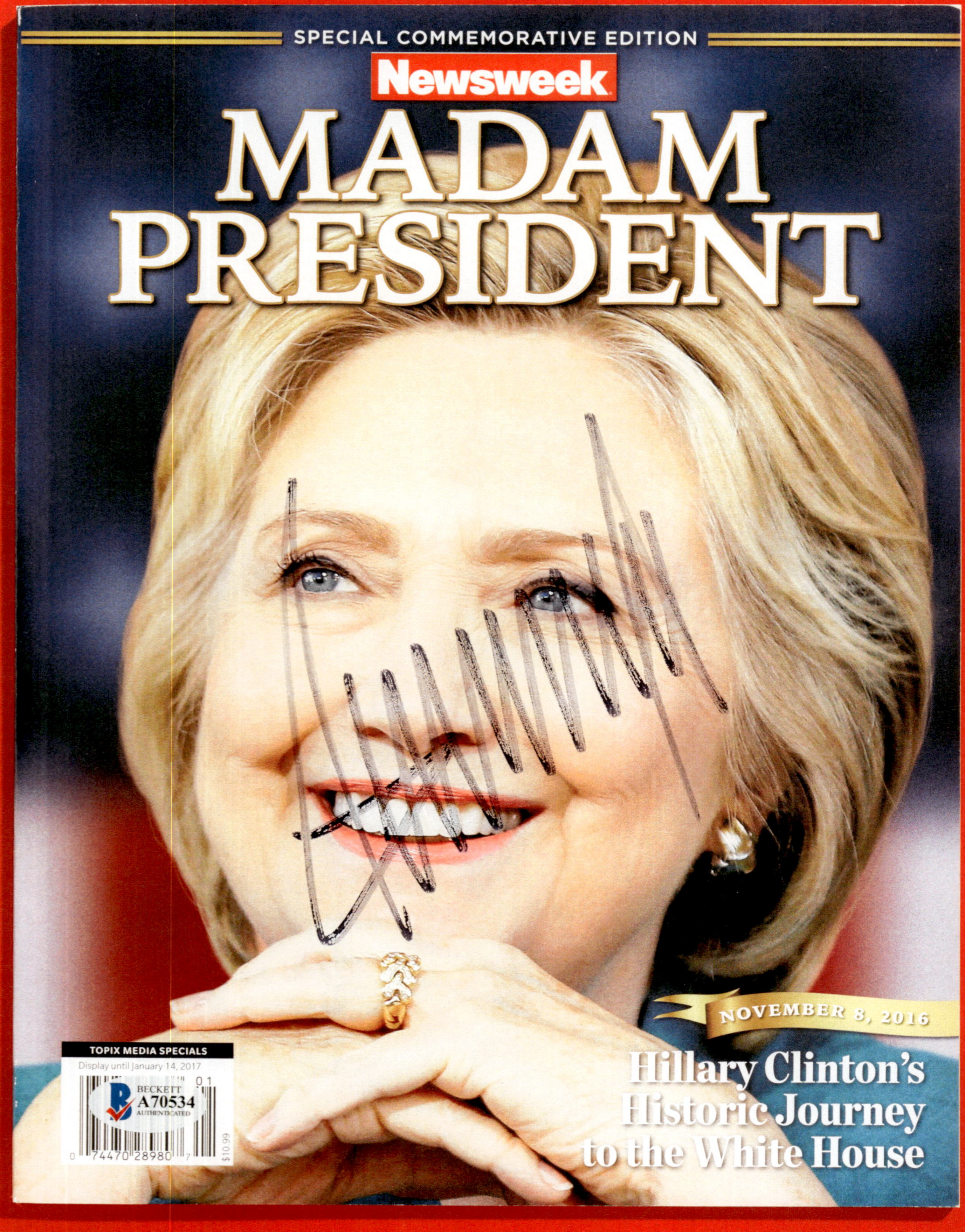

TIME MAGAZINE, AUGUST 31, 2015
SIGNED DONALD TRUMP

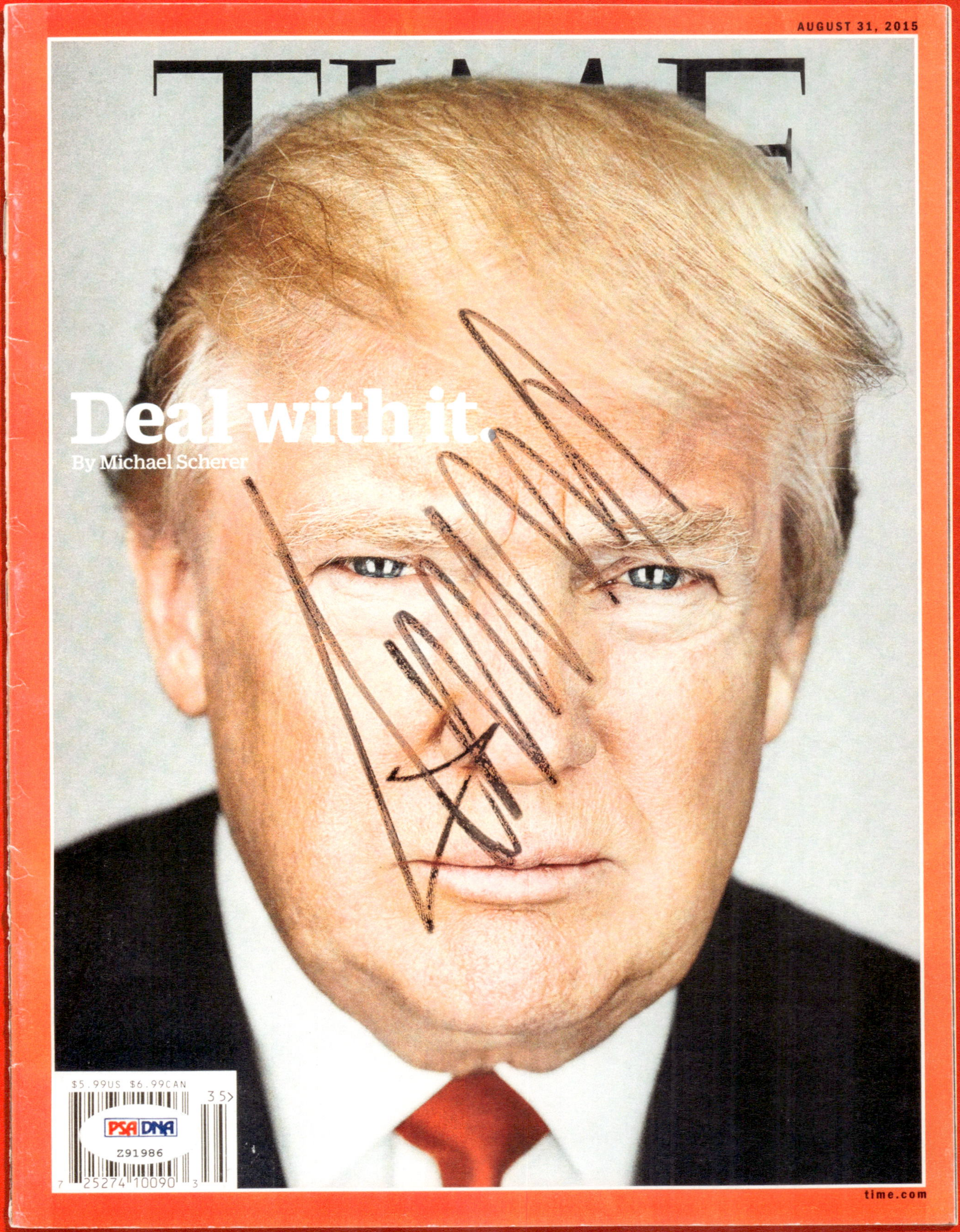

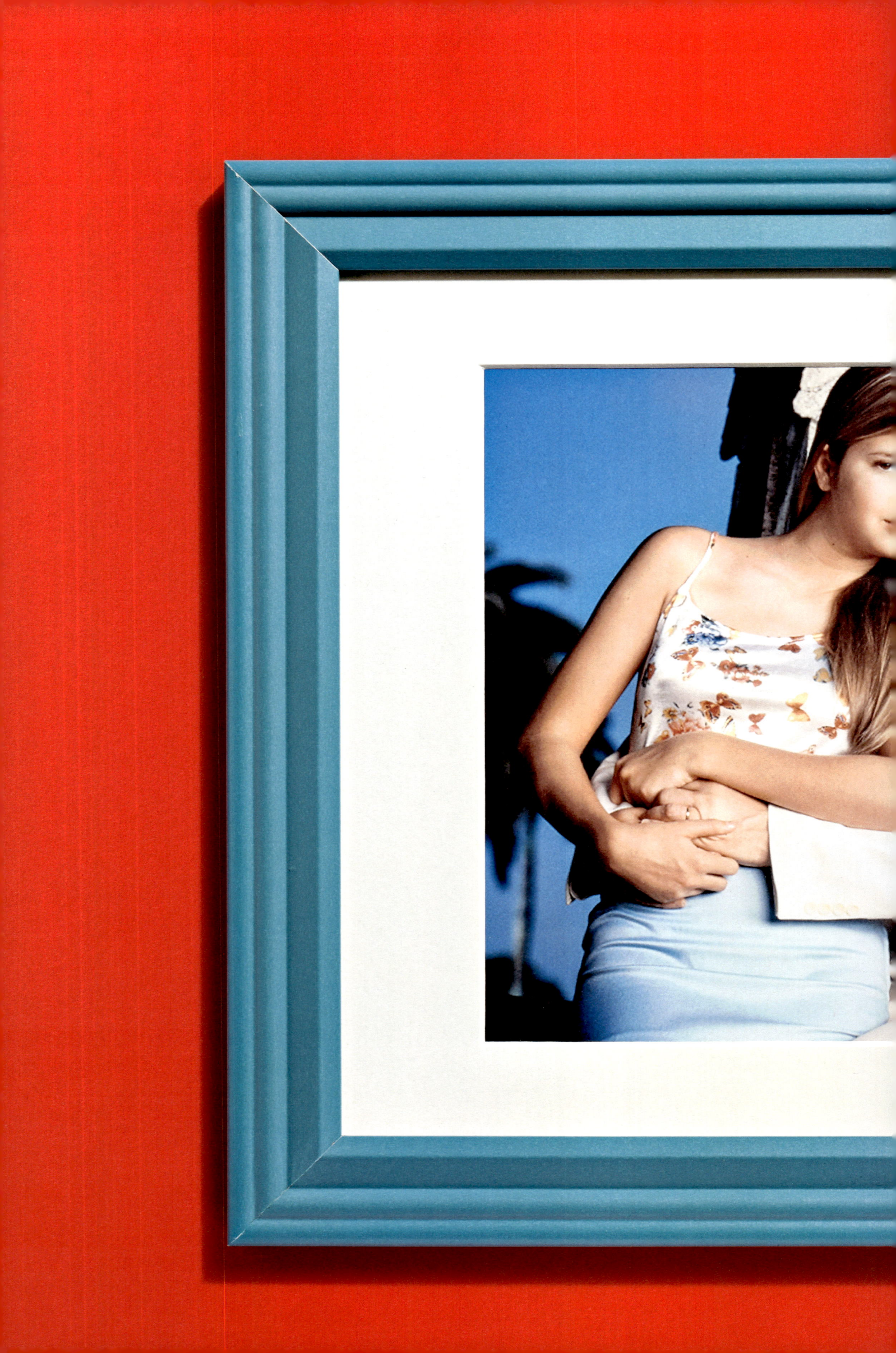

SIGNED PHOTOGRAPH OF IVANKA AND DONALD TRUMP
AT MAR-A-LAGO, PALM BEACH, 1996

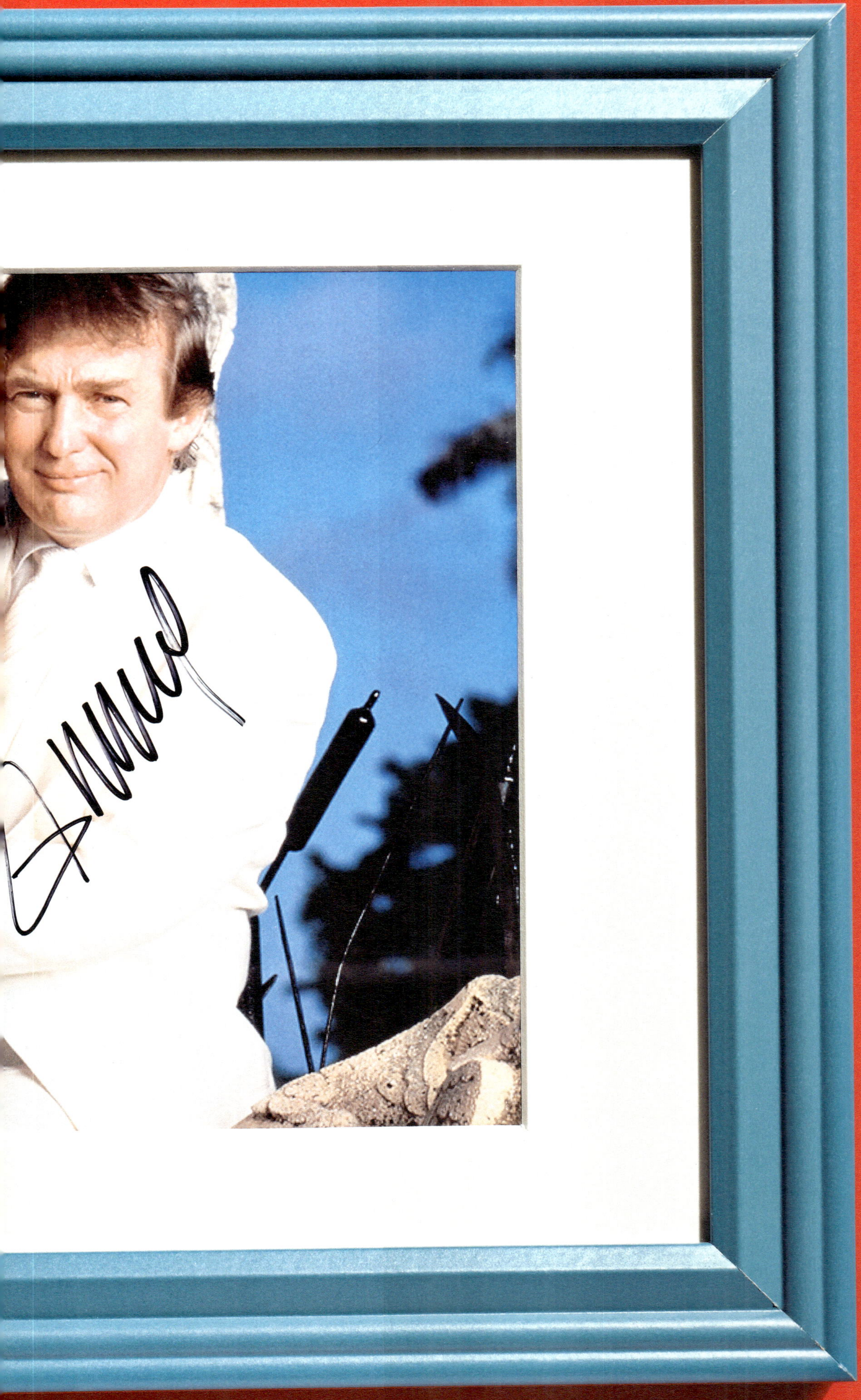

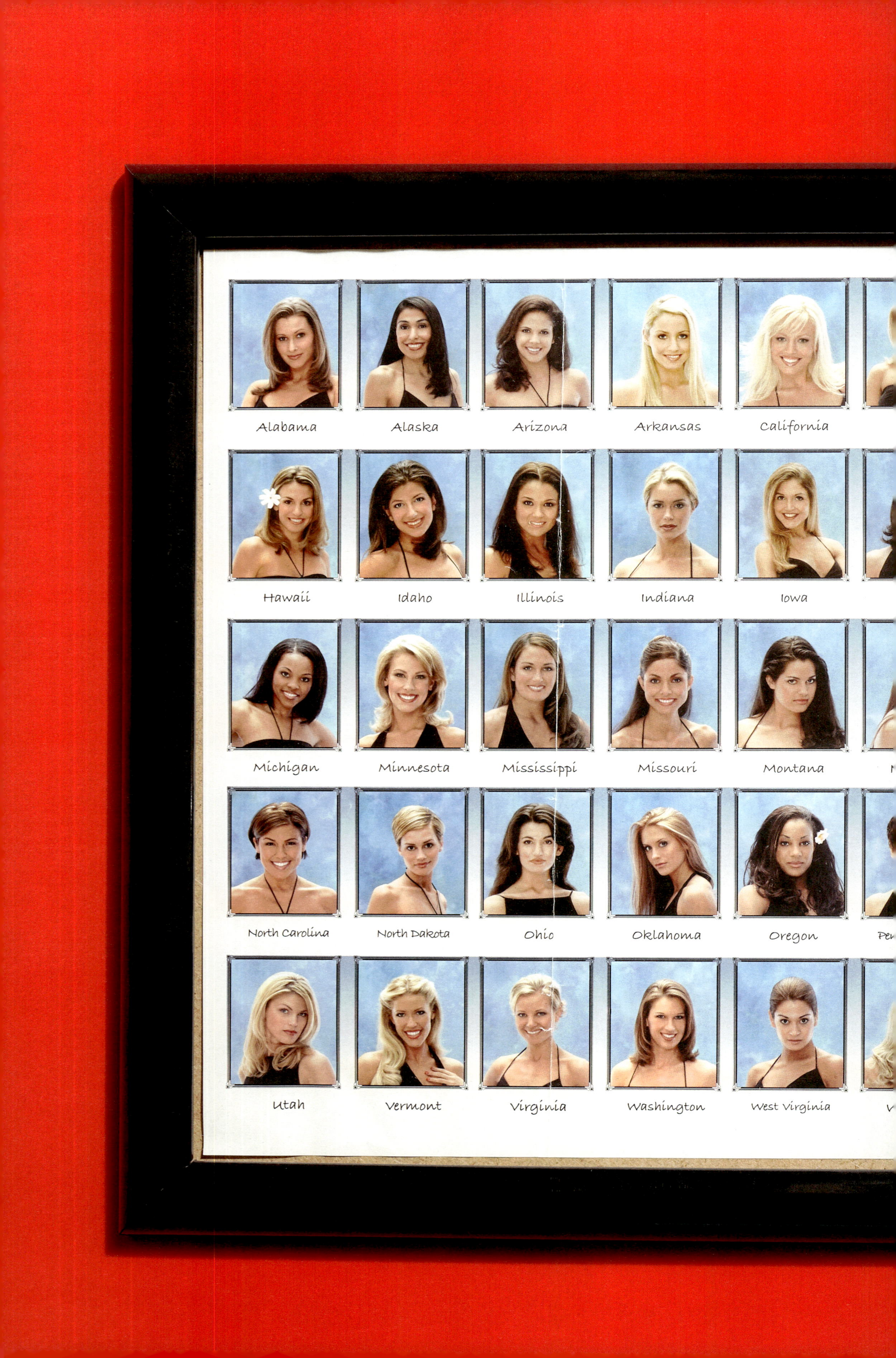
Alabama
Alaska
Arizona
Arkansas
California
Hawaii
Idaho
Illinois
Indiana
Iowa
Michigan
Minnesota
Mississippi
Missouri
Montana
North Carolina
North Dakota
Ohio
Oklahoma
Oregon
Utah
Vermont
Virginia
Washington
West Virginia

MISS USA PAGEANT POSTER, 2001
THE PAGEANT WAS OWNED BY DONALD TRUMP FROM 1996 TO 2015

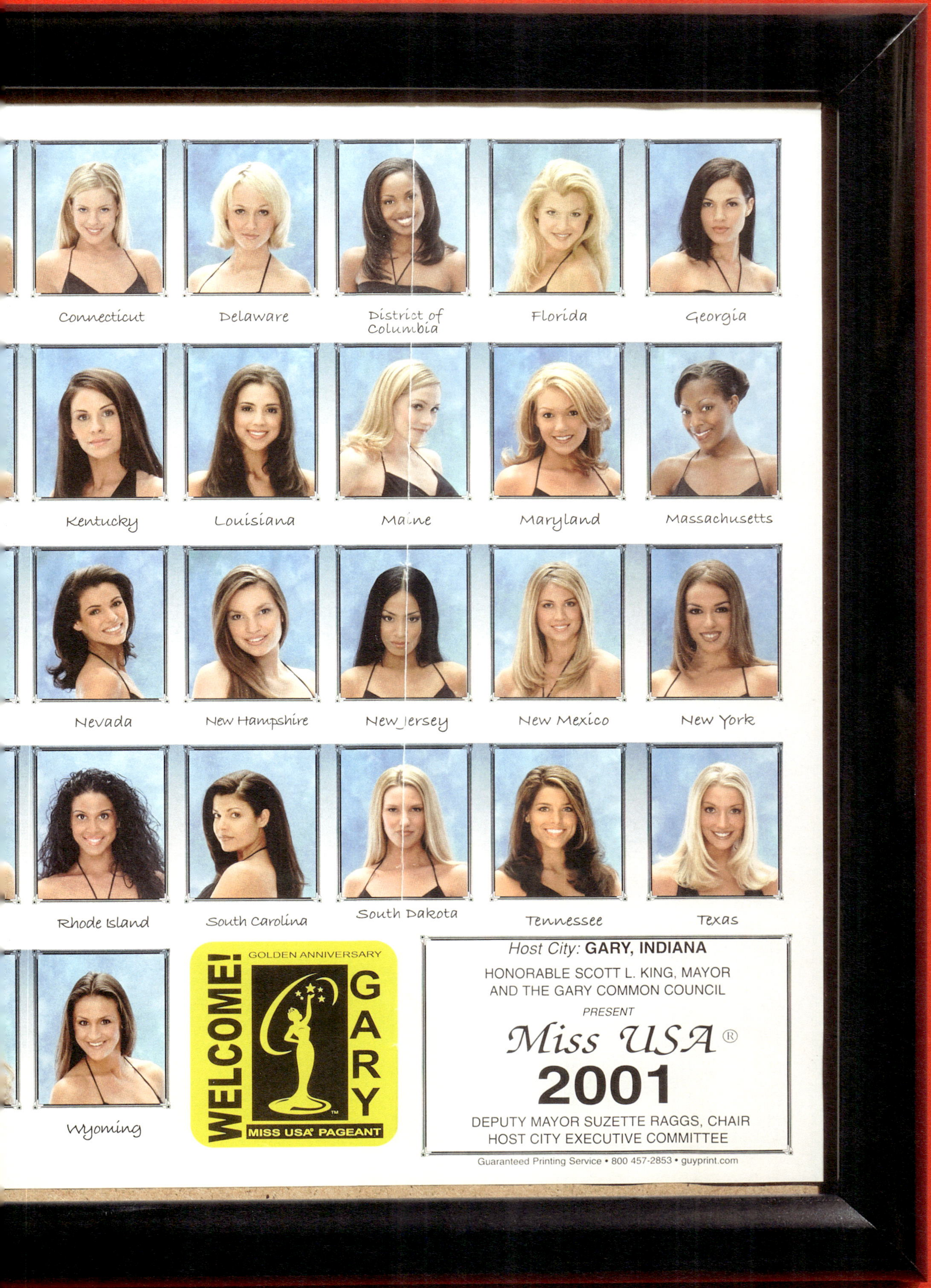

TIME MAGAZINE, JUNE 18, 2018
SIGNED DONALD TRUMP

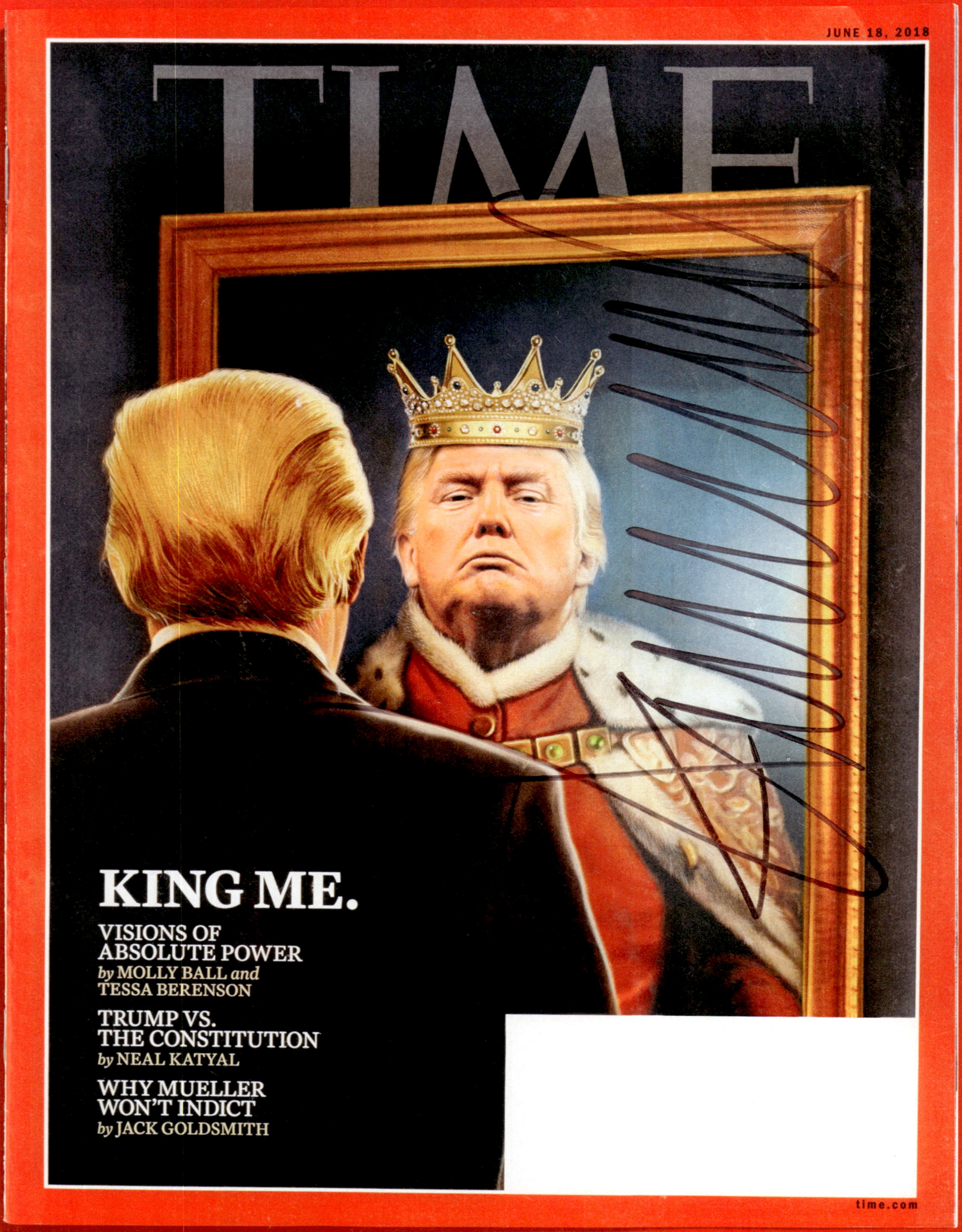

TRUMP FACE PLACARD
SIGNED DONALD TRUMP

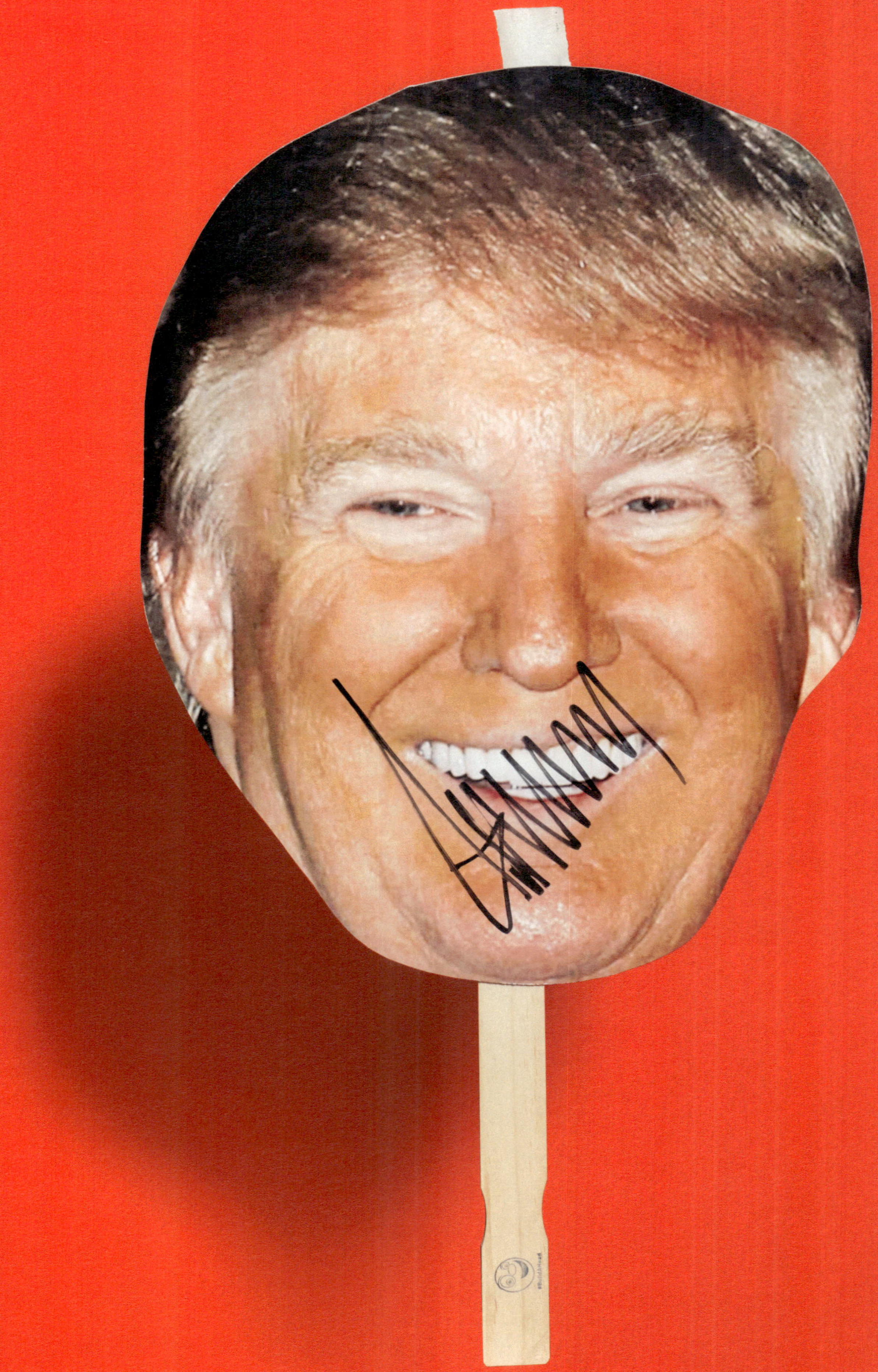

TRUMP TAJ MAHAL LIMITED EDITION DONALD J. TRUMP BOBBLEHEAD

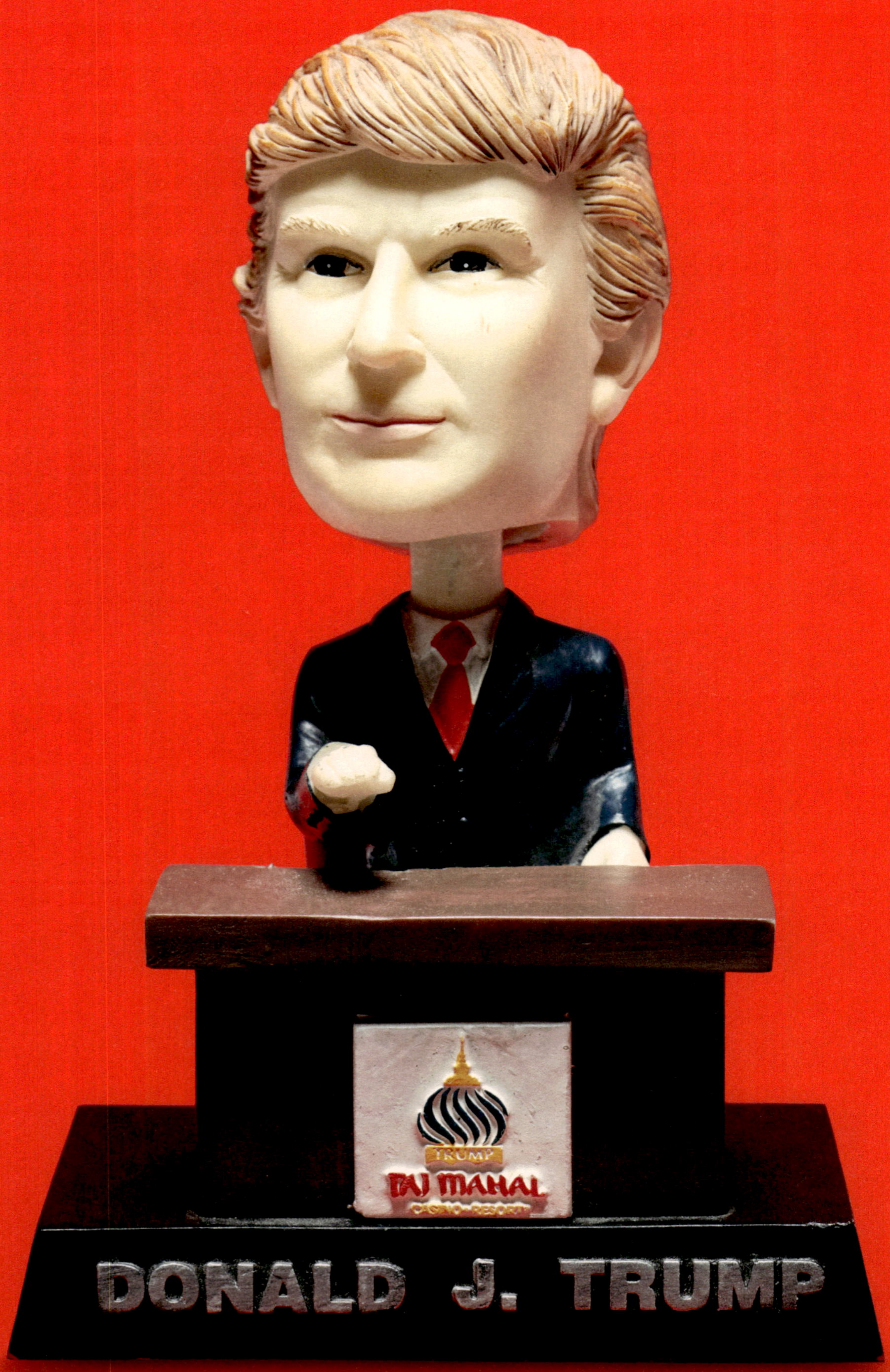

SIGNED PHOTOGRAPH OF DONALD TRUMP
AT SOUTH CAROLINA TEA PARTY COALITION CONVENTION, 2016

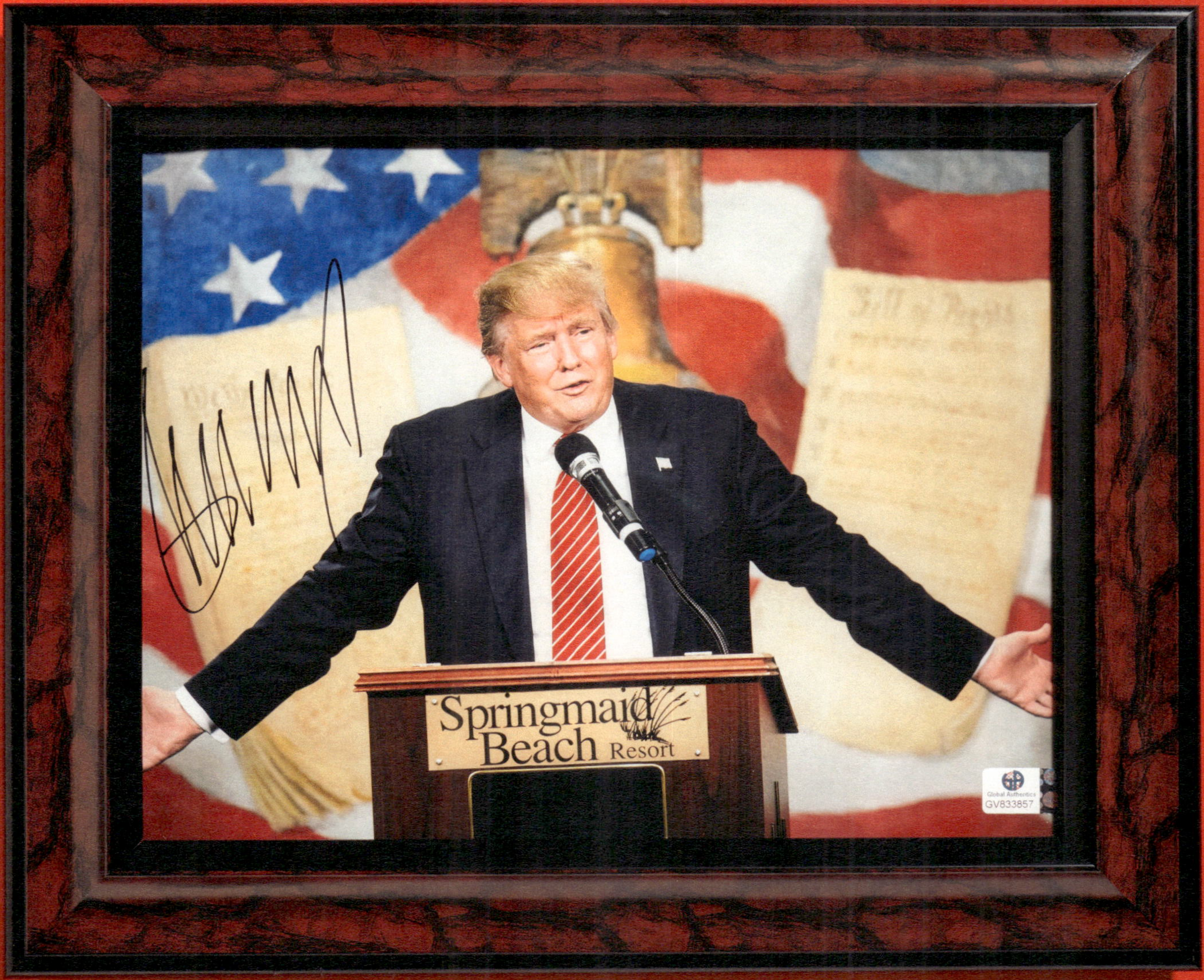

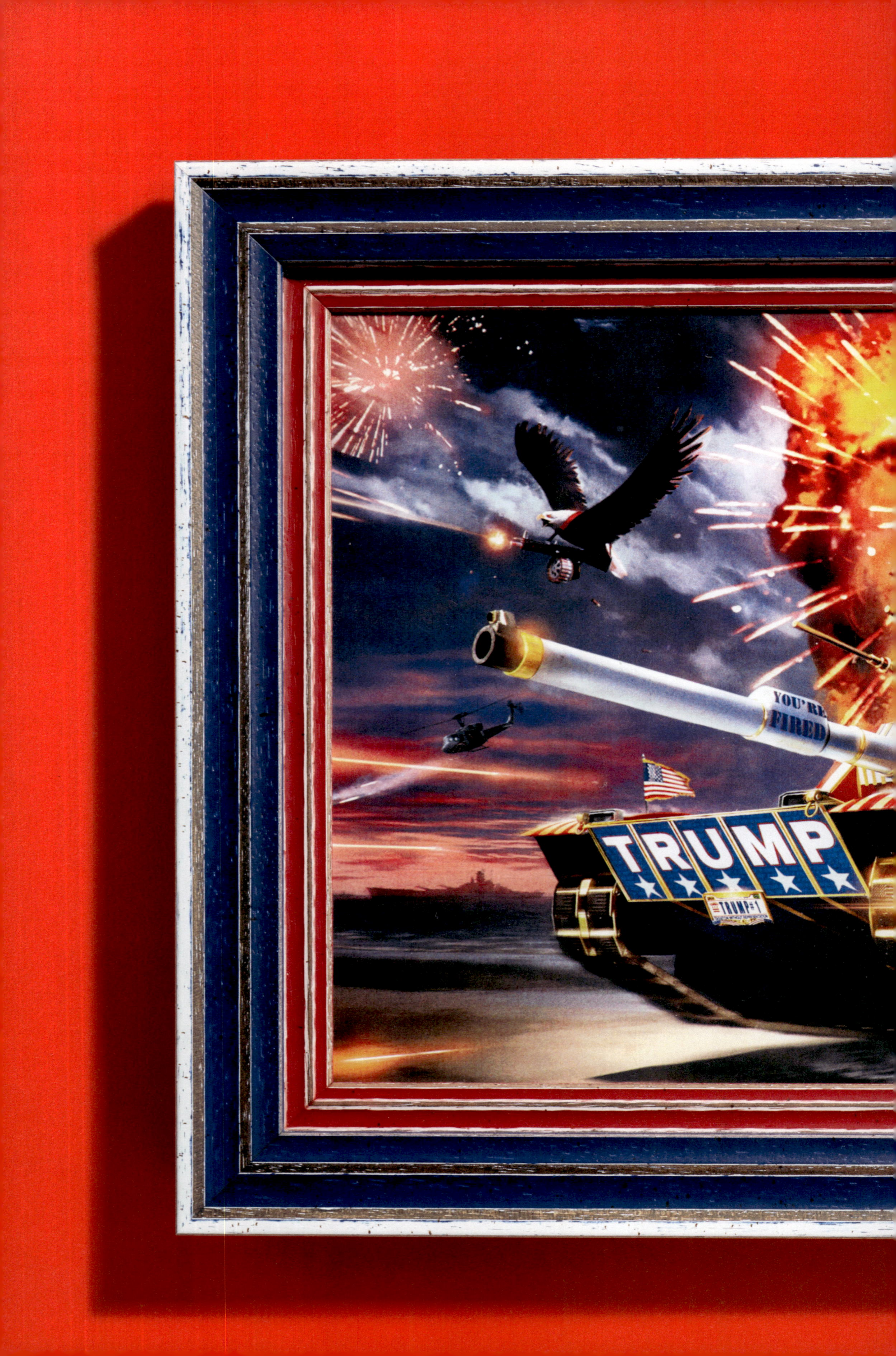
FIRED
TRUMP

"THE DONALD" ILLUSTRATION BY POLITICAL SATIRIST JASON HEUSER
FIRST UPLOADED TO DEVIANTART IN 2016
SIGNED DONALD TRUMP

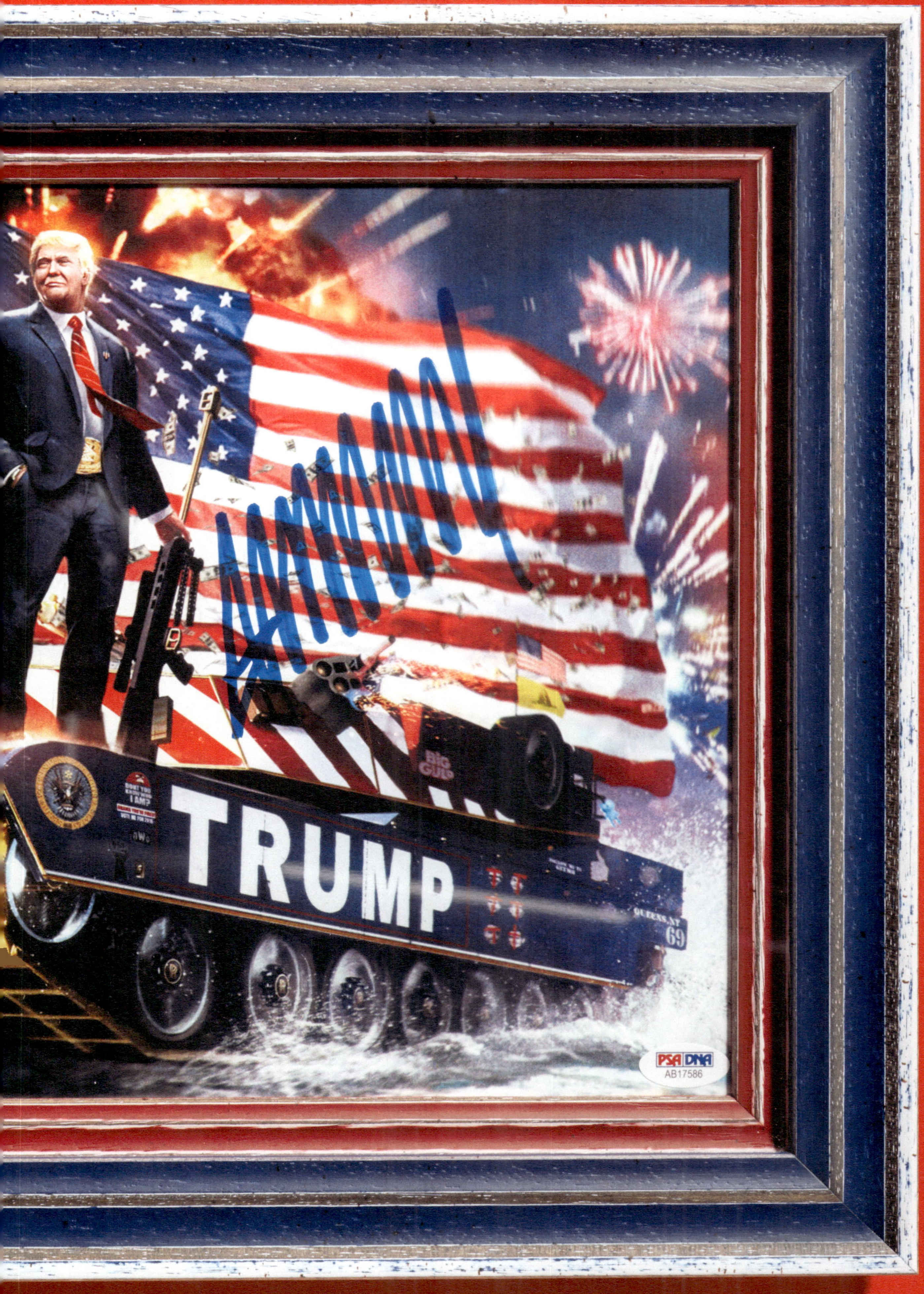

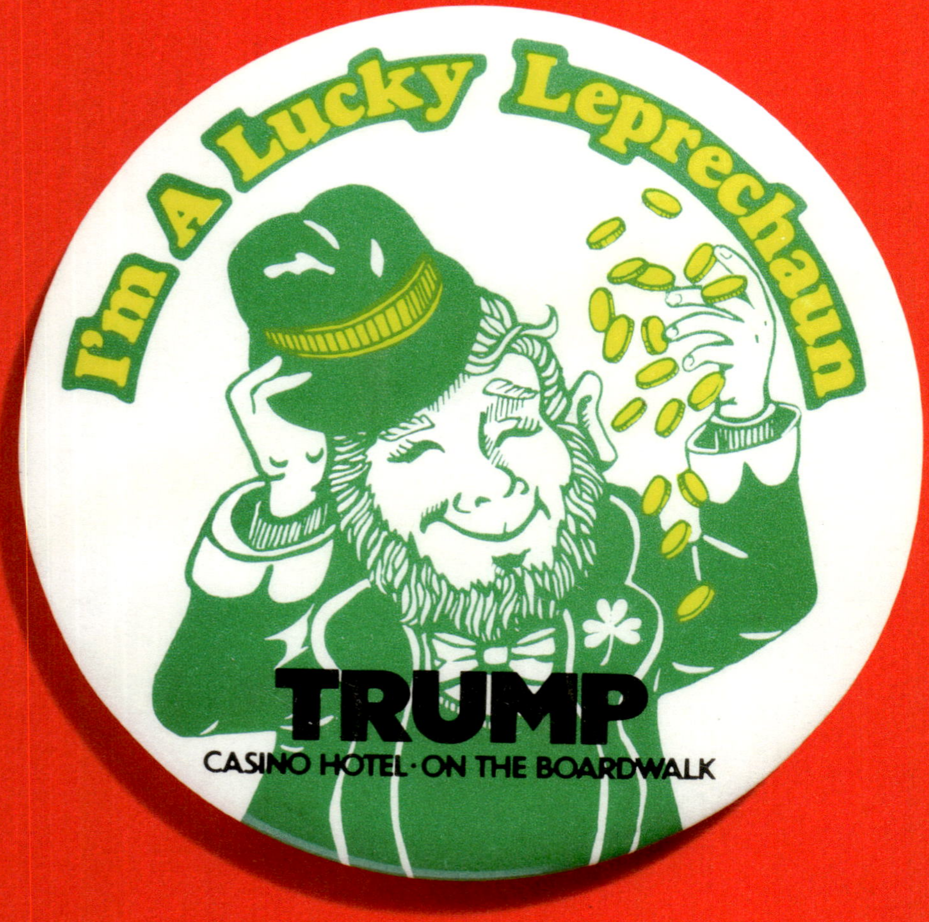
I'm A Lucky Leprechaun
TRUMP
CASINO HOTEL · ON THE BOARDWALK

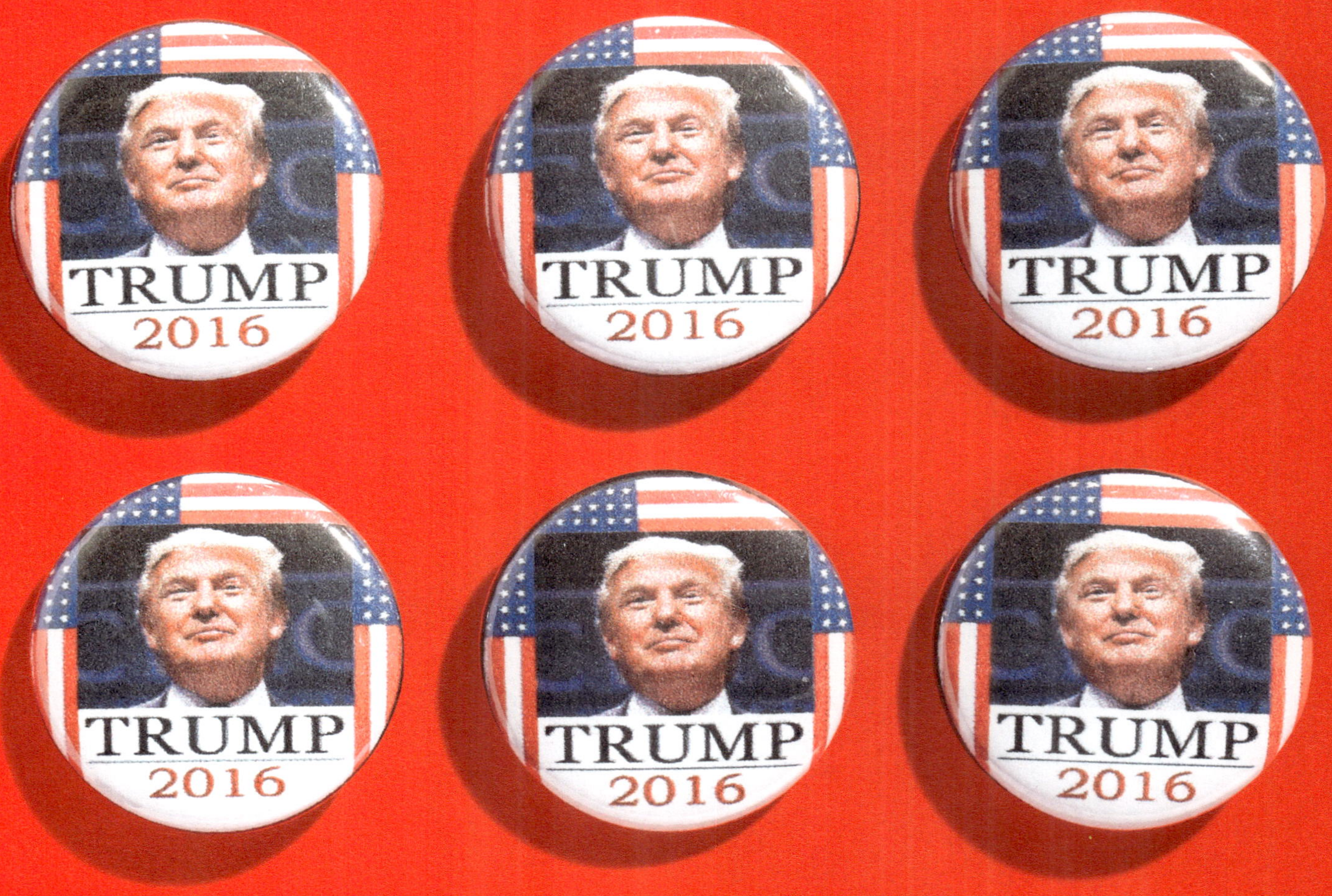
TRUMP
2016
TRUMP
2016
TRUMP
2016
TRUMP
2016
TRUMP
2016
TRUMP
2016

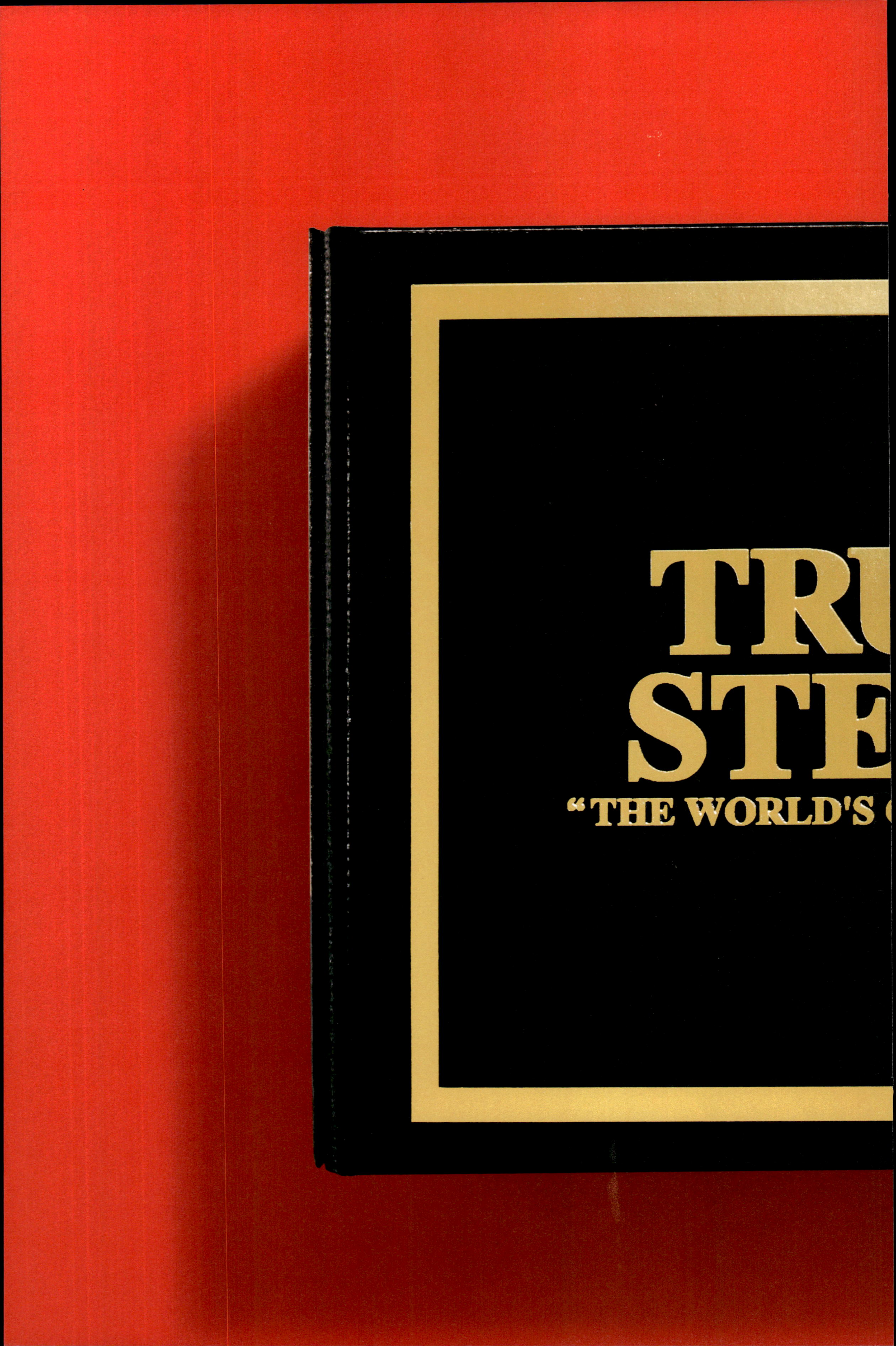
TRU
STE
“THE WORLD'S

TRUMP STEAKS BOX
LAUNCHED EXCLUSIVELY THROUGH THE SHARPER IMAGE AND QVC IN MAY 2007 AND DISCONTINUED AFTER TWO MONTHS. BOXES WERE PRICED BETWEEN $199 AND $999

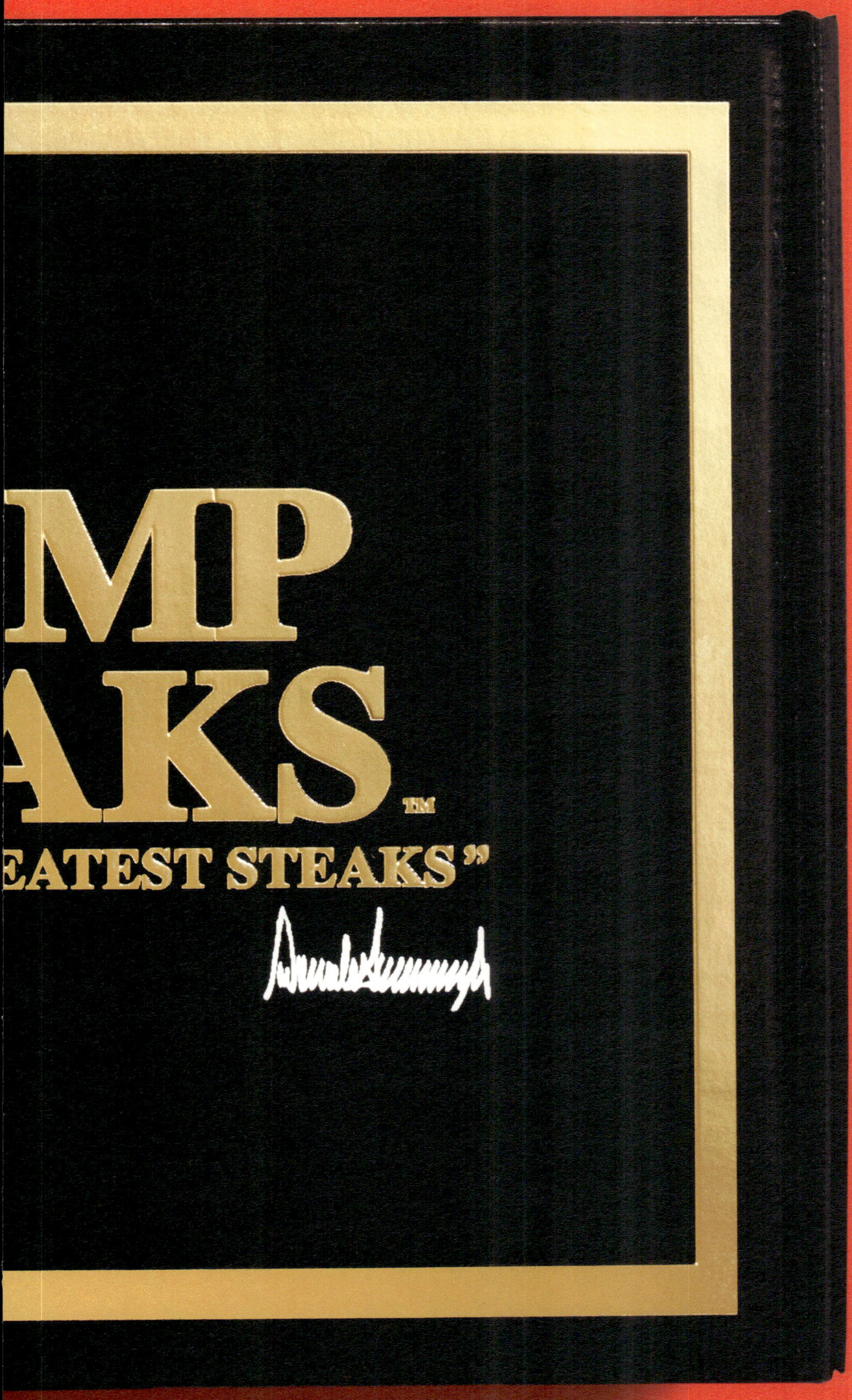

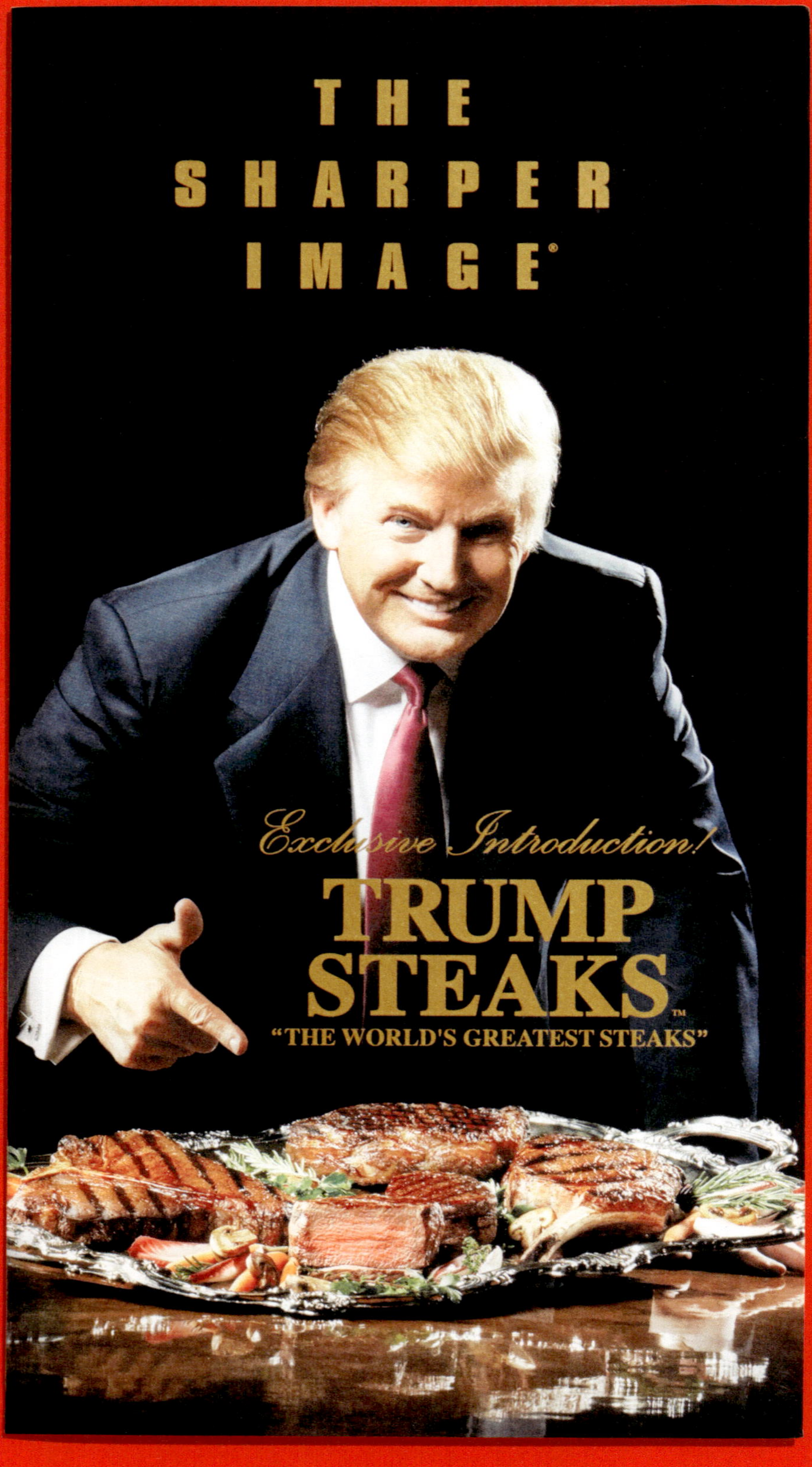
THE
SHARPER
IMAGE®
Exclusive Introduction!
TRUMP
STEAKS™
"THE WORLD'S GREATEST STEAKS"

NEW YORK POST, JUNE 30, 1991

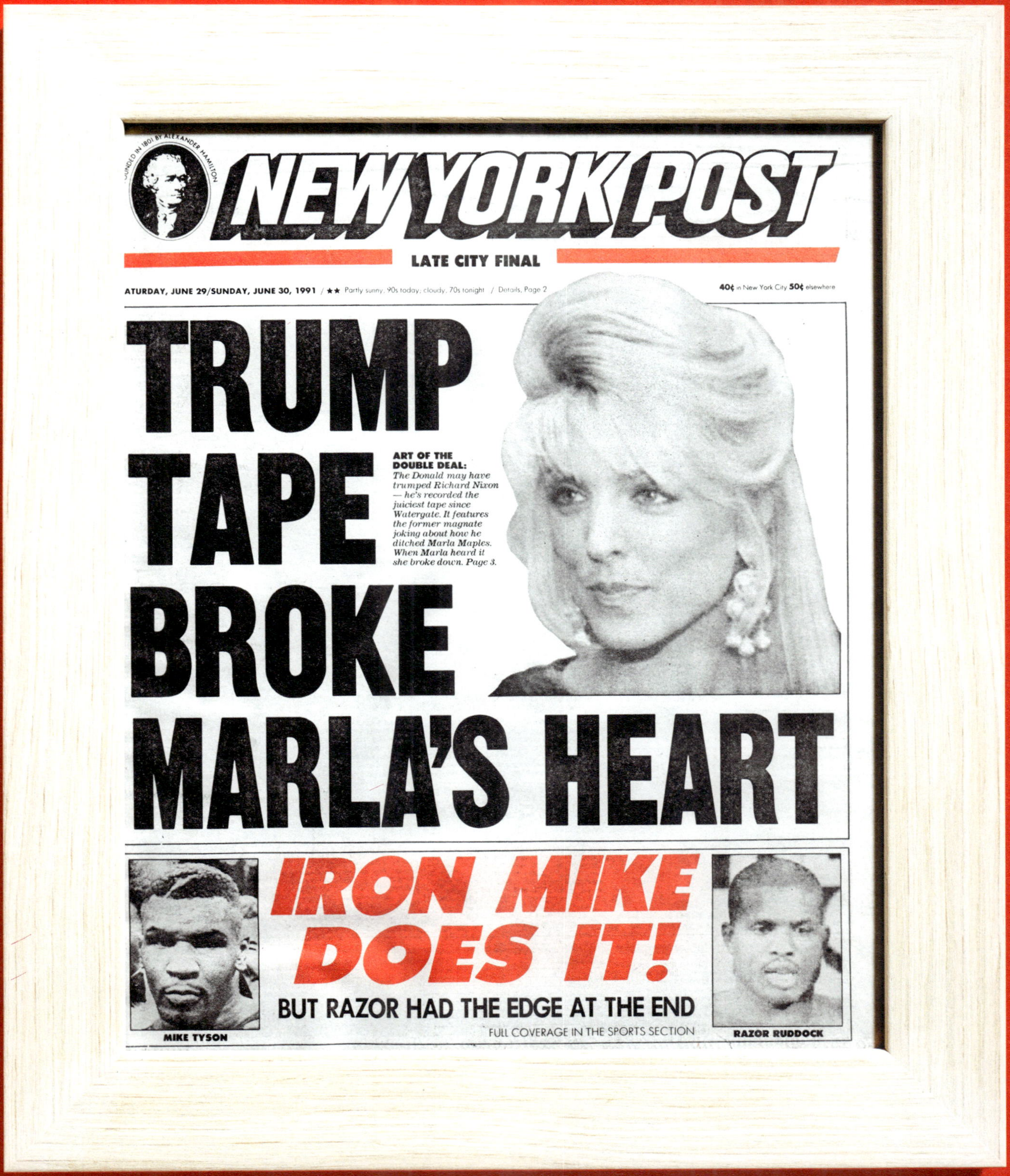

NEW YORK POST

LATE CITY FINAL

ATURDAY, JUNE 29/SUNDAY, JUNE 30, 1991 / ★★ Partly sunny, 90s today; cloudy, 70s tonight / Details, Page 2

40¢ in New York City 50¢ elsewhere

TRUMP TAPE BROKE MARLA'S HEART

ART OF THE DOUBLE DEAL: *The Donald may have trumped Richard Nixon — he's recorded the juiciest tape since Watergate. It features the former magnate joking about how he ditched Marla Maples. When Marla heard it she broke down. Page 3.*

IRON MIKE DOES IT!

BUT RAZOR HAD THE EDGE AT THE END

FULL COVERAGE IN THE SPORTS SECTION

MIKE TYSON

RAZOR RUDDOCK

NEW YORK POST, FEBRUARY 16, 1990

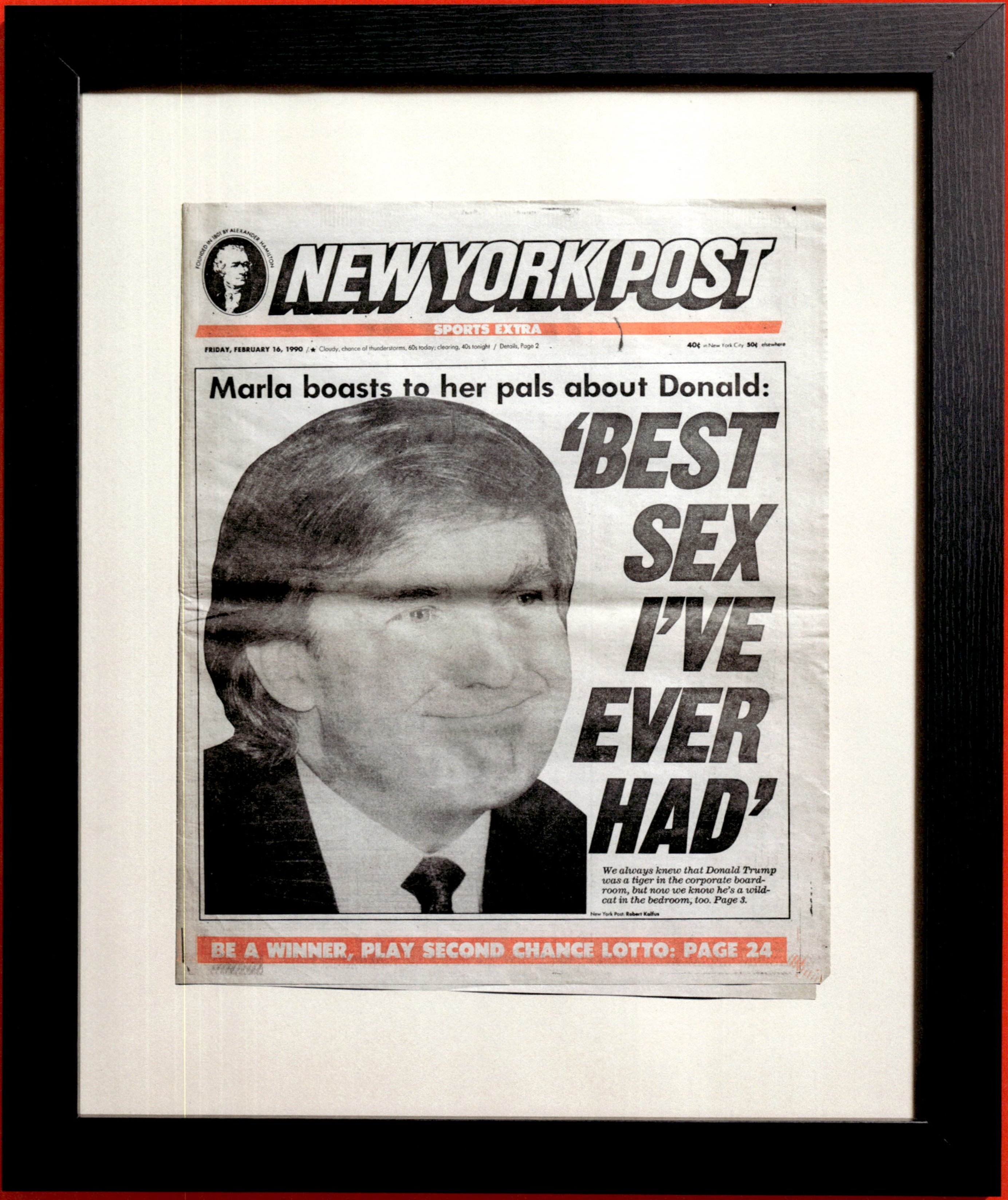

FOUNDED IN 1801 BY ALEXANDER HAMILTON

NEW YORK POST

SPORTS EXTRA

FRIDAY, FEBRUARY 16, 1990 / ★ Cloudy, chance of thunderstorms, 60s today; clearing, 40s tonight / Details, Page 2

40¢ in New York City 50¢ elsewhere

Marla boasts to her pals about Donald:

'BEST SEX I'VE EVER HAD'

We always knew that Donald Trump was a tiger in the corporate boardroom, but now we know he's a wildcat in the bedroom, too. Page 3.

New York Post: Robert Kalfus

BE A WINNER, PLAY SECOND CHANCE LOTTO: PAGE 24

**OFFICIAL TRUMP 2016 CAMPAIGN SIGN
SIGNED DONALD TRUMP**

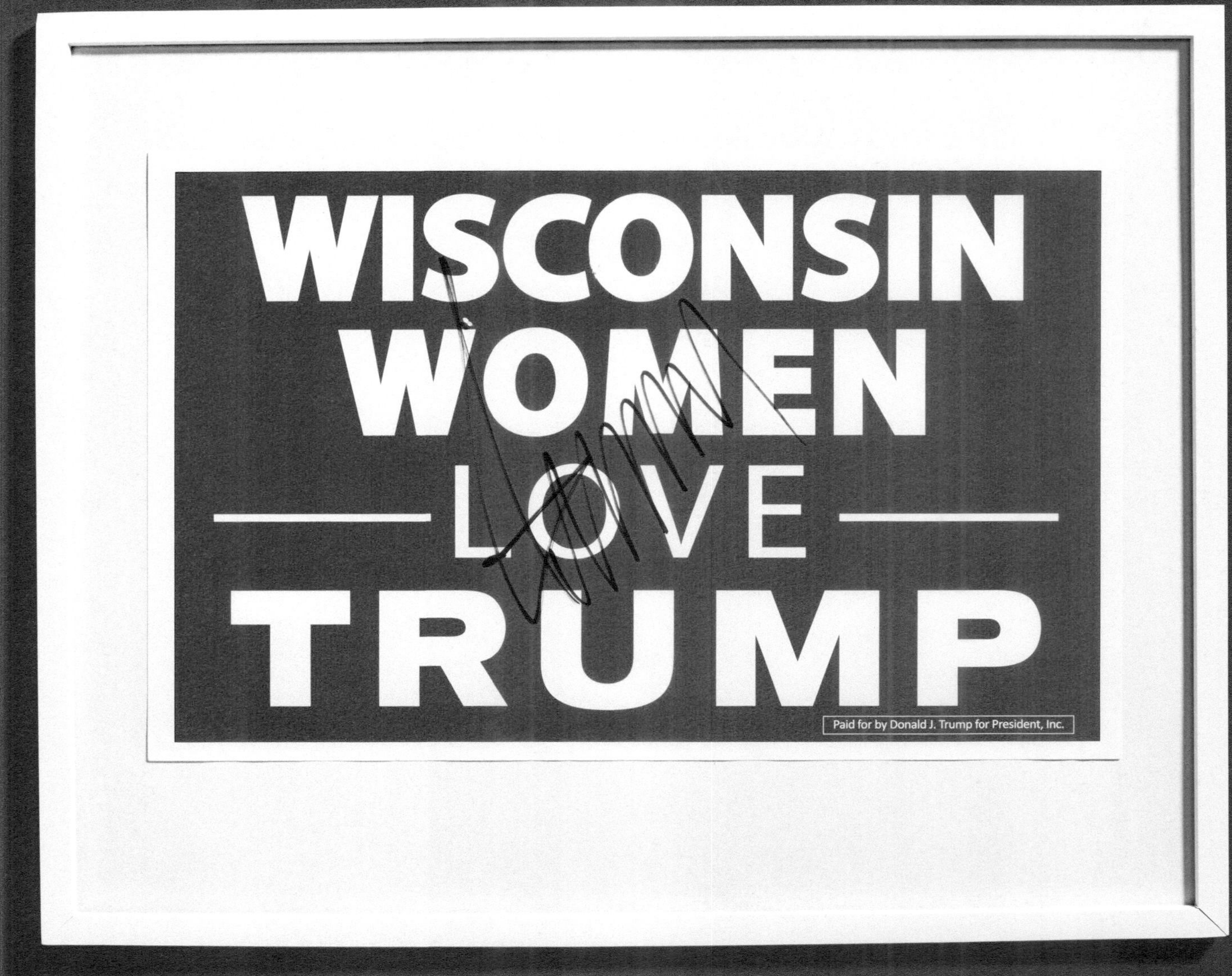

TRUMP MARINA HERRINGTON BIKER PATRIOT TEDDY BEAR, 2002

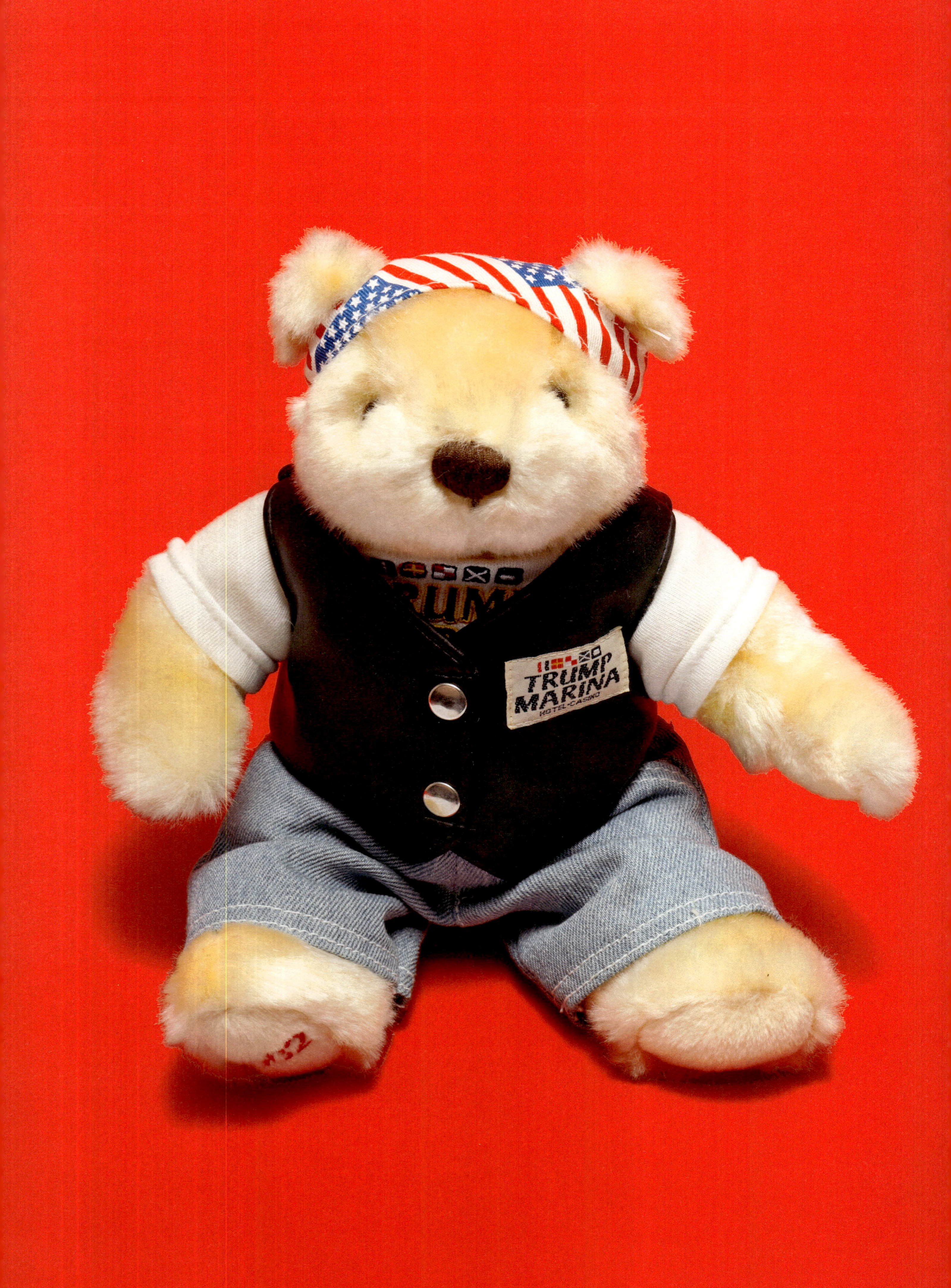

SIGNED PHOTOGRAPH OF DONALD TRUMP, 2016

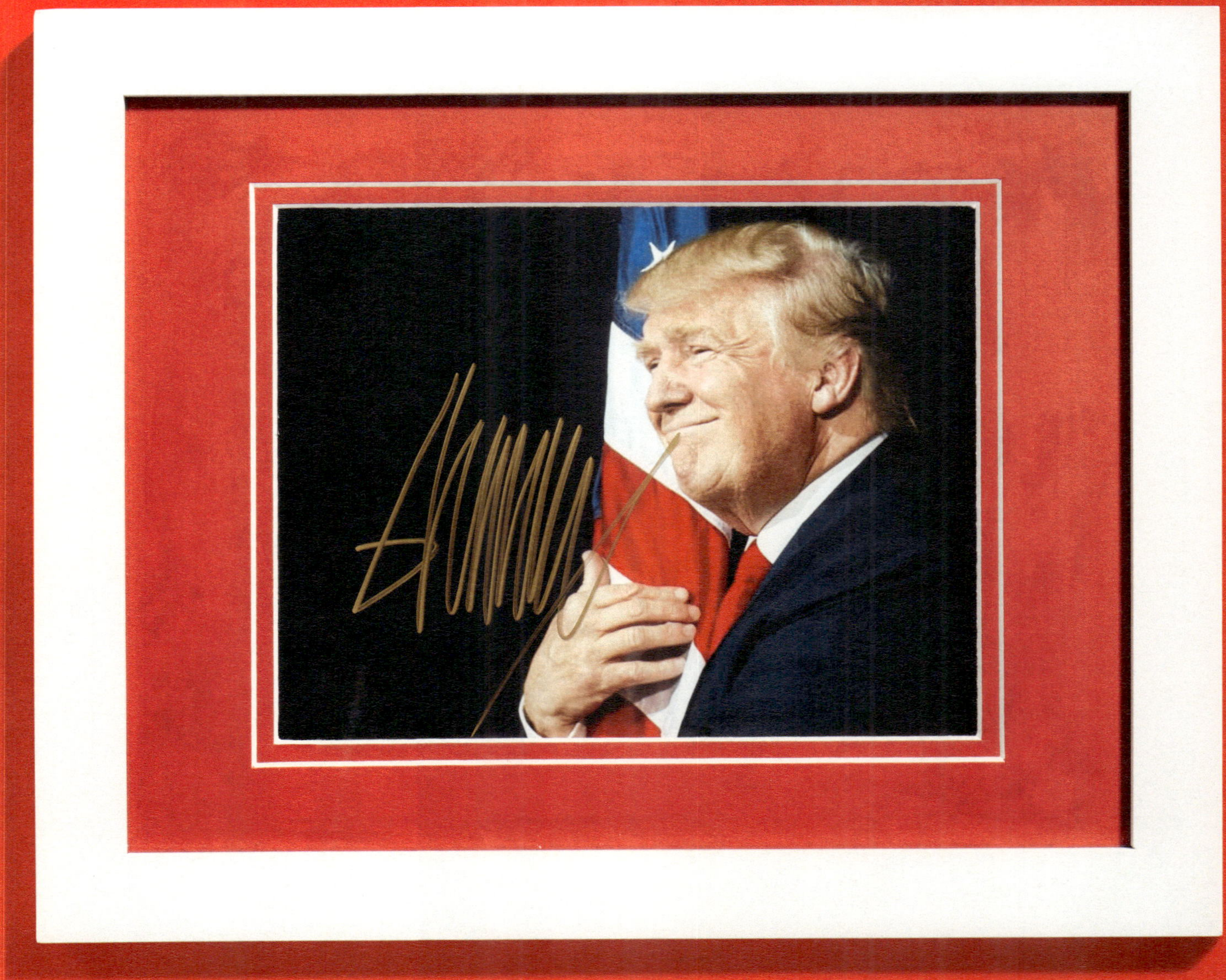

PLAYBOY MAGAZINE, MARCH 1990
SIGNED DONALD TRUMP

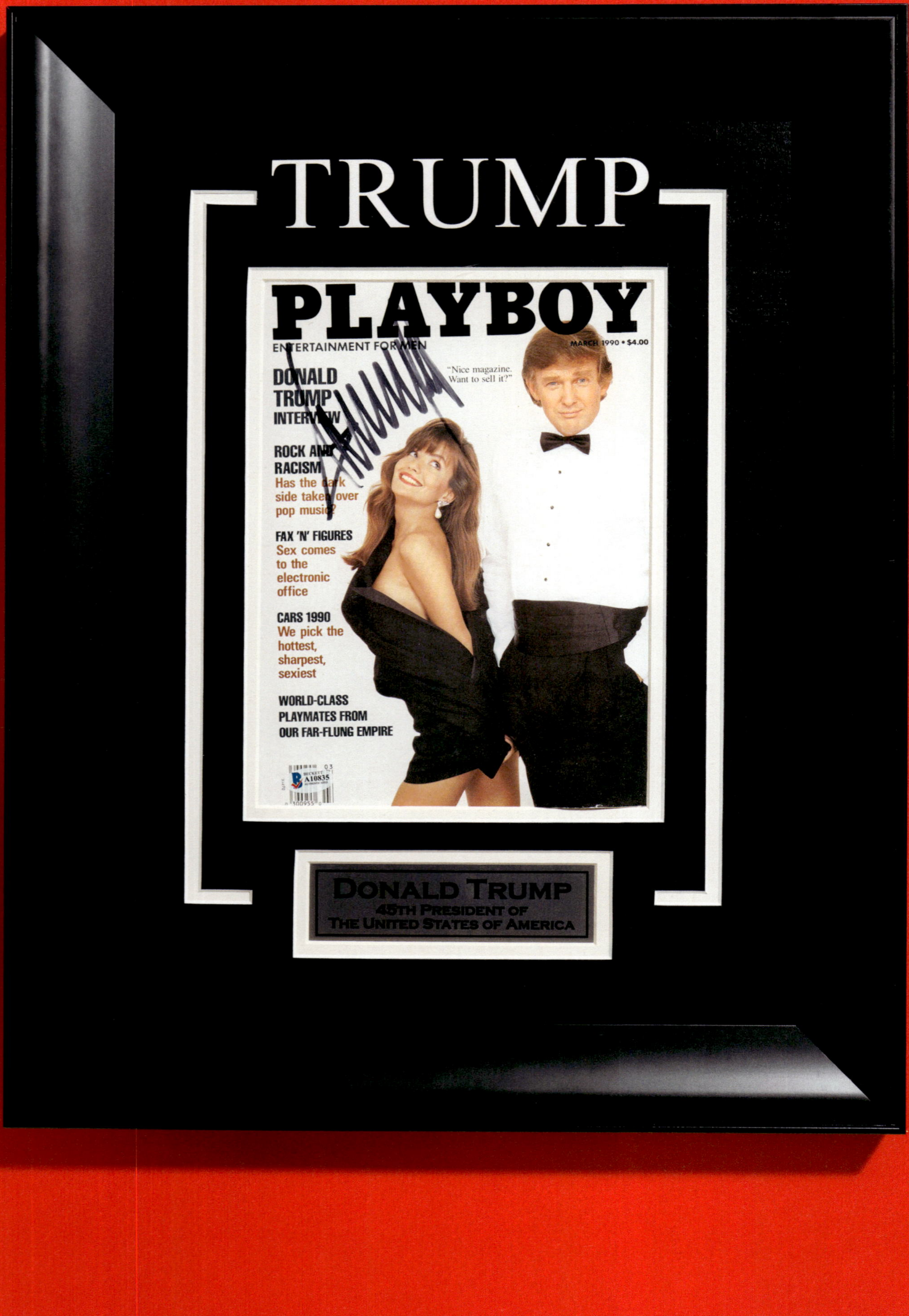

OFFICIAL TRUMP 2016 CAMPAIGN SIGN

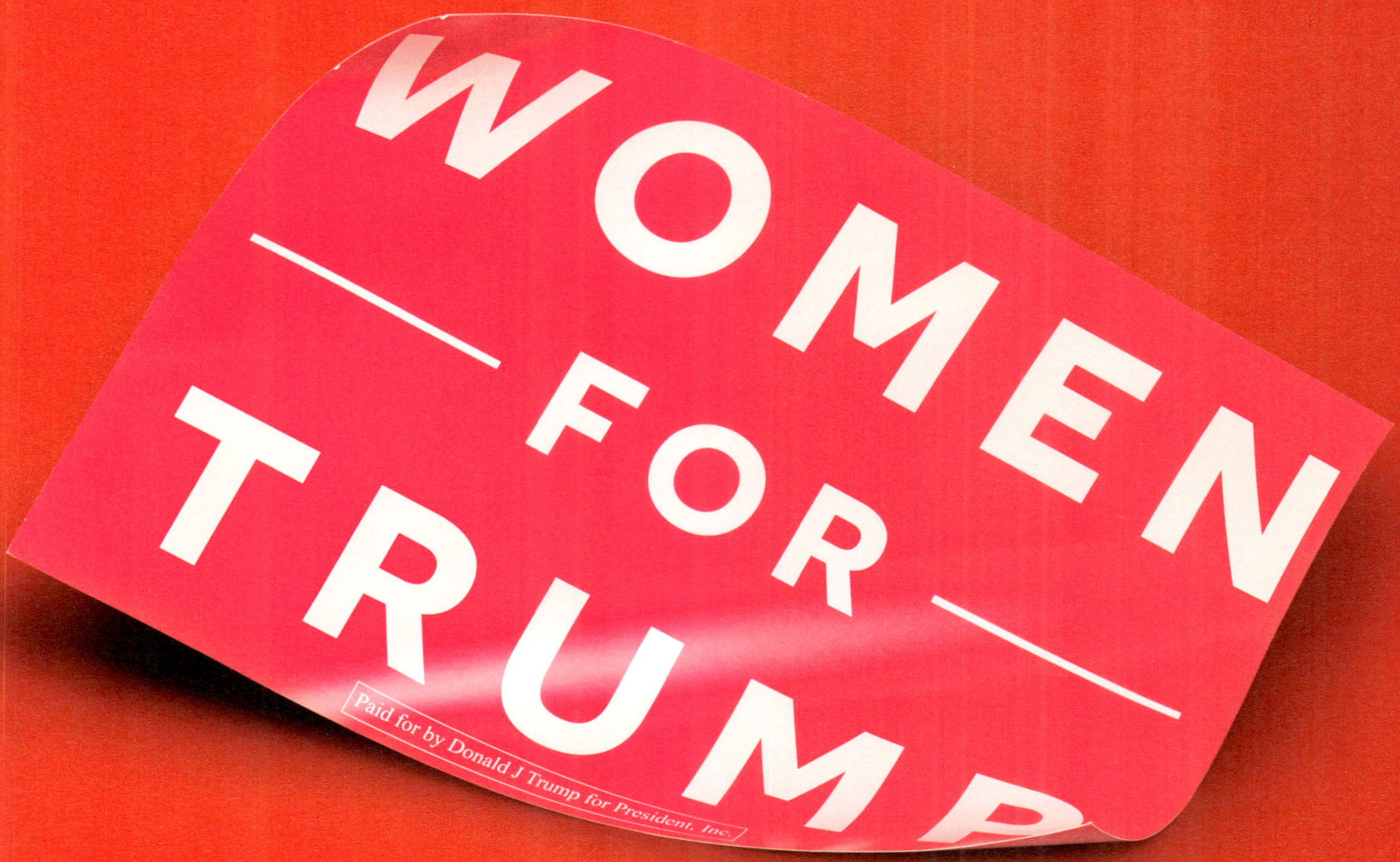

MAD MAGAZINE, APRIL 2007
IN DECEMBER 2006, ROSIE O'DONNELL AND DONALD TRUMP BEGAN A LONG-RUNNING PUBLIC FEUD. O'DONNELL CALLED TRUMP "A SNAKE-OIL SALESMAN" ON ABC'S THE VIEW. TRUMP THREATENED TO SUE, SAYING HE WOULD TAKE "LOTS OF MONEY FROM MY NICE, FAT LITTLE ROSIE"

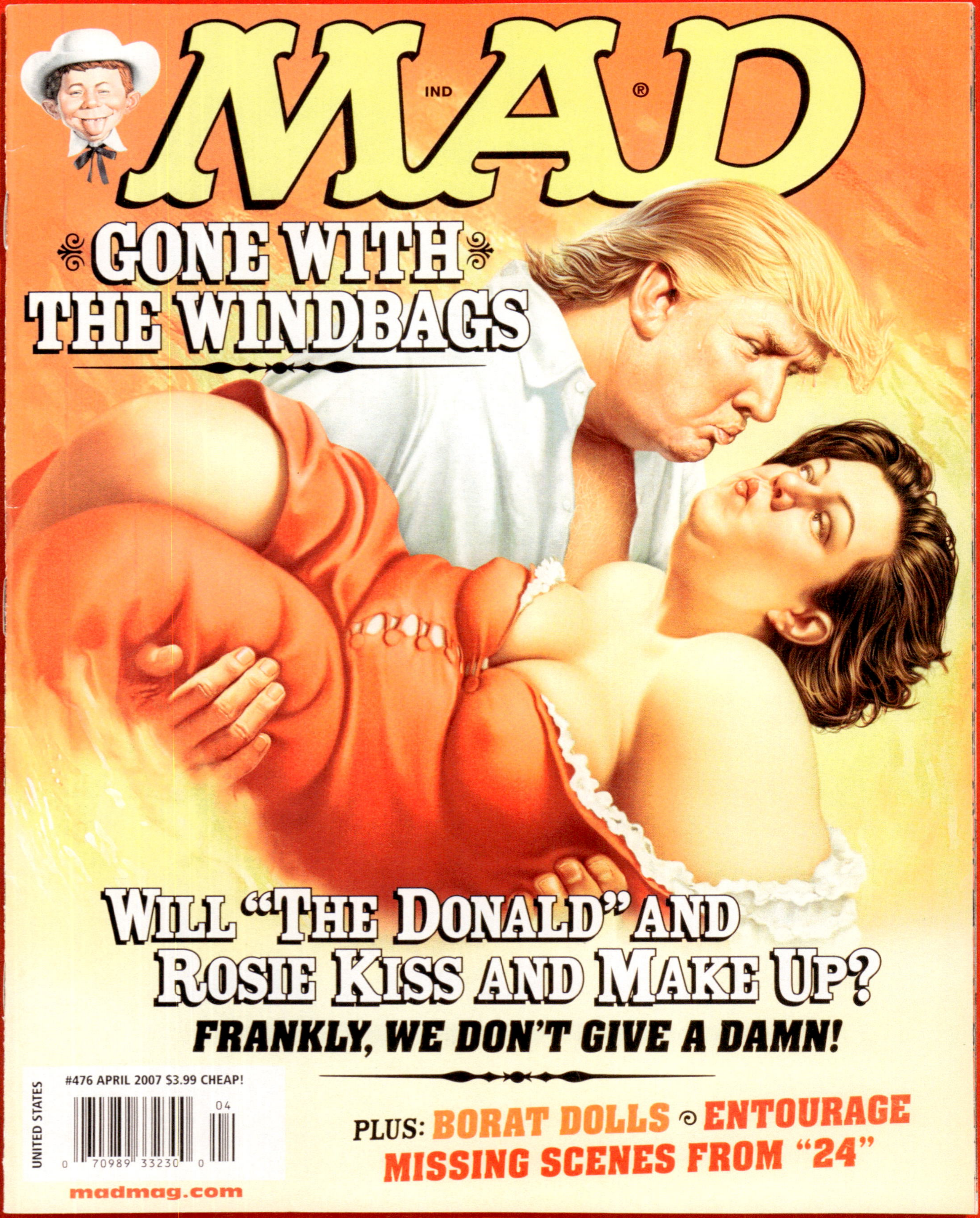

THE SYDNEY MORNING HERALD
SEPTEMBER 28, 2016

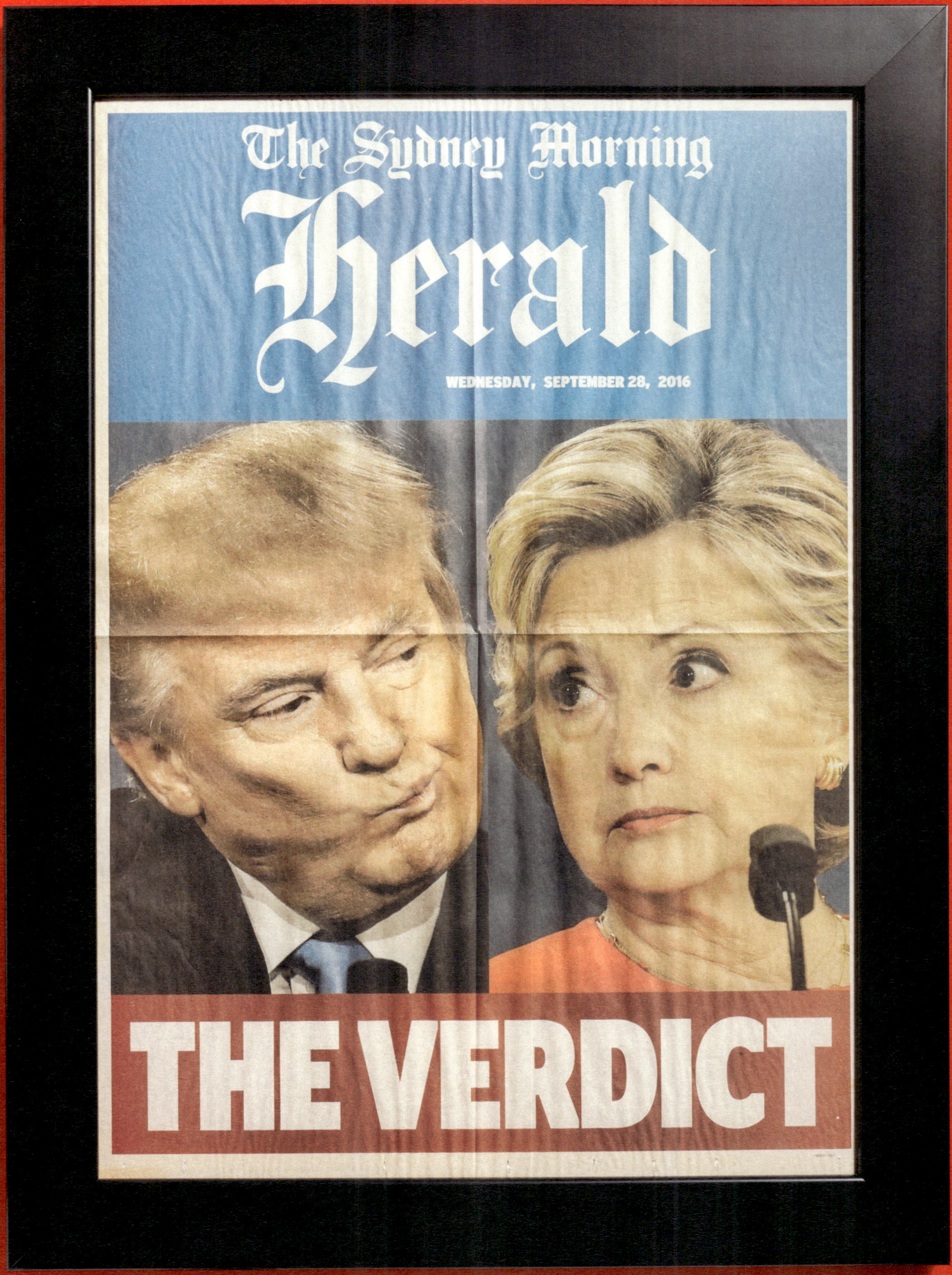
The Sydney Morning Herald

WEDNESDAY, SEPTEMBER 28, 2016

THE VERDICT

SIGNED PHOTOGRAPH OF DONALD TRUMP AT HIS DESK, 2015

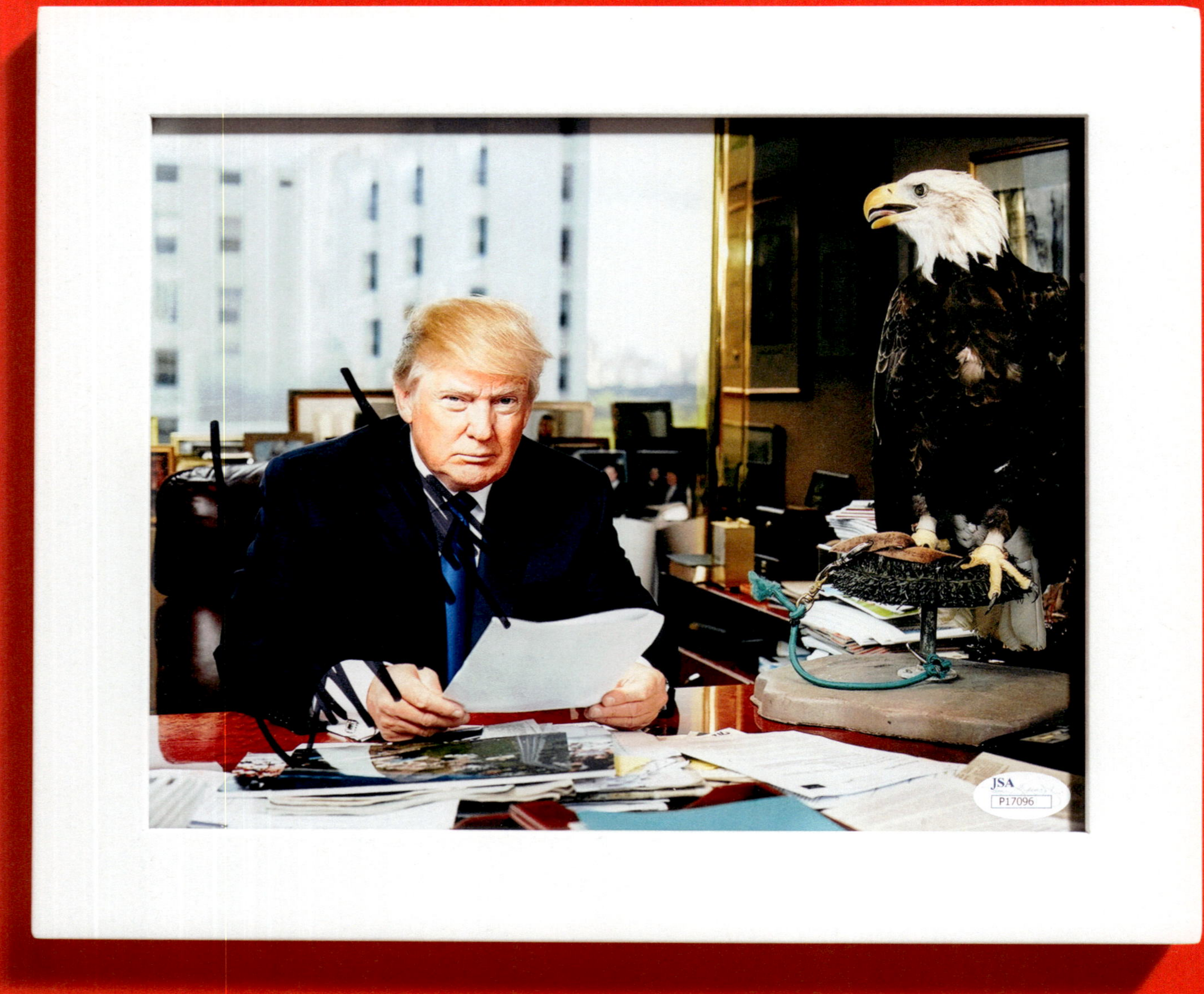

TRUMP 2016 CAMPAIGN RALLY HANDOUT
SIGNED DONALD TRUMP

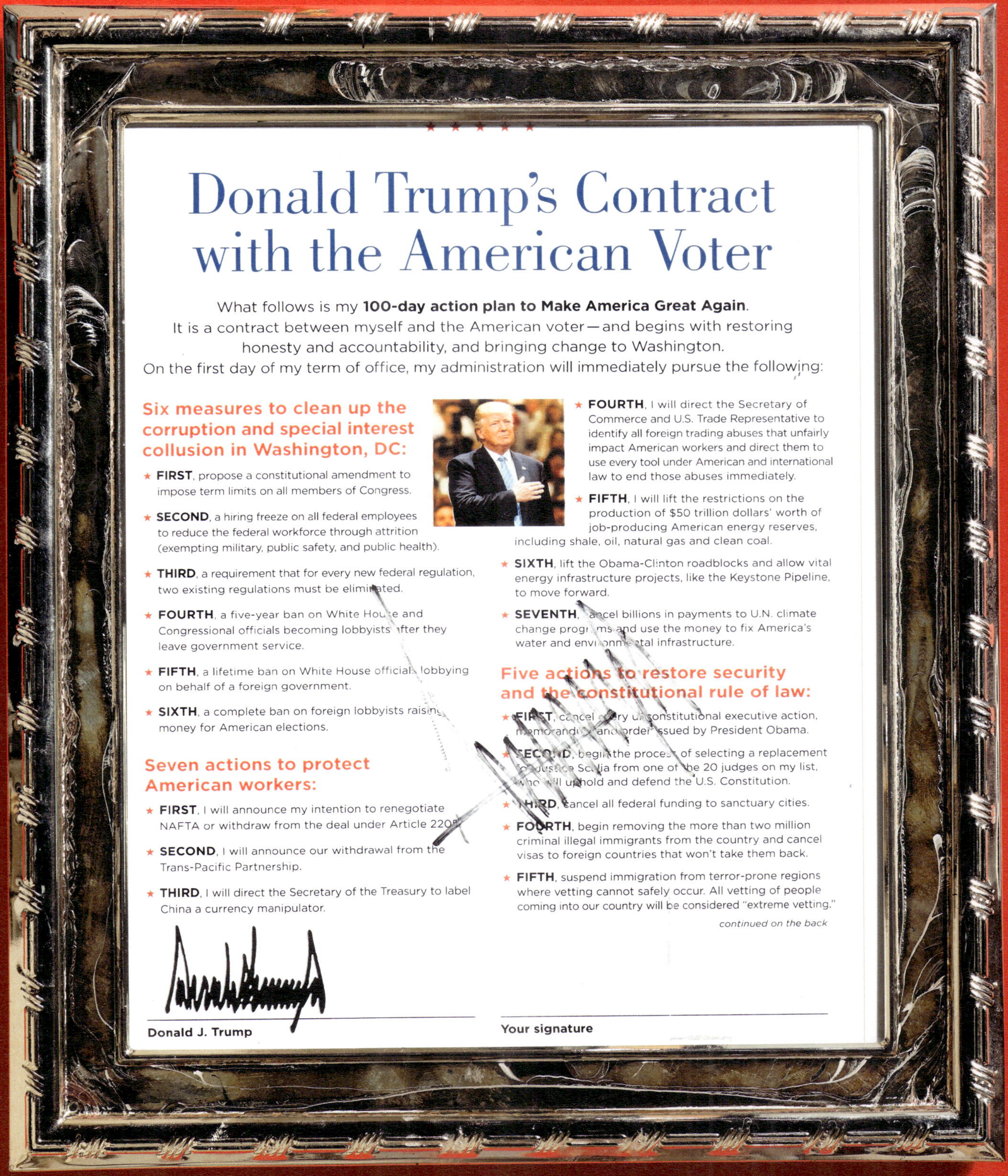

Donald Trump's Contract with the American Voter

What follows is my **100-day action plan to Make America Great Again**. It is a contract between myself and the American voter—and begins with restoring honesty and accountability, and bringing change to Washington. On the first day of my term of office, my administration will immediately pursue the following:

Six measures to clean up the corruption and special interest collusion in Washington, DC:

- ★ **FIRST**, propose a constitutional amendment to impose term limits on all members of Congress.
- ★ **SECOND**, a hiring freeze on all federal employees to reduce the federal workforce through attrition (exempting military, public safety, and public health).
- ★ **THIRD**, a requirement that for every new federal regulation, two existing regulations must be eliminated.
- ★ **FOURTH**, a five-year ban on White House and Congressional officials becoming lobbyists after they leave government service.
- ★ **FIFTH**, a lifetime ban on White House officials lobbying on behalf of a foreign government.
- ★ **SIXTH**, a complete ban on foreign lobbyists raising money for American elections.

Seven actions to protect American workers:

- ★ **FIRST**, I will announce my intention to renegotiate NAFTA or withdraw from the deal under Article 2205.
- ★ **SECOND**, I will announce our withdrawal from the Trans-Pacific Partnership.
- ★ **THIRD**, I will direct the Secretary of the Treasury to label China a currency manipulator.
- ★ **FOURTH**, I will direct the Secretary of Commerce and U.S. Trade Representative to identify all foreign trading abuses that unfairly impact American workers and direct them to use every tool under American and international law to end those abuses immediately.
- ★ **FIFTH**, I will lift the restrictions on the production of $50 trillion dollars' worth of job-producing American energy reserves, including shale, oil, natural gas and clean coal.
- ★ **SIXTH**, lift the Obama-Clinton roadblocks and allow vital energy infrastructure projects, like the Keystone Pipeline, to move forward.
- ★ **SEVENTH**, cancel billions in payments to U.N. climate change programs and use the money to fix America's water and environmental infrastructure.

Five actions to restore security and the constitutional rule of law:

- ★ **FIRST**, cancel every unconstitutional executive action, memorandum and orders issued by President Obama.
- ★ **SECOND**, begin the process of selecting a replacement for Justice Scalia from one of the 20 judges on my list, who will uphold and defend the U.S. Constitution.
- ★ **THIRD**, cancel all federal funding to sanctuary cities.
- ★ **FOURTH**, begin removing the more than two million criminal illegal immigrants from the country and cancel visas to foreign countries that won't take them back.
- ★ **FIFTH**, suspend immigration from terror-prone regions where vetting cannot safely occur. All vetting of people coming into our country will be considered "extreme vetting."

continued on the back

Donald J. Trump

Your signature

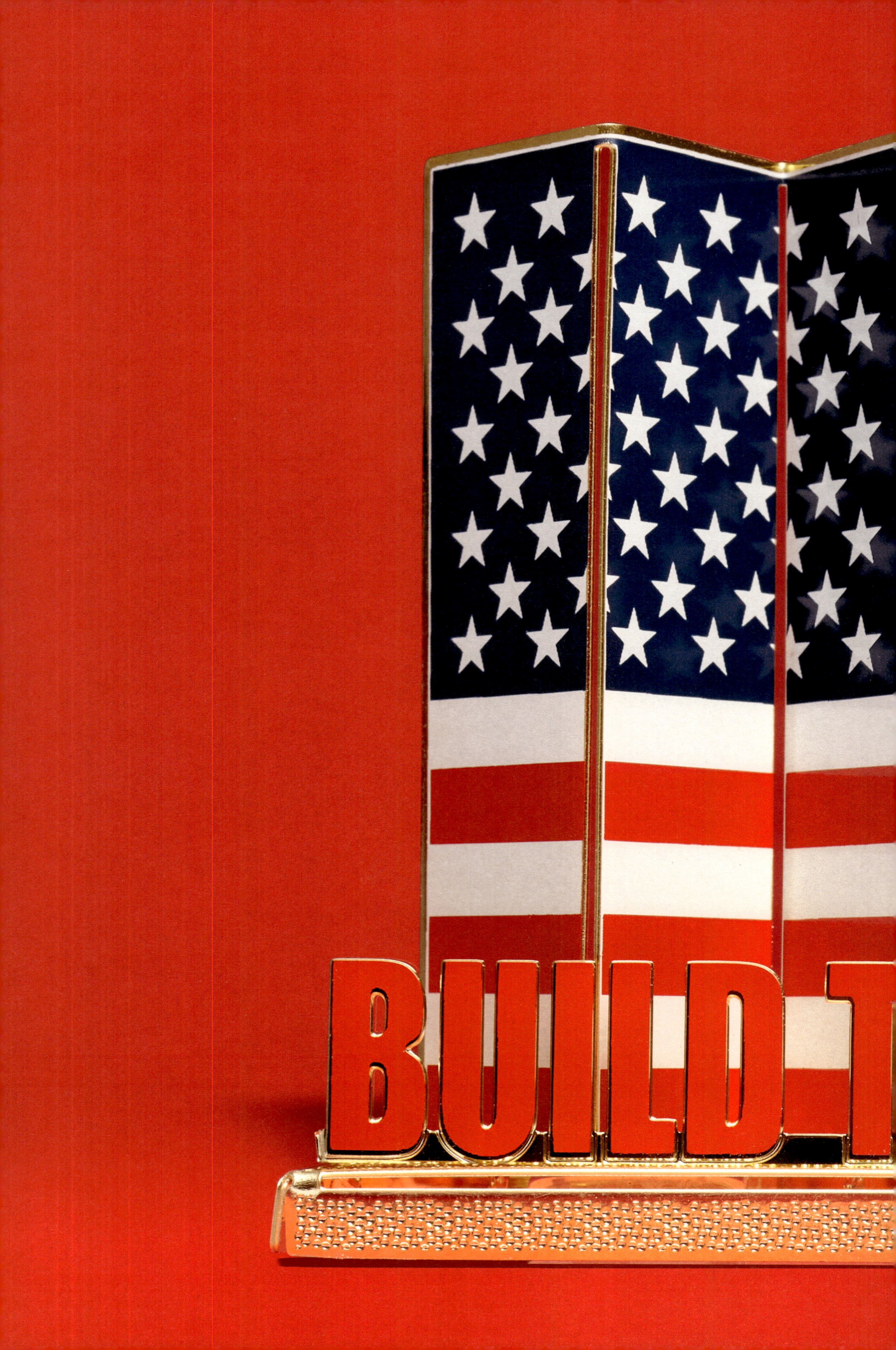
BUILD

LIMITED EDITION 24K GOLD "BUILD THE WALL" COLLECTIBLE
OFFICIAL WHITE HOUSE GIFT SHOP

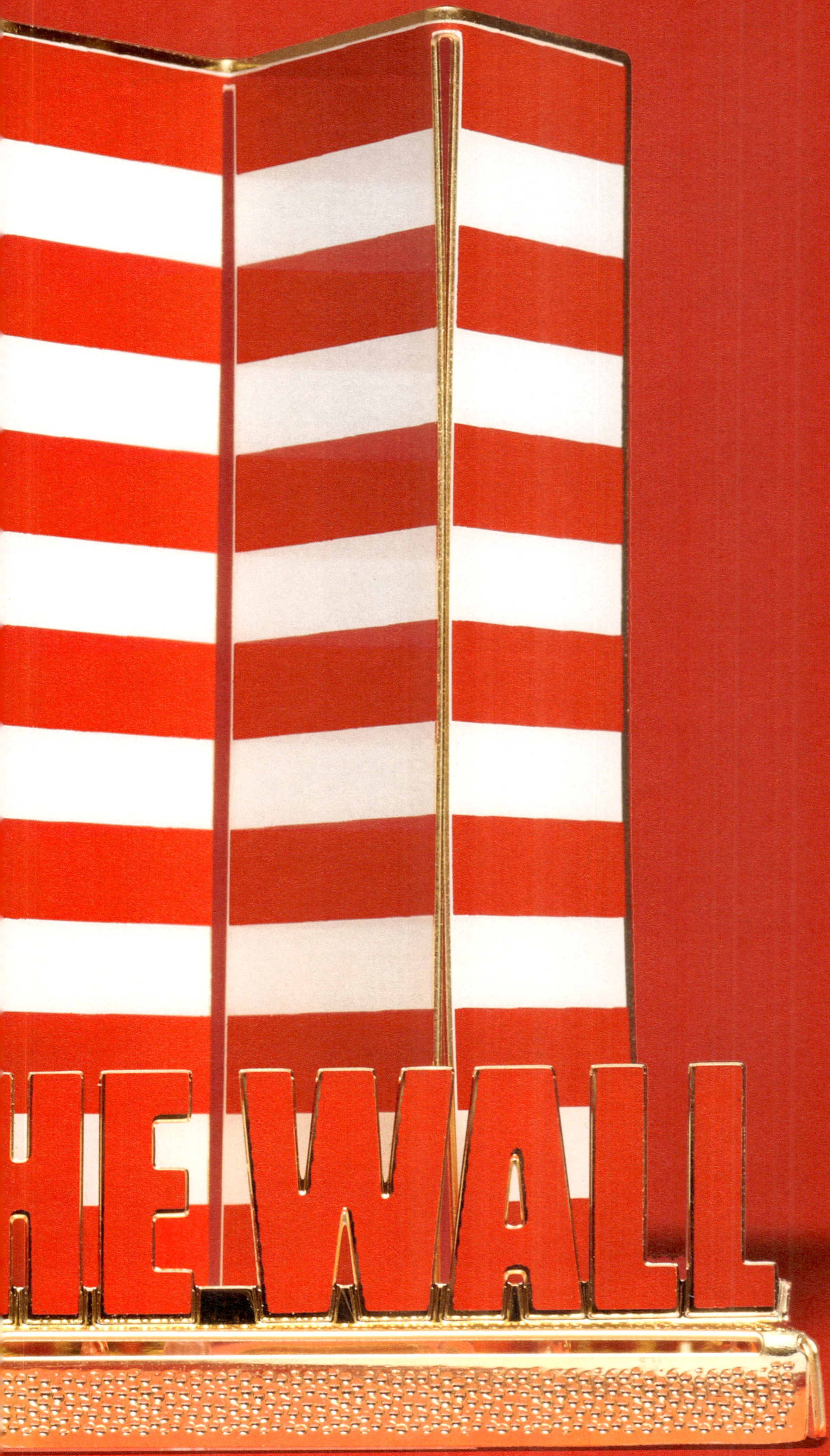

ABRAHAM LINCOLN FIVE-DOLLAR BILL
THOMAS JEFFERSON TEN-DOLLAR BILL
FAKE HILLARY PENITENTIARY 2016-DOLLAR BILL
SIGNED DONALD TRUMP

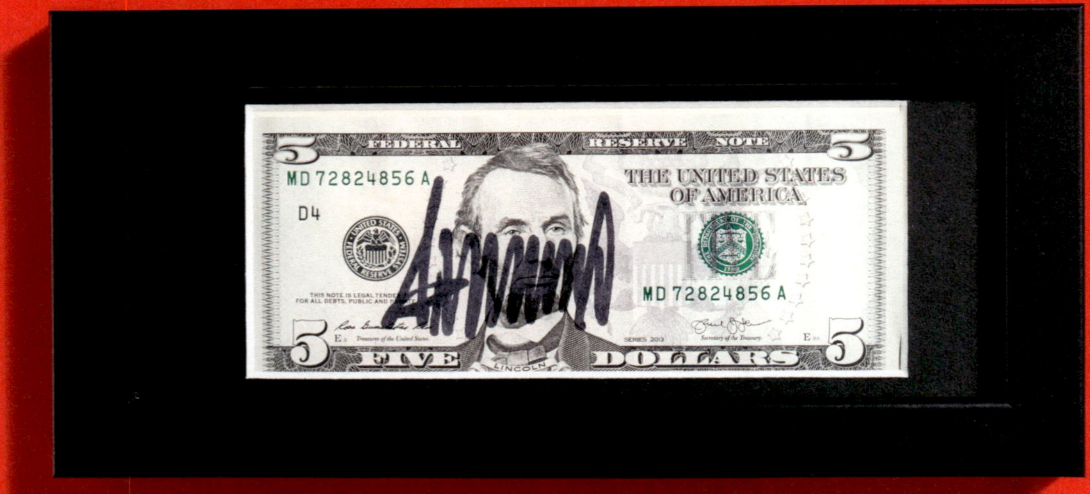

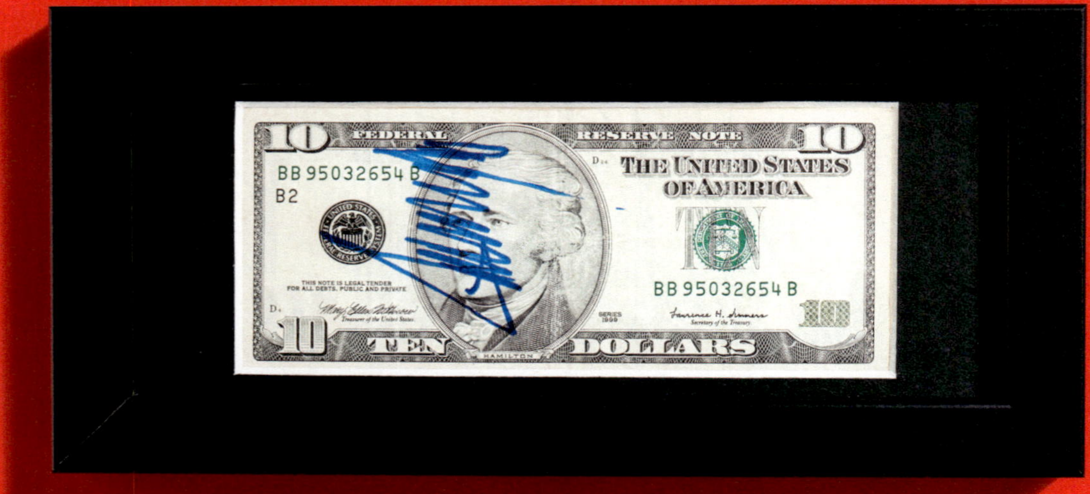

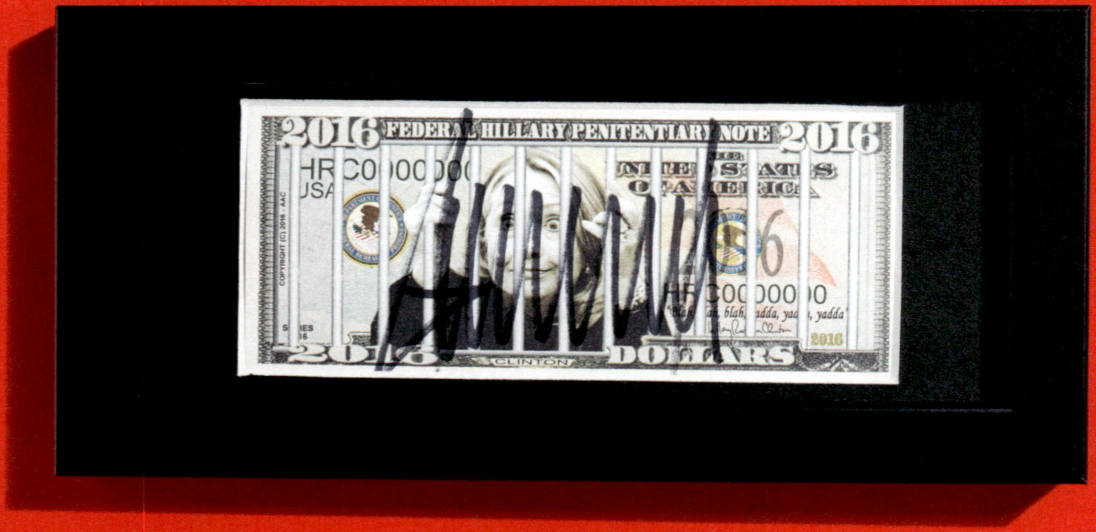

SIGNED PHOTOGRAPH OF DONALD TRUMP HOLDING
ONE MILLION DOLLARS AT THE TRUMP TAJ MAHAL, 1990

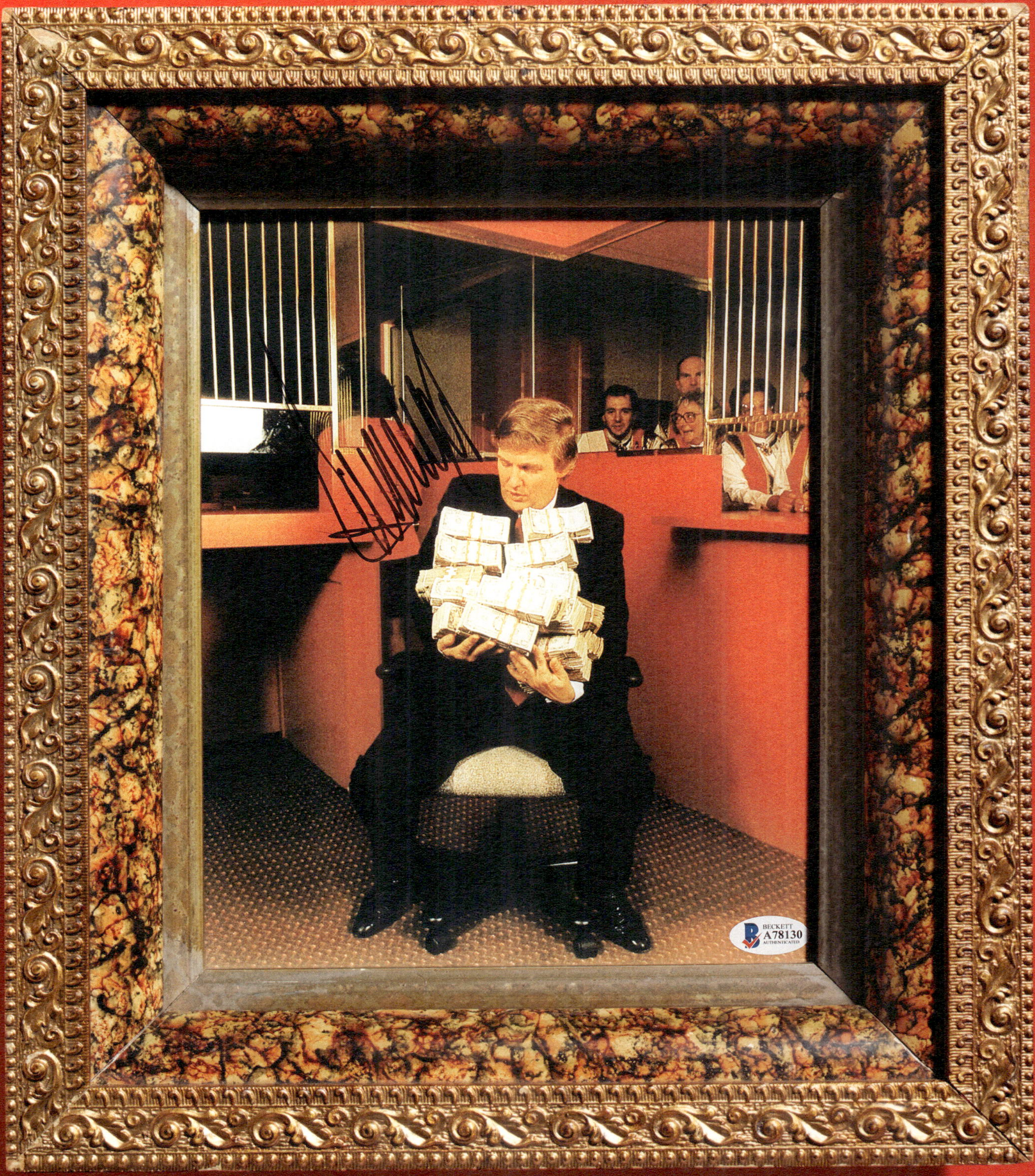

TRUMP TAJ MAHAL MOSCOW CIRCUS BADGE, 1990

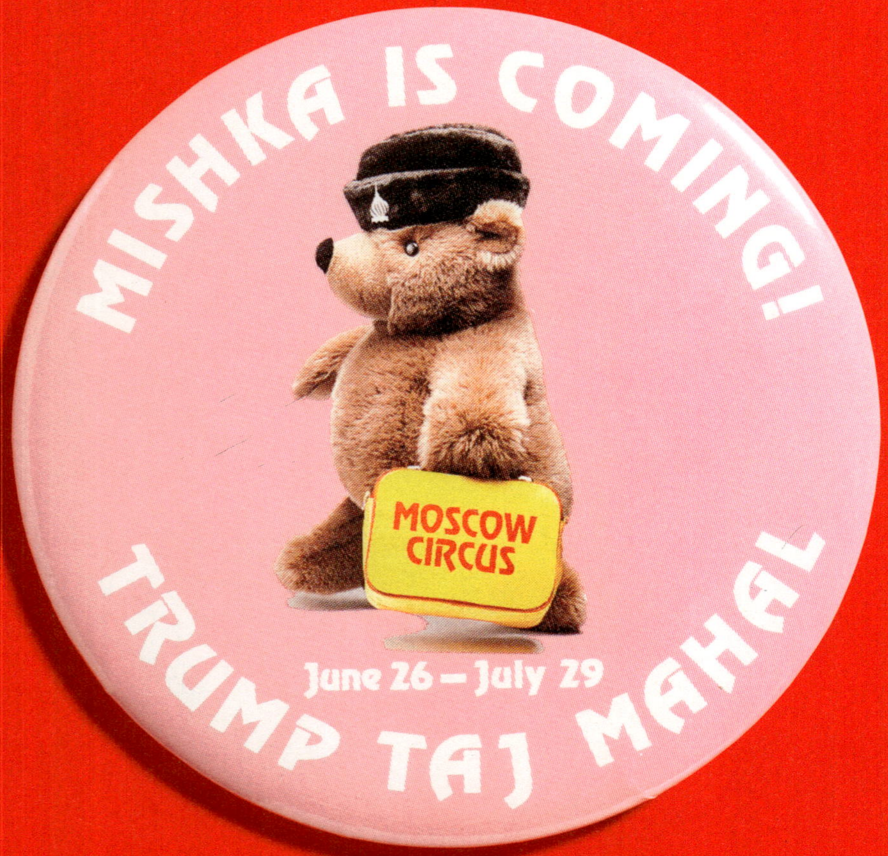

TIME MAGAZINE, JULY 30, 2018
SIGNED DONALD TRUMP

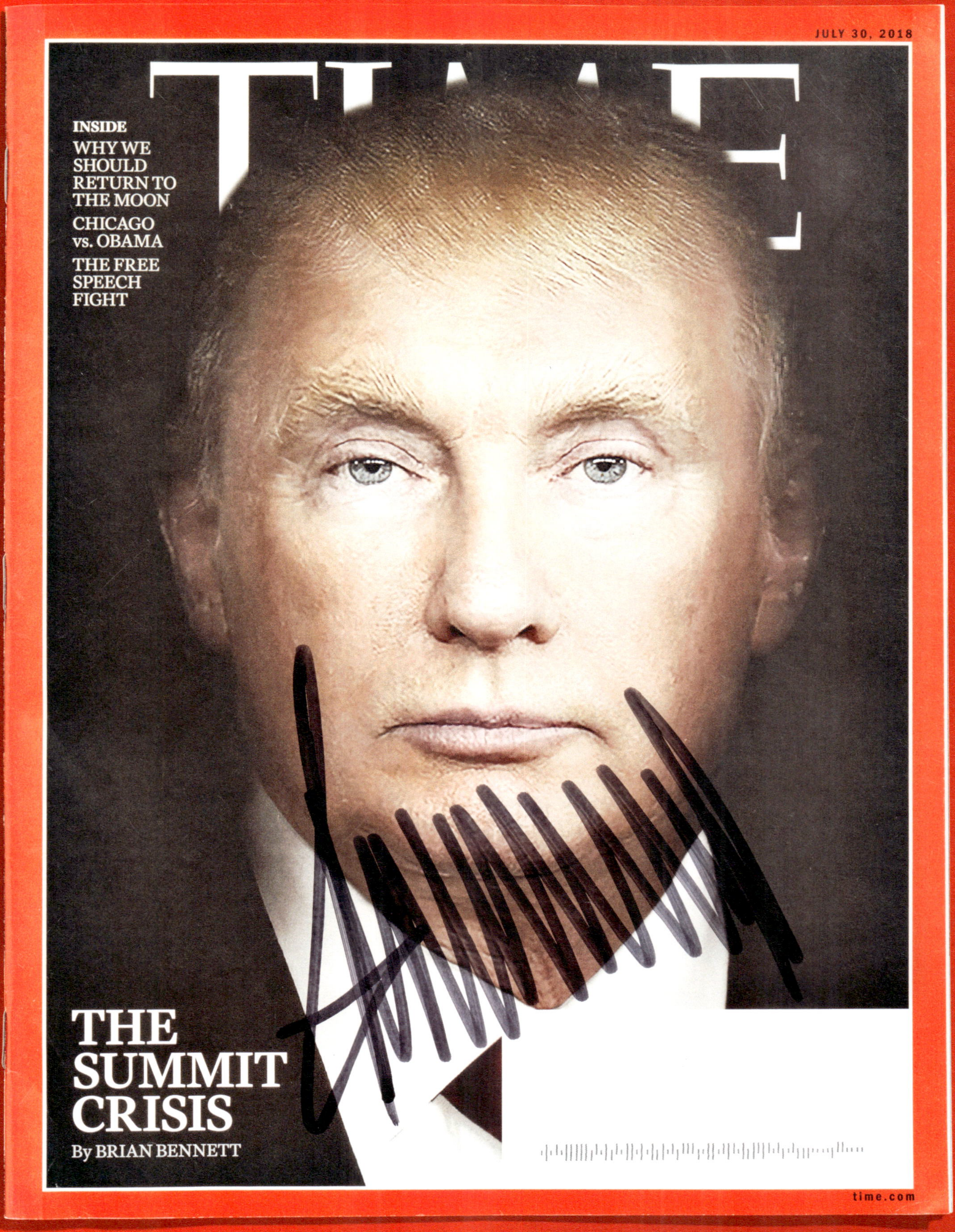

TRUMP MARINA JUKEBOX COOKIE JAR

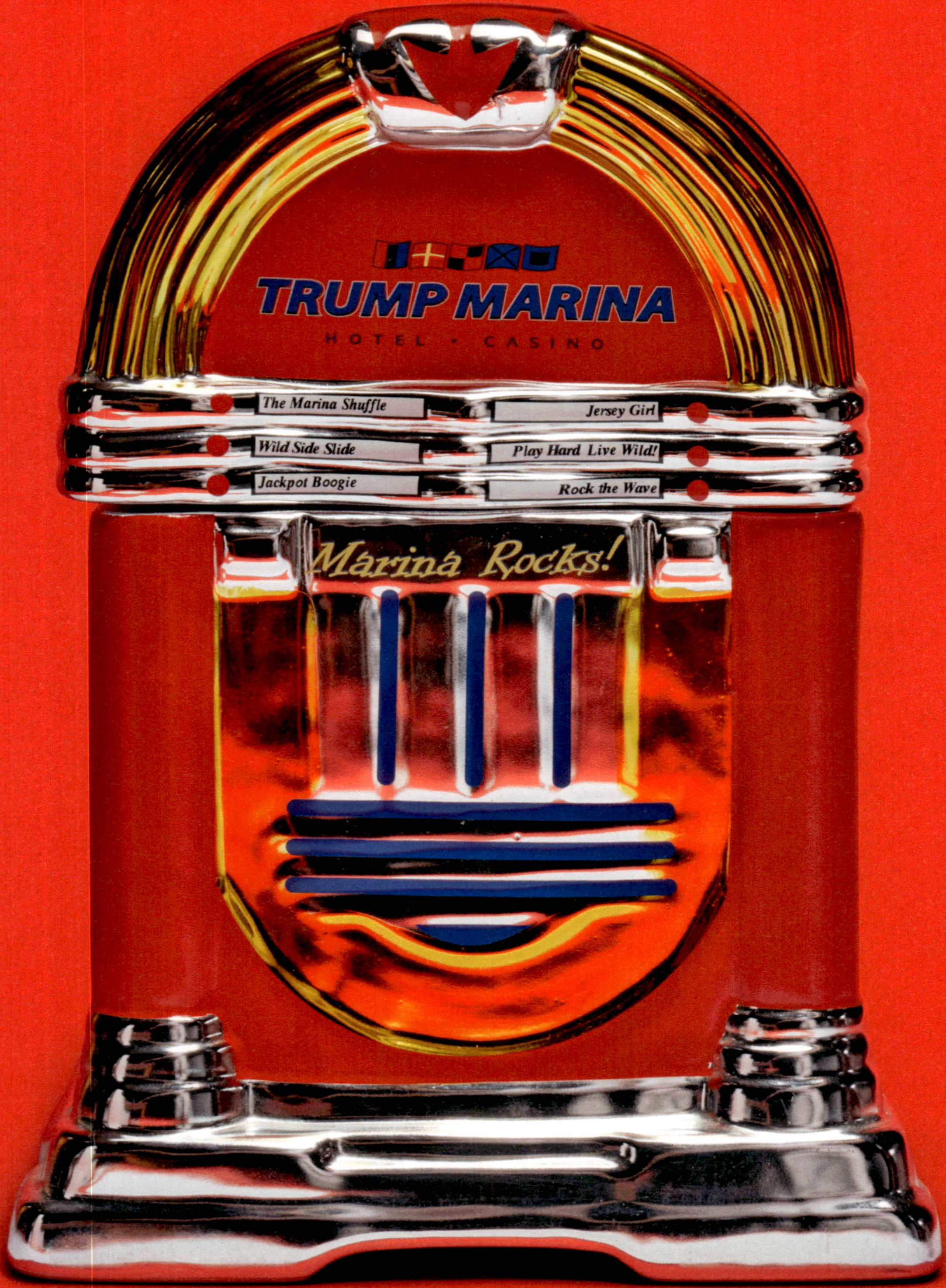

SIGNED 45TH PRESIDENT OF THE UNITED STATES PRINT

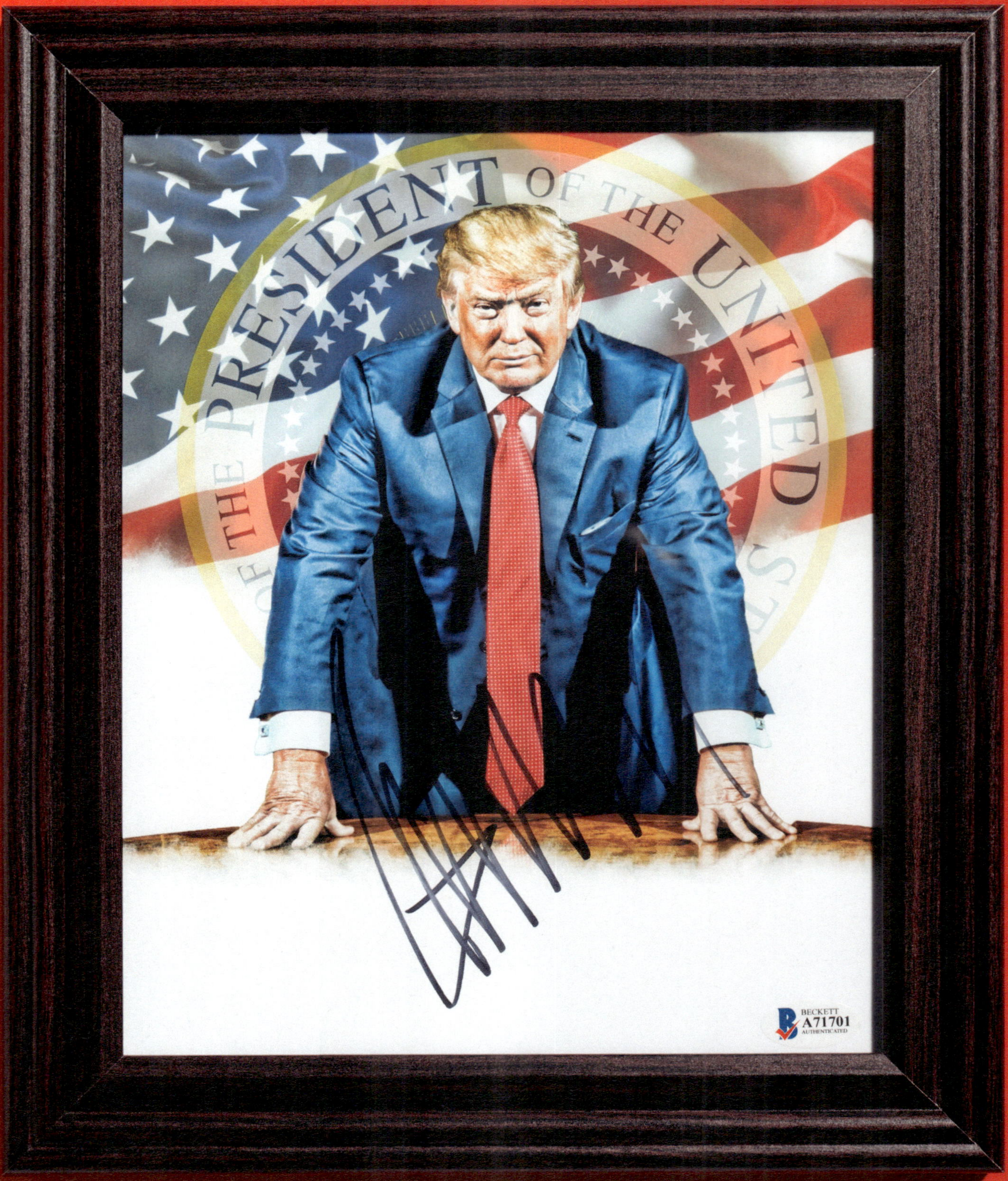

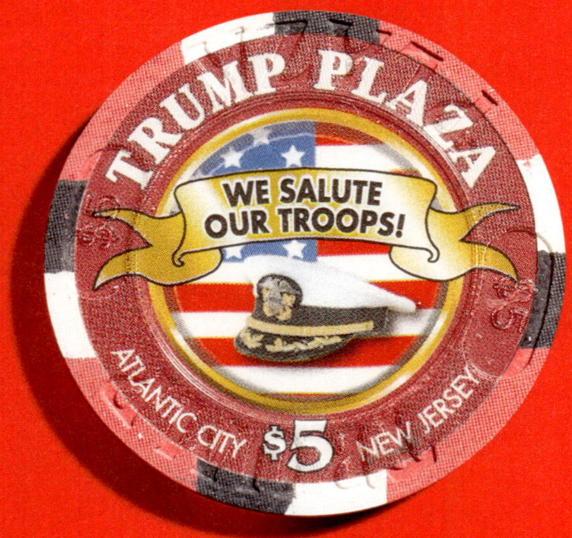
TRUMP PLAZA
WE SALUTE OUR TROOPS!
ATLANTIC CITY $5 NEW JERSEY

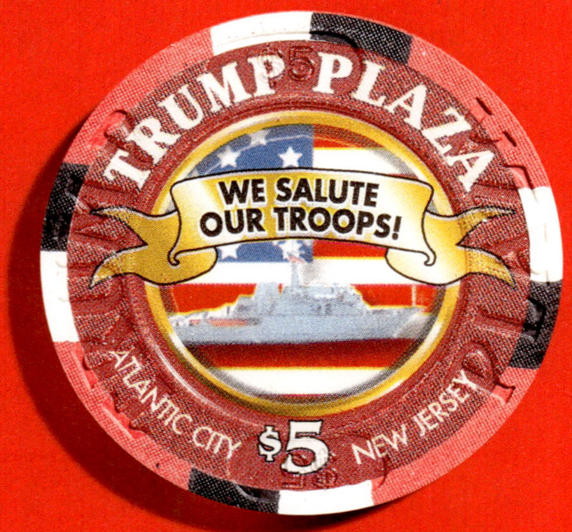
TRUMP PLAZA
WE SALUTE OUR TROOPS!
ATLANTIC CITY $5 NEW JERSEY

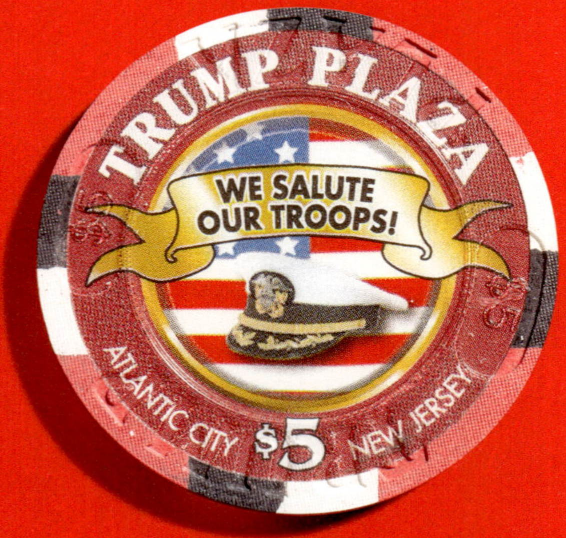
TRUMP PLAZA
WE SALUTE OUR TROOPS!
ATLANTIC CITY $5 NEW JERSEY

NEWSWEEK MAGAZINE
AUGUST 25 – SEPTEMBER 1, 2017

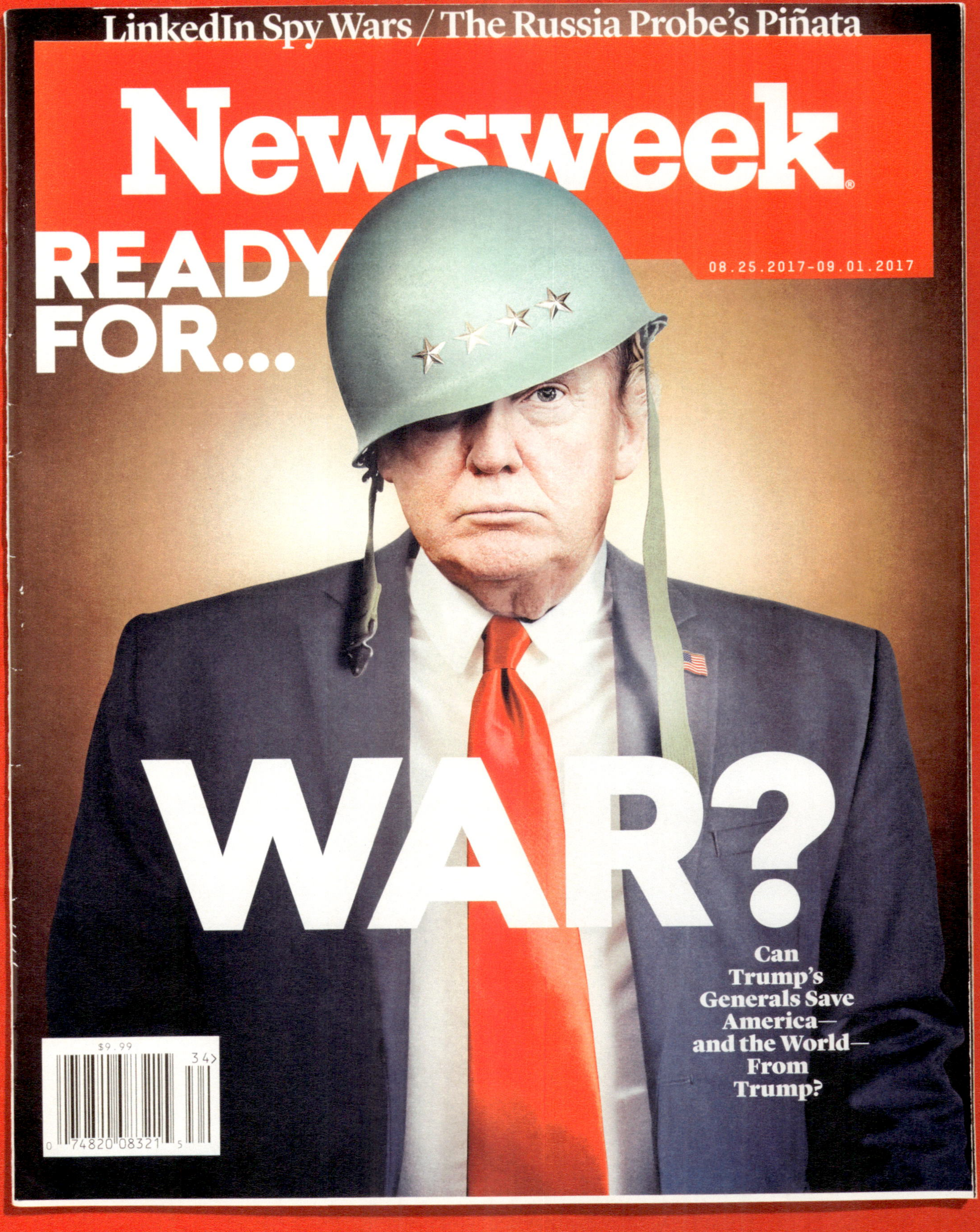

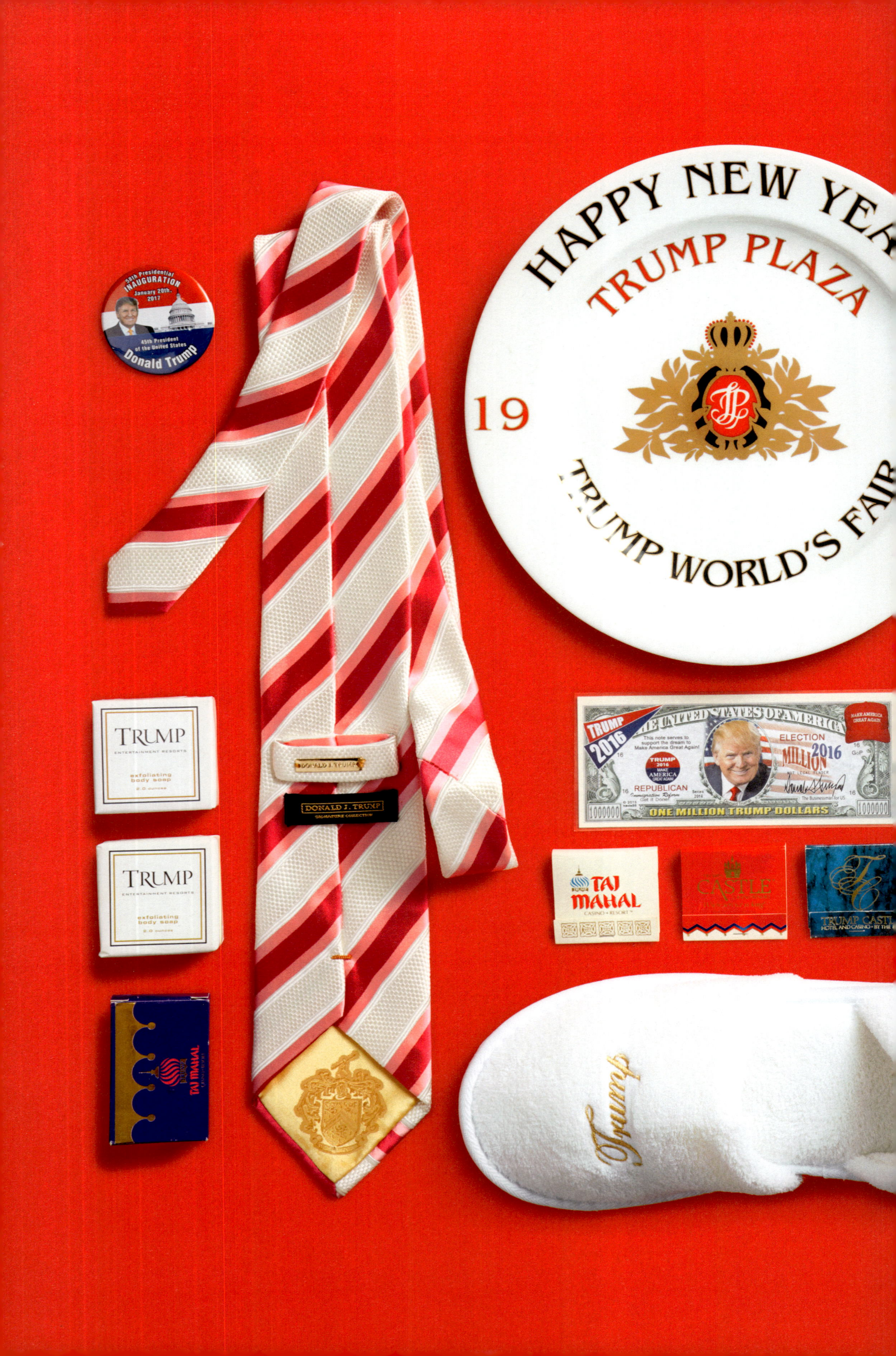

58th Presidential
INAUGURATION
January 20th, 2017
45th President
of the United States
Donald Trump
HAPPY NEW YEAR
TRUMP PLAZA
19
TRUMP WORLD'S FAIR
TRUMP
ENTERTAINMENT RESORTS
exfoliating
body soap
DONALD J. TRUMP
DONALD J. TRUMP
TRUMP
ENTERTAINMENT RESORTS
exfoliating
body soap
TRUMP
2016
ELECTION
MILLION
2016
REPUBLICAN
ONE MILLION TRUMP DOLLARS
TAJ MAHAL
CASINO • RESORT
CASTLE
TRUMP CASTLE
TAJ MAHAL
Trump

SELECTION OF TRUMP-BRANDED OBJECTS

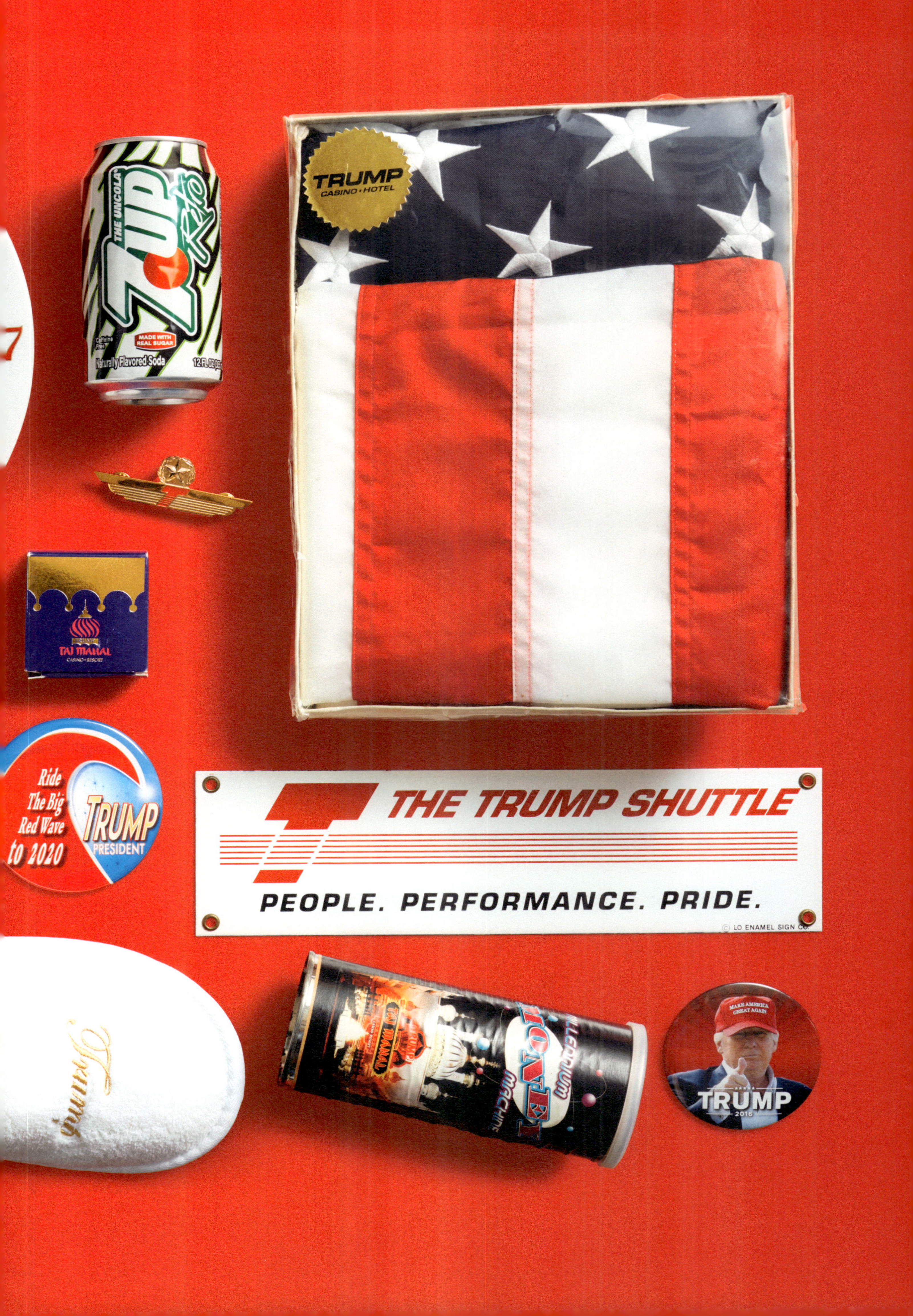

TRUMP PLAZA LEPRECHAUN SOFT TOY

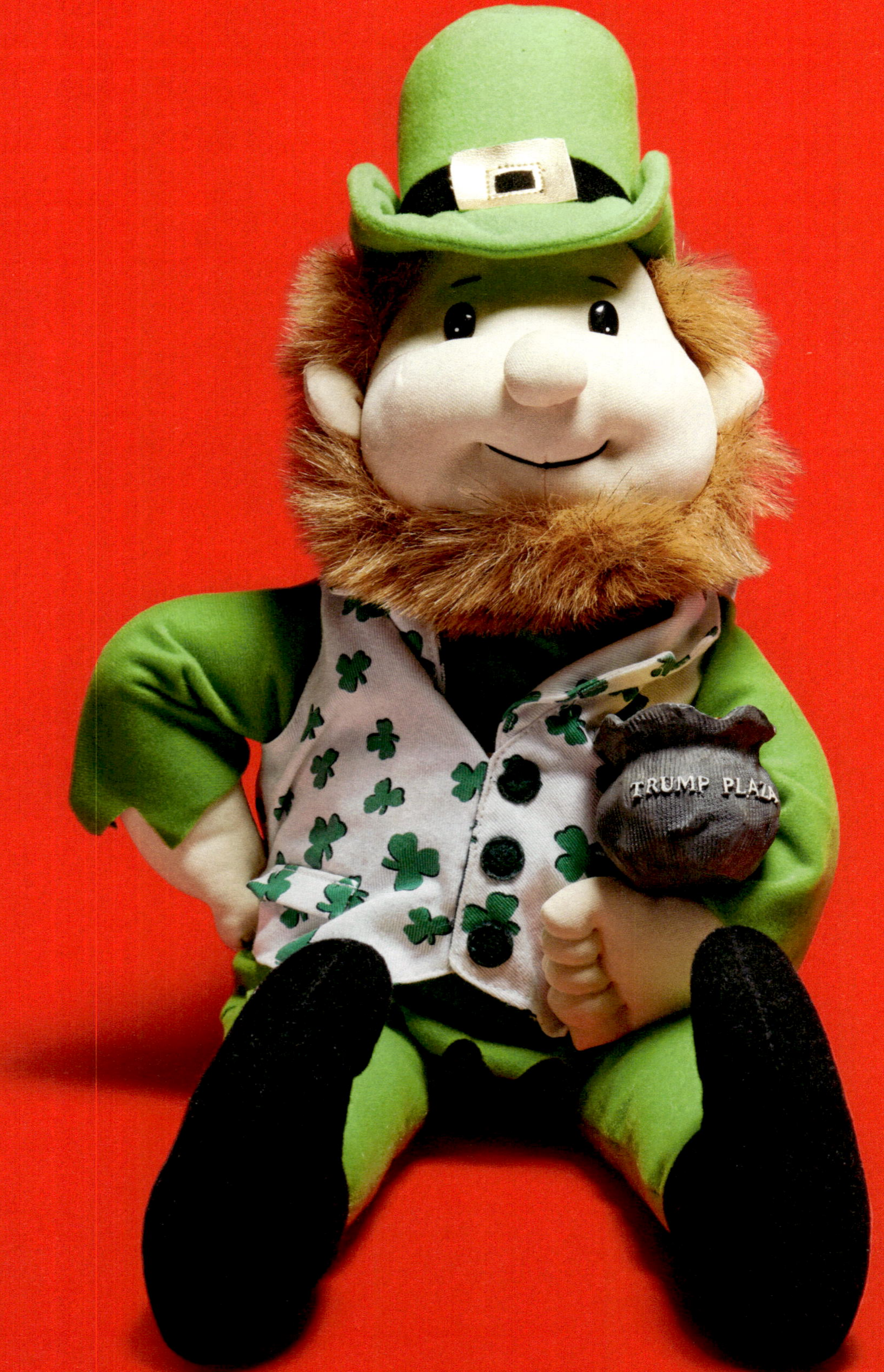

SIGNED PHOTOGRAPH OF DONALD TRUMP, 1989
COMMISSIONED FOR FEATURE ON AMERICAN BILLIONAIRES
BY FORTUNE MAGAZINE

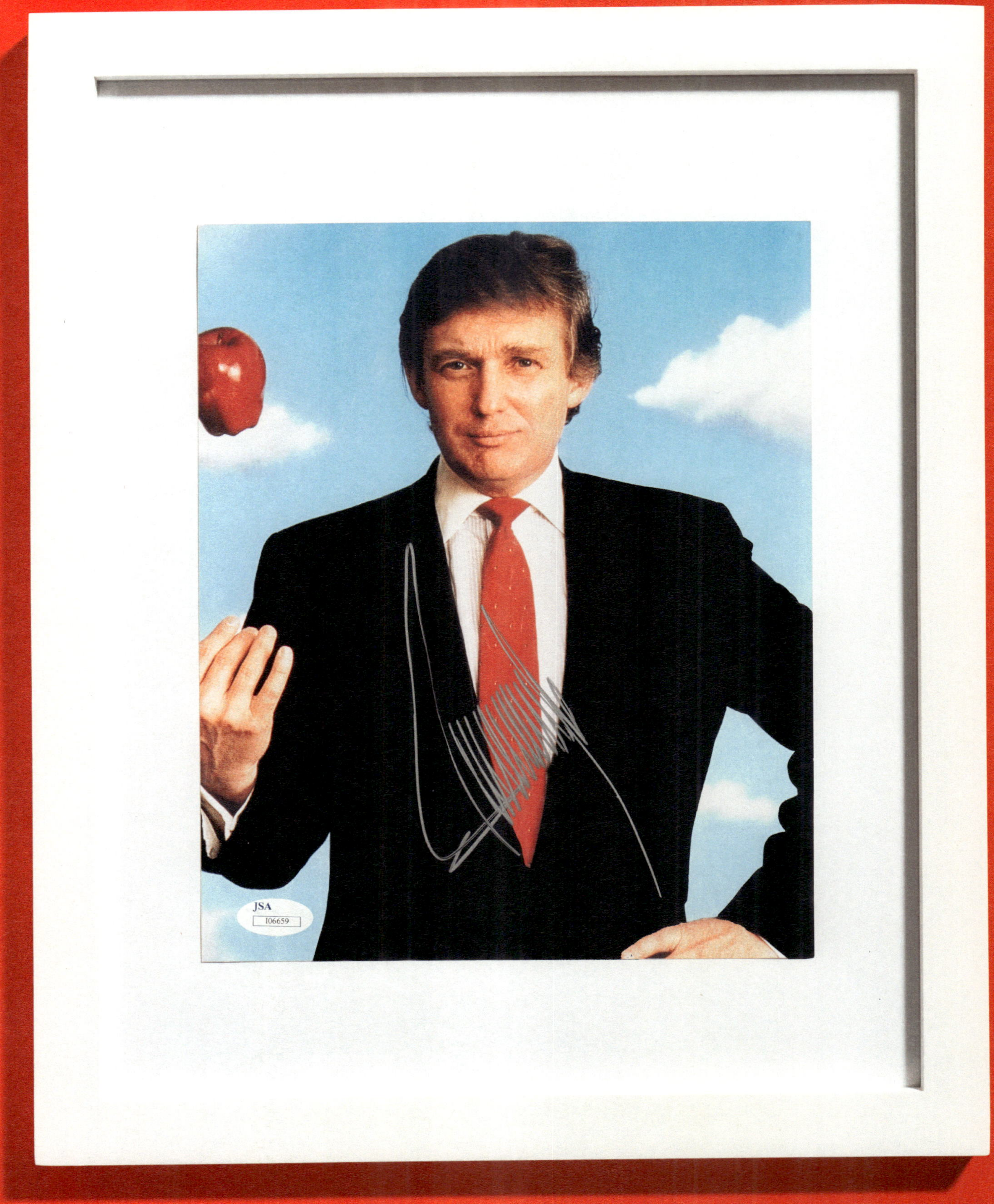

TIME MAGAZINE, JULY 23, 2018
SIGNED DONALD TRUMP

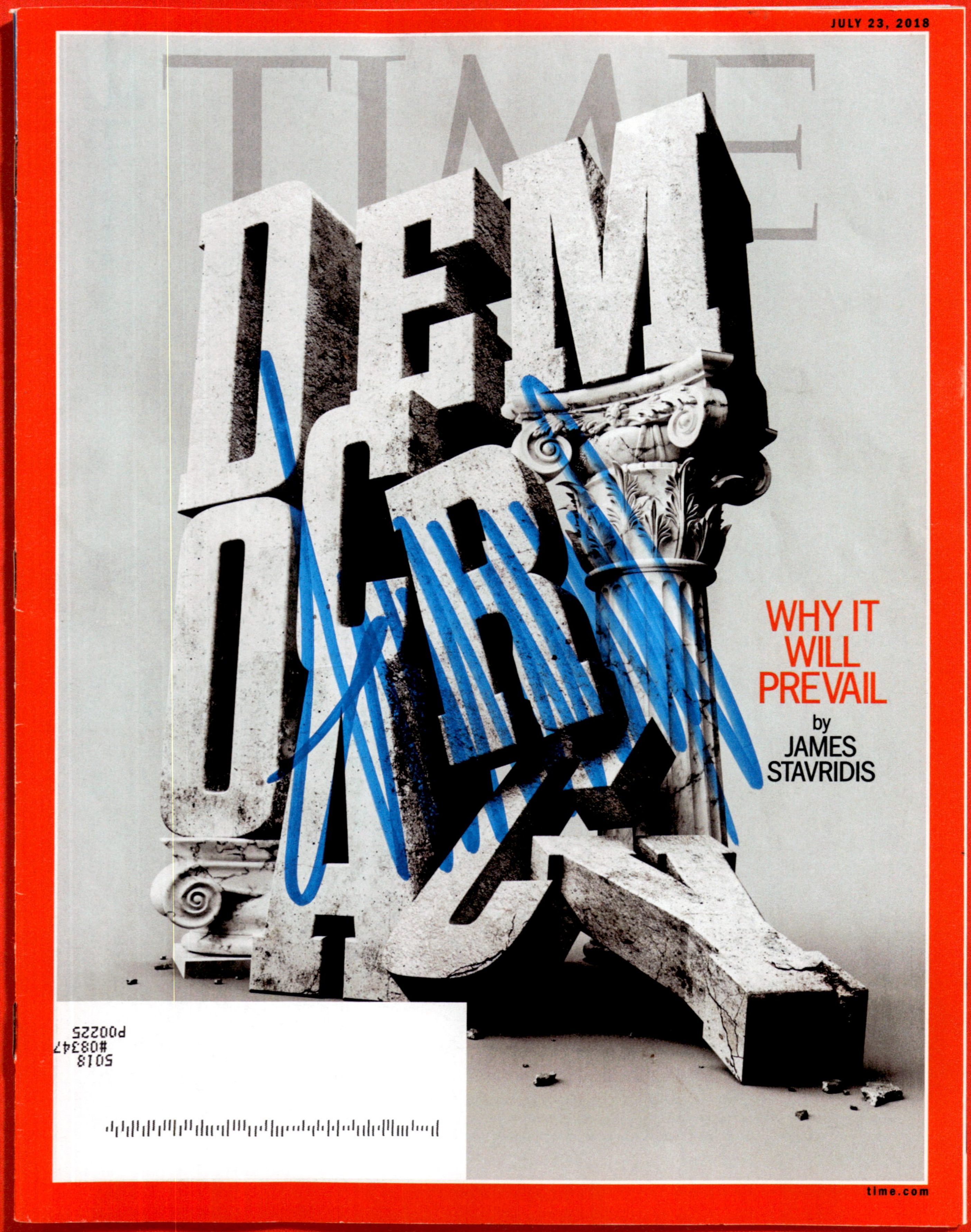

VANITY FAIR MAGAZINE, MARCH 1994
SIGNED DONALD TRUMP

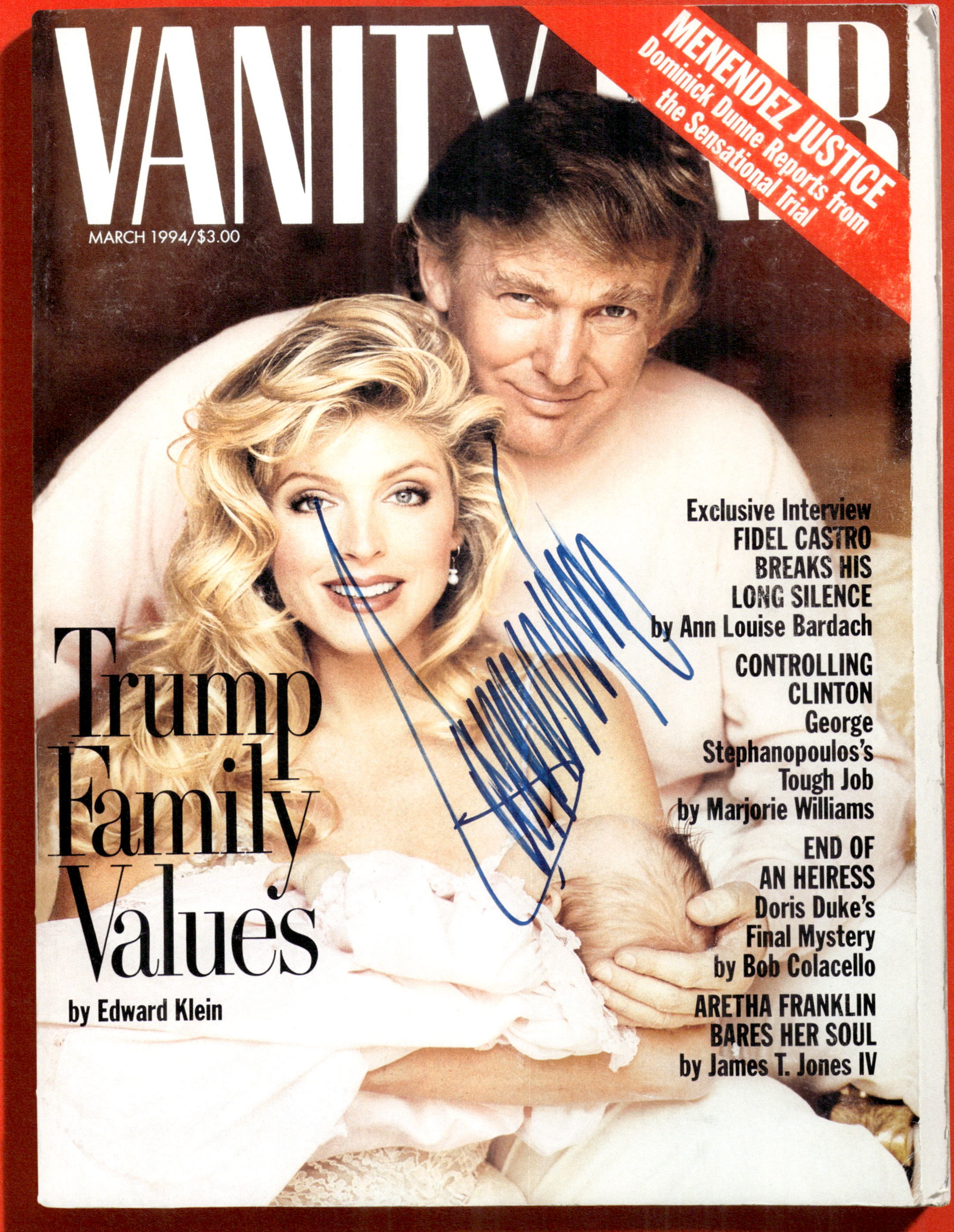

TRUMP'S CASTLE BRANDED COLLECTOR PLATE, MATCHSTICKS, BLANKET, AND FLASHLIGHT

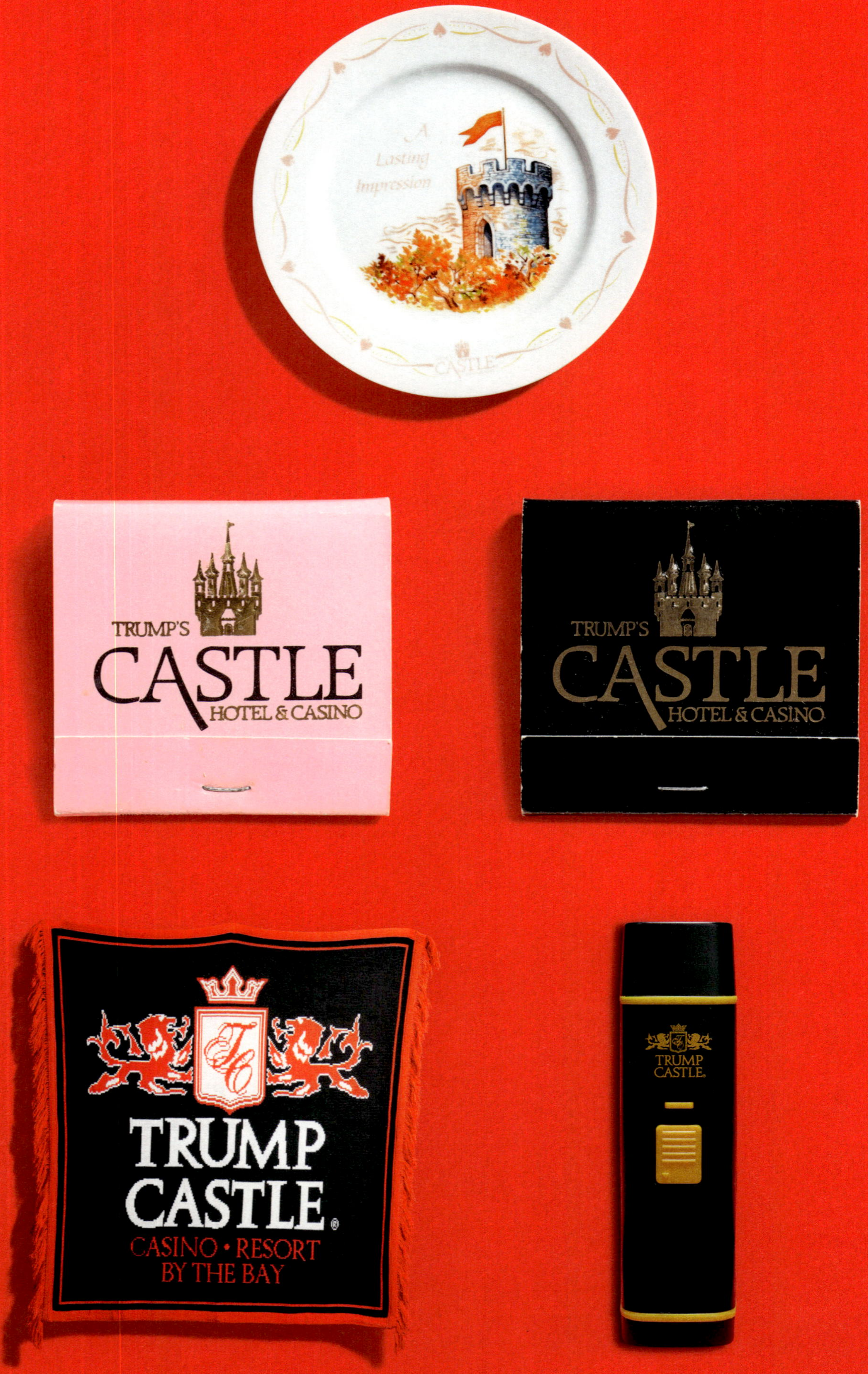

SIGNED PHOTOGRAPH OF DONALD TRUMP IN THE OVAL OFFICE

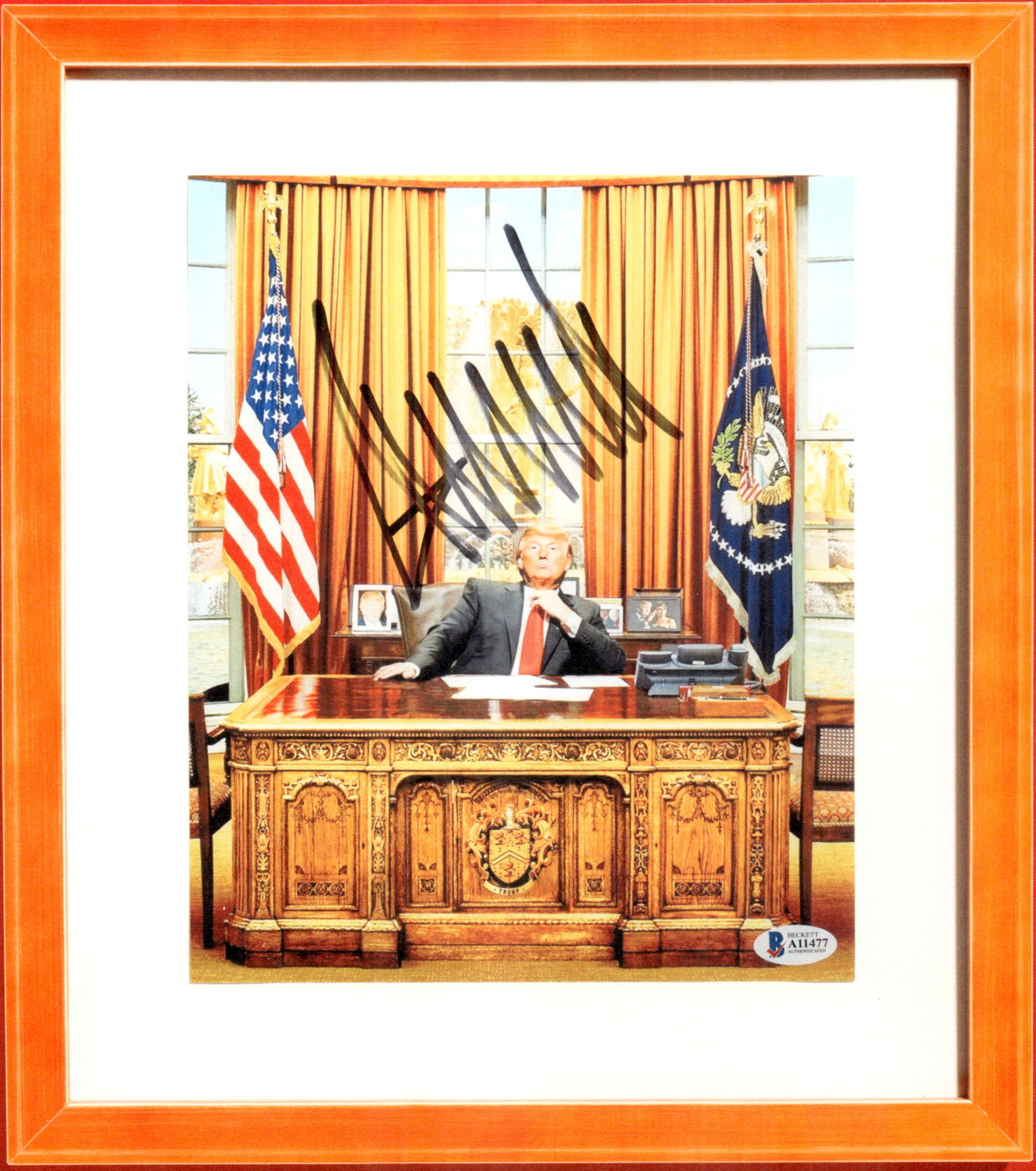

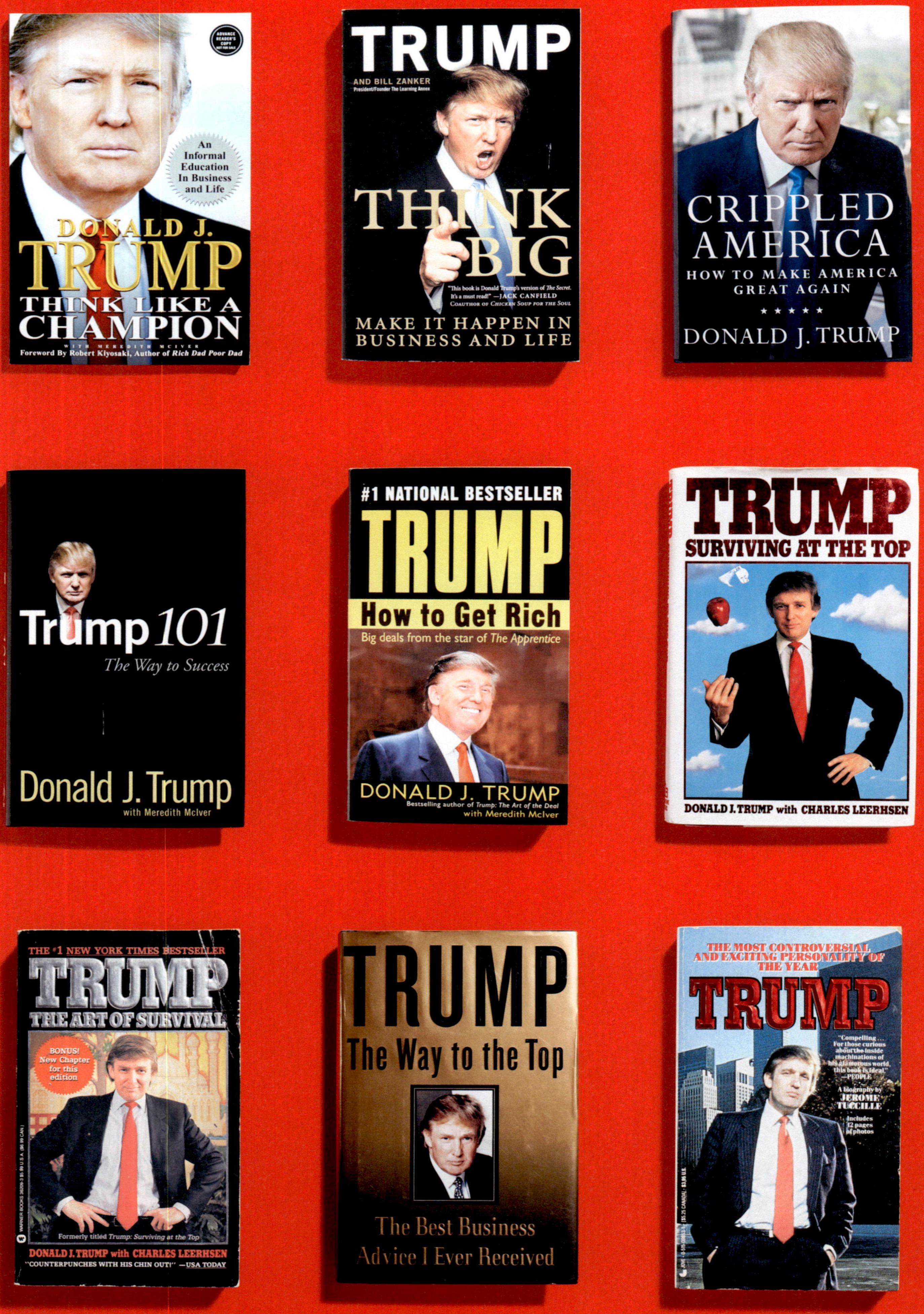
An Informal Education In Business and Life
DONALD J. TRUMP
THINK LIKE A CHAMPION
Foreword By Robert Kiyosaki, Author of Rich Dad Poor Dad
TRUMP
AND BILL ZANKER
THINK BIG
MAKE IT HAPPEN IN BUSINESS AND LIFE
CRIPPLED AMERICA
HOW TO MAKE AMERICA GREAT AGAIN
DONALD J. TRUMP
Trump 101
The Way to Success
Donald J. Trump
with Meredith McIver
#1 NATIONAL BESTSELLER
TRUMP
How to Get Rich
Big deals from the star of The Apprentice
DONALD J. TRUMP
with Meredith McIver
TRUMP
SURVIVING AT THE TOP
DONALD J. TRUMP with CHARLES LEERHSEN
THE #1 NEW YORK TIMES BESTSELLER
TRUMP
THE ART OF SURVIVAL
BONUS! New Chapter for this edition
Formerly titled Trump: Surviving at the Top
DONALD J. TRUMP with CHARLES LEERHSEN
"COUNTERPUNCHES WITH HIS CHIN OUT!" —USA TODAY
TRUMP
The Way to the Top
The Best Business Advice I Ever Received
THE MOST CONTROVERSIAL AND EXCITING PERSONALITY OF THE YEAR
TRUMP
A biography by JEROME TUCCILLE

TRUMP: THE ART OF THE DEAL BOOK, 1987
OVER ONE MILLION COPIES SOLD TO DATE
SIGNED DONALD TRUMP

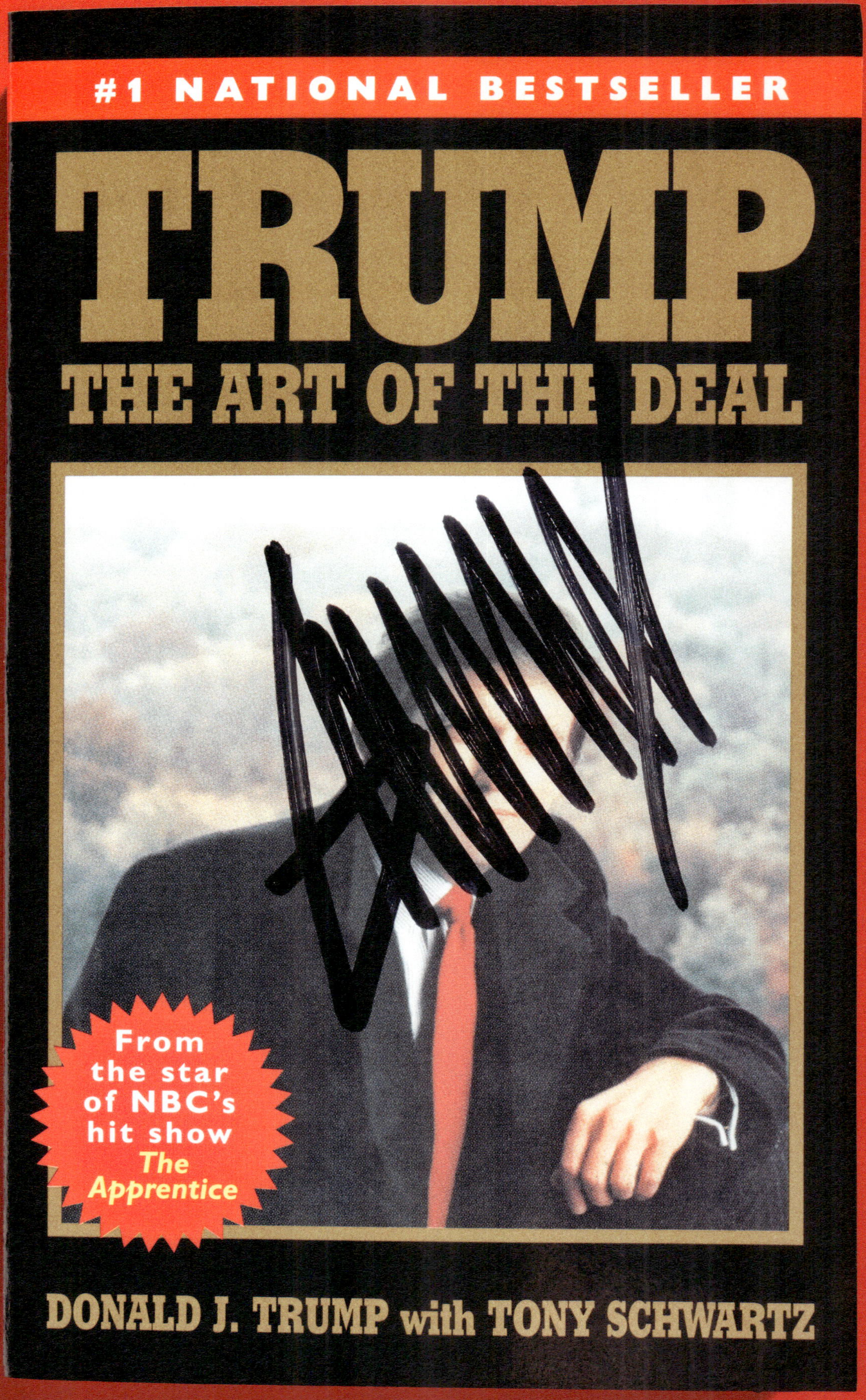

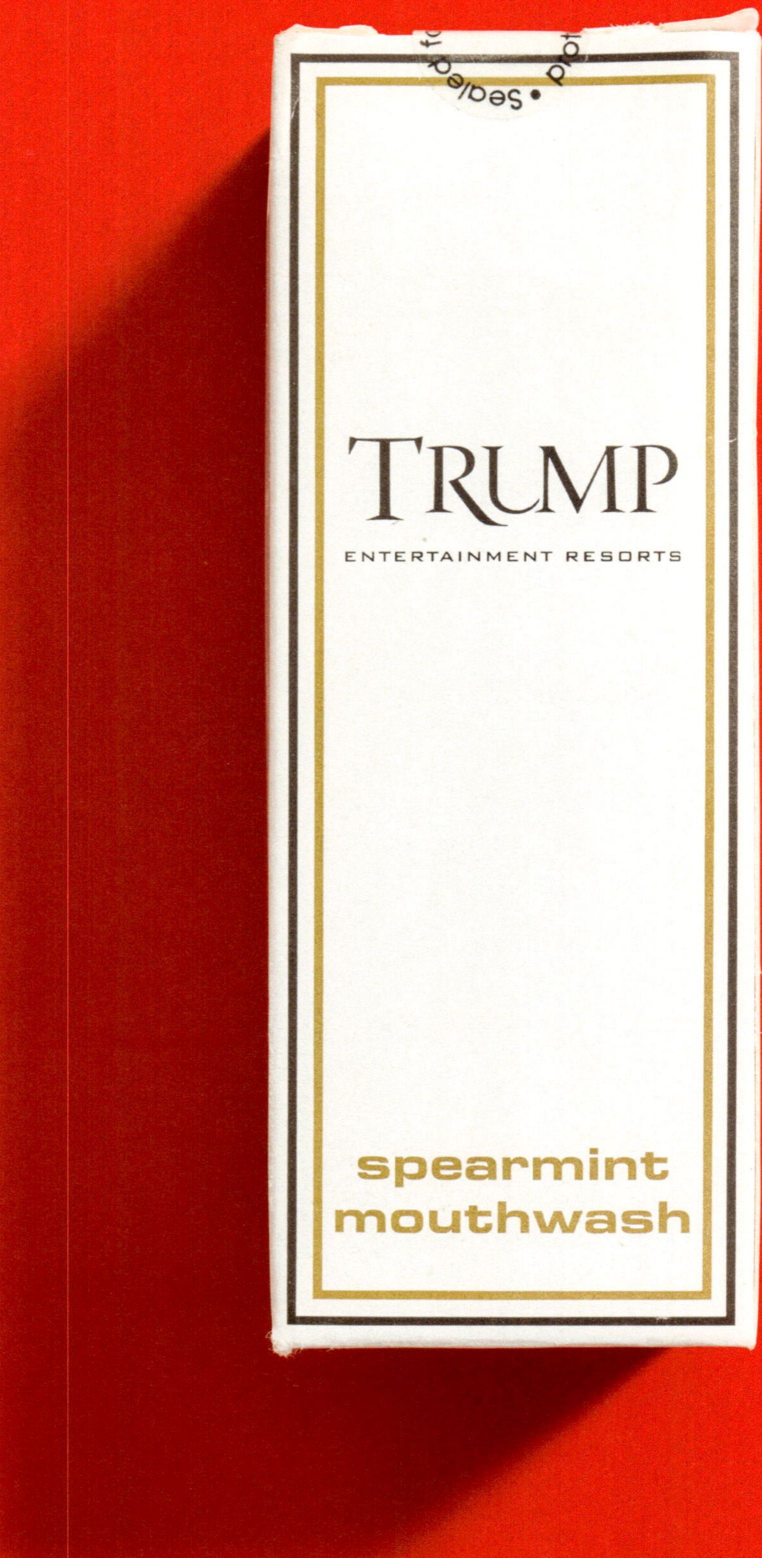
TRUMP
ENTERTAINMENT RESORTS
spearmint
mouthwash

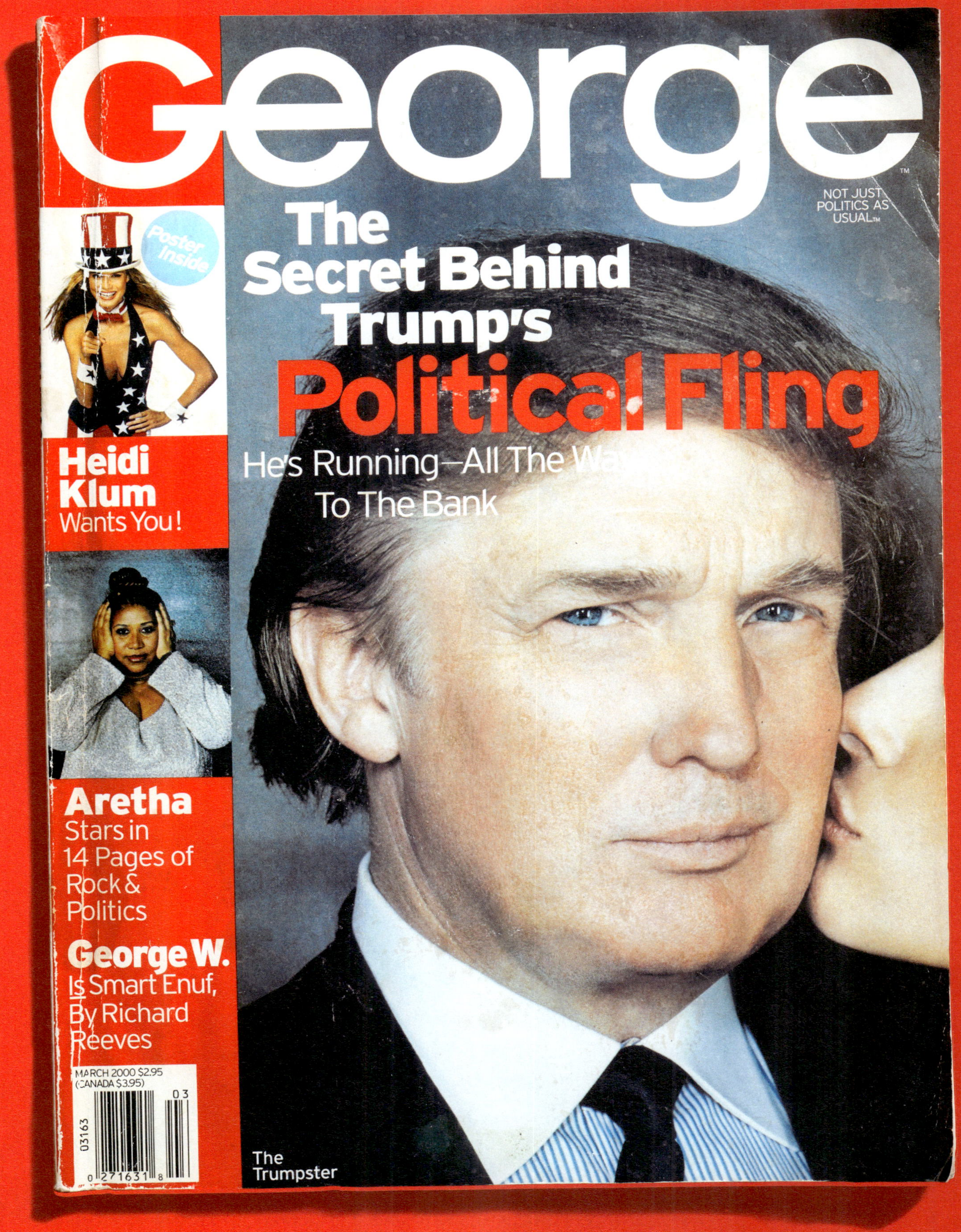
George
NOT JUST POLITICS AS USUAL
The Secret Behind Trump's Political Fling
He's Running—All The Way To The Bank
Poster Inside
Heidi Klum Wants You!
Aretha Stars in 14 Pages of Rock & Politics
George W. Is Smart Enuf, By Richard Reeves
MARCH 2000 $2.95 (CANADA $3.95)
The Trumpster

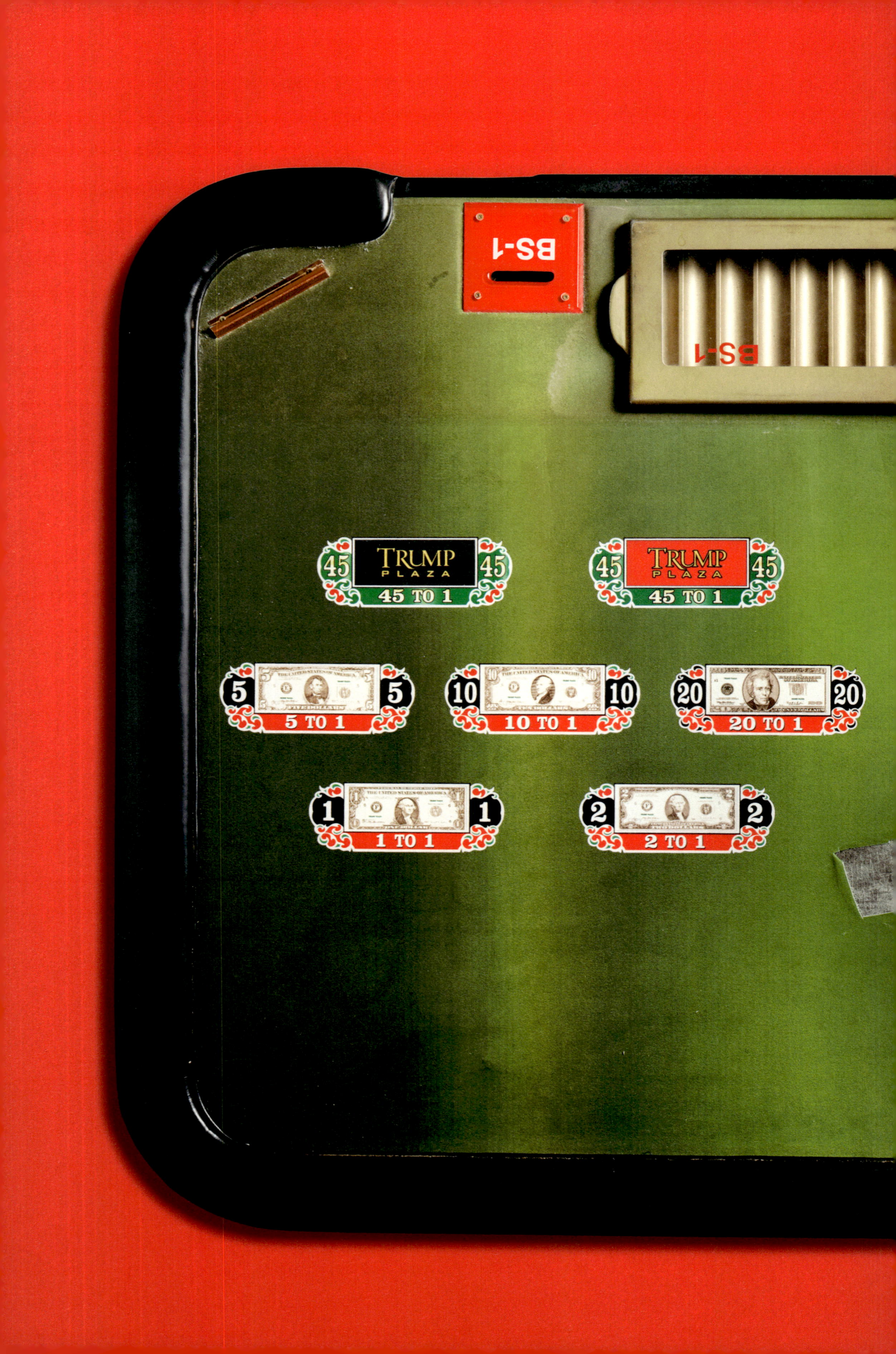
BS-1
BS-1
45 TRUMP PLAZA 45
45 TO 1
45 TRUMP PLAZA 45
45 TO 1
5 5
5 TO 1
10 10
10 TO 1
20 20
20 TO 1
1 1
1 TO 1
2 2
2 TO 1

TRUMP PLAZA BIG WHEEL TABLE
BIG WHEEL, SOMETIMES REFERRED TO AS BIG 6 OR WHEEL OF FORTUNE,
IS GENERALLY CONSIDERED THE CASINO GAME WITH THE WORST ODDS

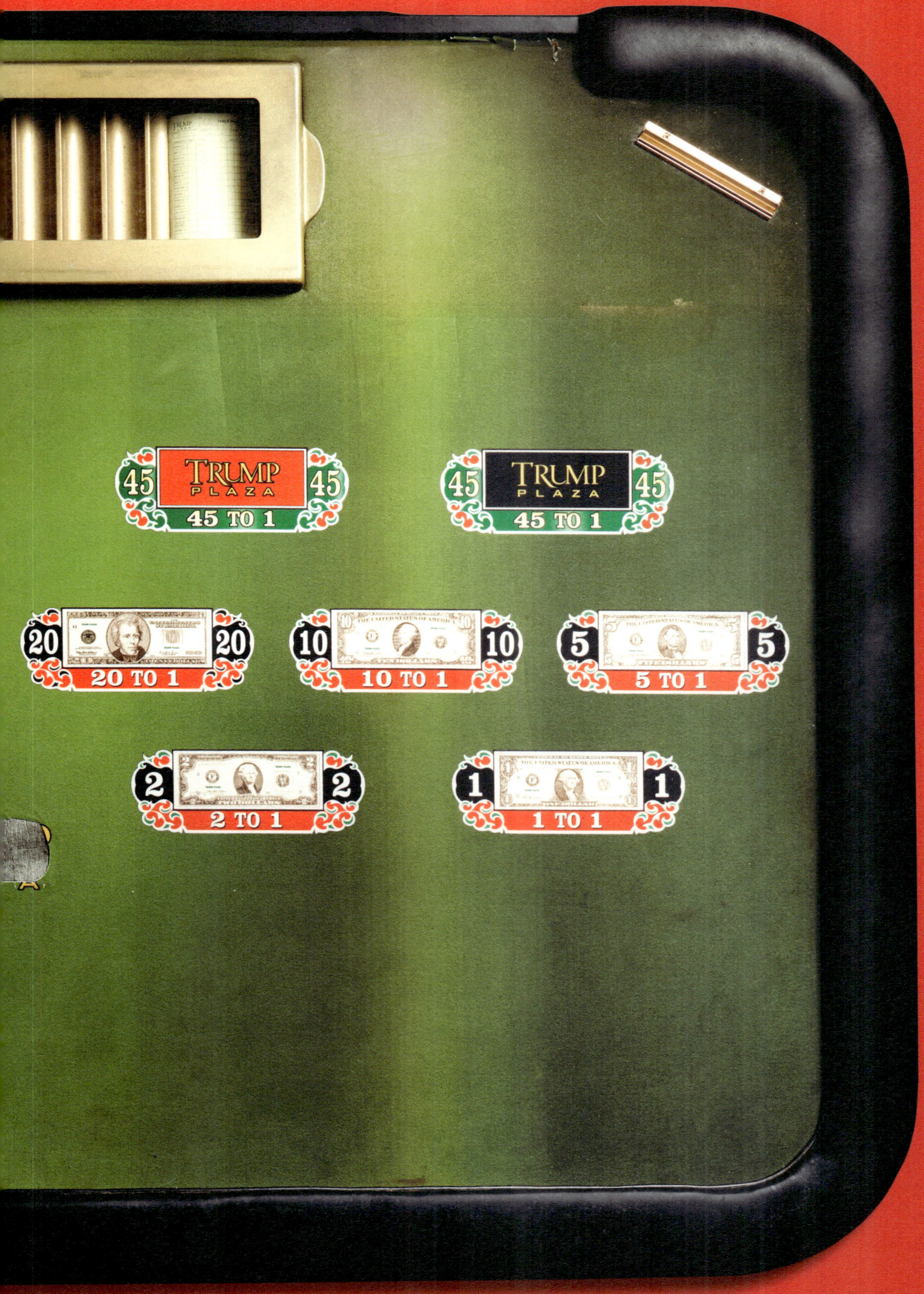

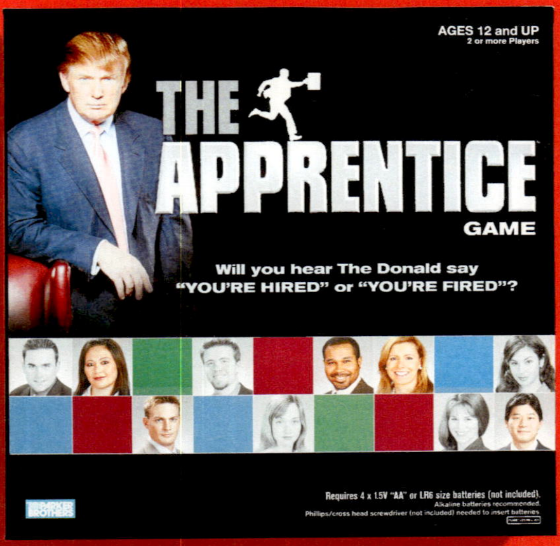
AGES 12 and UP
2 or more Players
THE APPRENTICE
GAME
Will you hear The Donald say
"YOU'RE HIRED" or "YOU'RE FIRED"?
Requires 4 x 1.5V "AA" or LR6 size batteries (not included).
Alkaline batteries recommended.

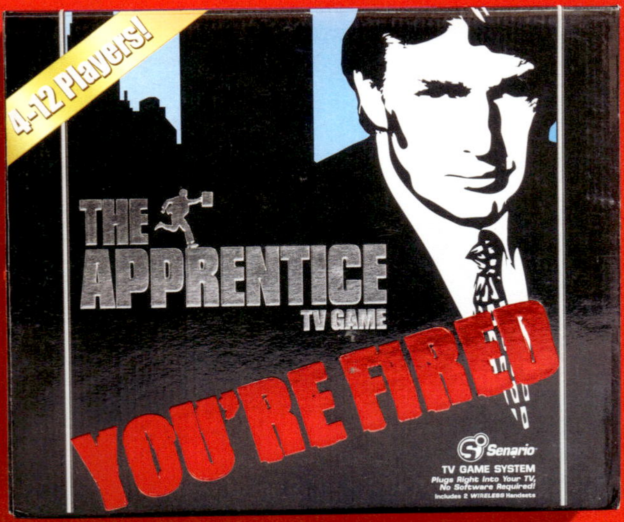
4-12 Players!
THE APPRENTICE
TV GAME
YOU'RE FIRED
Senario
TV GAME SYSTEM
Plugs Right Into Your TV,
No Software Required!

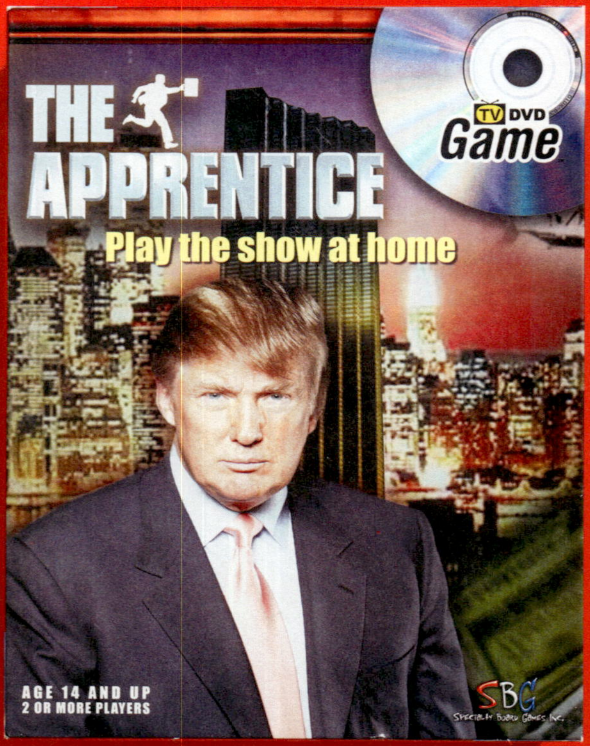
THE APPRENTICE
TV DVD
Game
Play the show at home
AGE 14 AND UP
2 OR MORE PLAYERS
SBG

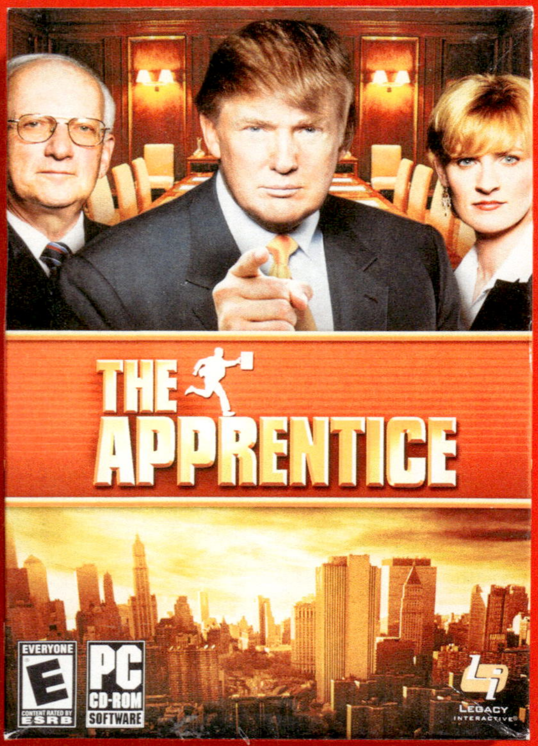
THE APPRENTICE
EVERYONE
E
PC
CD-ROM
SOFTWARE
LEGACY
INTERACTIVE

TV GUIDE, FEBRUARY 7–13, 2004
DONALD TRUMP HOSTED NBC'S THE APPRENTICE REALITY TV SHOW FOR 14 SEASONS FROM 2004 TO 2015

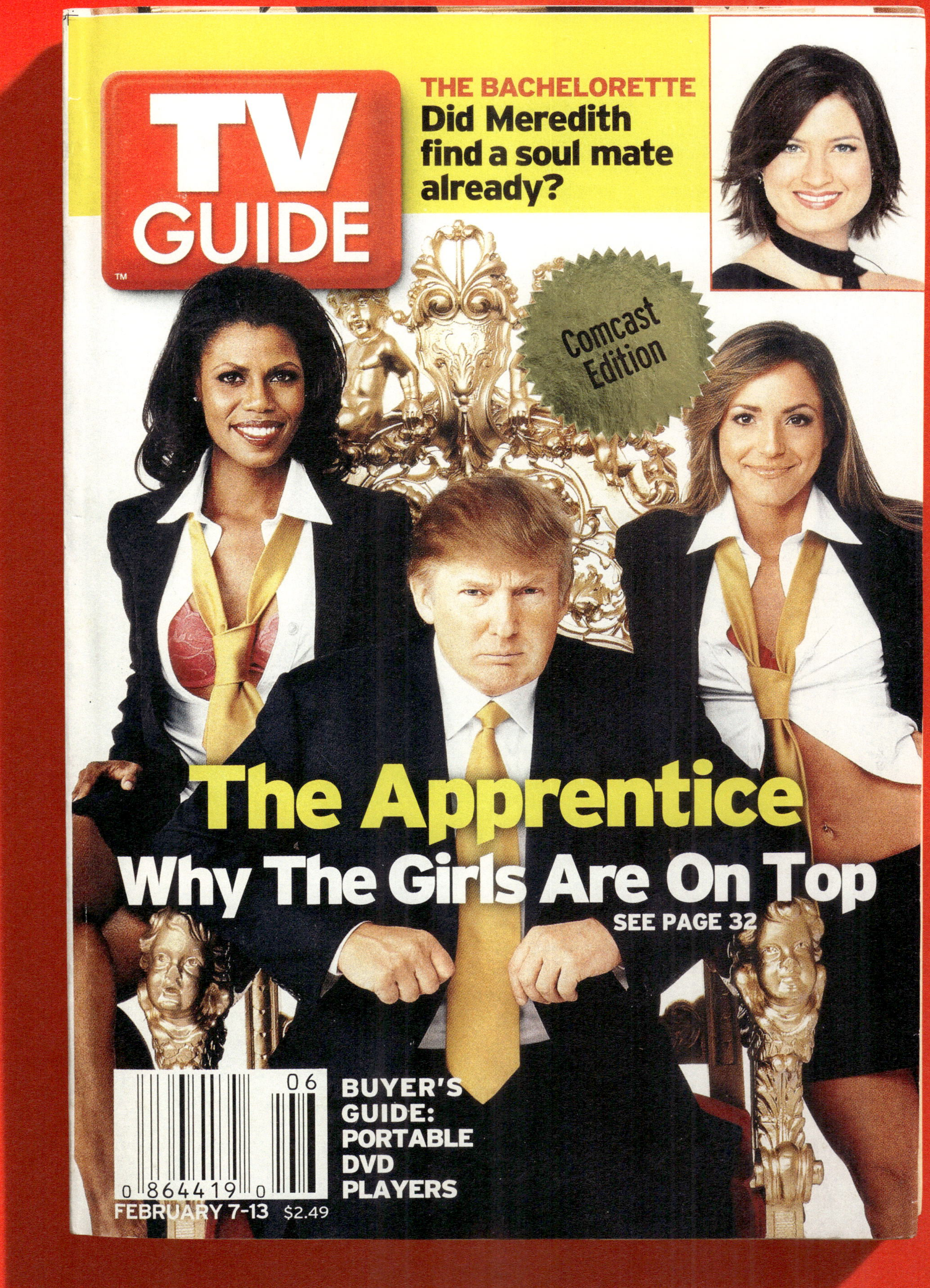

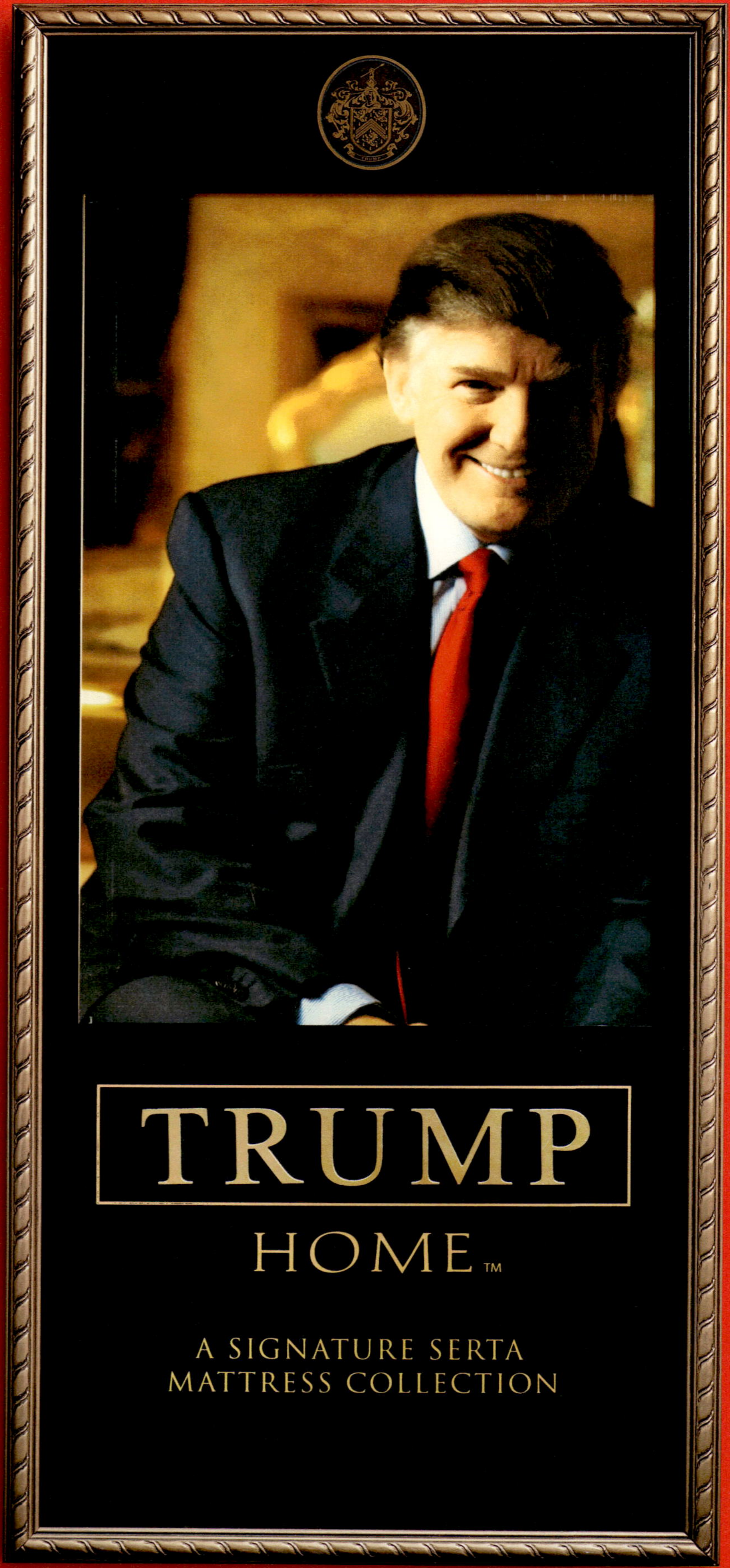
TRUMP
HOME™
A SIGNATURE SERTA
MATTRESS COLLECTION

DONALD J. TRUMP SIGNATURE COLLECTION TIE

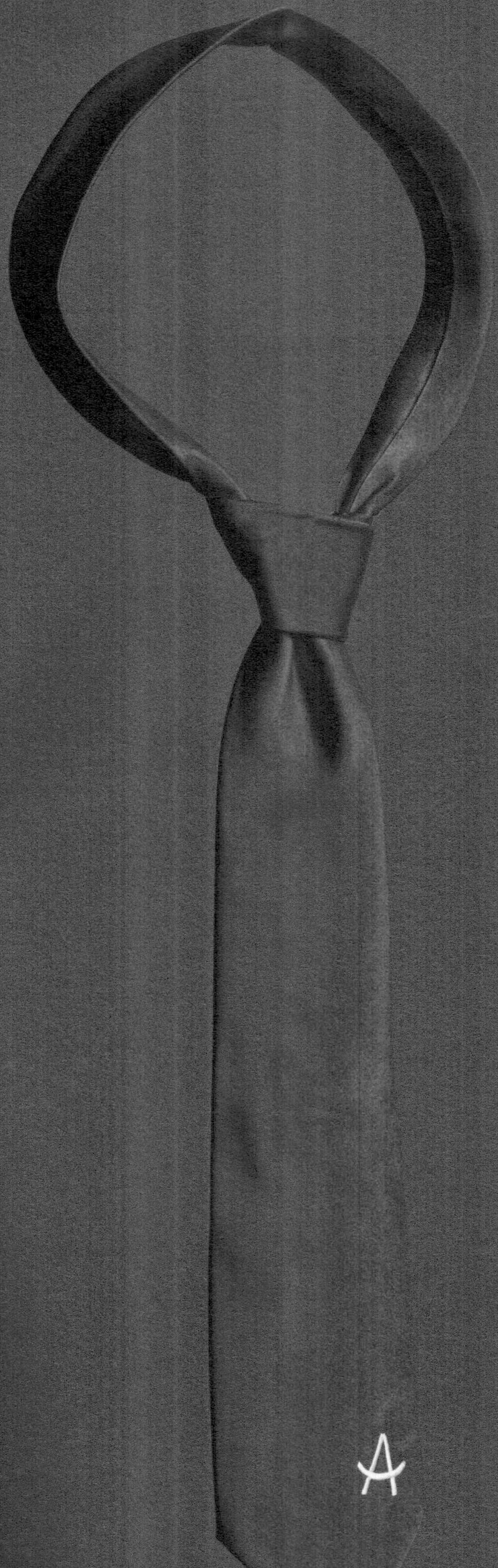

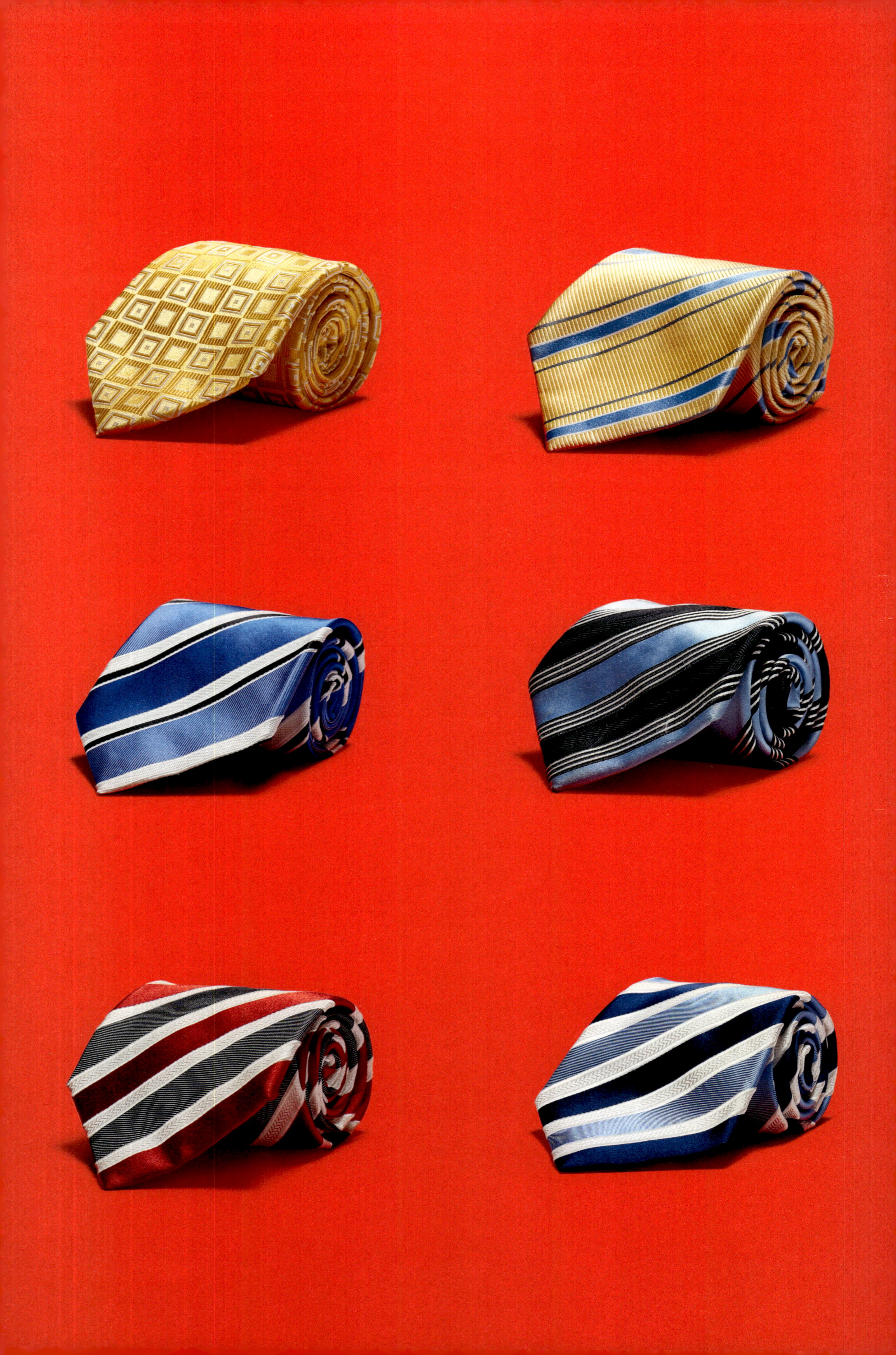

DONALD J. TRUMP SIGNATURE COLLECTION TIES

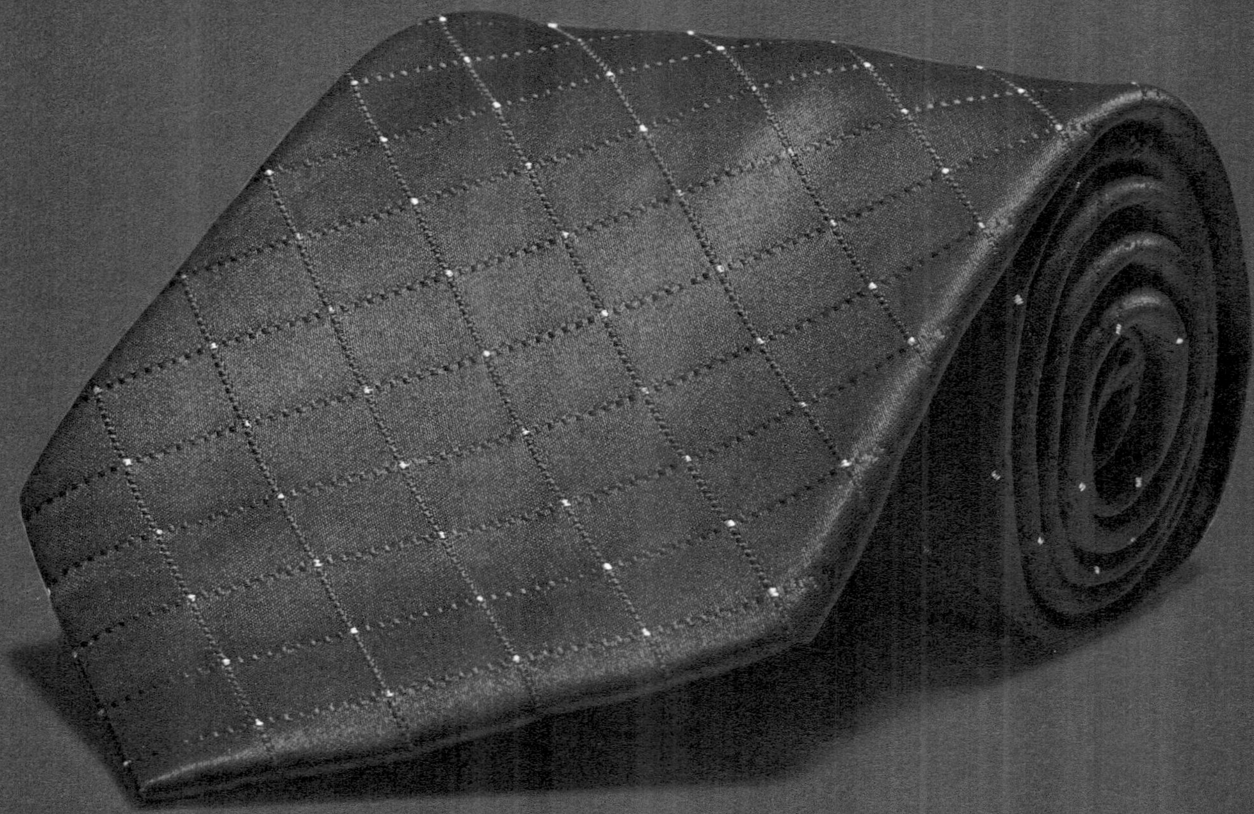

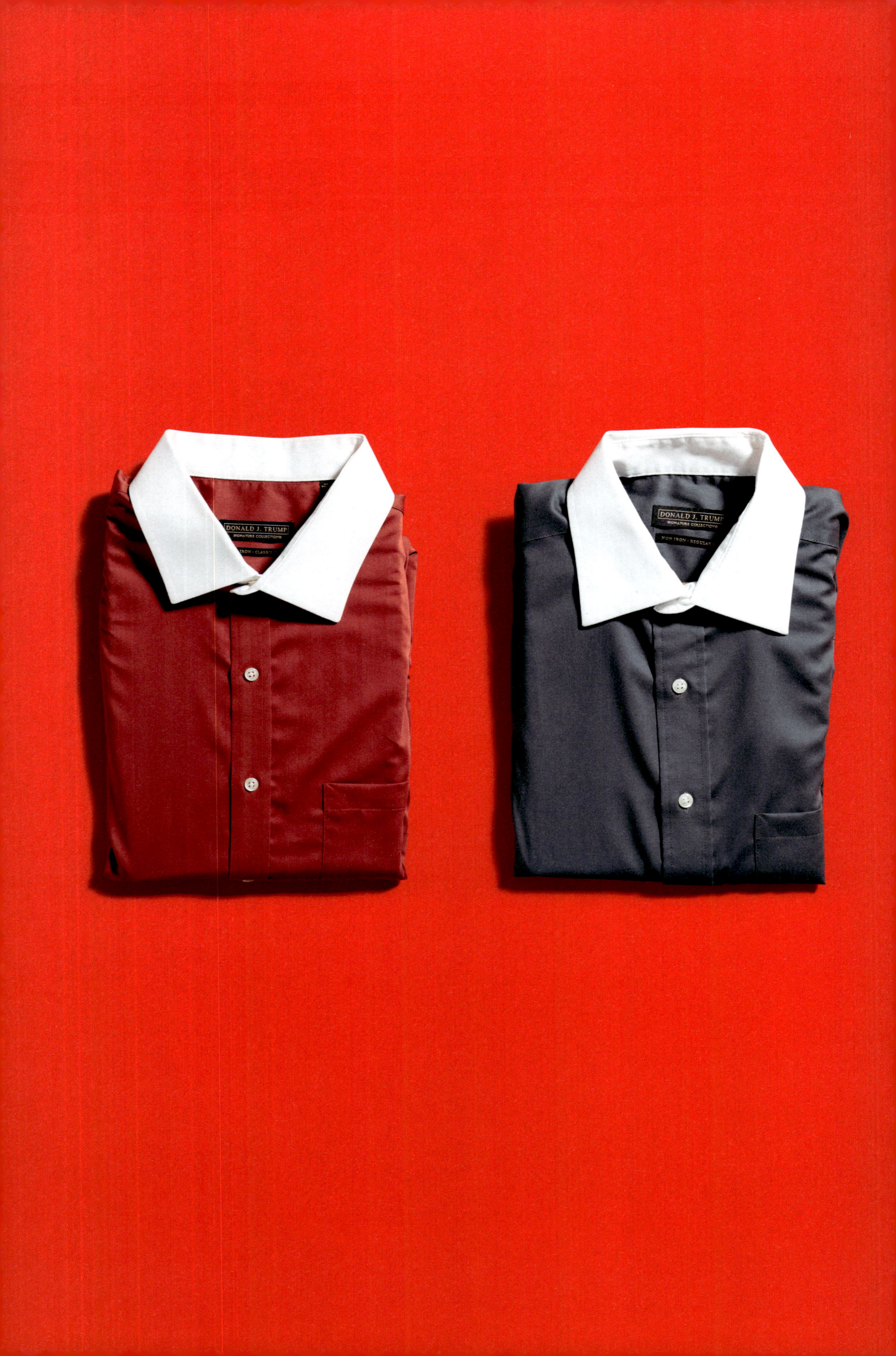
DONALD J. TRUMP
DONALD J. TRUMP

DONALD J. TRUMP SIGNATURE COLLECTION SHIRTS

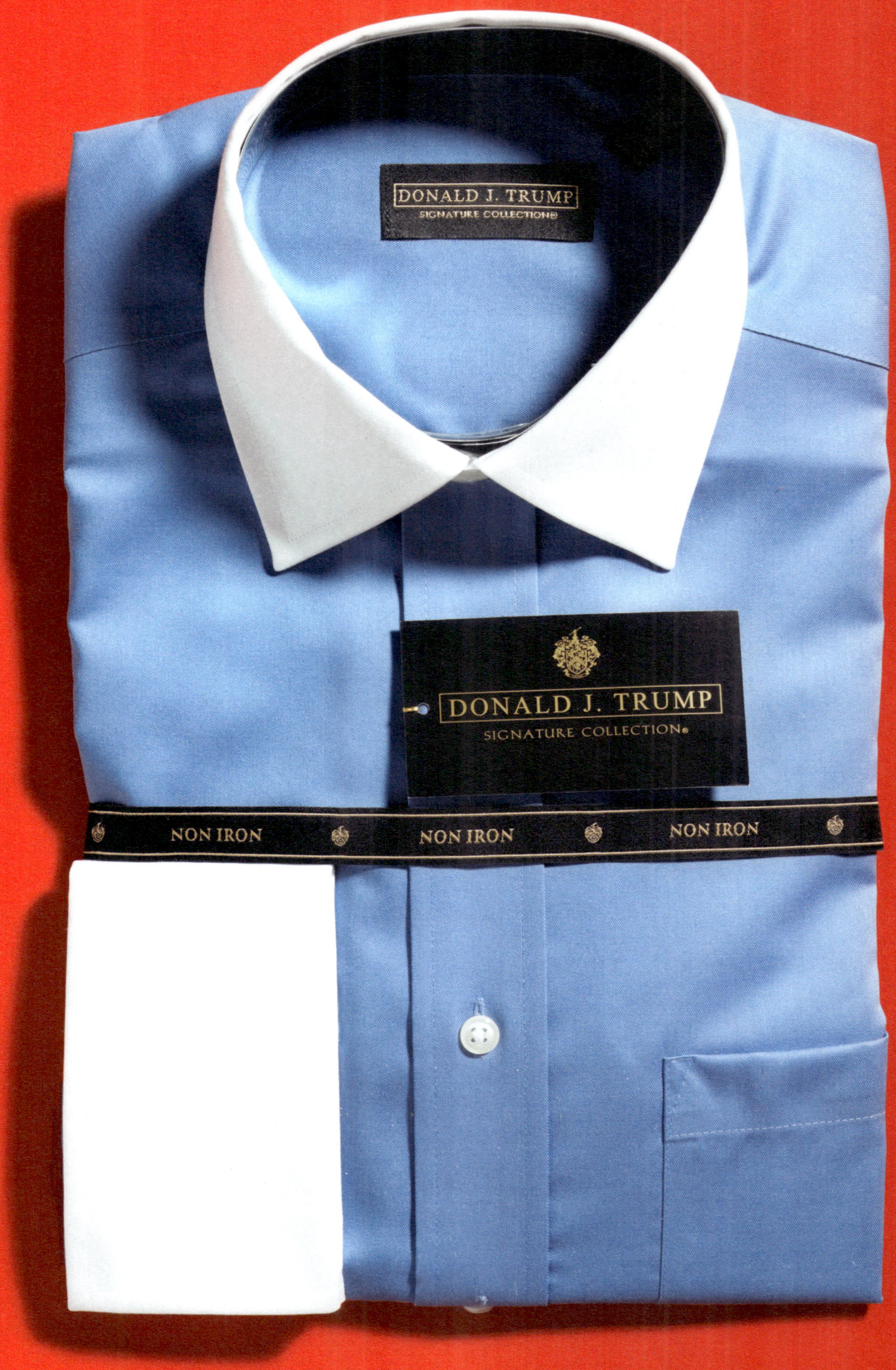

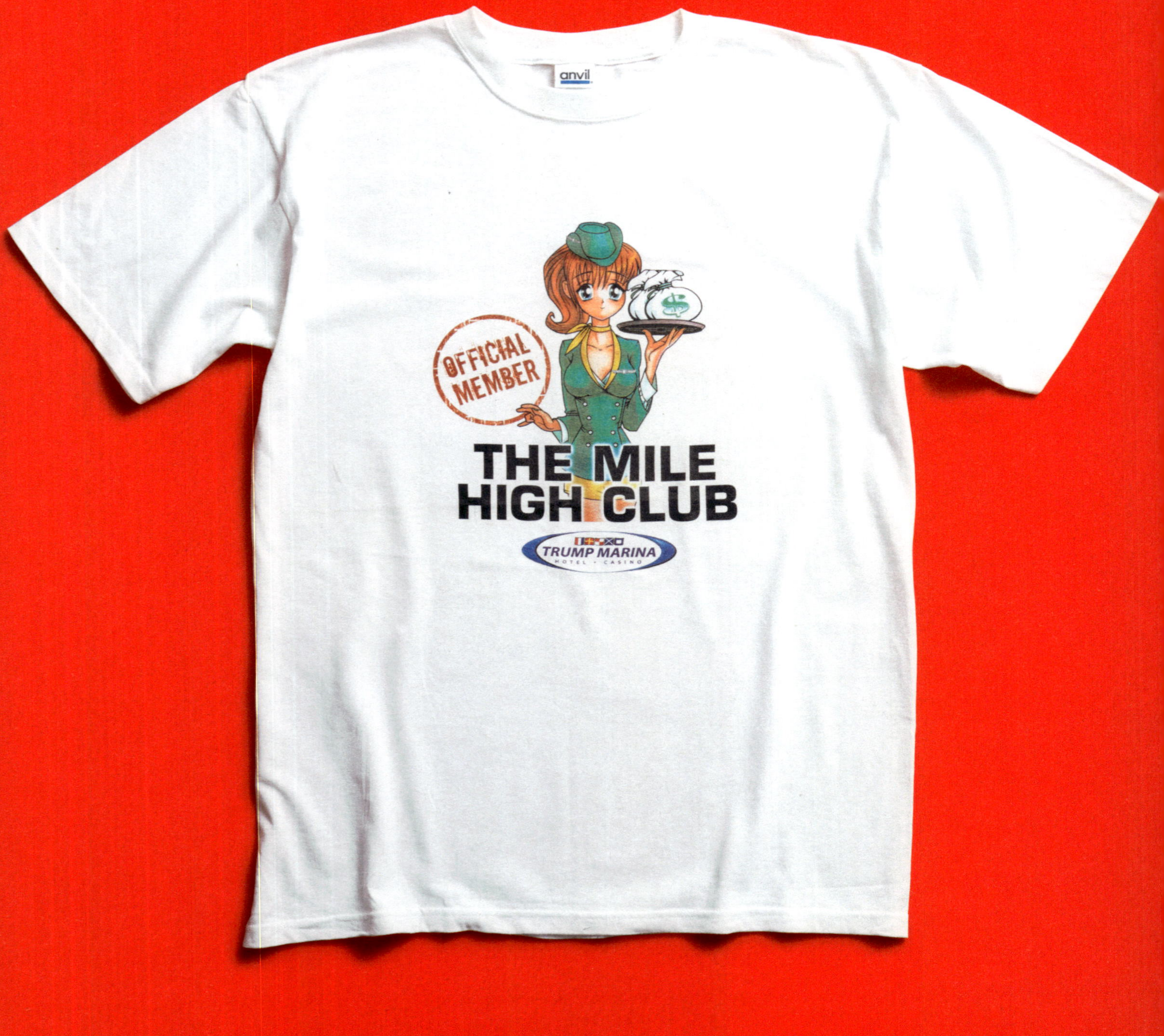
anvil
OFFICIAL MEMBER
THE MILE HIGH CLUB
TRUMP MARINA
HOTEL • CASINO

SELECTION OF EPHEMERA FROM THE TRUMP SHUTTLE
THE AIRLINE WAS OWNED BY DONALD TRUMP FROM 1989 TO 1992,
OPERATING HOURLY FLIGHTS FROM NEW YORK CITY TO
BOSTON AND WASHINGTON, D.C.

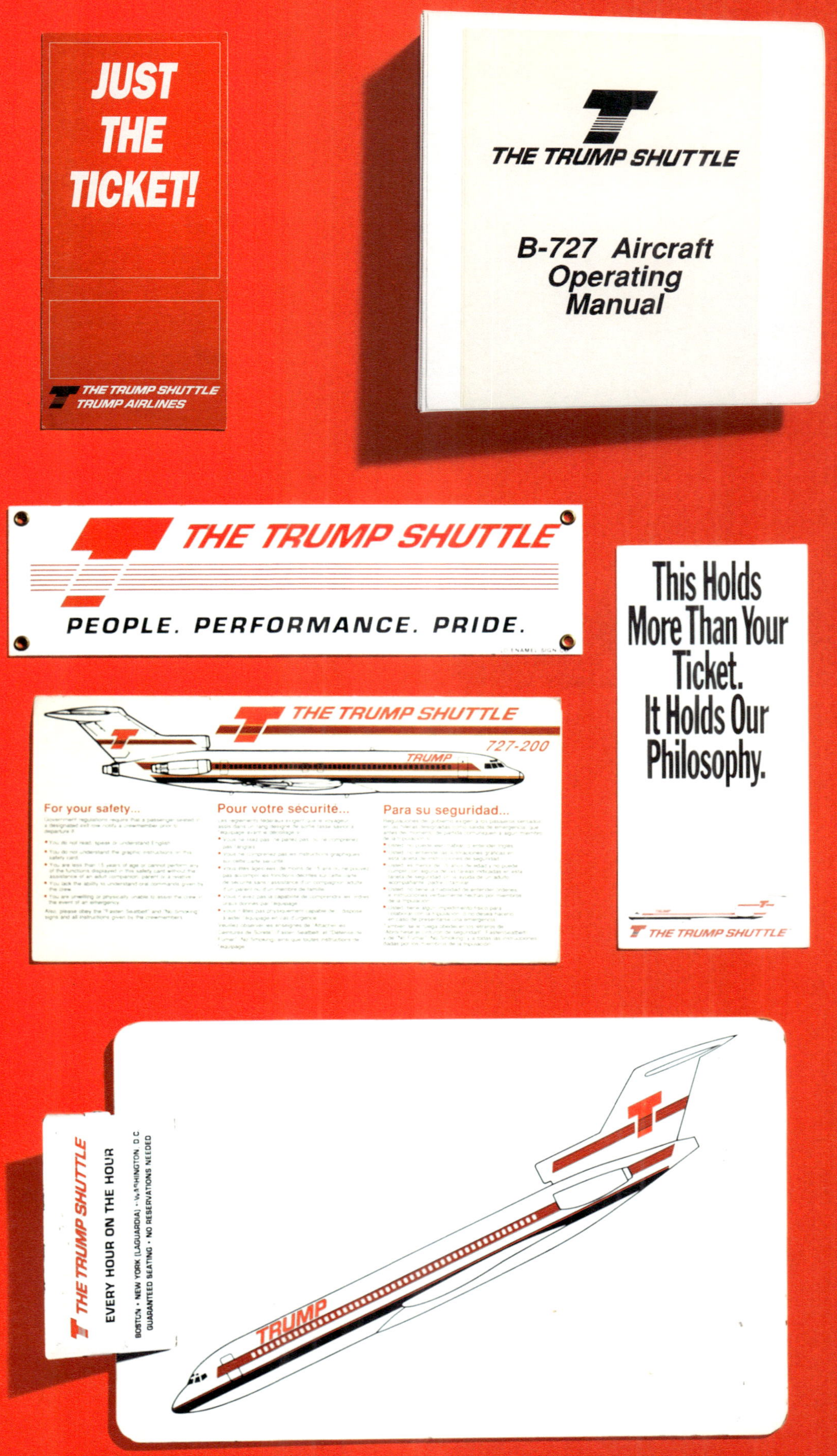

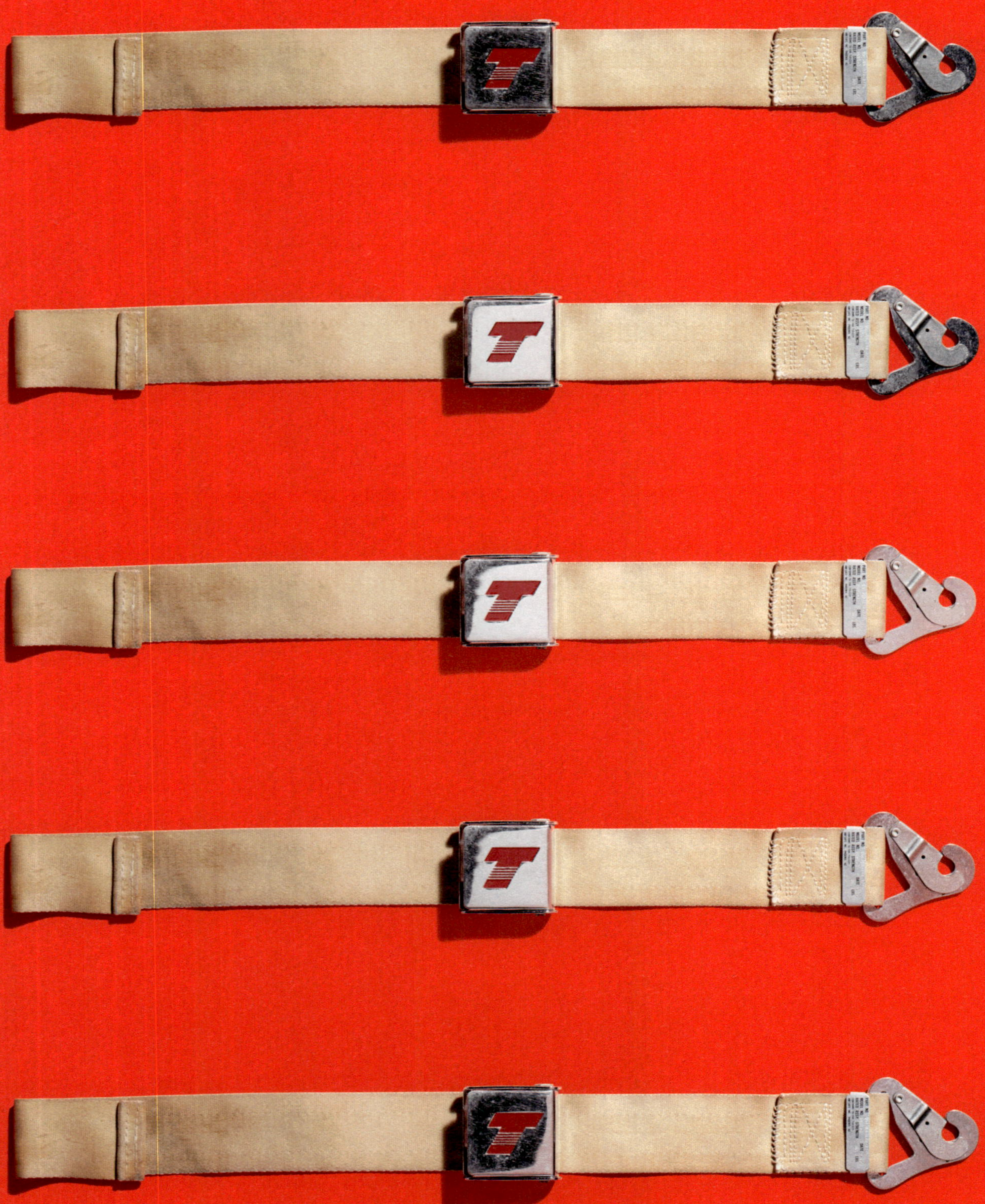

THE TRUMP SHUTTLE AIRLINE MAIL BAG
TRUMP TAJ MAHAL BALSA WOOD PLANE
THE TRUMP SHUTTLE PILOT BADGE

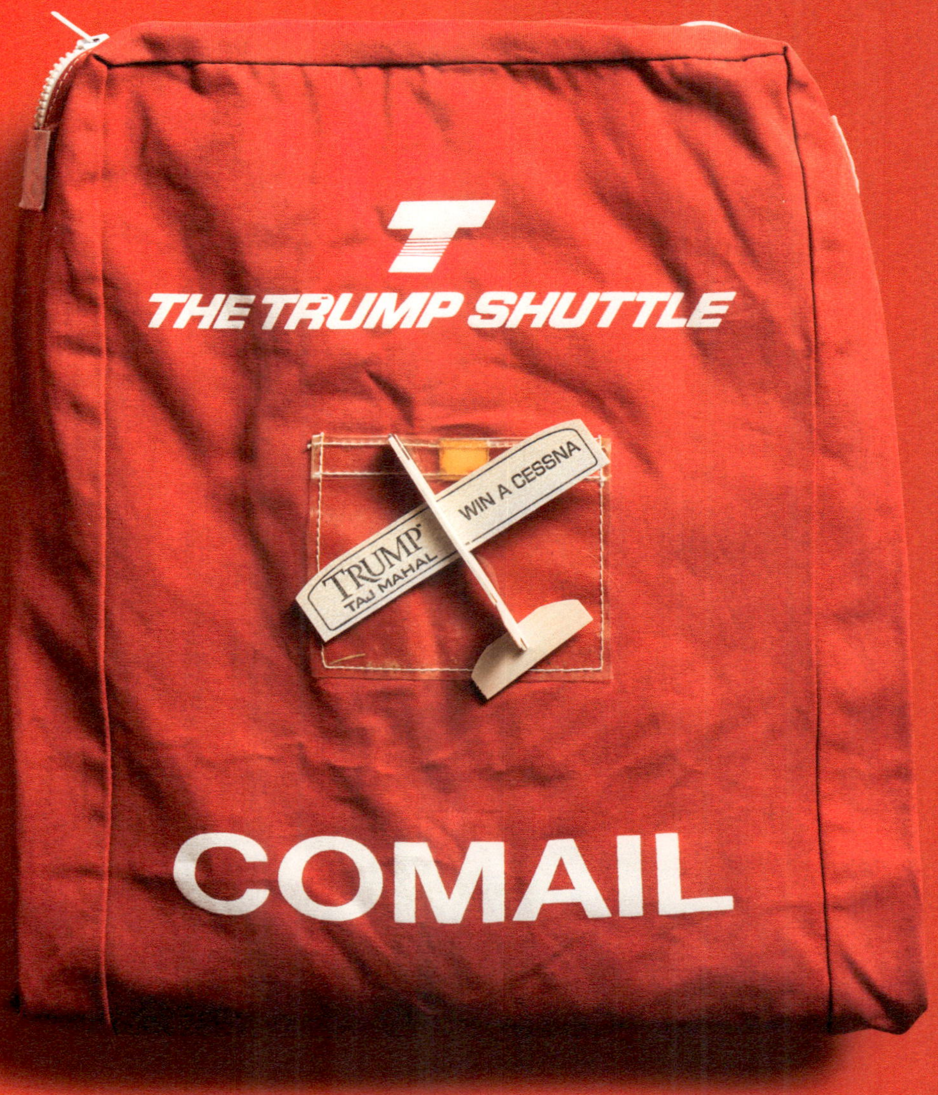

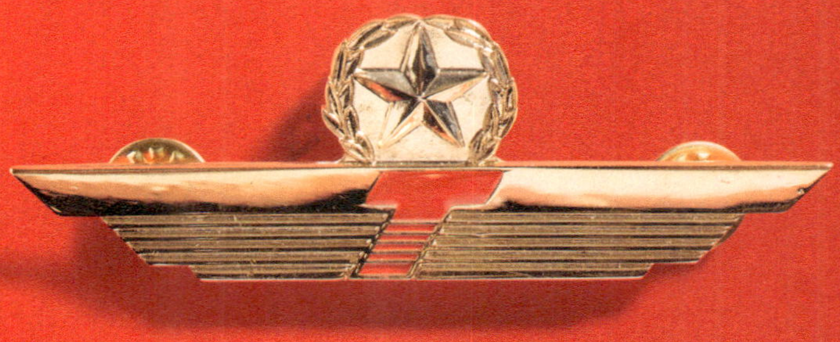

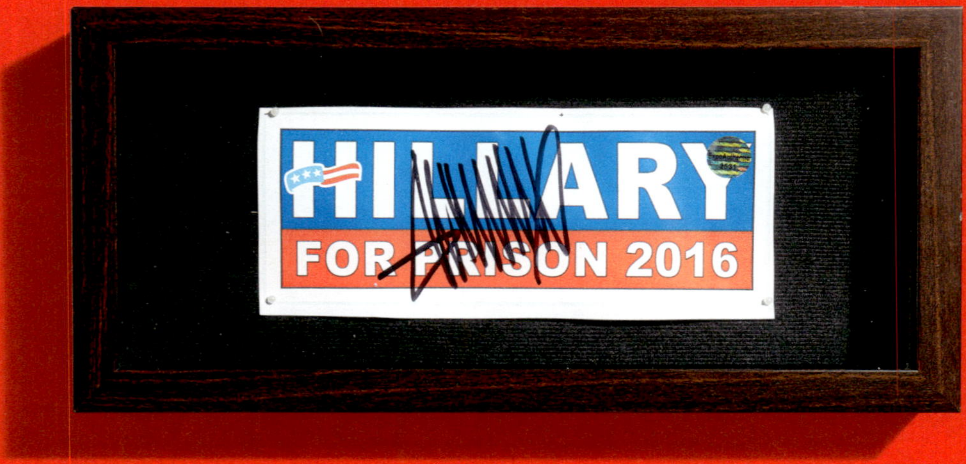
HILLARY
FOR PRISON 2016

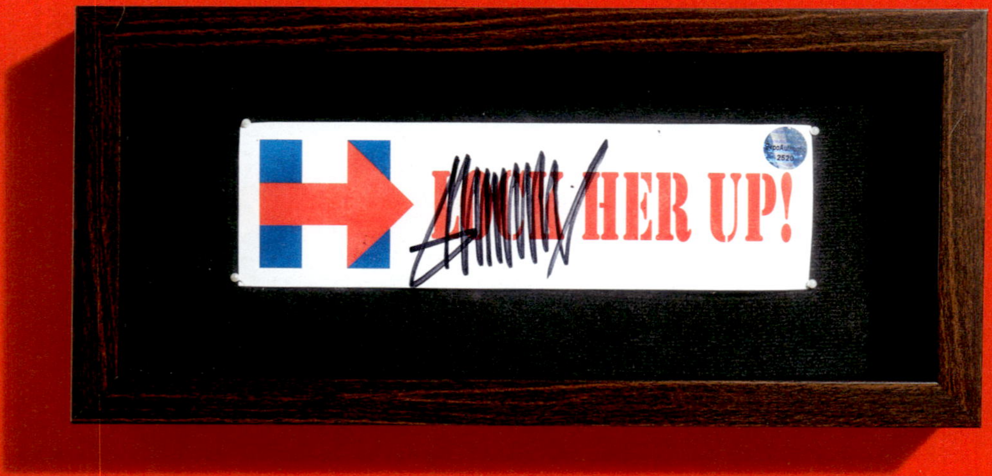
HER UP!

TRUMP TAJ MAHAL SECURITY GUARD UNIFORM WITH
MAKE AMERICA GREAT AGAIN BASEBALL CAP

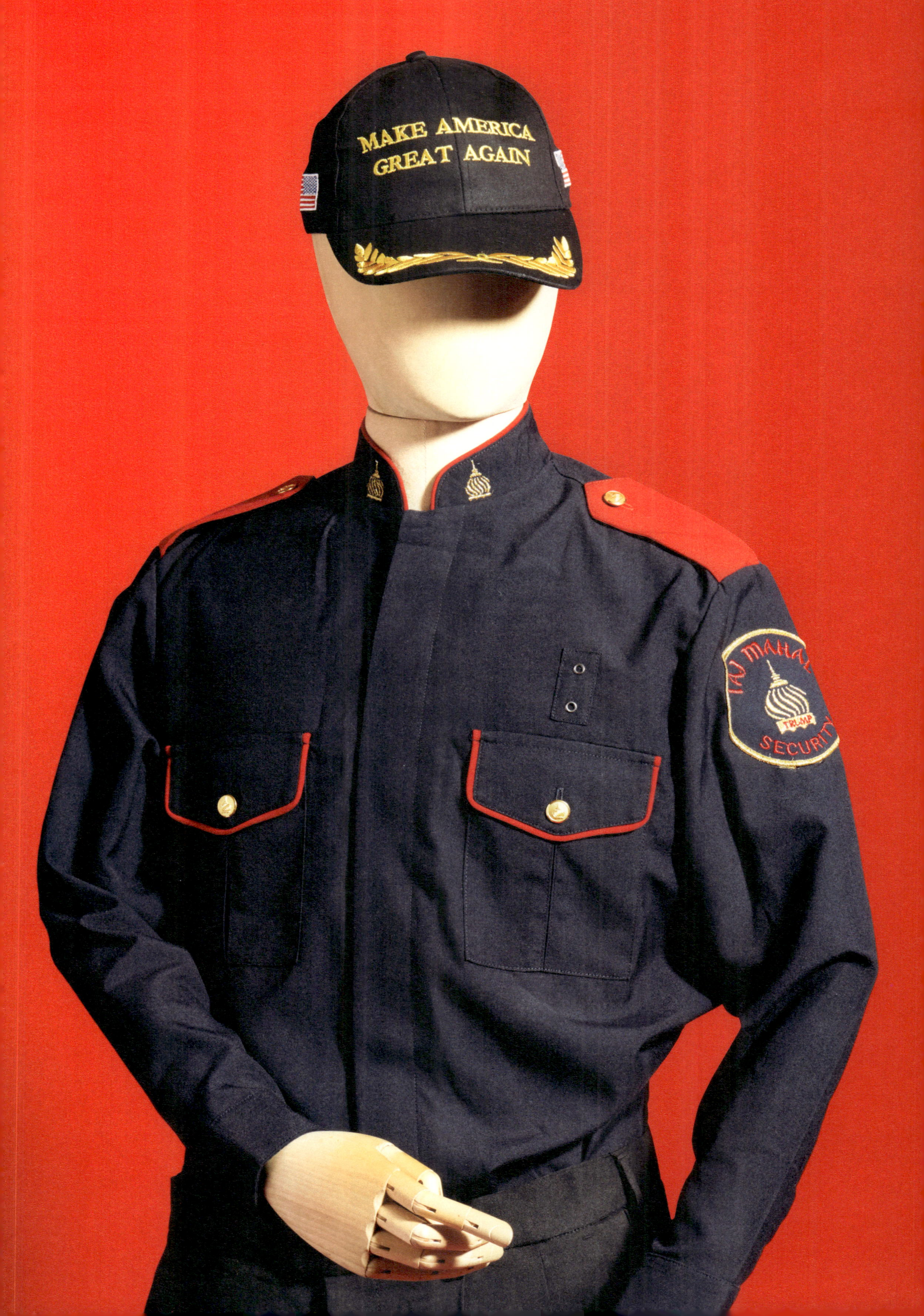

SEAL OF THE PRESIDENT OF THE UNITED STATES OFFICIAL GOLF BALL

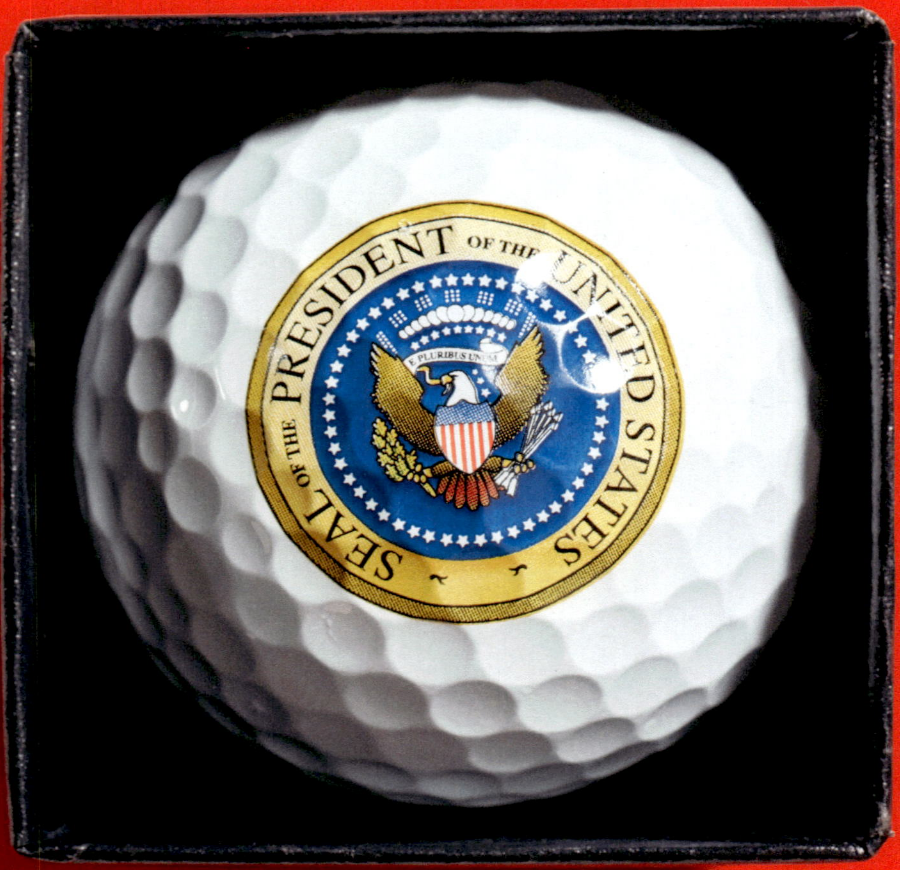

US CONSTITUTION PAMPHLET SIGNED INSIDE BY DONALD TRUMP AND LIEUTENANT MICHAEL FLYNN, HIS EX-NATIONAL SECURITY ADVISOR

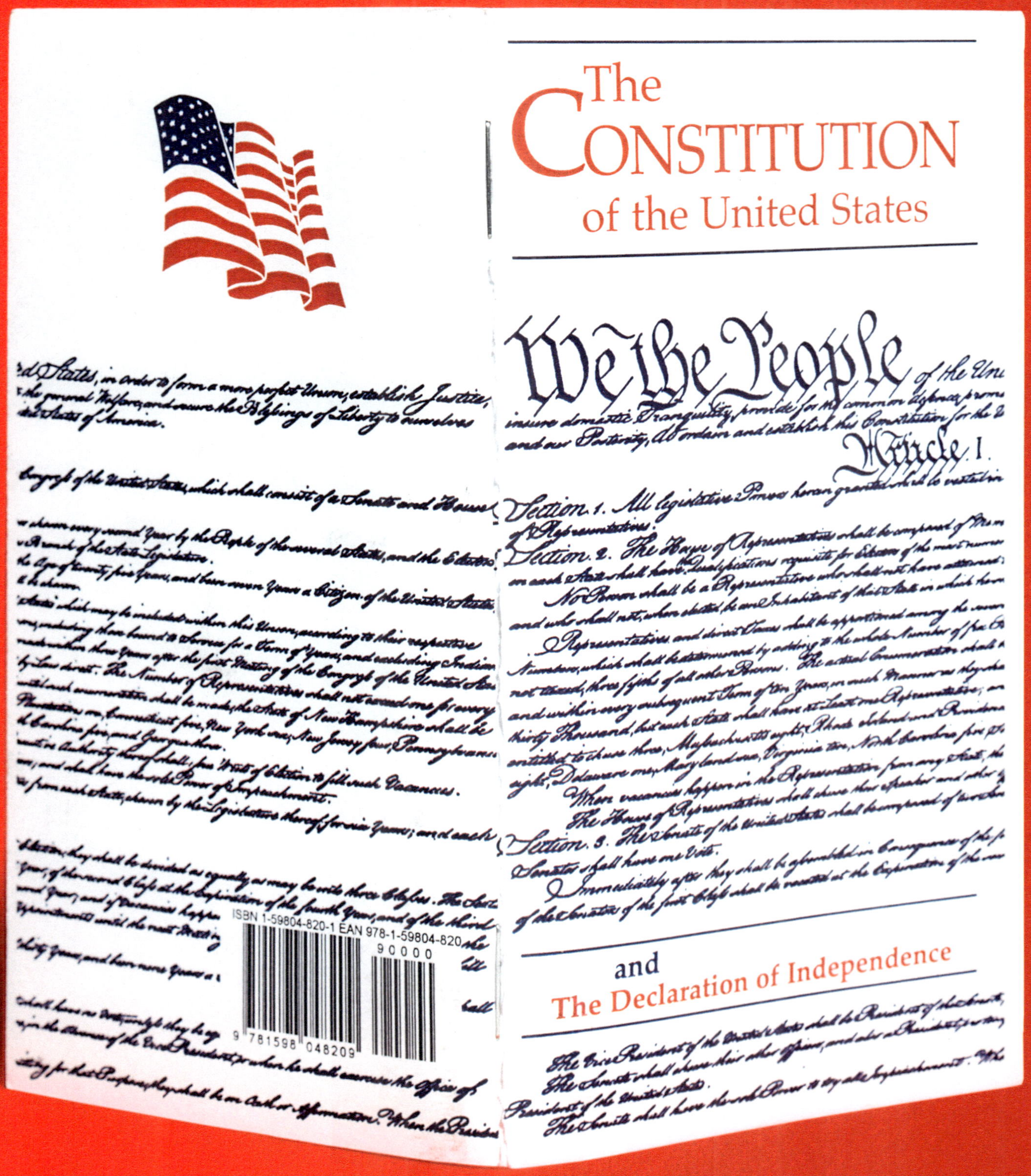

TRUMP TOWERS II GRAND OPENING BADGE
JAN 20, 2013 MARKS THE DATE OF PRESIDENT OBAMA'S SECOND TERM PRIVATE SWEARING-IN CEREMONY AT THE WHITE HOUSE

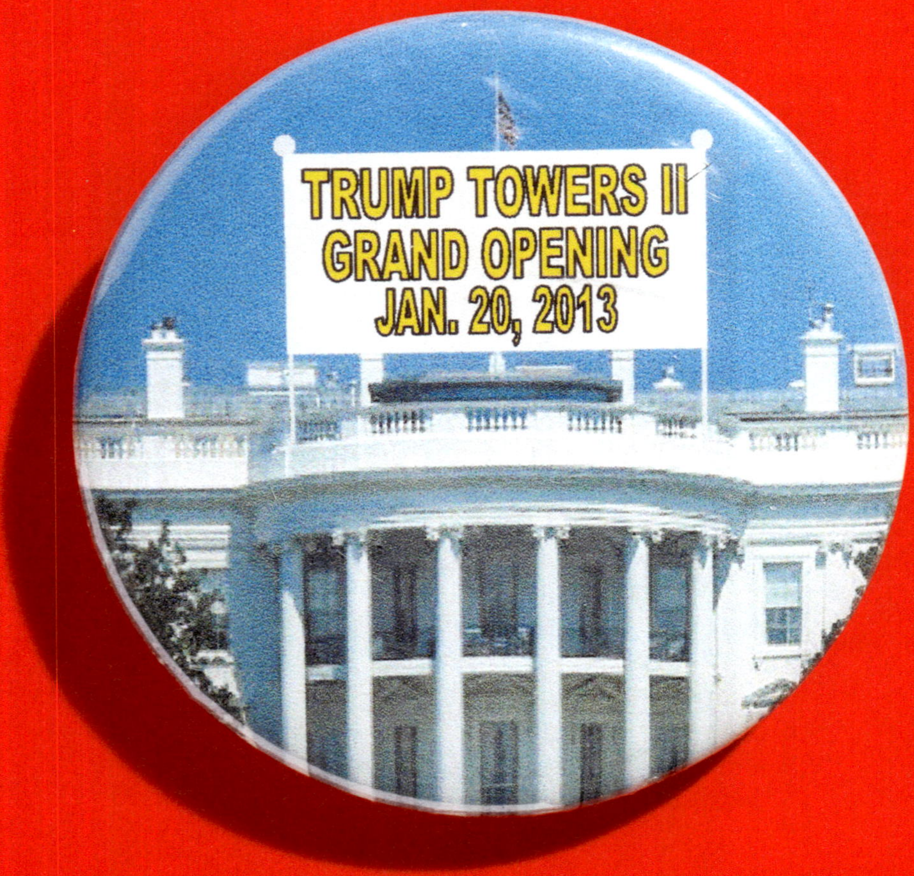

TRUMP: THE BEST REAL ESTATE ADVICE I EVER RECEIVED BOOK, 2006

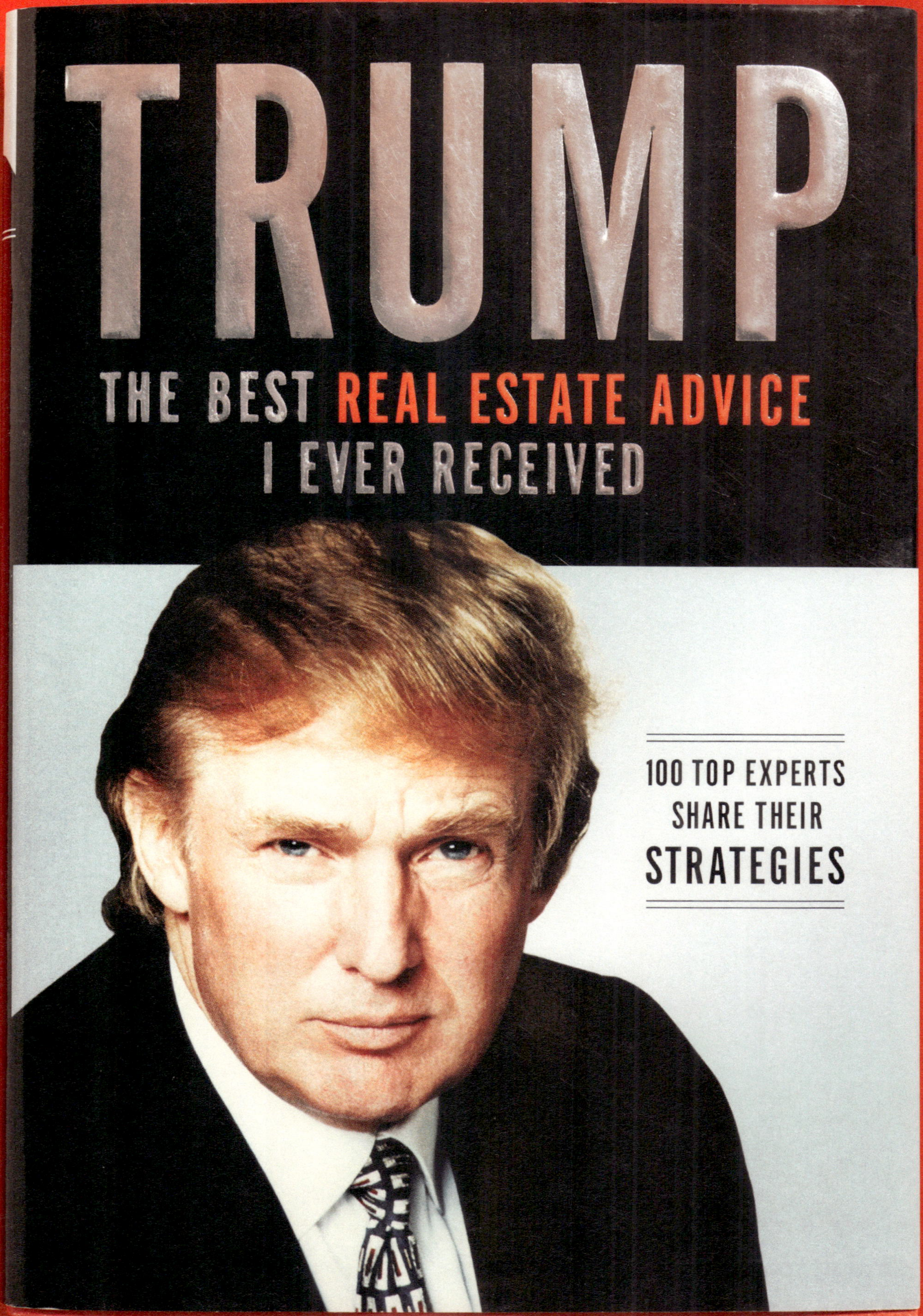

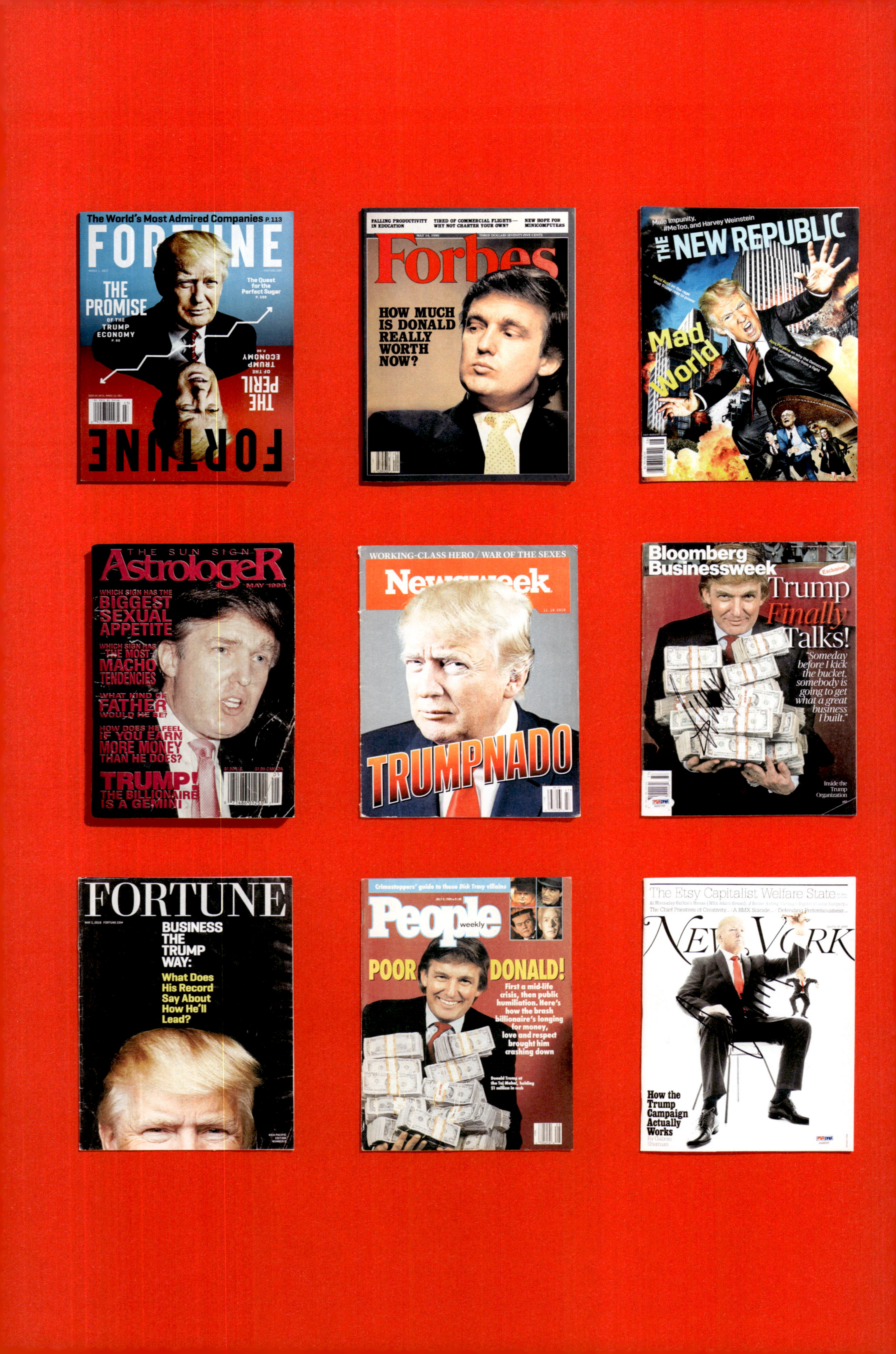

The World's Most Admired Companies P. 113
FORTUNE
THE PROMISE OF THE TRUMP ECONOMY
The Quest for the Perfect Sugar
THE PERIL OF THE TRUMP ECONOMY
FORTUNE
FALLING PRODUCTIVITY IN EDUCATION
TIRED OF COMMERCIAL FLIGHTS— WHY NOT CHARTER YOUR OWN?
NEW HOPE FOR MINICOMPUTERS
Forbes
HOW MUCH IS DONALD REALLY WORTH NOW?
Male Impunity, #MeToo, and Harvey Weinstein
THE NEW REPUBLIC
Mad World
THE SUN SIGN ASTROLOGER
MAY 1990
WHICH SIGN HAS THE BIGGEST SEXUAL APPETITE
WHICH SIGN HAS THE MOST MACHO TENDENCIES
WHAT KIND OF FATHER WOULD HE BE?
HOW DOES HE FEEL IF YOU EARN MORE MONEY THAN HE DOES?
TRUMP! THE BILLIONAIRE IS A GEMINI
WORKING-CLASS HERO / WAR OF THE SEXES
Newsweek
TRUMPNADO
Bloomberg Businessweek
Exclusive!
Trump Finally Talks!
"Someday before I kick the bucket, somebody is going to get what a great business I built."
Inside the Trump Organization
FORTUNE
BUSINESS THE TRUMP WAY:
What Does His Record Say About How He'll Lead?
Crimestoppers' guide to those Dick Tracy villains
People weekly
POOR DONALD!
First a mid-life crisis, then public humiliation. Here's how the brash billionaire's longing for money, love and respect brought him crashing down
The Etsy Capitalist Welfare State
NEW YORK
How the Trump Campaign Actually Works

SELECTION OF SIGNED AND UNSIGNED MAGAZINE COVERS FEATURING DONALD TRUMP, FROM 1990 TO 2019

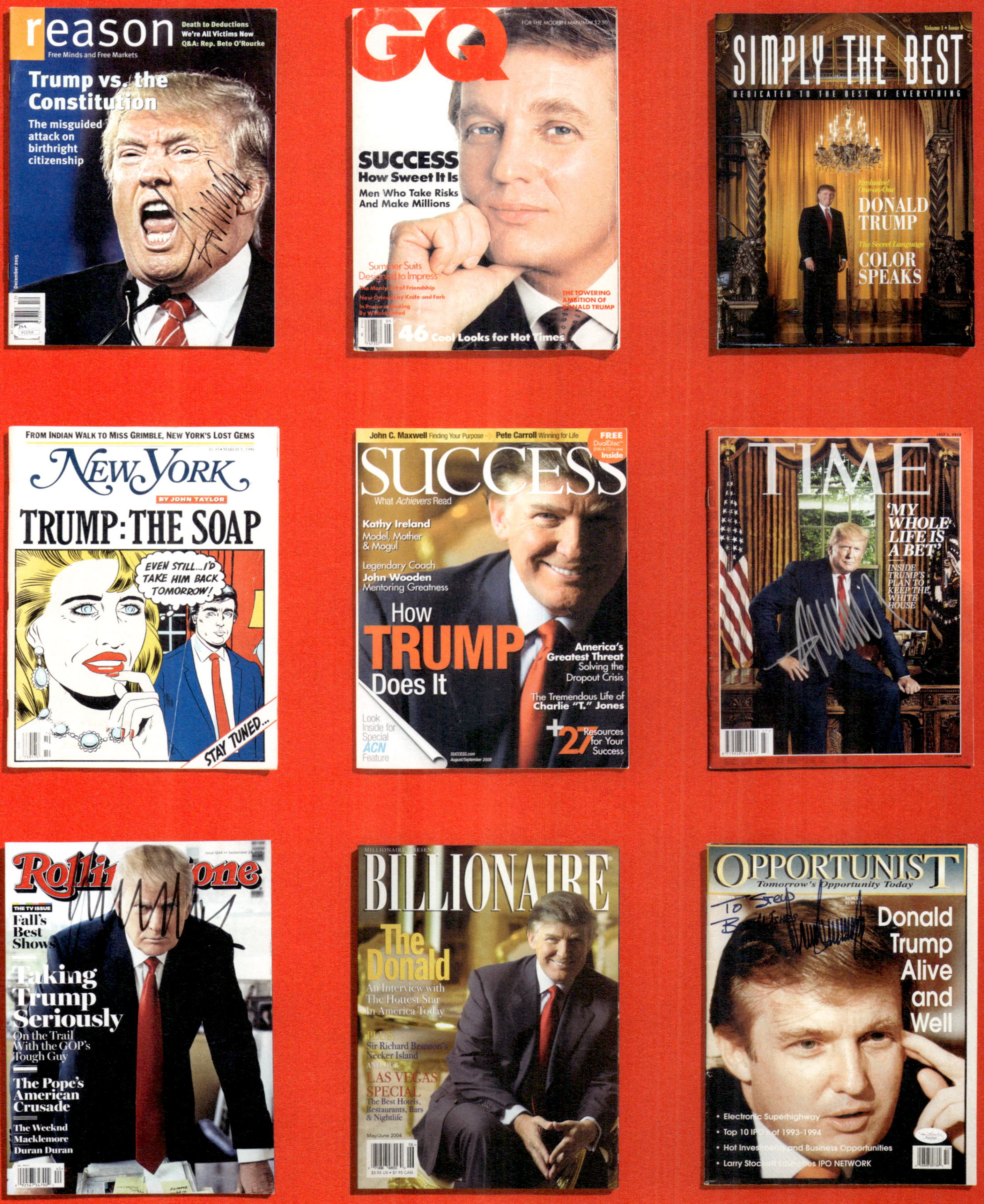

LIST OF TRUMP ORGANIZATION PROPERTIES SIGNED DONALD TRUMP

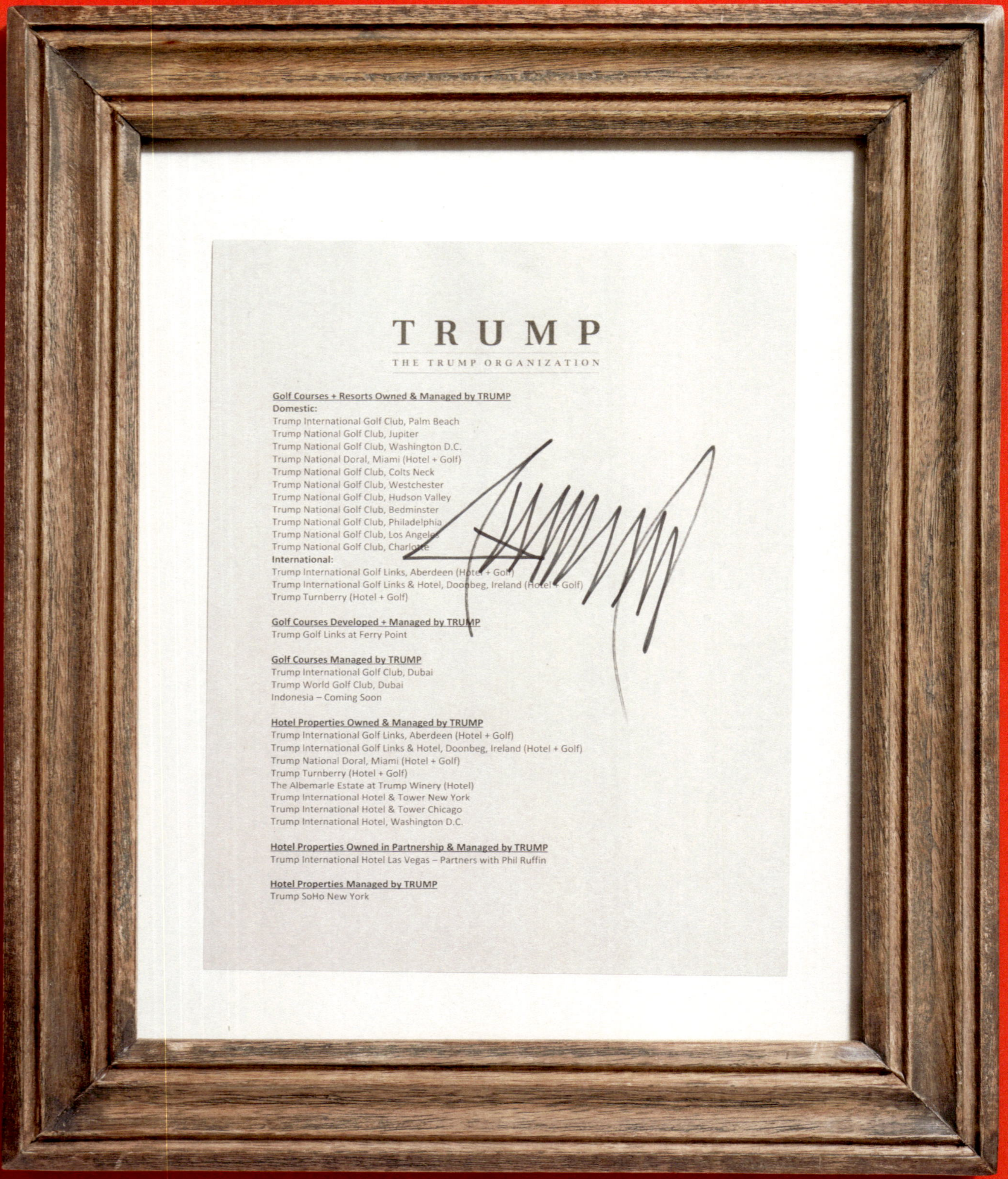

TRUMP

THE TRUMP ORGANIZATION

Golf Courses + Resorts Owned & Managed by TRUMP
Domestic:
Trump International Golf Club, Palm Beach
Trump National Golf Club, Jupiter
Trump National Golf Club, Washington D.C.
Trump National Doral, Miami (Hotel + Golf)
Trump National Golf Club, Colts Neck
Trump National Golf Club, Westchester
Trump National Golf Club, Hudson Valley
Trump National Golf Club, Bedminster
Trump National Golf Club, Philadelphia
Trump National Golf Club, Los Angeles
Trump National Golf Club, Charlotte
International:
Trump International Golf Links, Aberdeen (Hotel + Golf)
Trump International Golf Links & Hotel, Doonbeg, Ireland (Hotel + Golf)
Trump Turnberry (Hotel + Golf)

Golf Courses Developed + Managed by TRUMP
Trump Golf Links at Ferry Point

Golf Courses Managed by TRUMP
Trump International Golf Club, Dubai
Trump World Golf Club, Dubai
Indonesia – Coming Soon

Hotel Properties Owned & Managed by TRUMP
Trump International Golf Links, Aberdeen (Hotel + Golf)
Trump International Golf Links & Hotel, Doonbeg, Ireland (Hotel + Golf)
Trump National Doral, Miami (Hotel + Golf)
Trump Turnberry (Hotel + Golf)
The Albemarle Estate at Trump Winery (Hotel)
Trump International Hotel & Tower New York
Trump International Hotel & Tower Chicago
Trump International Hotel, Washington D.C.

Hotel Properties Owned in Partnership & Managed by TRUMP
Trump International Hotel Las Vegas – Partners with Phil Ruffin

Hotel Properties Managed by TRUMP
Trump SoHo New York

TRUMP TAJ MAHAL POKER CHAMPIONSHIP FLYER, 1996

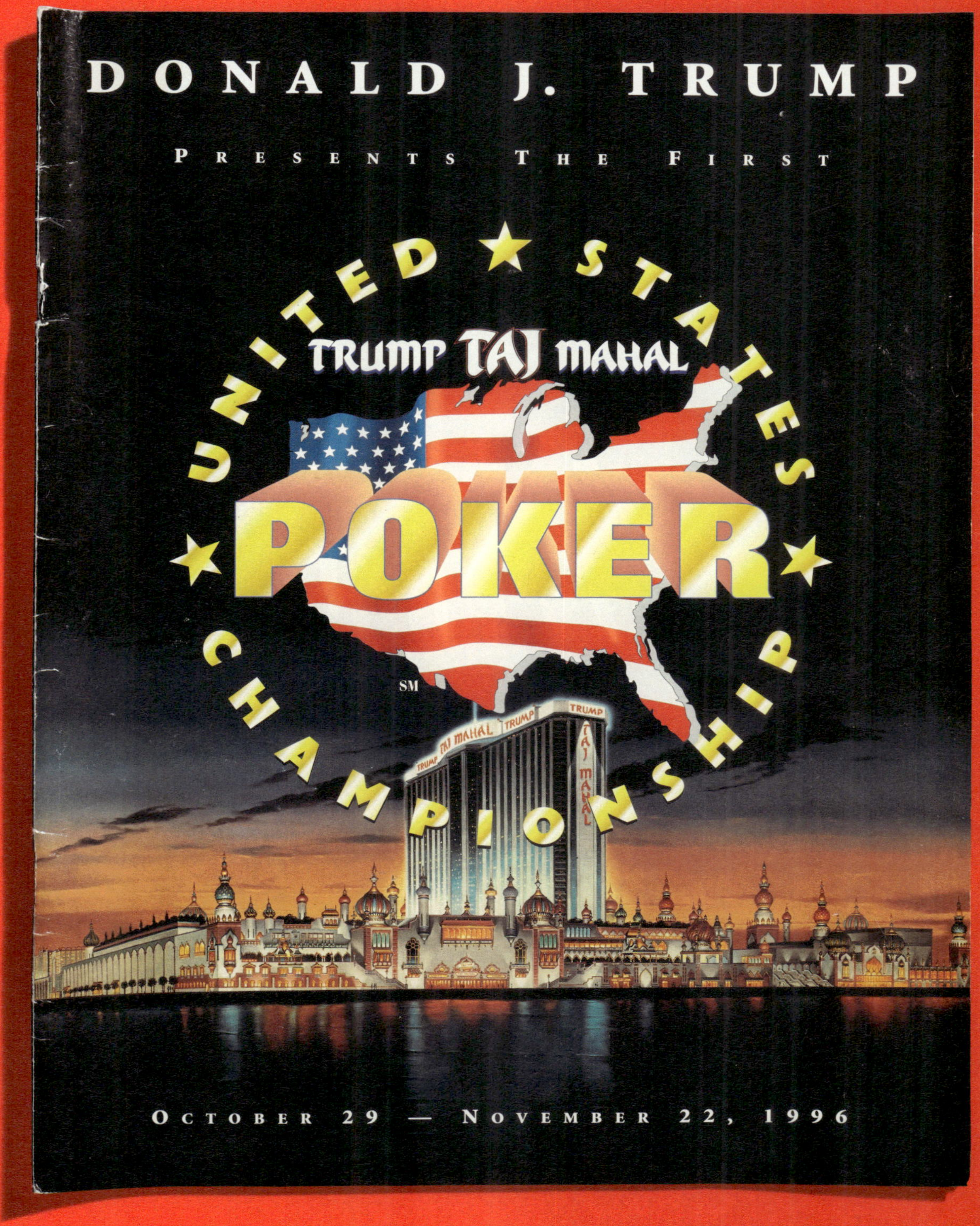

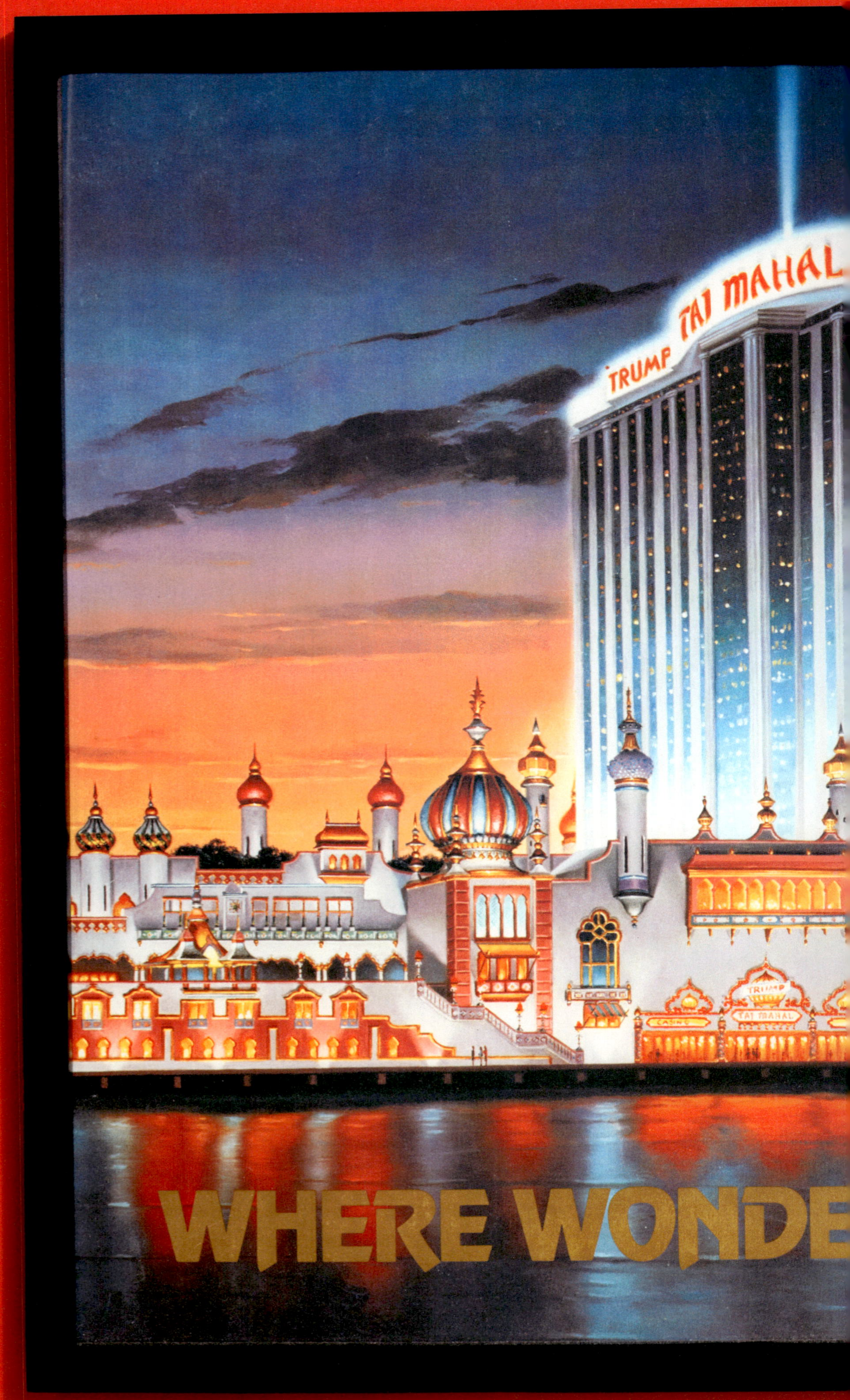
TRUMP TAJ MAHAL
WHERE WONDE

TRUMP TAJ MAHAL POSTER, 1990
THE TRUMP TAJ MAHAL WAS BUILT FOR $1.2 BILLION IN 1990 AND SOLD FOR $50 MILLION IN 2009 TO HARD ROCK INTERNATIONAL

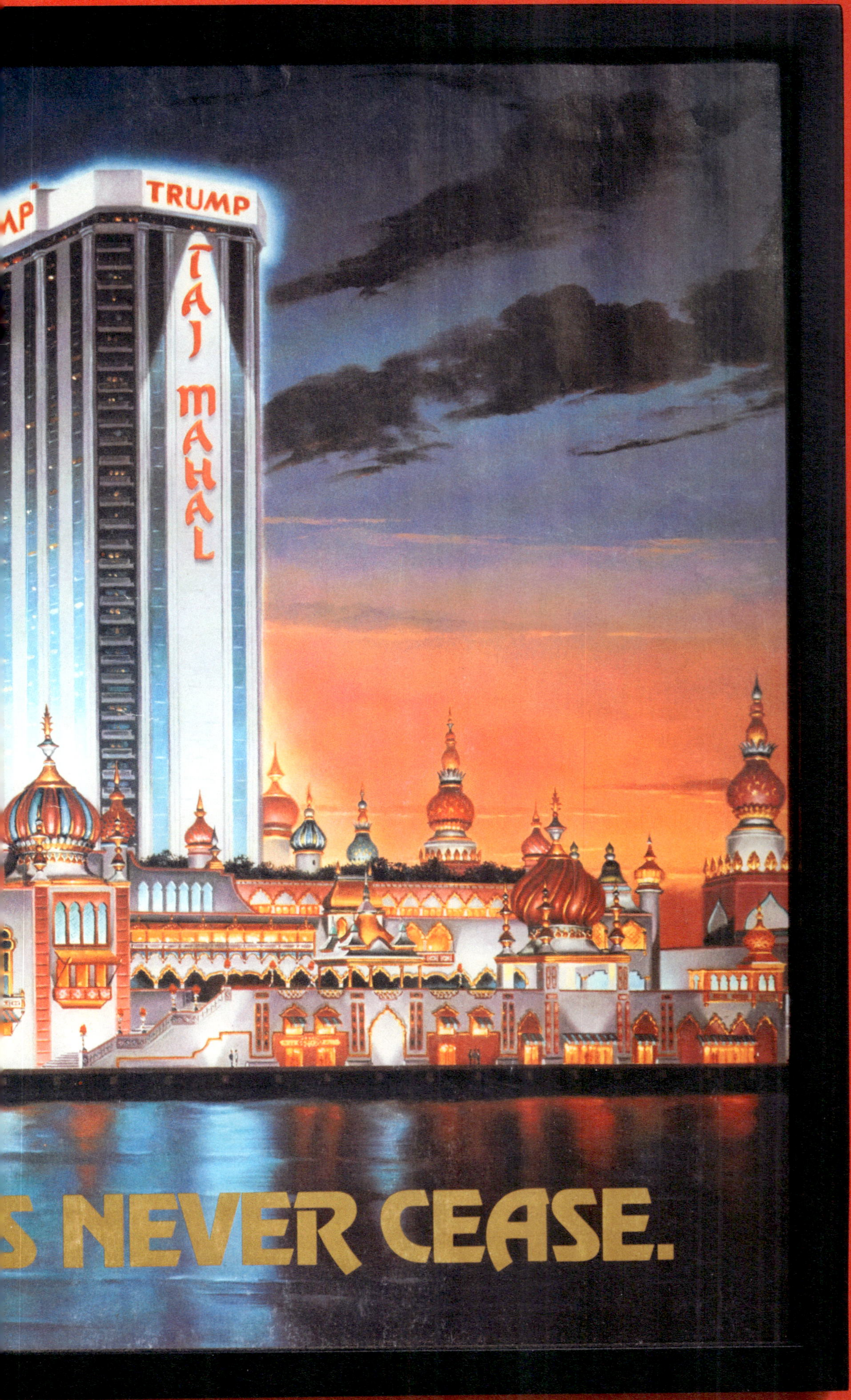

TRUMP TAJ MAHAL BALLPOINT PENS

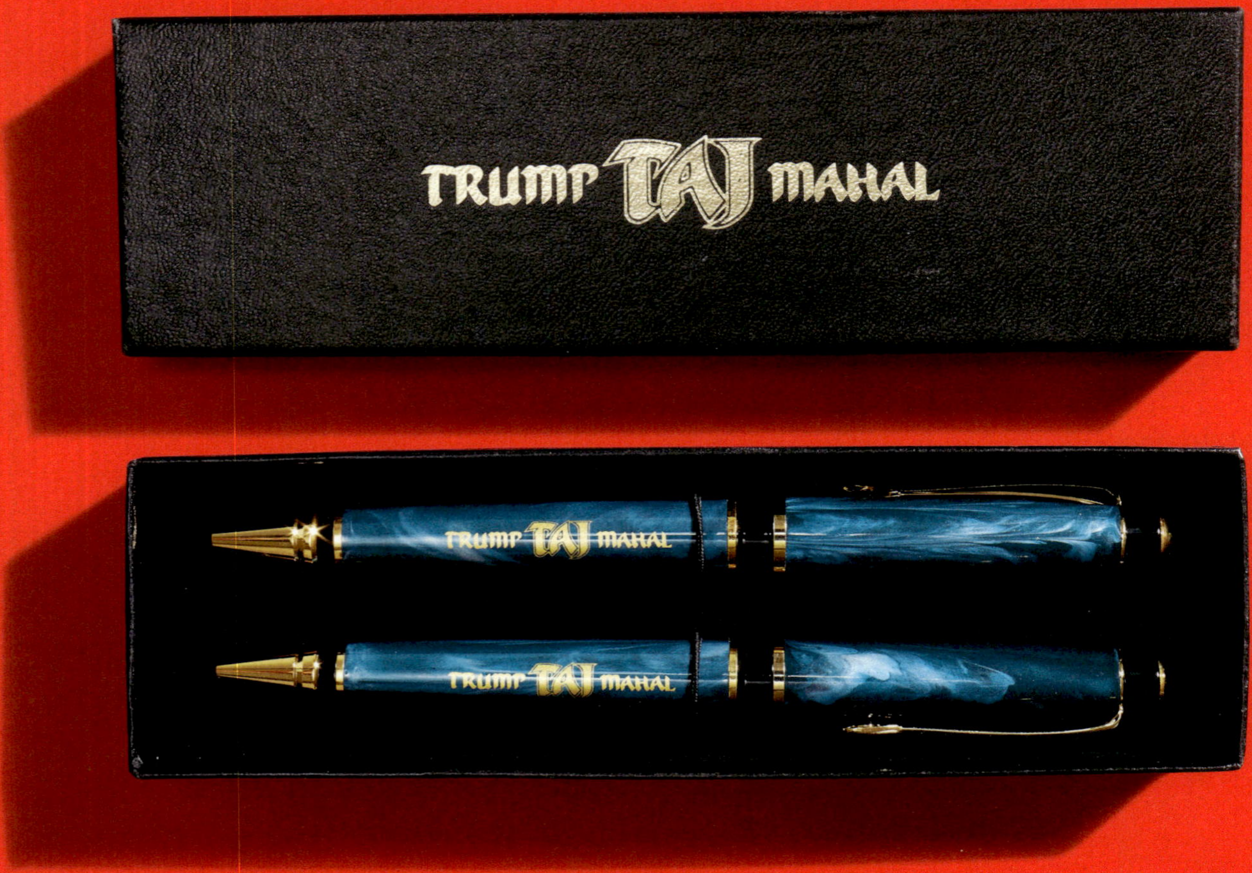

SIGNATURE PAGE OF CONTRACT FOR DONALD TRUMP'S THIRD CASINO IN ATLANTIC CITY, OCTOBER 22, 1987

SIGNATURES

Pursuant to the requirements of the Securities Act of 1933, as amended, each Registrant certifies that it has reasonable grounds to believe that it meets all of the requirements for filing on Form S-3 and has duly caused this Registration Statement to be signed on its behalf by the undersigned, thereunto duly authorized, in the City of Atlantic City, State of New Jersey, on October 22, 1987.

RESORTS INTERNATIONAL HOTEL FINANCING, INC.

By: ______________________
(Matthew B. Kearney)
Vice President

RESORTS INTERNATIONAL, INC.

By: ______________________
(Matthew B. Kearney)
Vice President-Finance

KNOW ALL MEN BY THESE PRESENTS, that each person whose signature appears below, constitutes and appoints Donald J. Trump, Robert S. Trump and Matthew B. Kearney, and each of them, his true and lawful attorneys-in-fact and agents, with full power of substitution and resubstitution for him and in his name, place and stead, in any and all capacities, to sign any or all amendments to this Registration Statement and to file the same with exhibits thereto, and other documents in connection therewith with the Securities and Exchange Commission, granting unto said attorneys-in-fact and agents full power and authority to do and perform each and every act and thing requisite and necessary to be done in or about the premises, as fully and to all intents and confirming all that said attorneys-in-fact and agents, or their substitute or substitutes, may lawfully do or come to be done by virtue thereof.

Pursuant to the requirements of the Securities Act of 1933, as amended, this Registration Statement has been signed by the following persons in the capacities and on the date indicated:

Signature	Title Resorts International Hotel Financing, Inc.	Title Resorts International, Inc.	Date
(Donald J. Trump)	Chairman of the Board of Directors	Chairman of the Board of Directors	October 22, 1987
(Robert S. Trump)	Vice Chairman of the Board of Directors	Vice Chairman of the Board of Directors	October 22, 1987
(I.G. Davis, Jr.)	President (Chief Executive Officer) and Director	President (Chief Executive Officer)	October 22, 1987
(George A. Barscillo, Jr.)		Director	October 22, 1987
(William Druz)		Director	October 22, 1987
(Harvey I. Freeman)	Director	Director	October 22, 1987
(Mitchell Sviridoff)		Director	October 22, 1987
(Matthew B. Kearney)	Vice President (Chief Financial Officer)	Vice President — Finance (Chief Financial Officer)	October 22, 1987
(David G. Bowden)	Controller (Chief Accounting Officer)	Vice President— Controller, Assistant Secretary (Chief Accounting Officer)	October 22, 1987

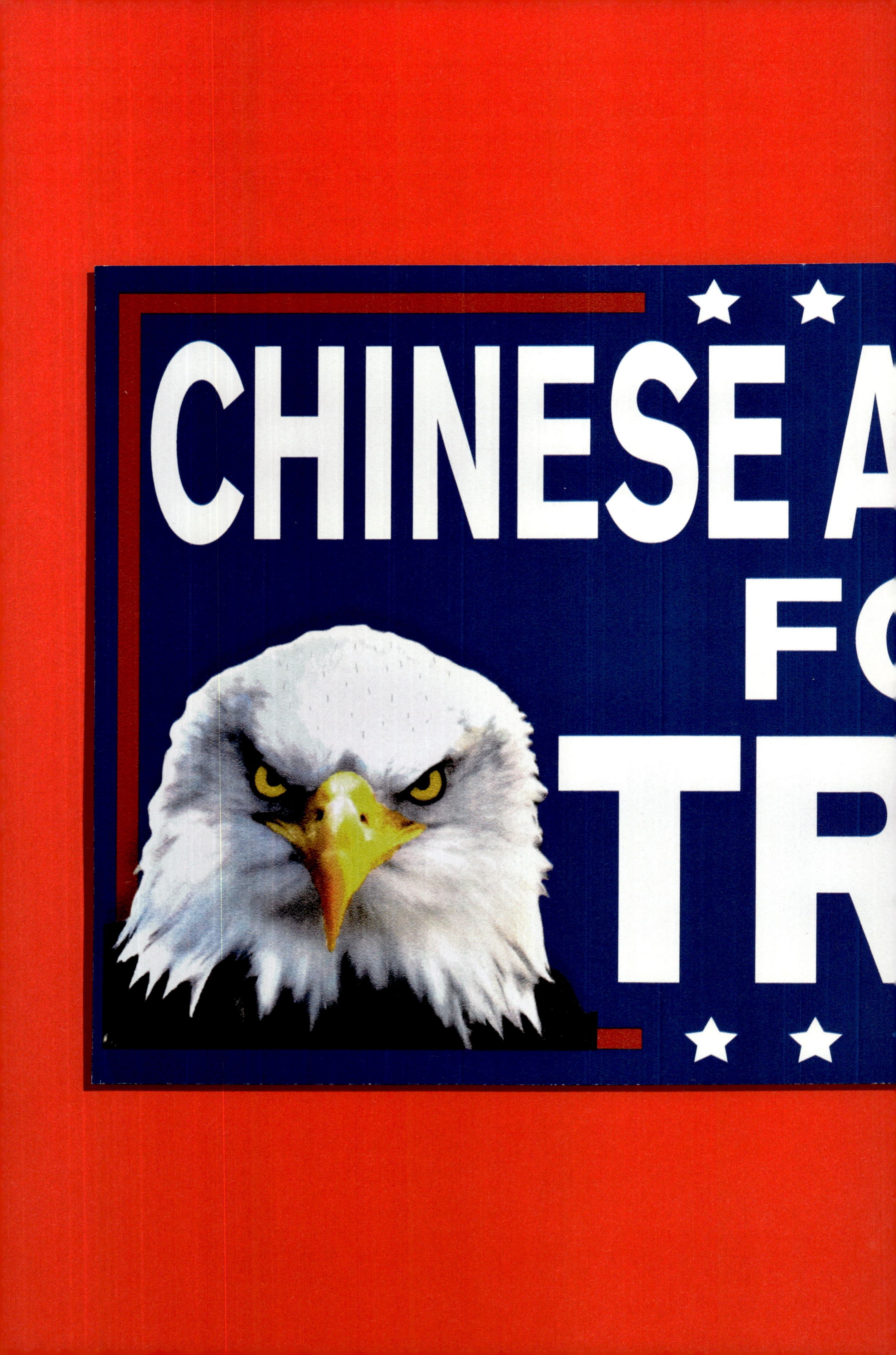
CHINESE A
F
TR

UNOFFICIAL TRUMP 2016 CAMPAIGN SIGN

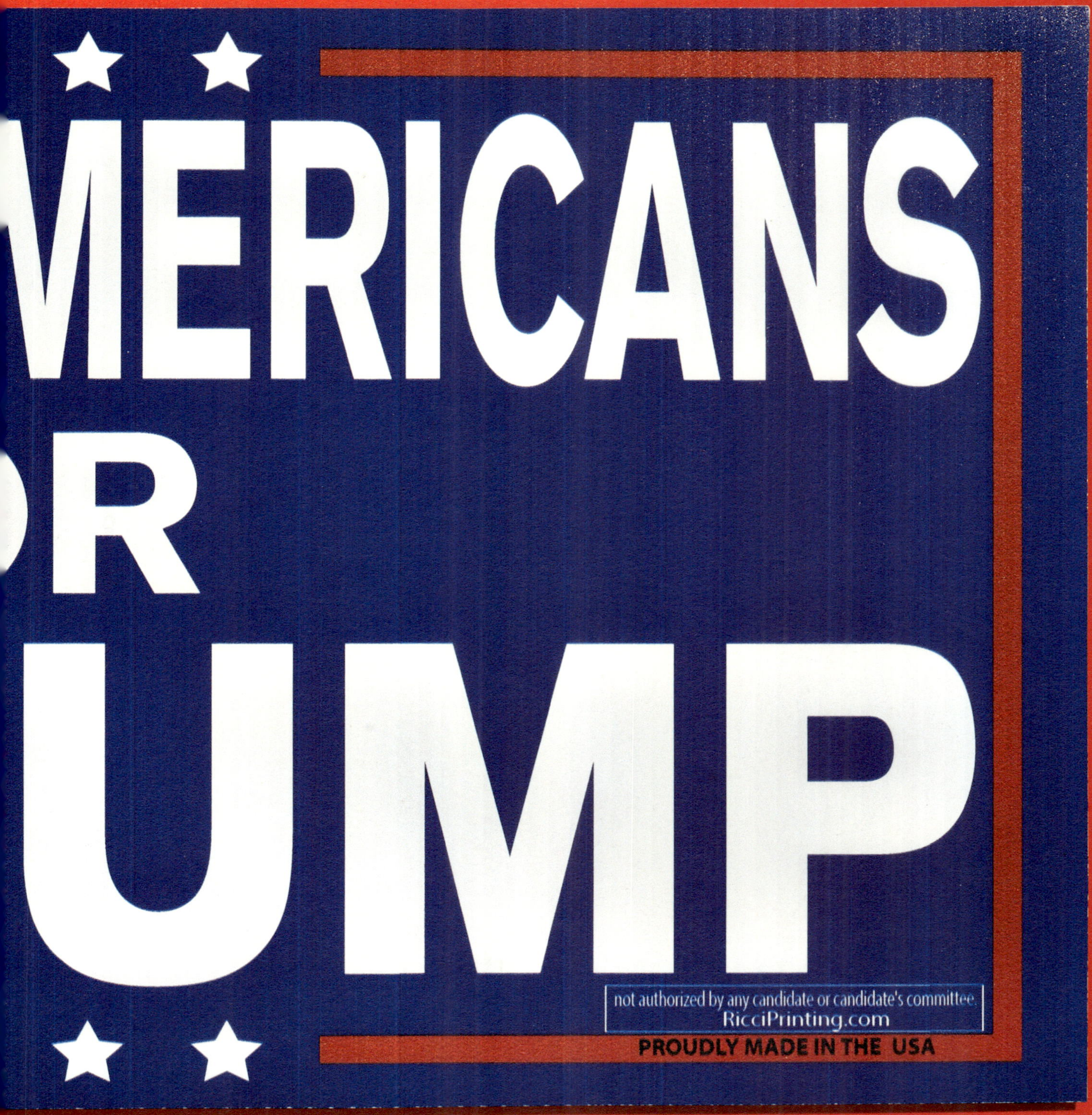

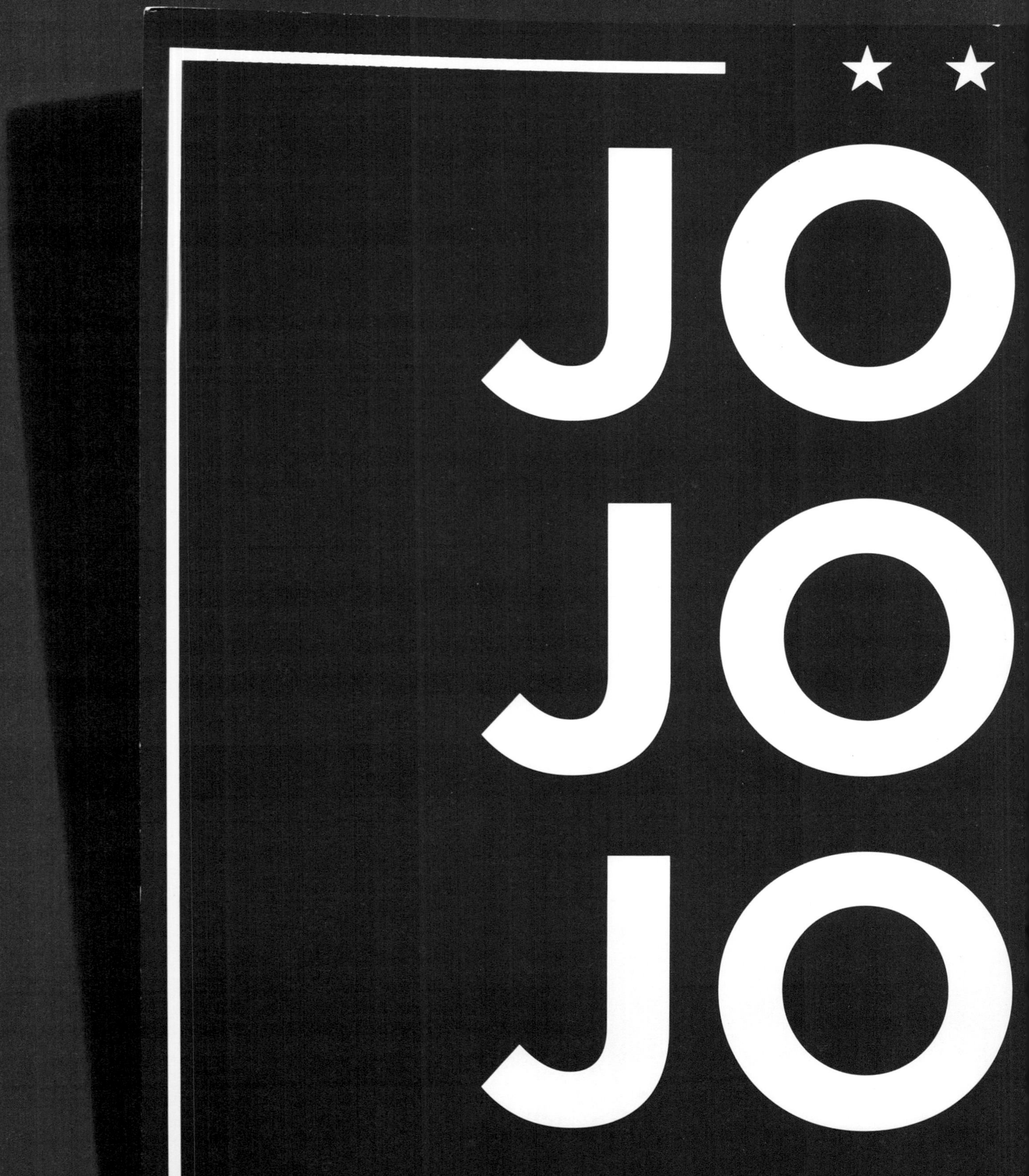
JO
JO
JO

OFFICIAL TRUMP 2020 CAMPAIGN SIGN

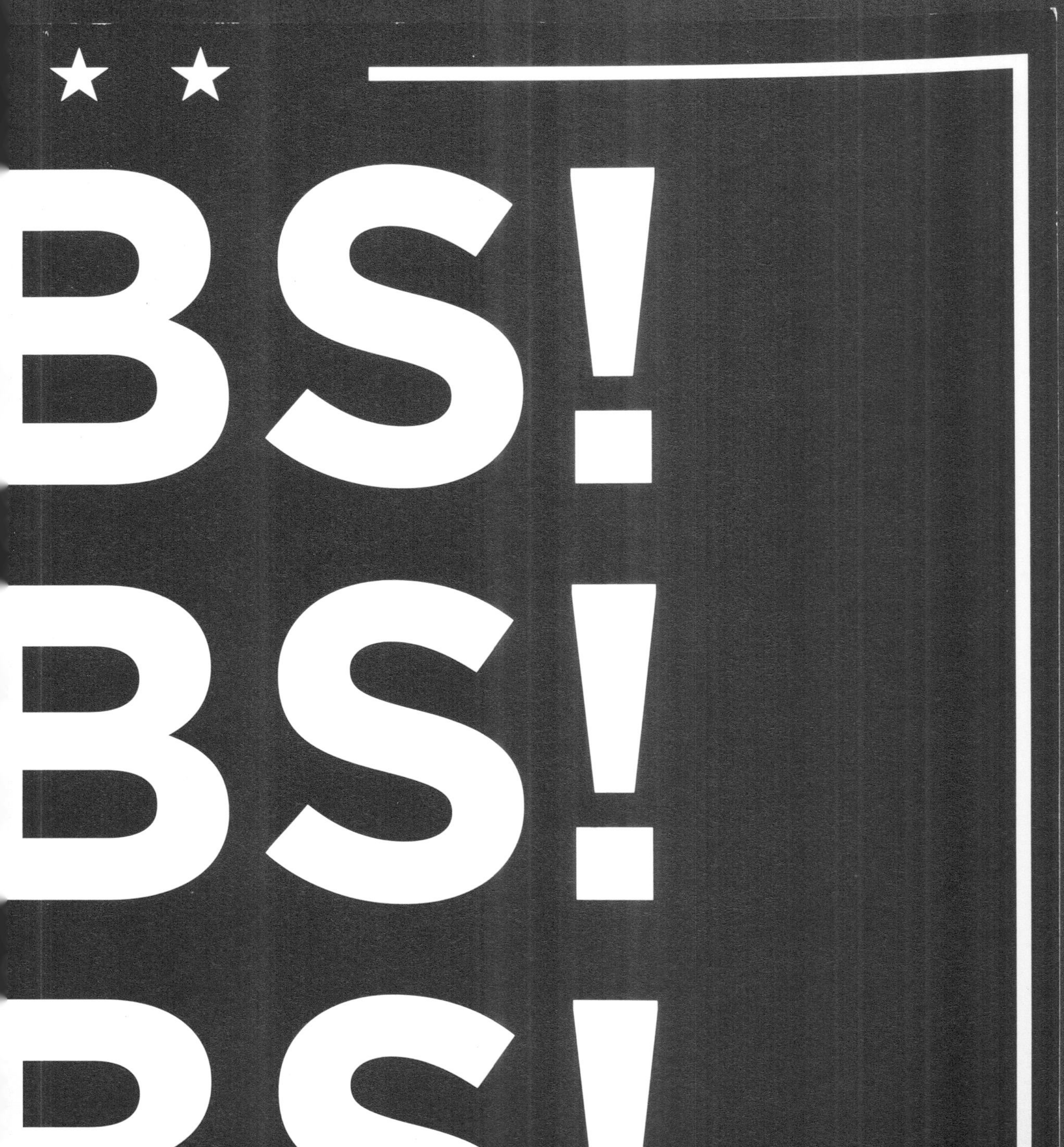

SECOND AMENDMENT PRINT
PROMOTING THE CONSTITUTIONAL RIGHT
OF THE PEOPLE TO KEEP AND BEAR ARMS
SIGNED DONALD TRUMP

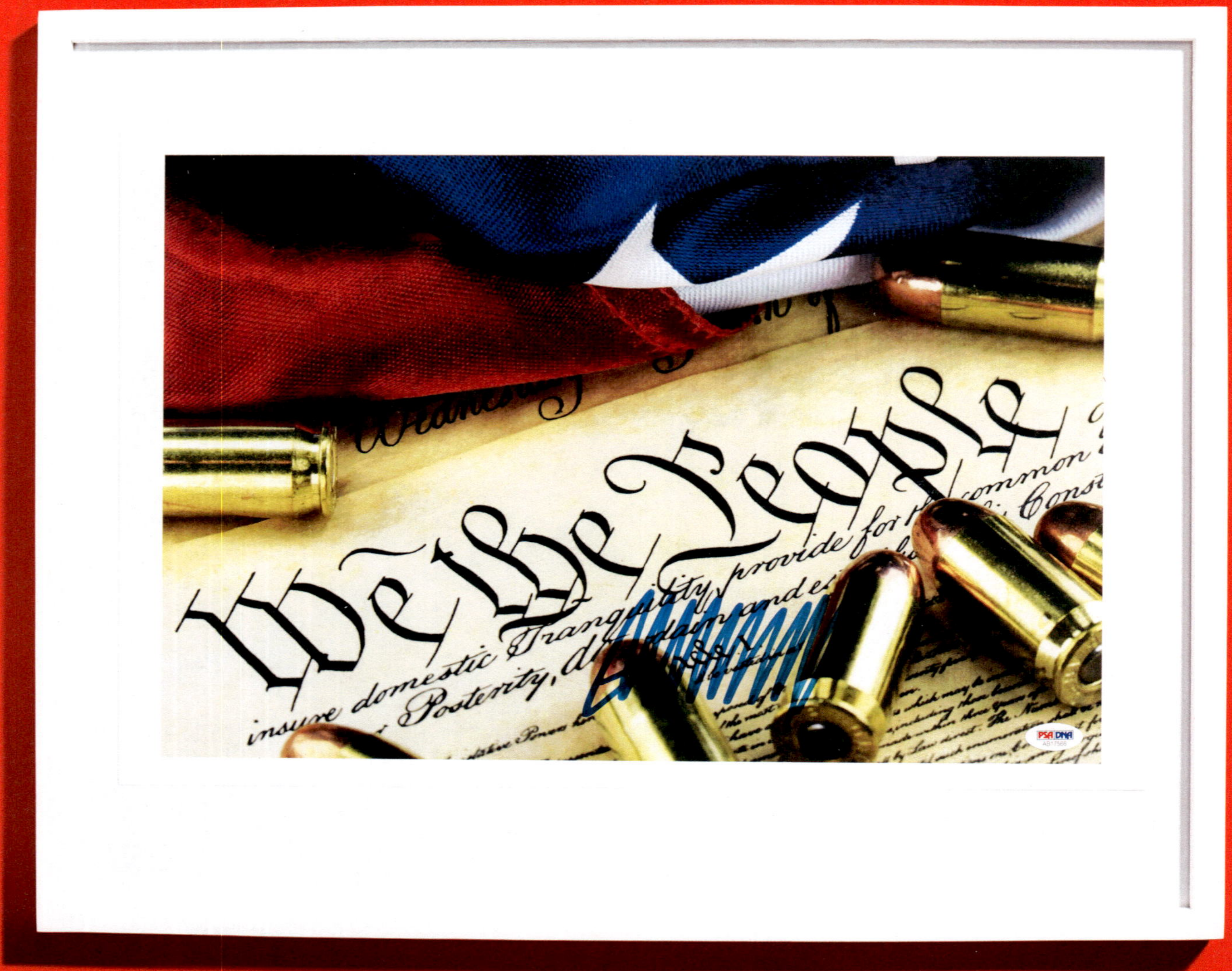

PHOTOGRAPH OF VLADIMIR PUTIN ON HORSEBACK
SIGNED DONALD TRUMP

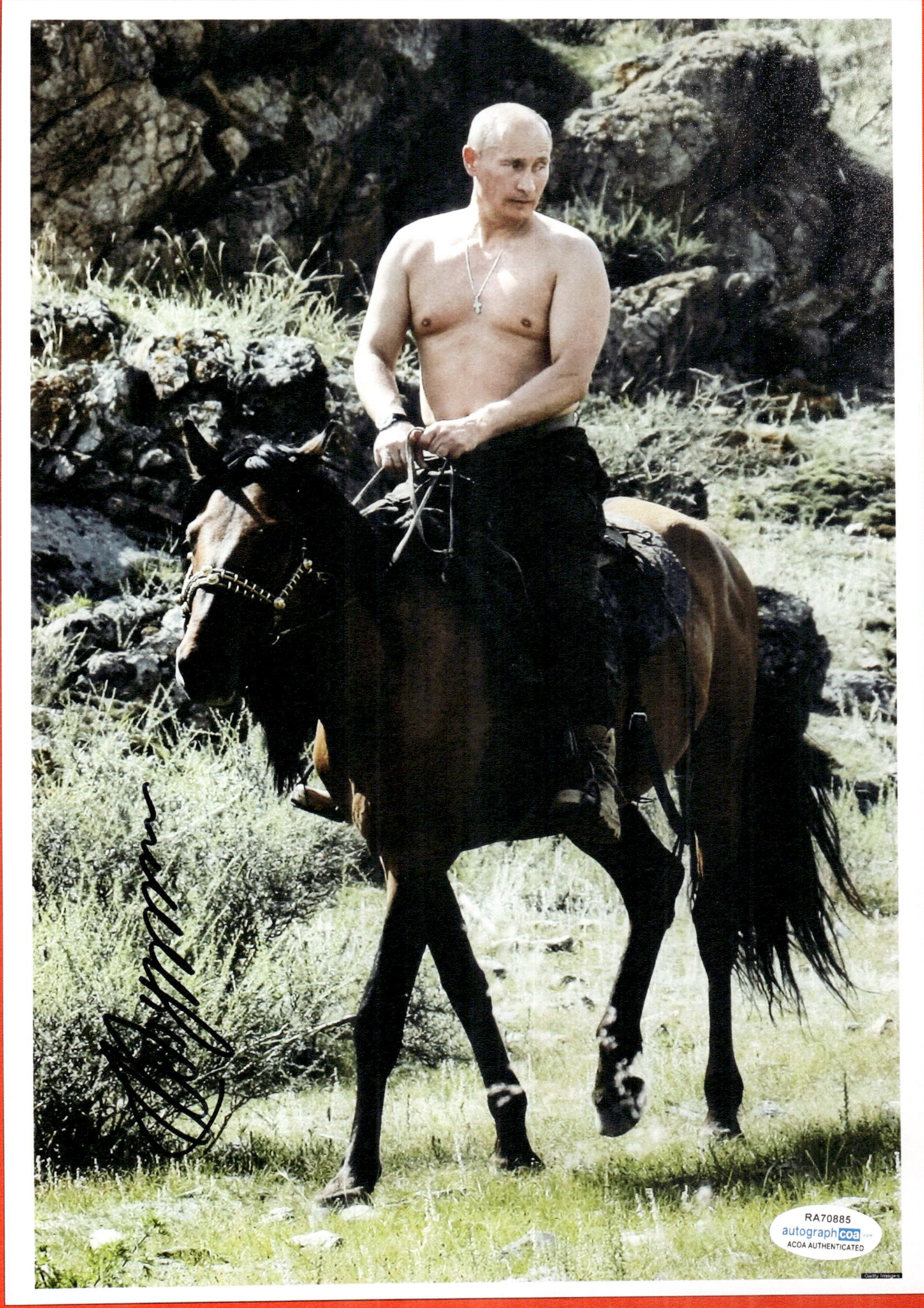

TRUMP 2016 CAMPAIGN PLEDGE ON IMMIGRATION REFORM
SIGNED DONALD TRUMP

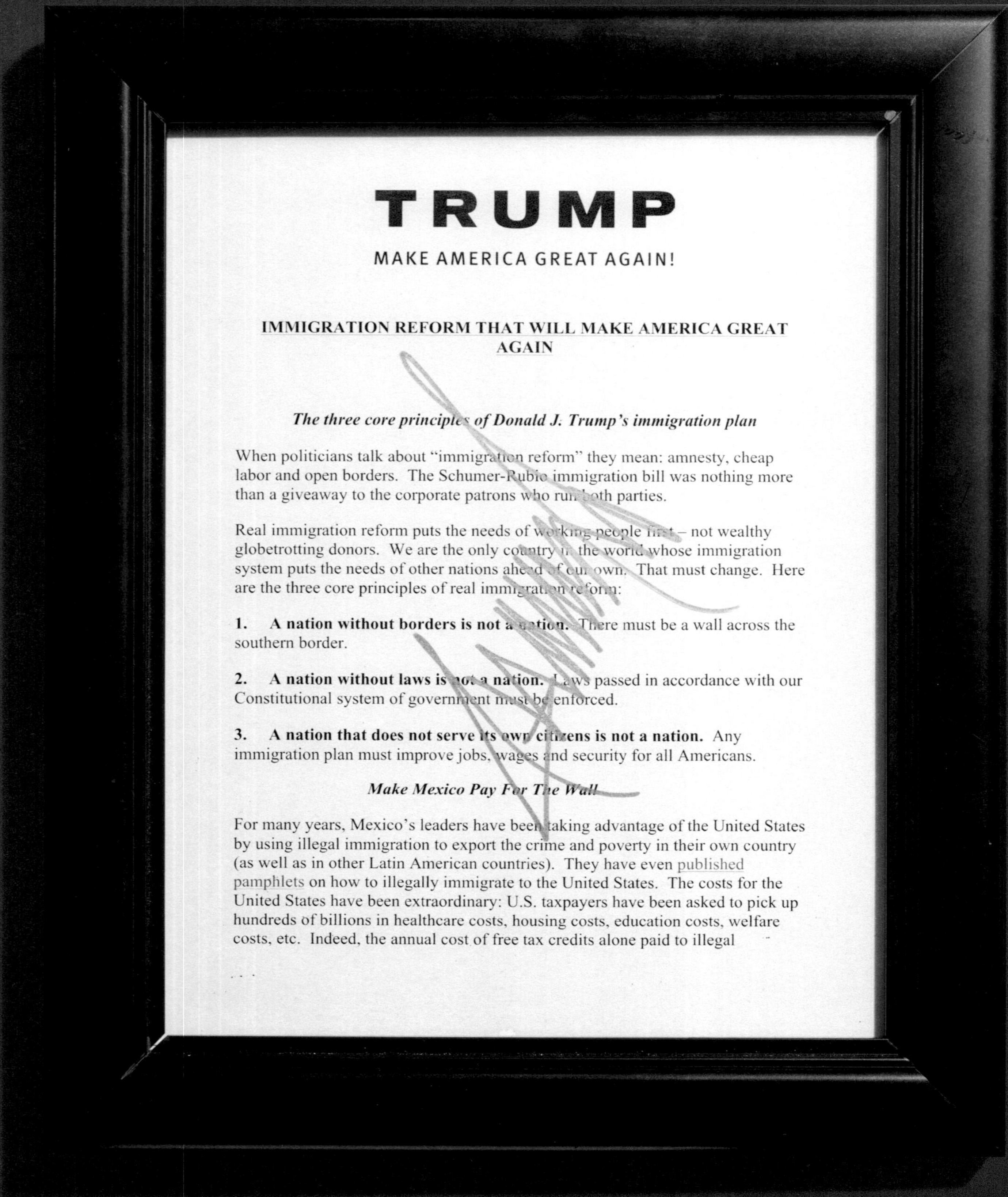

TRUMP

MAKE AMERICA GREAT AGAIN!

IMMIGRATION REFORM THAT WILL MAKE AMERICA GREAT AGAIN

The three core principles of Donald J. Trump's immigration plan

When politicians talk about "immigration reform" they mean: amnesty, cheap labor and open borders. The Schumer-Rubio immigration bill was nothing more than a giveaway to the corporate patrons who run both parties.

Real immigration reform puts the needs of working people first – not wealthy globetrotting donors. We are the only country in the world whose immigration system puts the needs of other nations ahead of our own. That must change. Here are the three core principles of real immigration reform:

1. **A nation without borders is not a nation.** There must be a wall across the southern border.

2. **A nation without laws is not a nation.** Laws passed in accordance with our Constitutional system of government must be enforced.

3. **A nation that does not serve its own citizens is not a nation.** Any immigration plan must improve jobs, wages and security for all Americans.

Make Mexico Pay For The Wall

For many years, Mexico's leaders have been taking advantage of the United States by using illegal immigration to export the crime and poverty in their own country (as well as in other Latin American countries). They have even published pamphlets on how to illegally immigrate to the United States. The costs for the United States have been extraordinary: U.S. taxpayers have been asked to pick up hundreds of billions in healthcare costs, housing costs, education costs, welfare costs, etc. Indeed, the annual cost of free tax credits alone paid to illegal

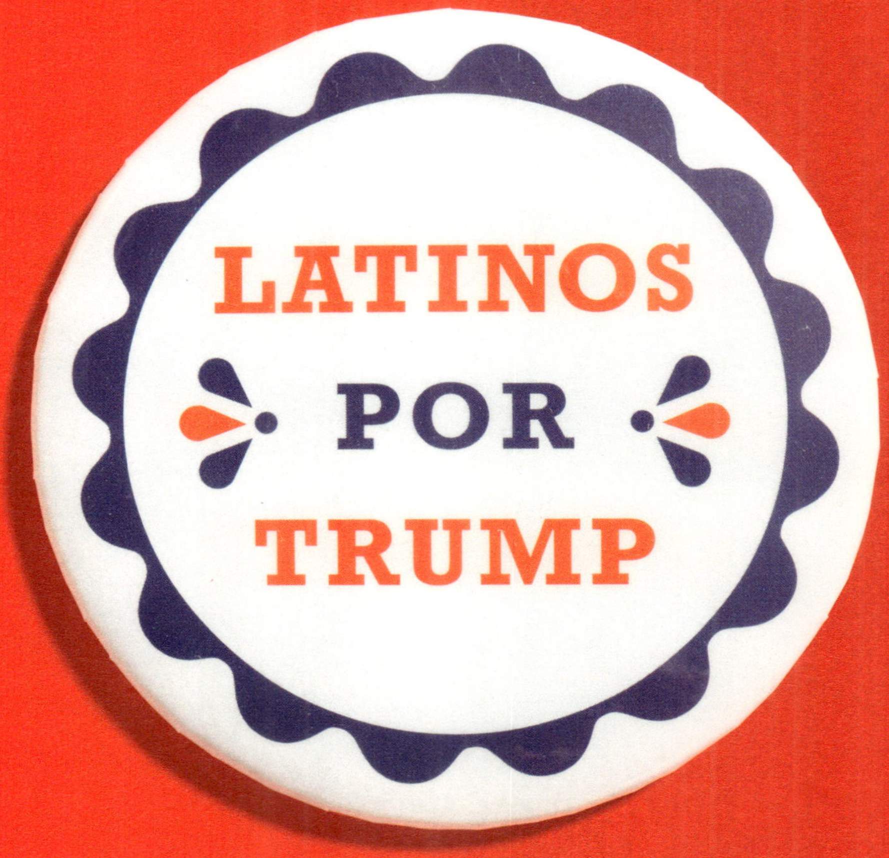
LATINOS
POR
TRUMP

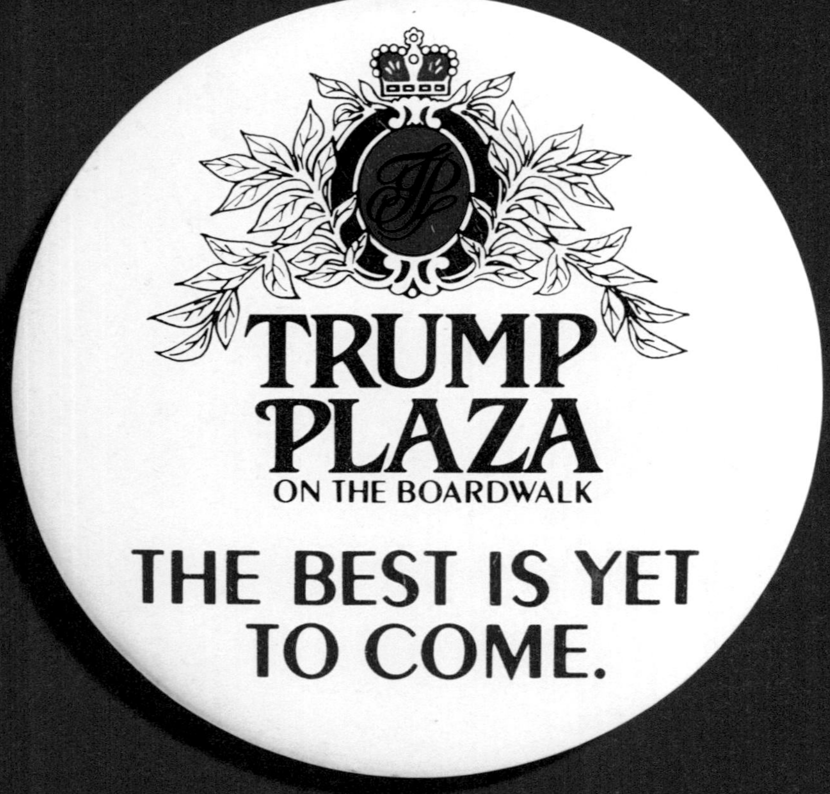
TP
TRUMP
PLAZA
ON THE BOARDWALK
THE BEST IS YET
TO COME.

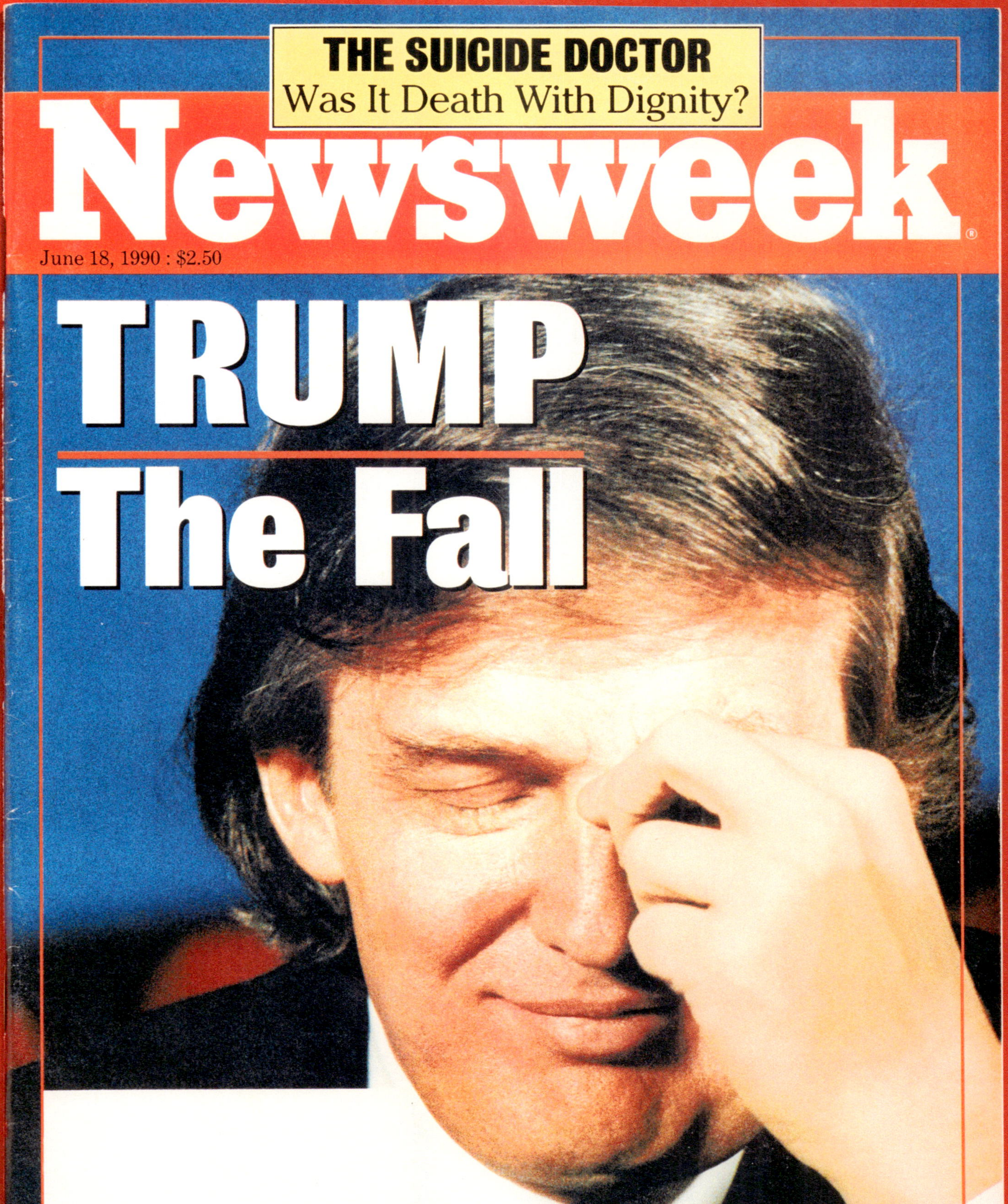
THE SUICIDE DOCTOR
Was It Death With Dignity?
Newsweek
June 18, 1990 : $2.50
TRUMP
The Fall

AMERICAN FLAG BOXING GLOVES
SIGNED DONALD TRUMP

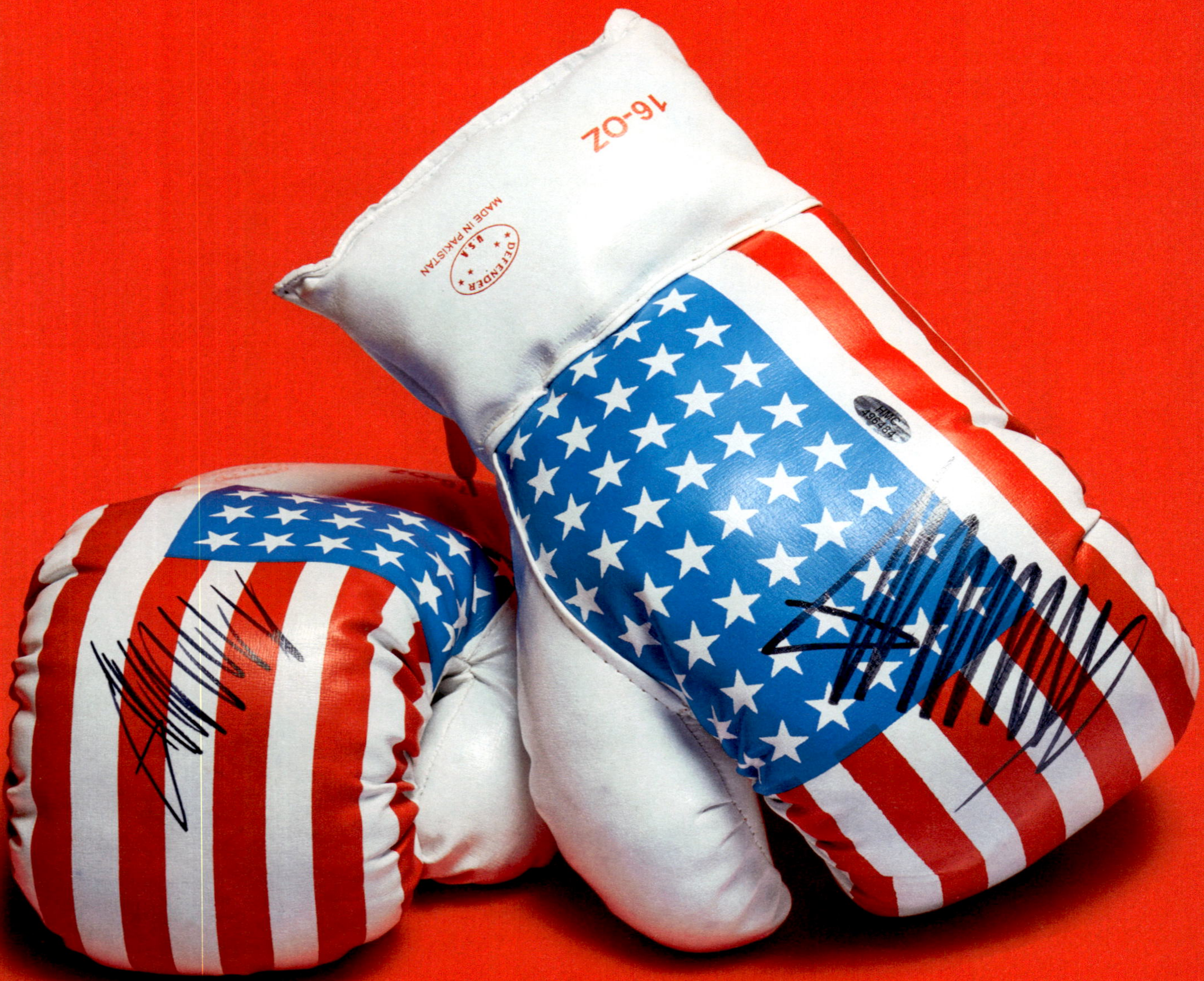

MELANIA AND DONALD TRUMP WEDDING CAKE, JANUARY 22, 2005
CHOCOLATE TRUFFLE CAKE WITH SINGLE SUGAR-SPUN BUTTERCREAM
ROSE AND GOLD FLAKES PRESENTED AS A WEDDING FAVOR TO
350 GUESTS, INCLUDING RUDY GIULIANI, HEIDI KLUM,
P. DIDDY, SHAQUILLE O'NEAL, SIMON COWELL,
SENATOR HILLARY CLINTON AND PRESIDENT BILL CLINTON

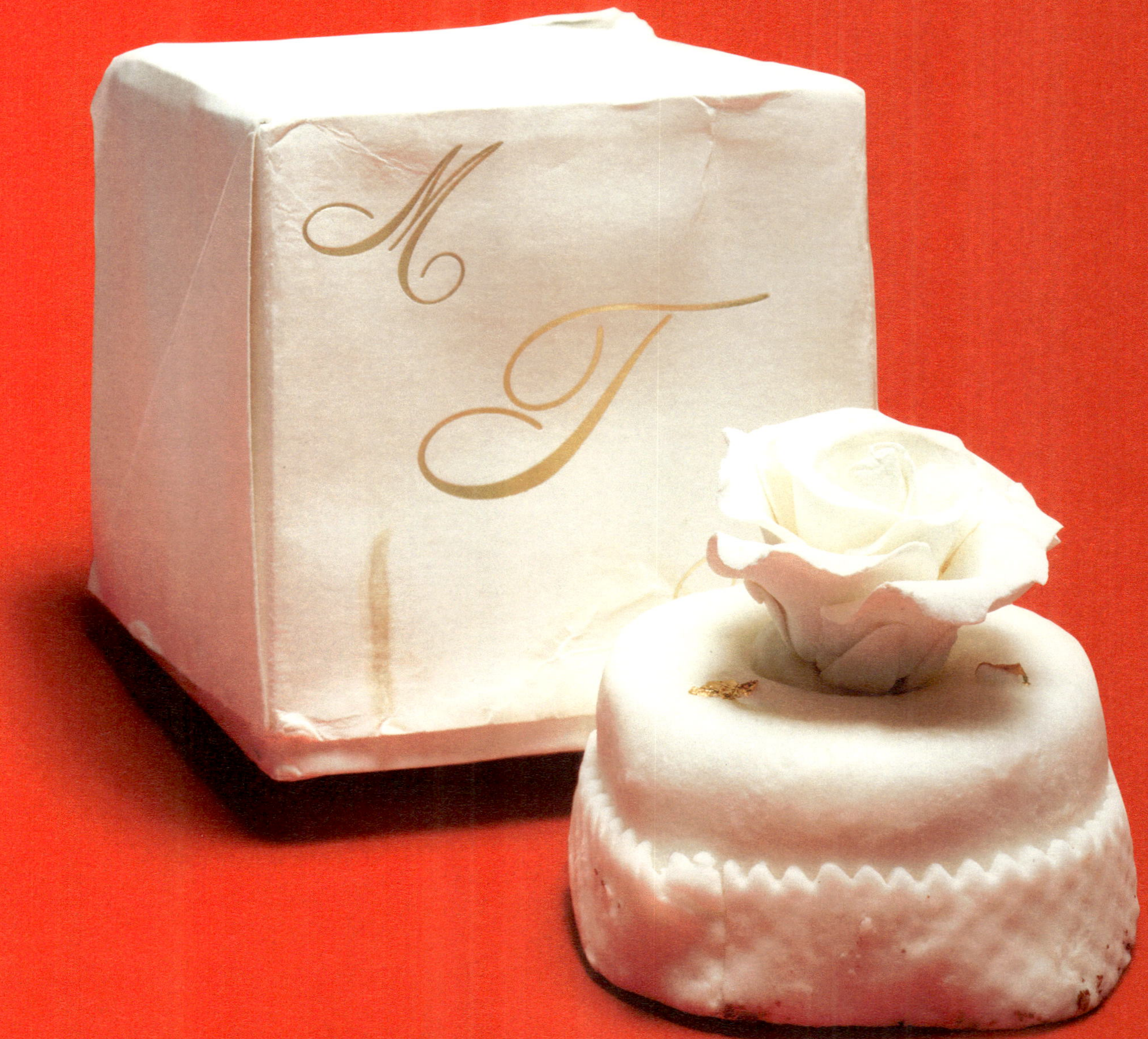

OFFICIAL PROGRAM: HOLYFIELD VS. MCDONAGH
TRUMP PLAZA, JUNE 1, 1990

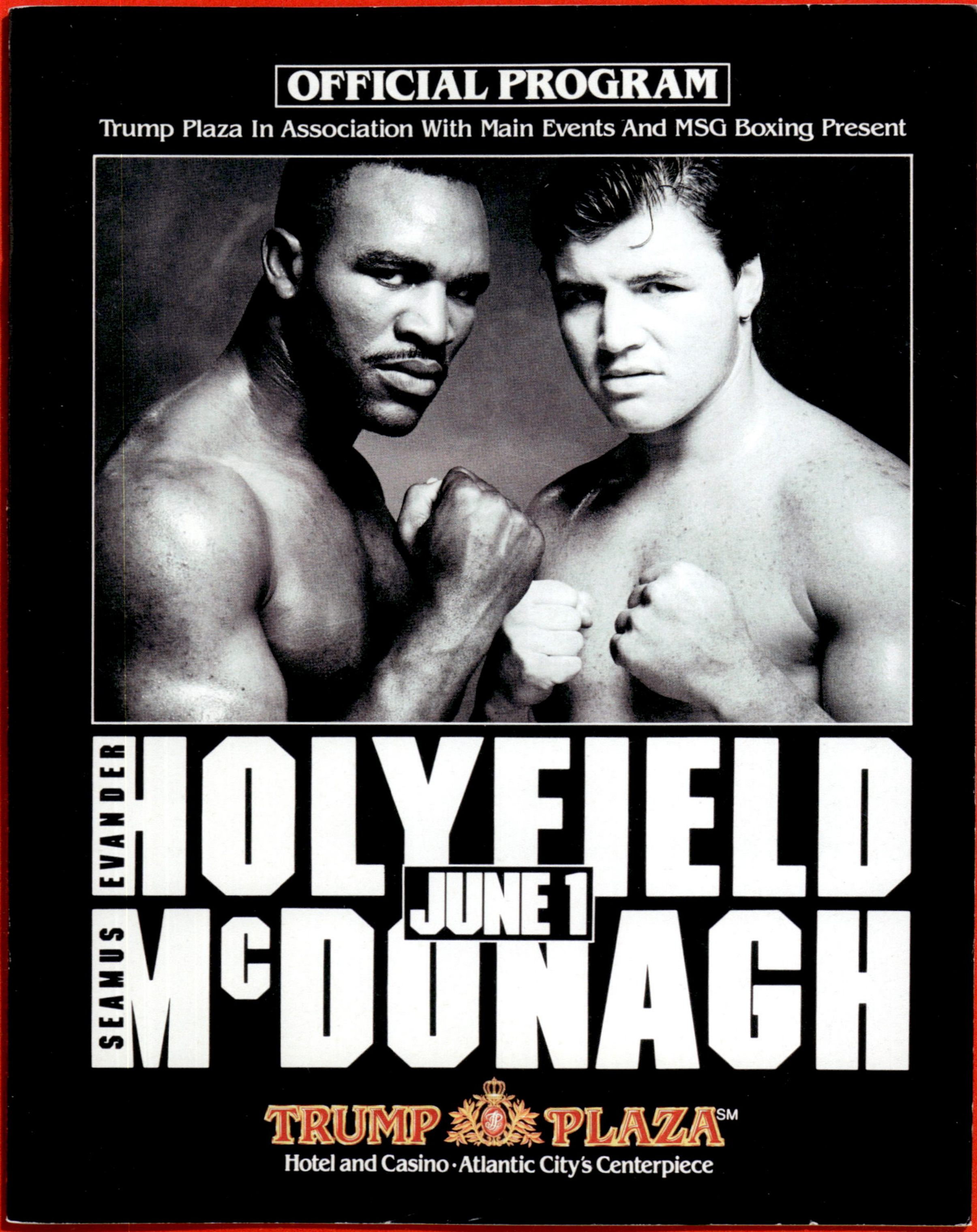

OFFICIAL PROGRAM: TYSON VS. HOLMES
WORLD HEAVYWEIGHT CHAMPIONSHIP
TRUMP PLAZA, JANUARY 22, 1988

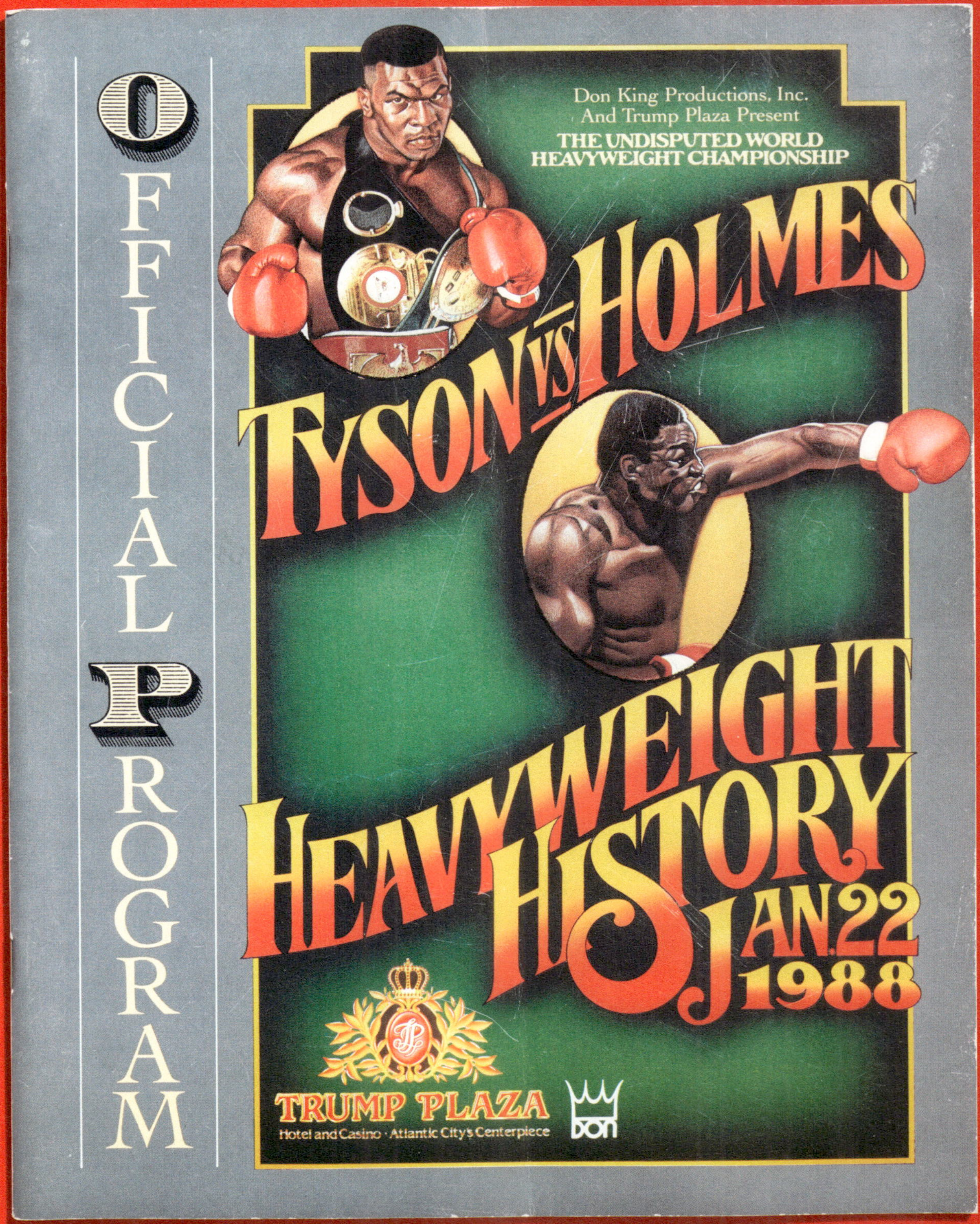

FRONT ROW TICKET: TYSON VS. BIGGS
WORLD HEAVYWEIGHT CHAMPIONSHIP
TRUMP PLAZA, OCTOBER 16, 1987

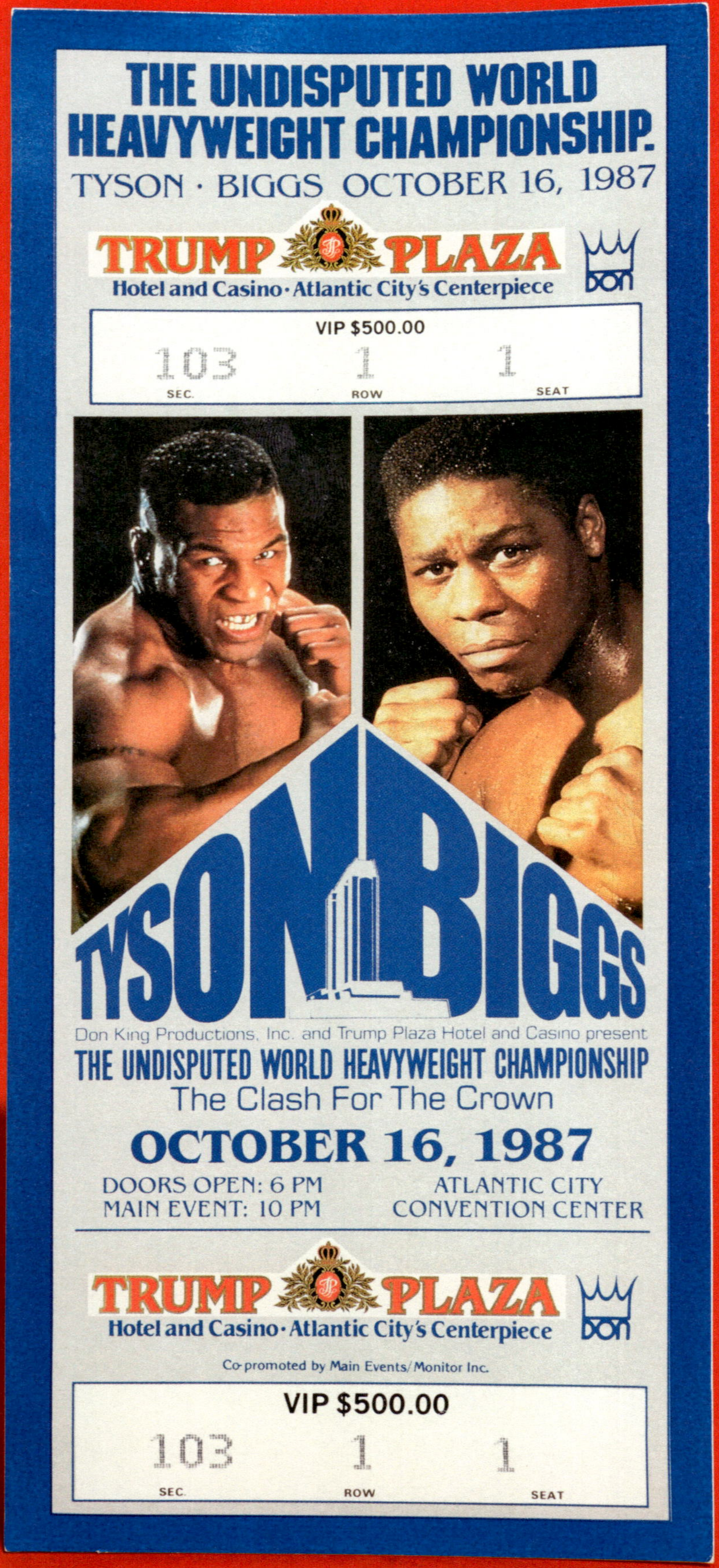

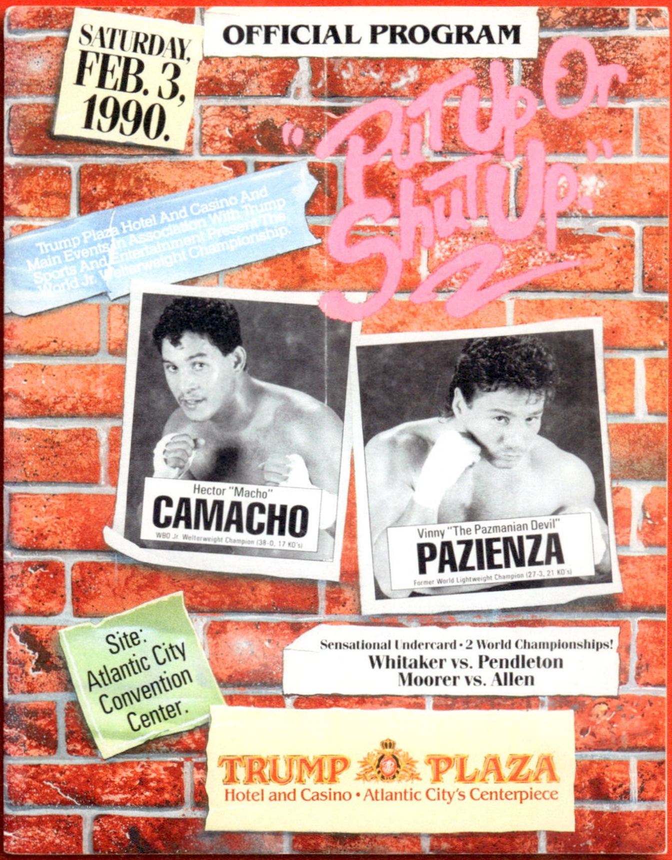
SATURDAY, FEB. 3, 1990.
OFFICIAL PROGRAM
"Put Up Or Shut Up"
Hector "Macho"
CAMACHO
Vinny "The Pazmanian Devil"
PAZIENZA
Site: Atlantic City Convention Center.
Sensational Undercard • 2 World Championships!
Whitaker vs. Pendleton
Moorer vs. Allen
TRUMP PLAZA
Hotel and Casino • Atlantic City's Centerpiece

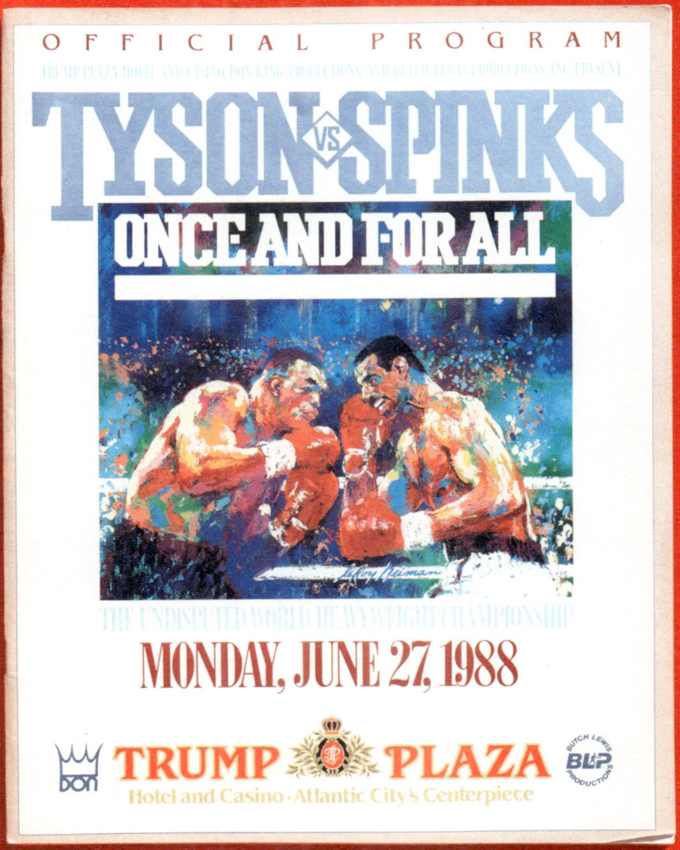
OFFICIAL PROGRAM
TYSON VS SPINKS
ONCE AND FOR ALL
THE UNDISPUTED WORLD HEAVYWEIGHT CHAMPIONSHIP
MONDAY, JUNE 27, 1988
TRUMP PLAZA
Hotel and Casino • Atlantic City's Centerpiece

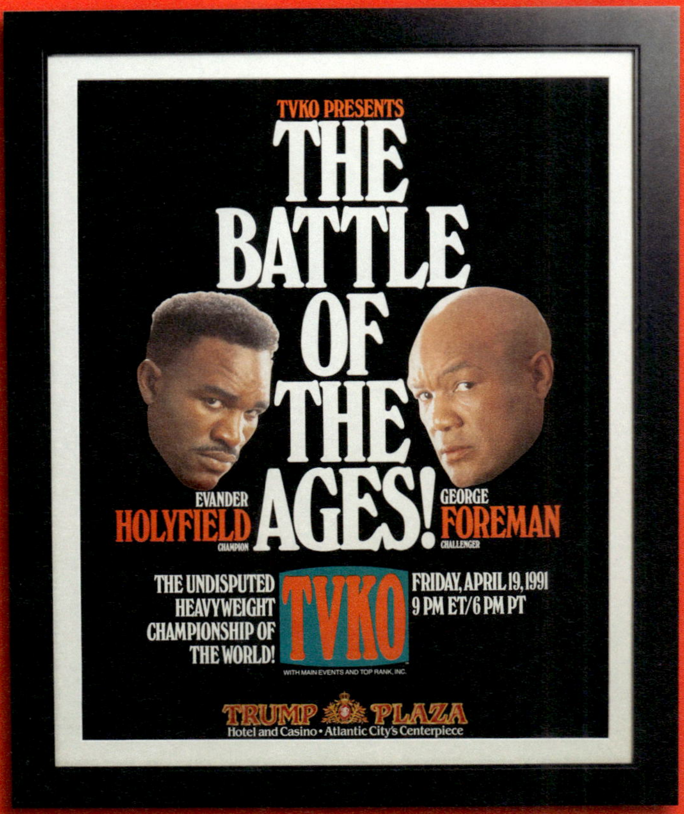
TVKO PRESENTS
THE BATTLE OF THE AGES!
EVANDER
HOLYFIELD
CHAMPION
GEORGE
FOREMAN
CHALLENGER
THE UNDISPUTED HEAVYWEIGHT CHAMPIONSHIP OF THE WORLD!
TVKO
FRIDAY, APRIL 19, 1991
9 PM ET/6 PM PT
TRUMP PLAZA
Hotel and Casino • Atlantic City's Centerpiece

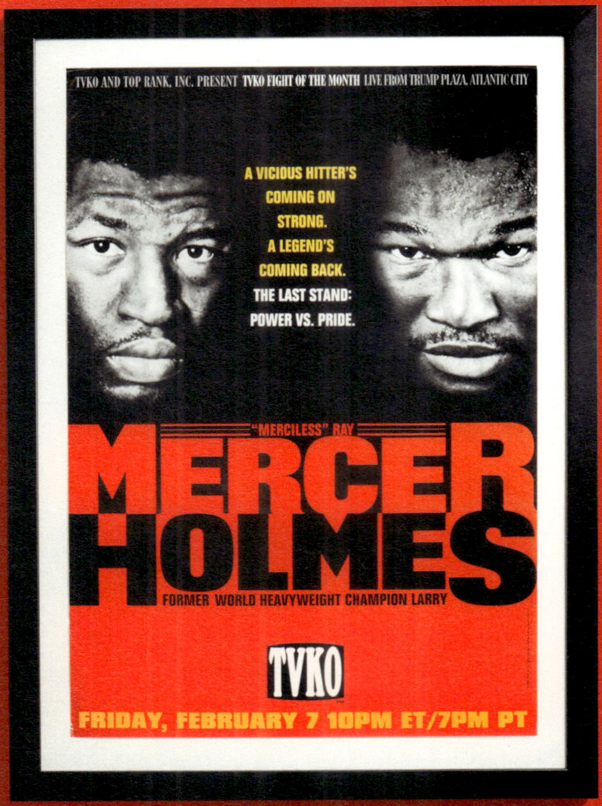
TVKO AND TOP RANK, INC. PRESENT TVKO FIGHT OF THE MONTH LIVE FROM TRUMP PLAZA, ATLANTIC CITY
A VICIOUS HITTER'S COMING ON STRONG.
A LEGEND'S COMING BACK.
THE LAST STAND: POWER VS. PRIDE.
"MERCILESS" RAY
MERCER
HOLMES
FORMER WORLD HEAVYWEIGHT CHAMPION LARRY
TVKO
FRIDAY, FEBRUARY 7 10PM ET/7PM PT

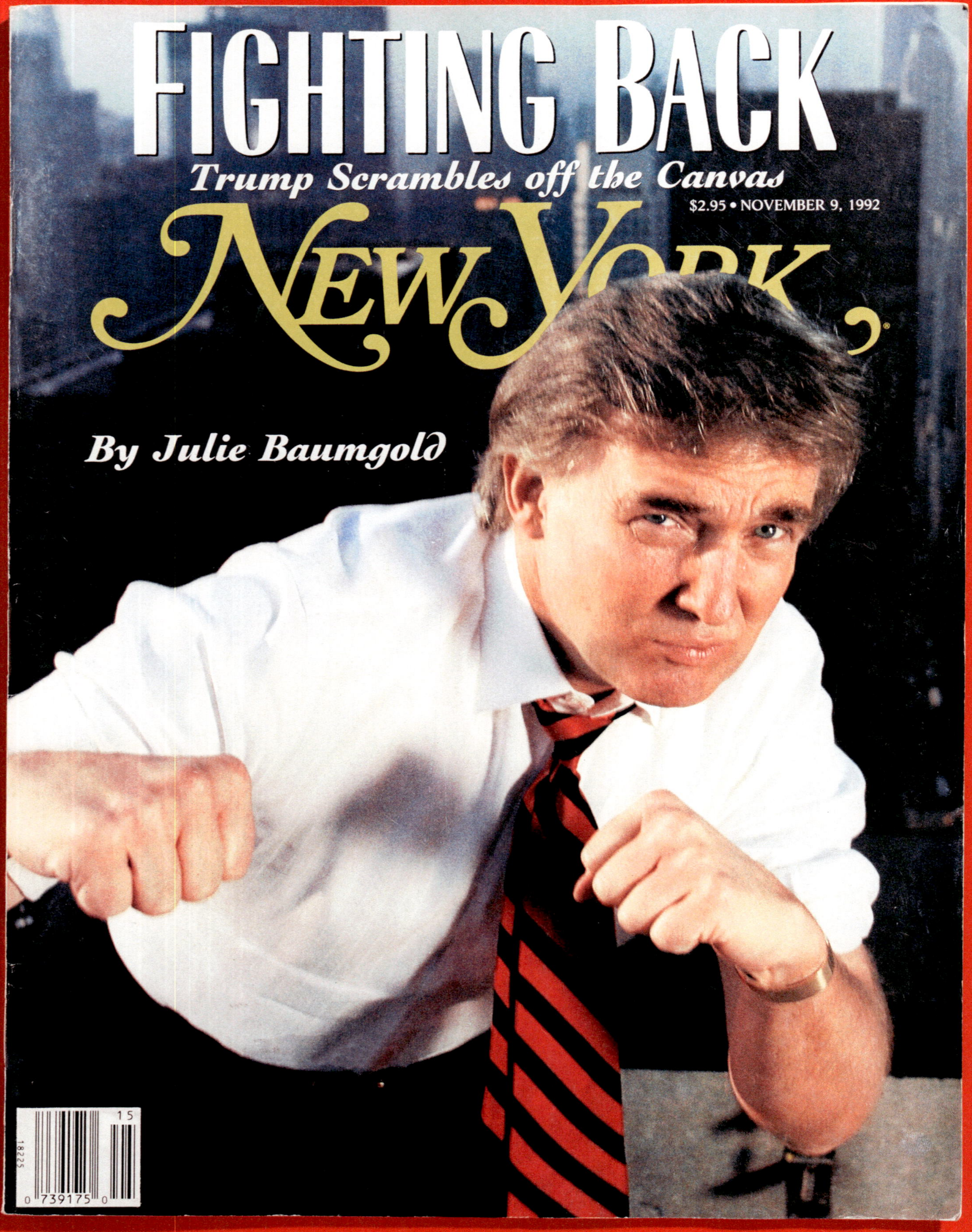
FIGHTING BACK
Trump Scrambles off the Canvas
$2.95 • NOVEMBER 9, 1992
NEW YORK
By Julie Baumgold

SUPERHERO-THEMED NEW YEAR'S EVE PARTY INVITATION, TRUMP PLAZA

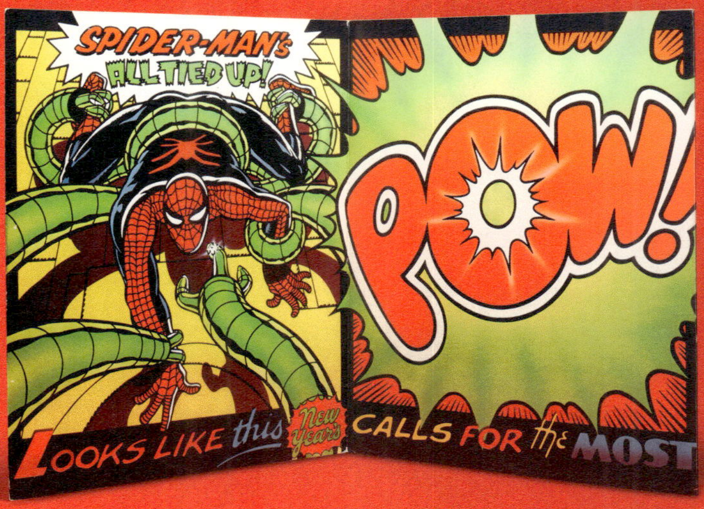

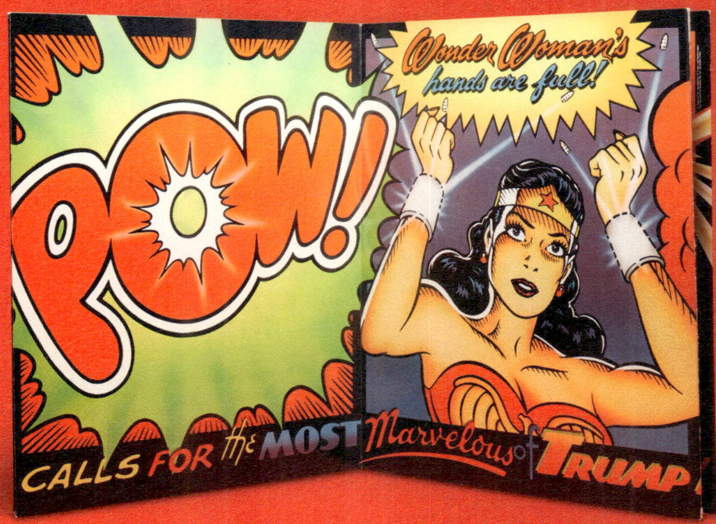

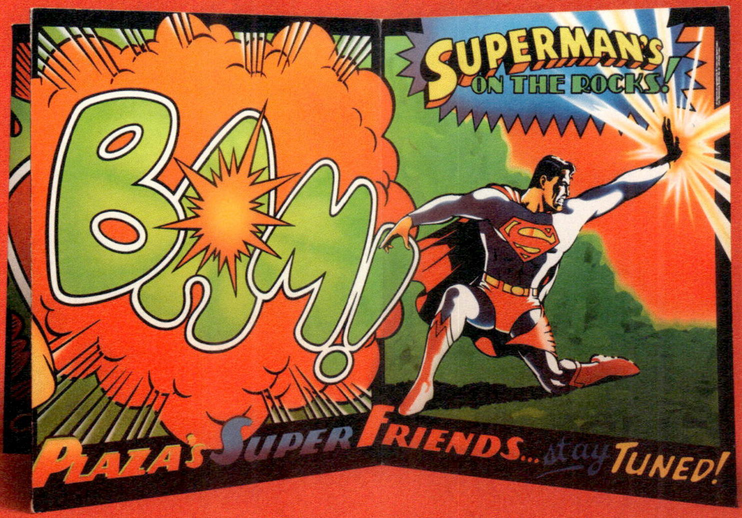

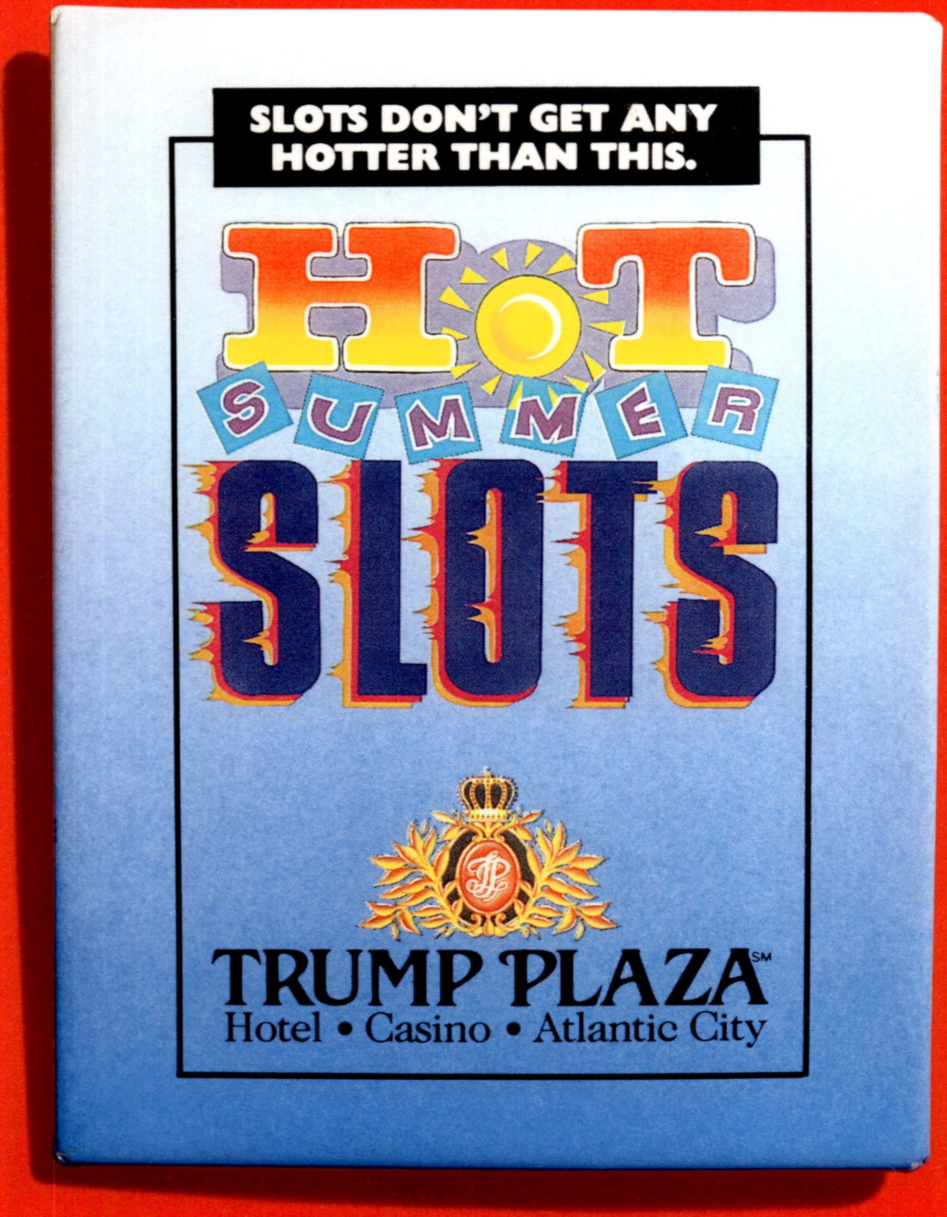
SLOTS DON'T GET ANY
HOTTER THAN THIS.
HOT
SUMMER
SLOTS
TRUMP PLAZA℠
Hotel • Casino • Atlantic City

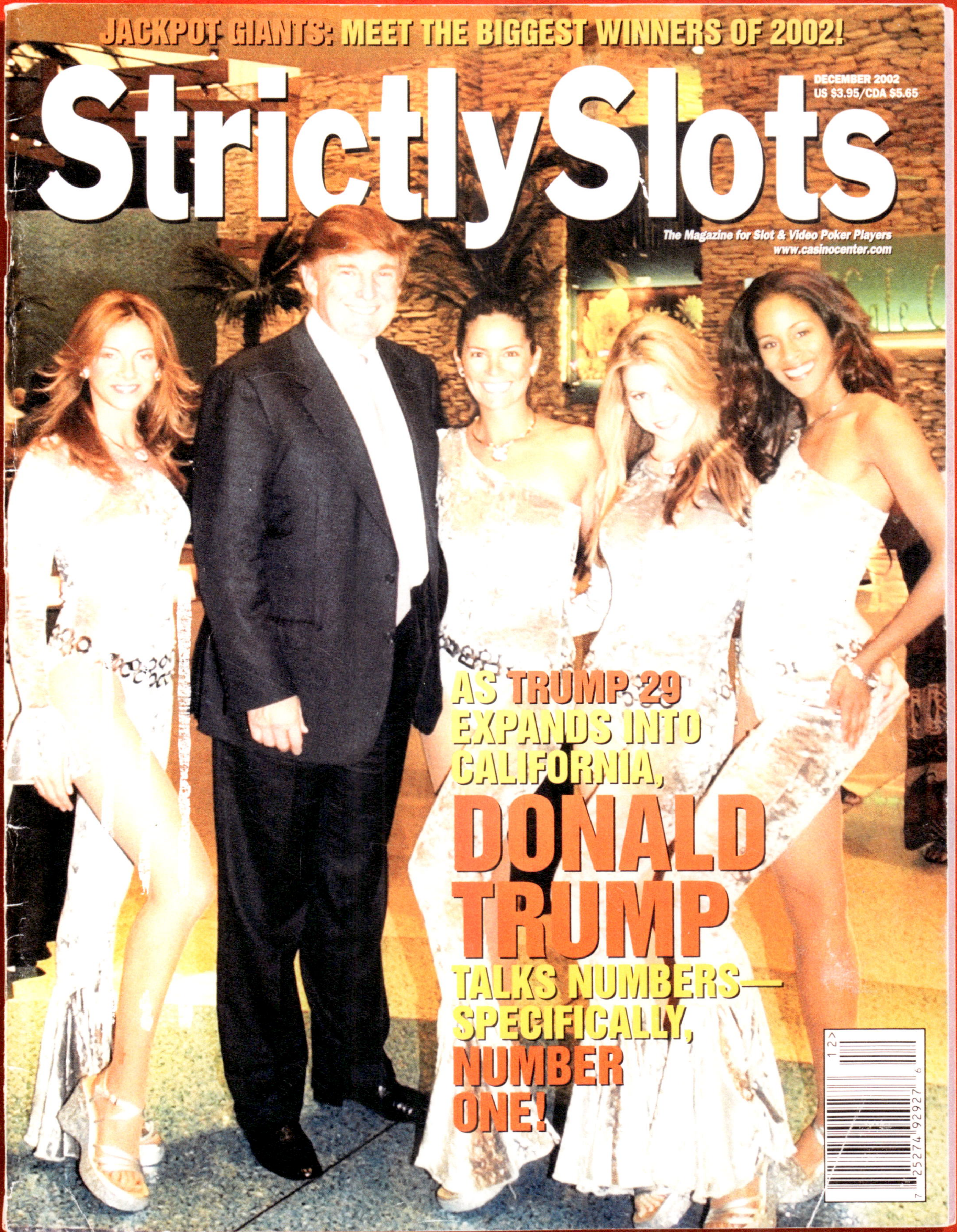
JACKPOT GIANTS: MEET THE BIGGEST WINNERS OF 2002!
StrictlySlots
DECEMBER 2002
US $3.95/CDA $5.65
The Magazine for Slot & Video Poker Players
www.casinocenter.com
AS TRUMP 29 EXPANDS INTO CALIFORNIA,
DONALD TRUMP
TALKS NUMBERS—SPECIFICALLY, NUMBER ONE!

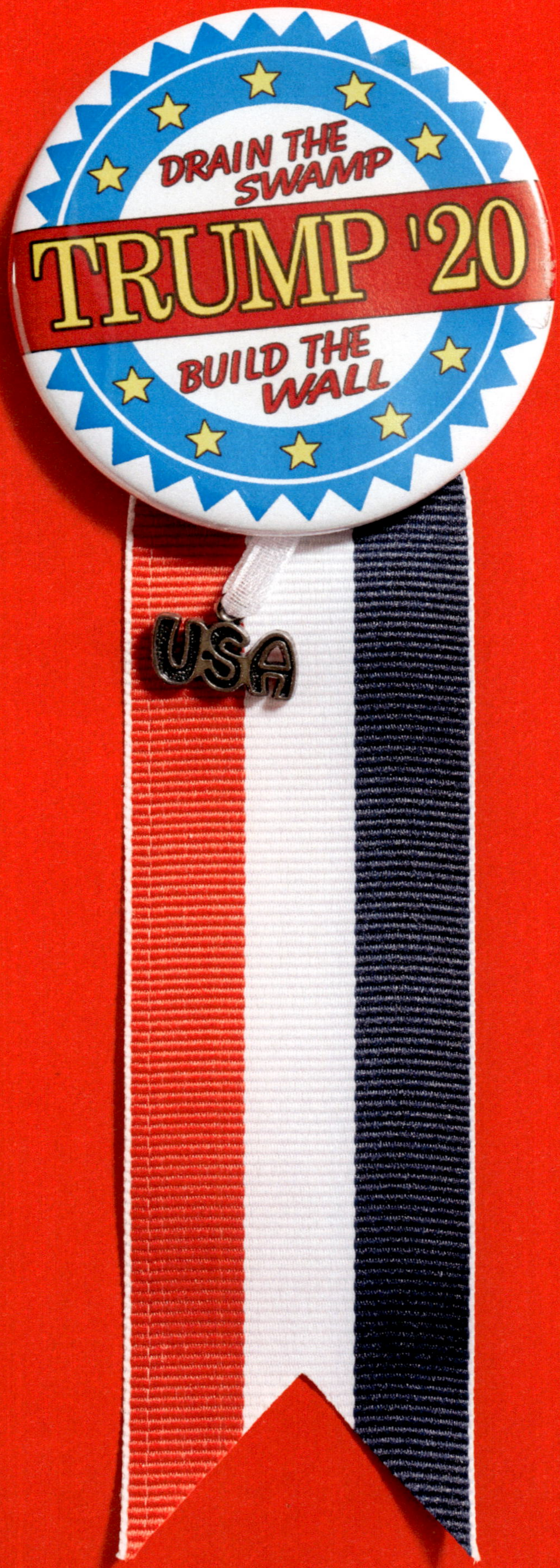
DRAIN THE SWAMP
TRUMP '20
BUILD THE WALL
USA

TRUMP TAJ MAHAL ROOM KEY AND DO NOT DISTURB DOOR SIGN

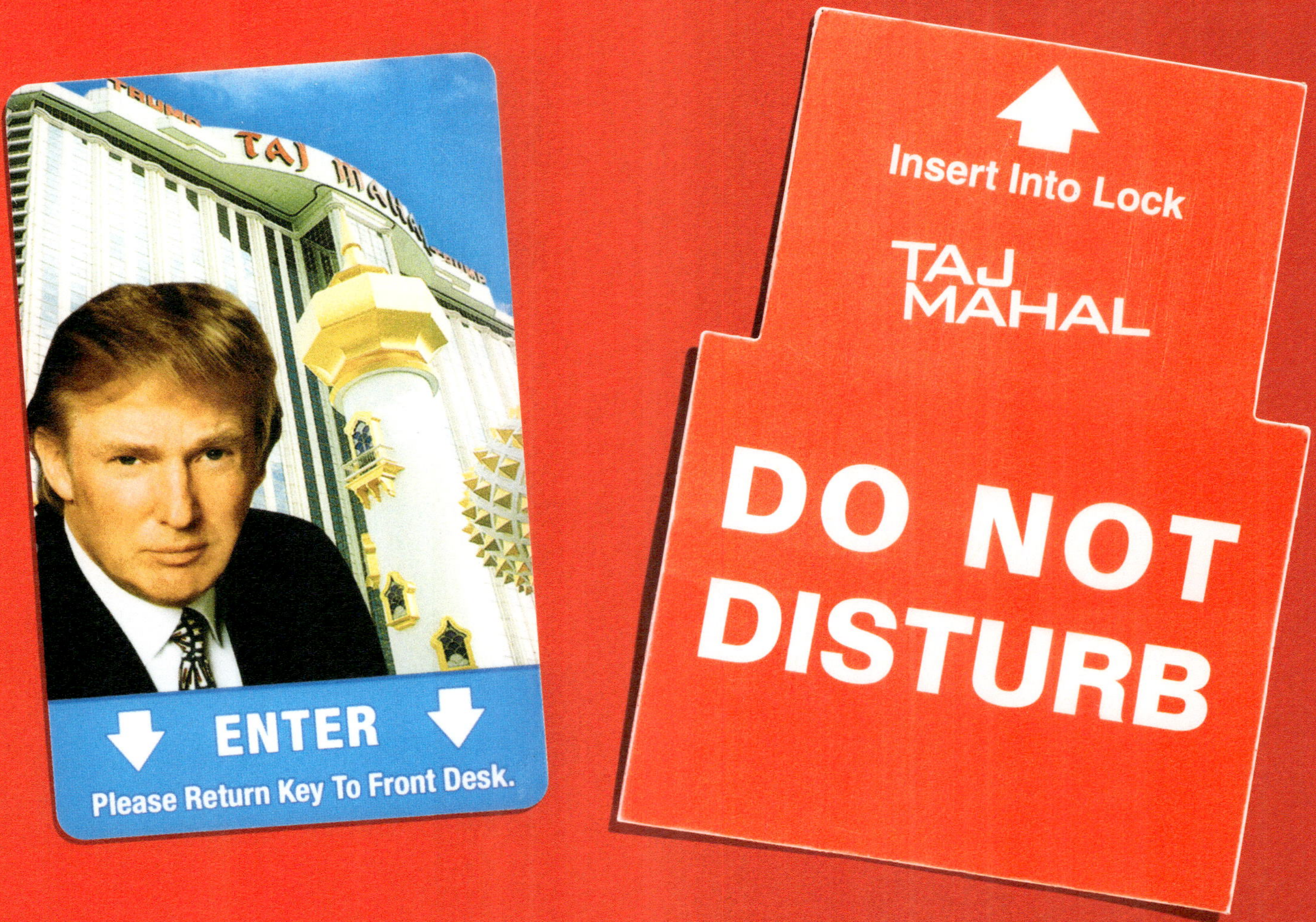

THE CELEBRITY APPRENTICE 7UP CAN
TRUMP CASINO COIN, CHIP AND TOKEN BUCKET

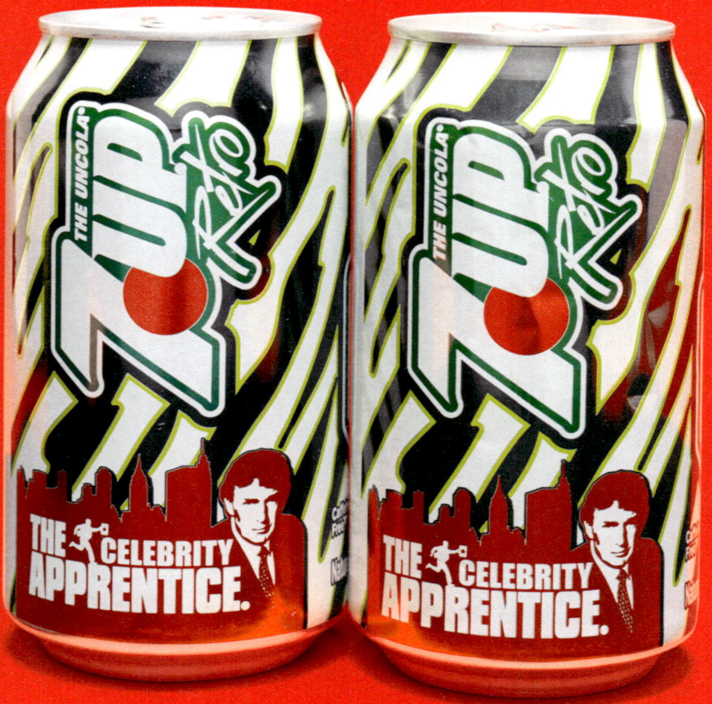

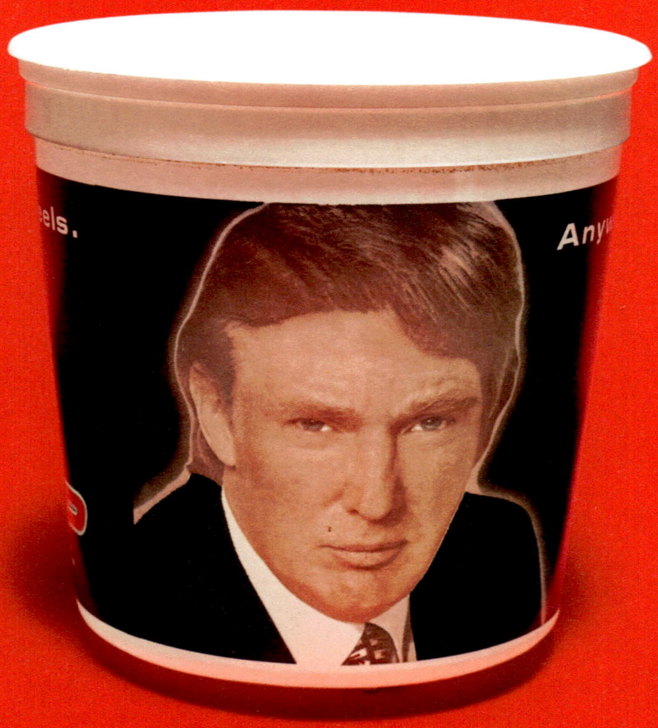

THE APPRENTICE SPECIAL EDITION
TRUMP ICE PURE SPRING WATER

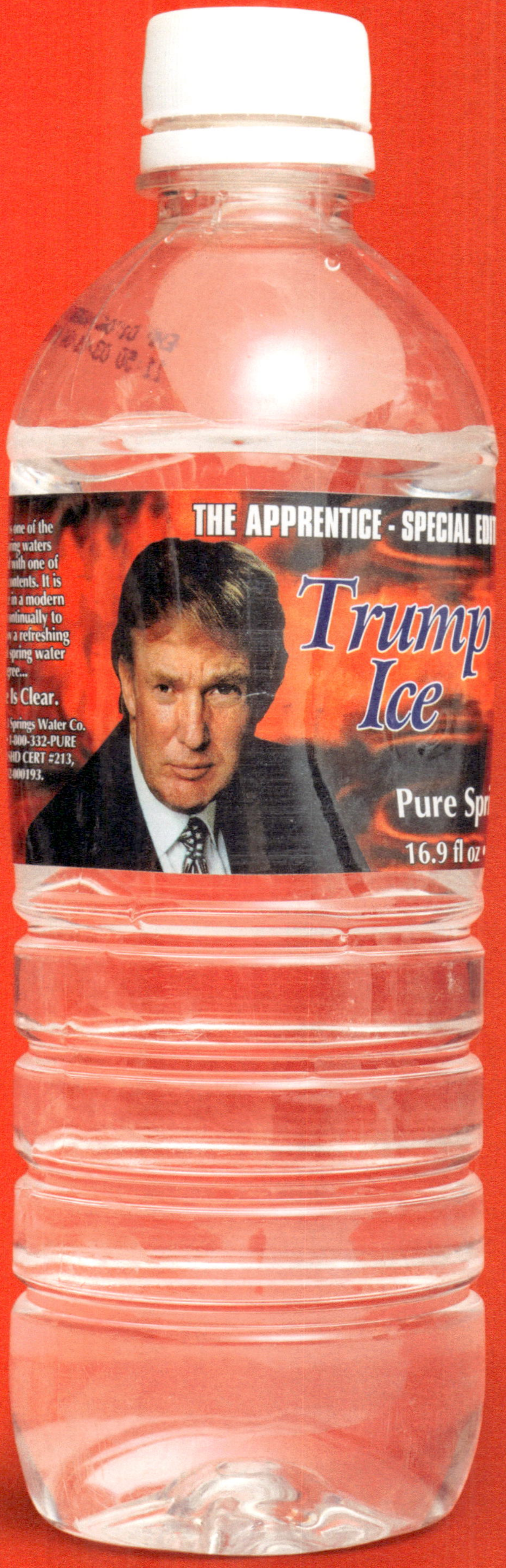

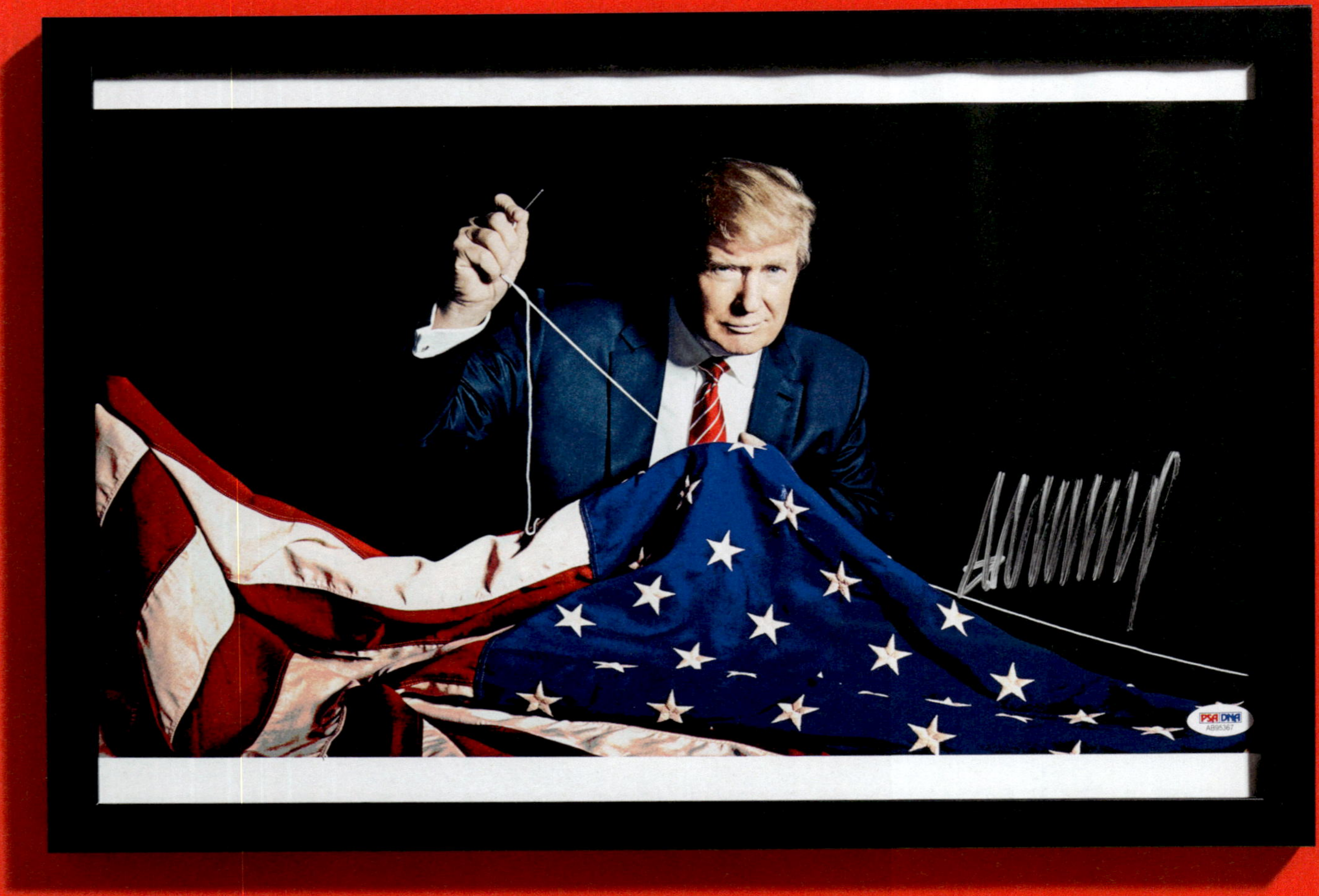

ESQUIRE MAGAZINE, FEBRUARY 2016
SIGNED DONALD TRUMP

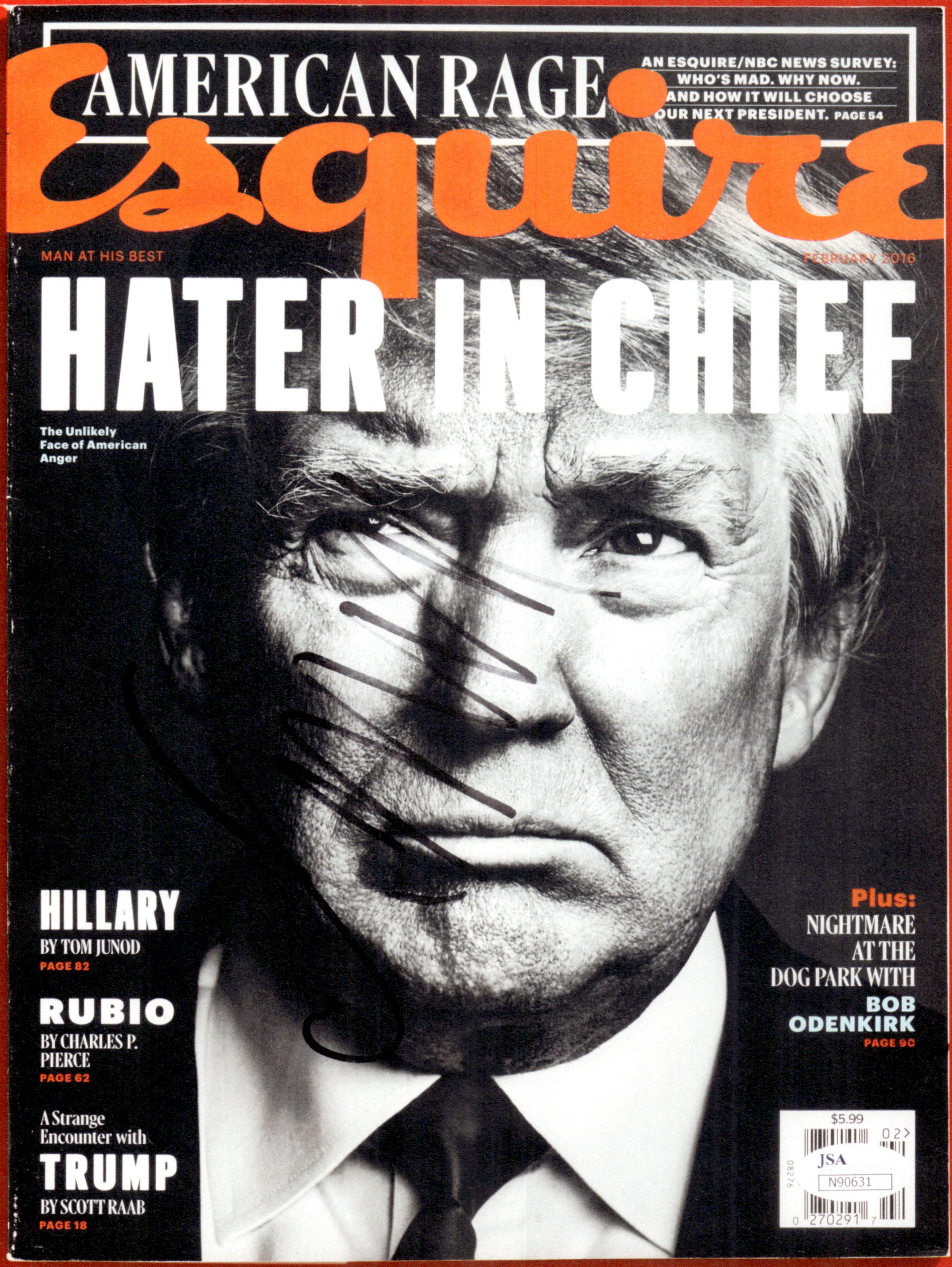

TV LAND AWARDS POSTER, 2006
DONALD TRUMP AND THE ICONIC VILLAIN J.R. EWING (PLAYED BY LARRY HAGMAN) FROM THE TV SHOW "DALLAS"

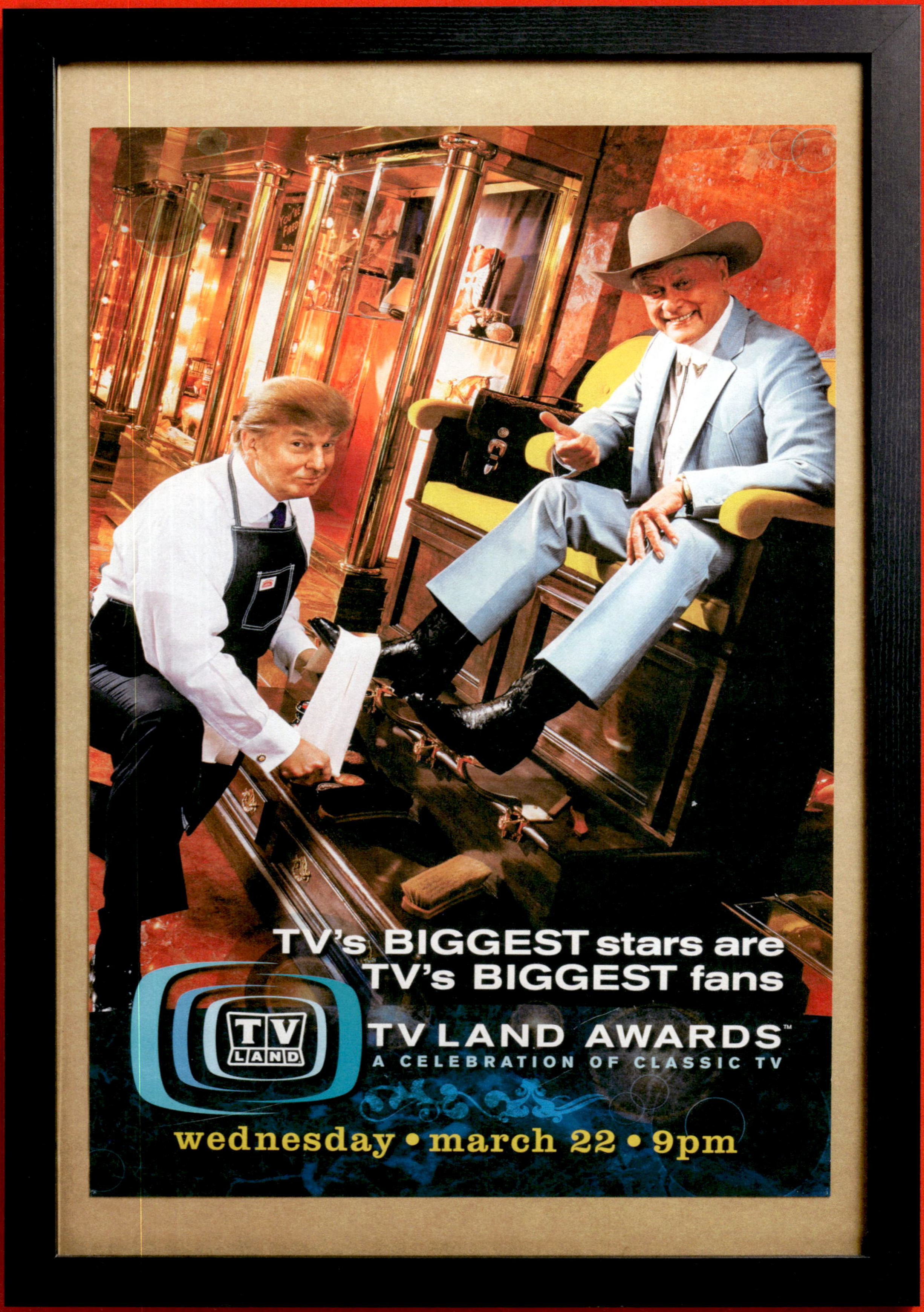

RECOMMENDATION COVER LETTER FOR LE CLUB, A NEW YORK MEMBERS ONLY RESTAURANT, NIGHTCLUB AND CELEBRITY HANGOUT, JANUARY 14, 1982

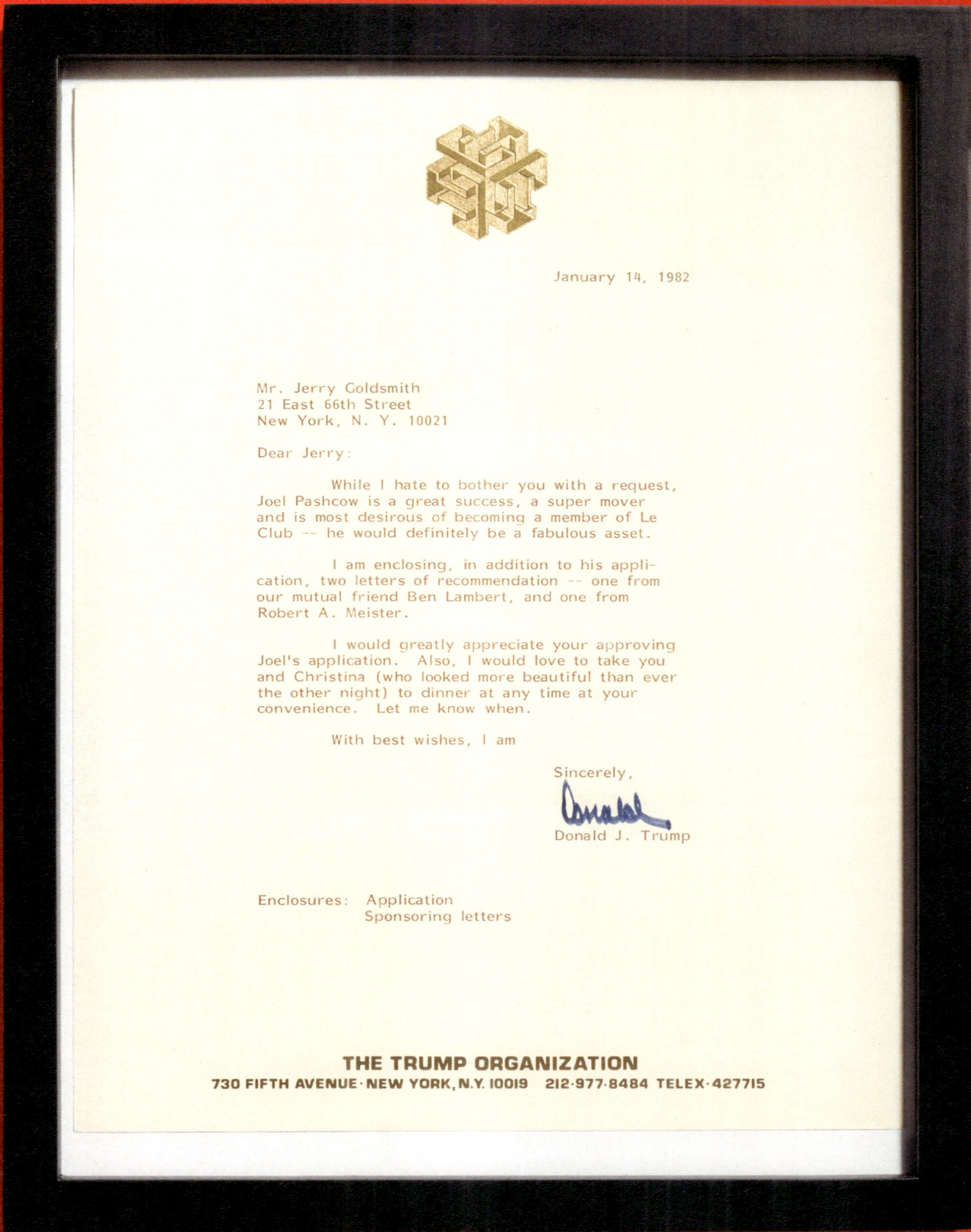

January 14, 1982

Mr. Jerry Goldsmith
21 East 66th Street
New York, N. Y. 10021

Dear Jerry:

While I hate to bother you with a request, Joel Pashcow is a great success, a super mover and is most desirous of becoming a member of Le Club -- he would definitely be a fabulous asset.

I am enclosing, in addition to his application, two letters of recommendation -- one from our mutual friend Ben Lambert, and one from Robert A. Meister.

I would greatly appreciate your approving Joel's application. Also, I would love to take you and Christina (who looked more beautiful than ever the other night) to dinner at any time at your convenience. Let me know when.

With best wishes, I am

Sincerely,

Donald

Donald J. Trump

Enclosures: Application
Sponsoring letters

THE TRUMP ORGANIZATION
730 FIFTH AVENUE · NEW YORK, N.Y. 10019 212·977·8484 TELEX·427715

SUCCESS BY TRUMP BOXED EAU DE TOILETTE SPRAY FOR MEN

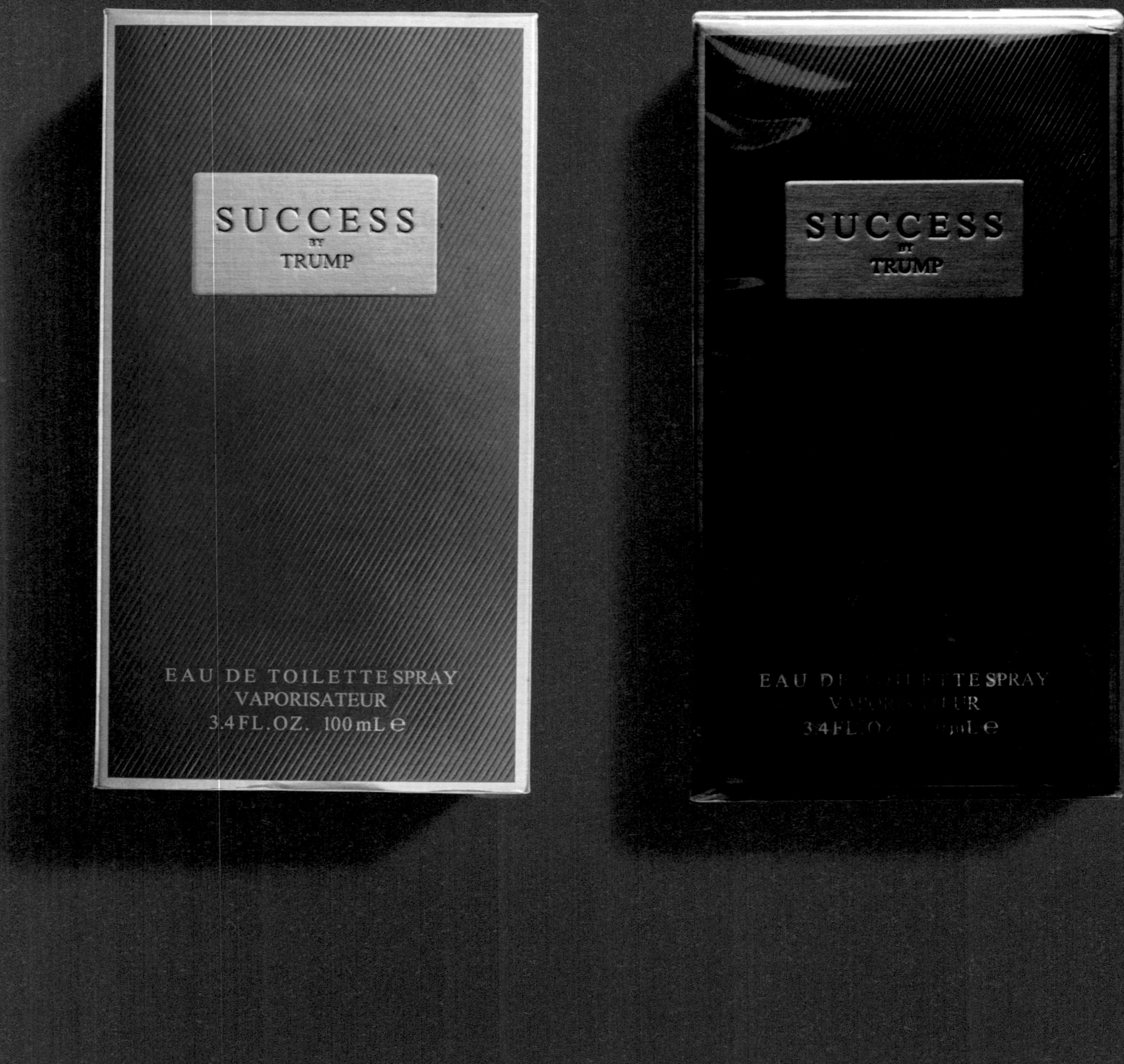

SUCCESS BY TRUMP ALCHOHOL-FREE DEODORANT FOR MEN

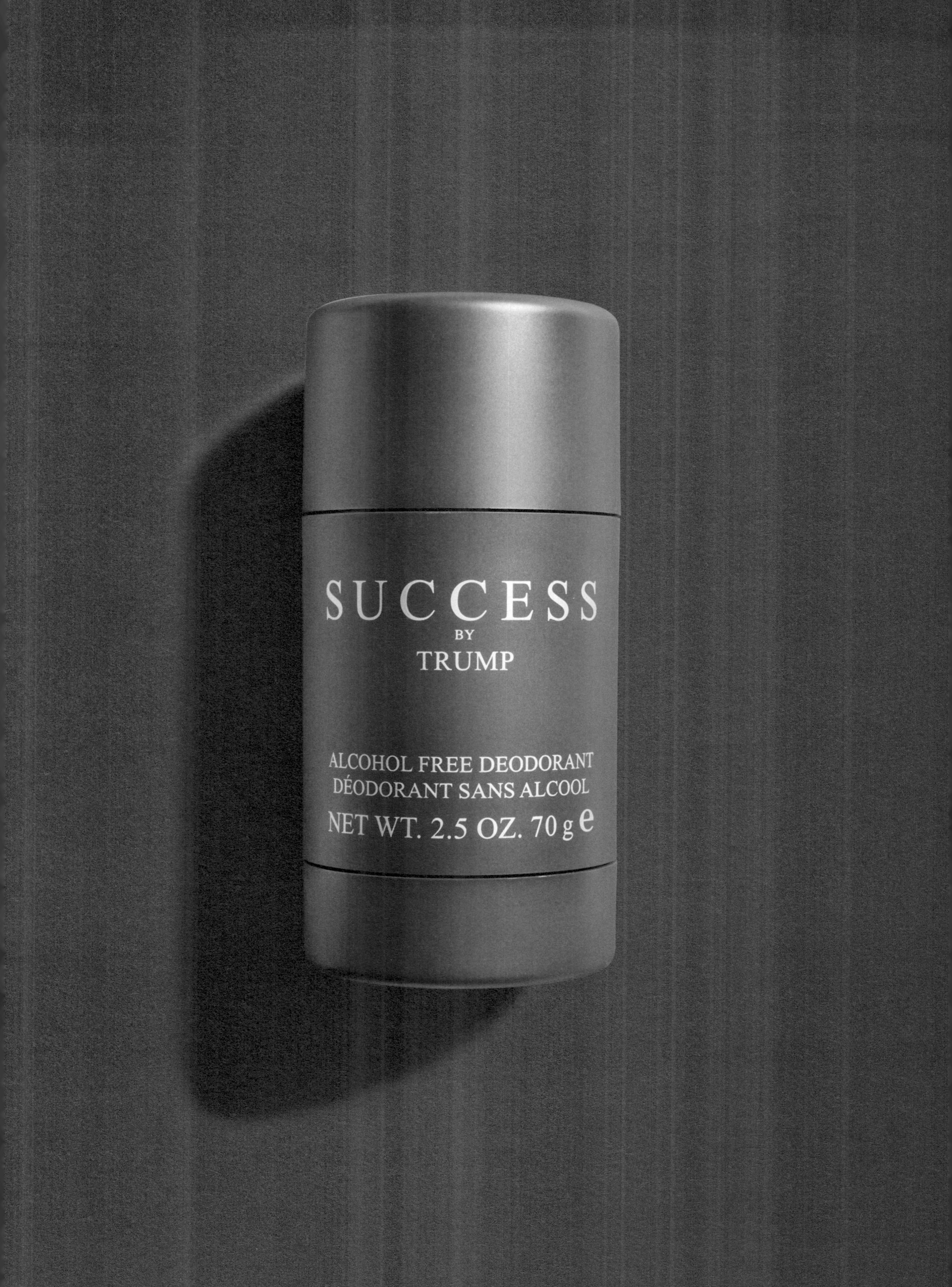

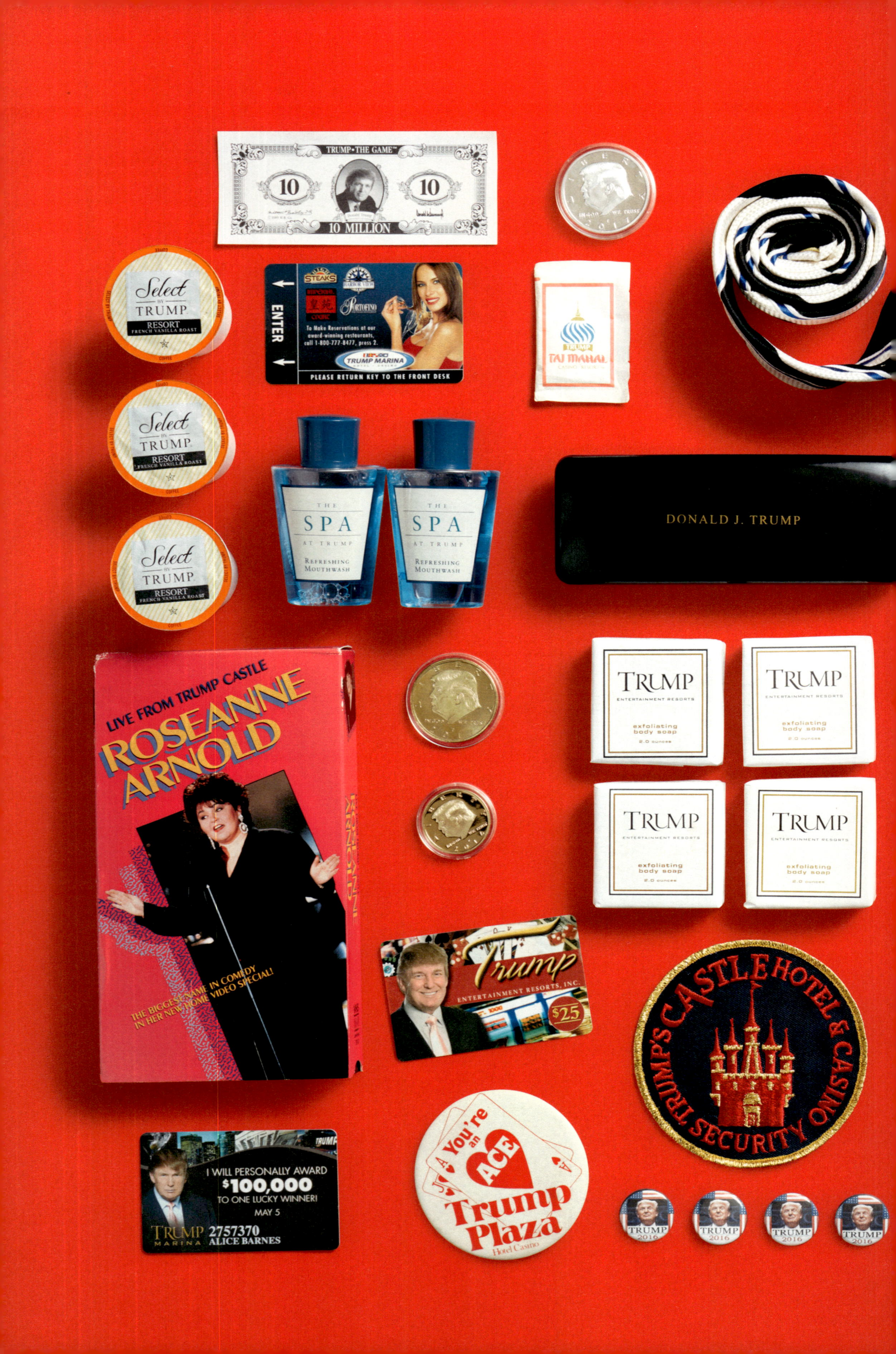

TRUMP • THE GAME
10
10
10 MILLION
Select
BY
TRUMP
RESORT
FRENCH VANILLA ROAST
ENTER
STEAKS
PORTOFINO
To Make Reservations at our award-winning restaurants, call 1-800-777-8477, press 2.
TRUMP MARINA
PLEASE RETURN KEY TO THE FRONT DESK
TRUMP
TAJ MAHAL
THE
SPA
AT TRUMP
REFRESHING
MOUTHWASH
DONALD J. TRUMP
LIVE FROM TRUMP CASTLE
ROSEANNE
ARNOLD
THE BIGGEST NAME IN COMEDY
IN HER NEW HOME VIDEO SPECIAL!
TRUMP
ENTERTAINMENT RESORTS
exfoliating
body soap
Trump
ENTERTAINMENT RESORTS, INC.
$25
TRUMP'S CASTLE HOTEL & CASINO
SECURITY
I WILL PERSONALLY AWARD
$100,000
TO ONE LUCKY WINNER!
MAY 5
TRUMP
MARINA
2757370
ALICE BARNES
You're an
ACE
Trump
Plaza
Hotel Casino
TRUMP
2016

SELECTION OF TRUMP-BRANDED OBJECTS

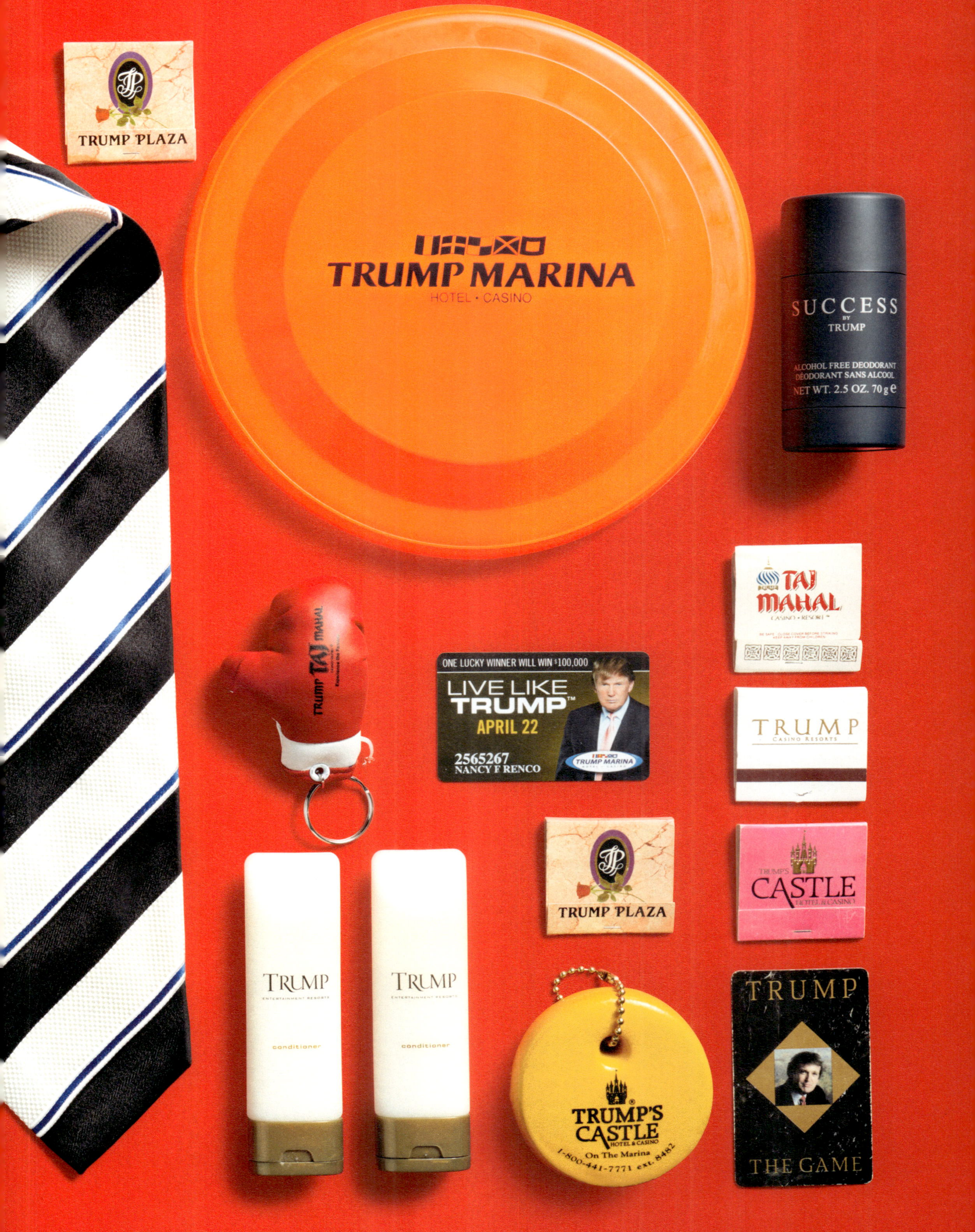

INVITATION POSTER FOR DONALD TRUMP'S 49TH BIRTHDAY PARTY
AT TRUMP'S CASTLE, JUNE 17, 1995

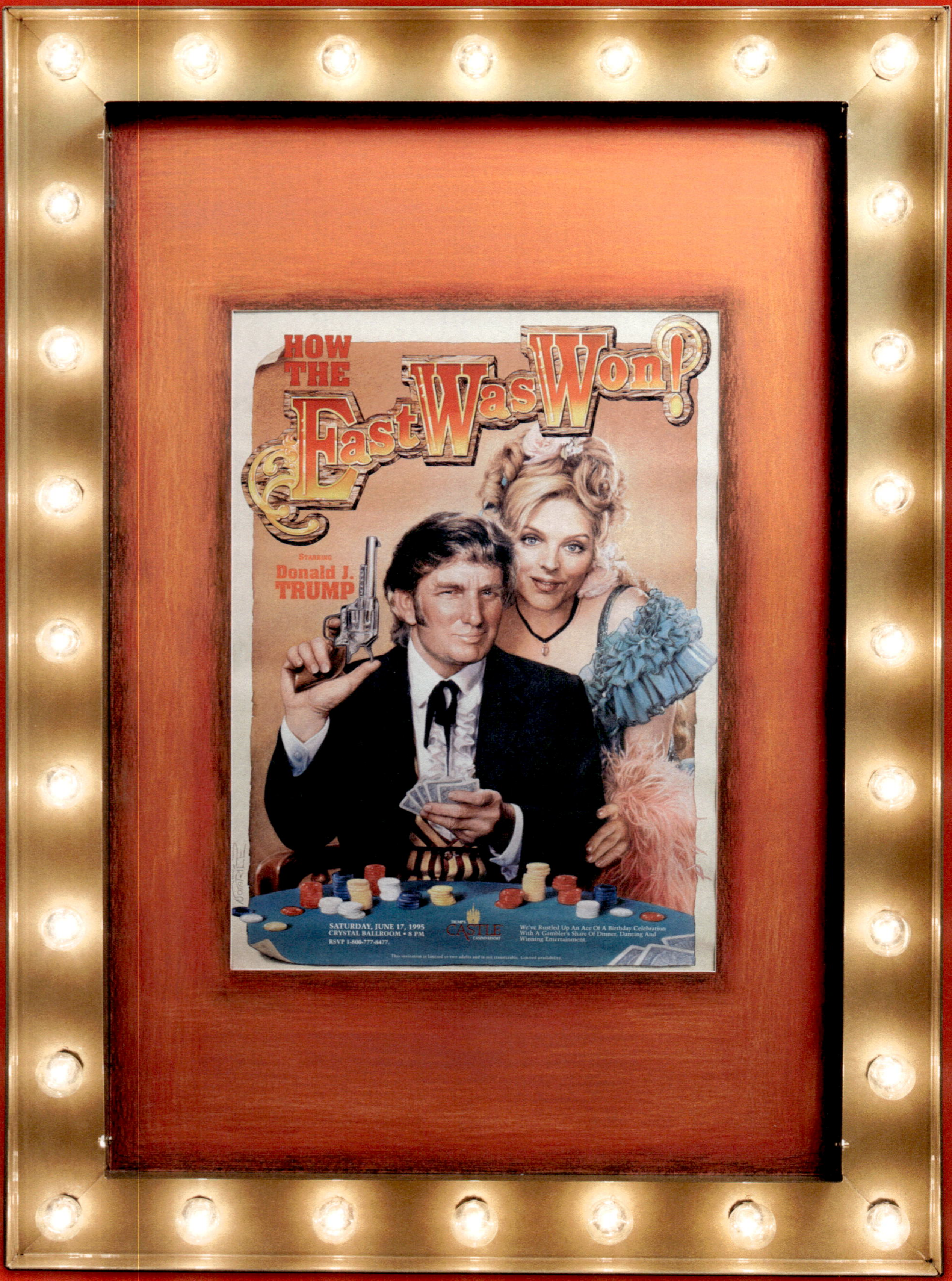

INVITATION POSTER FOR DONALD TRUMP'S 48TH BIRTHDAY PARTY
AT TRUMP'S CASTLE, JULY 23, 1994

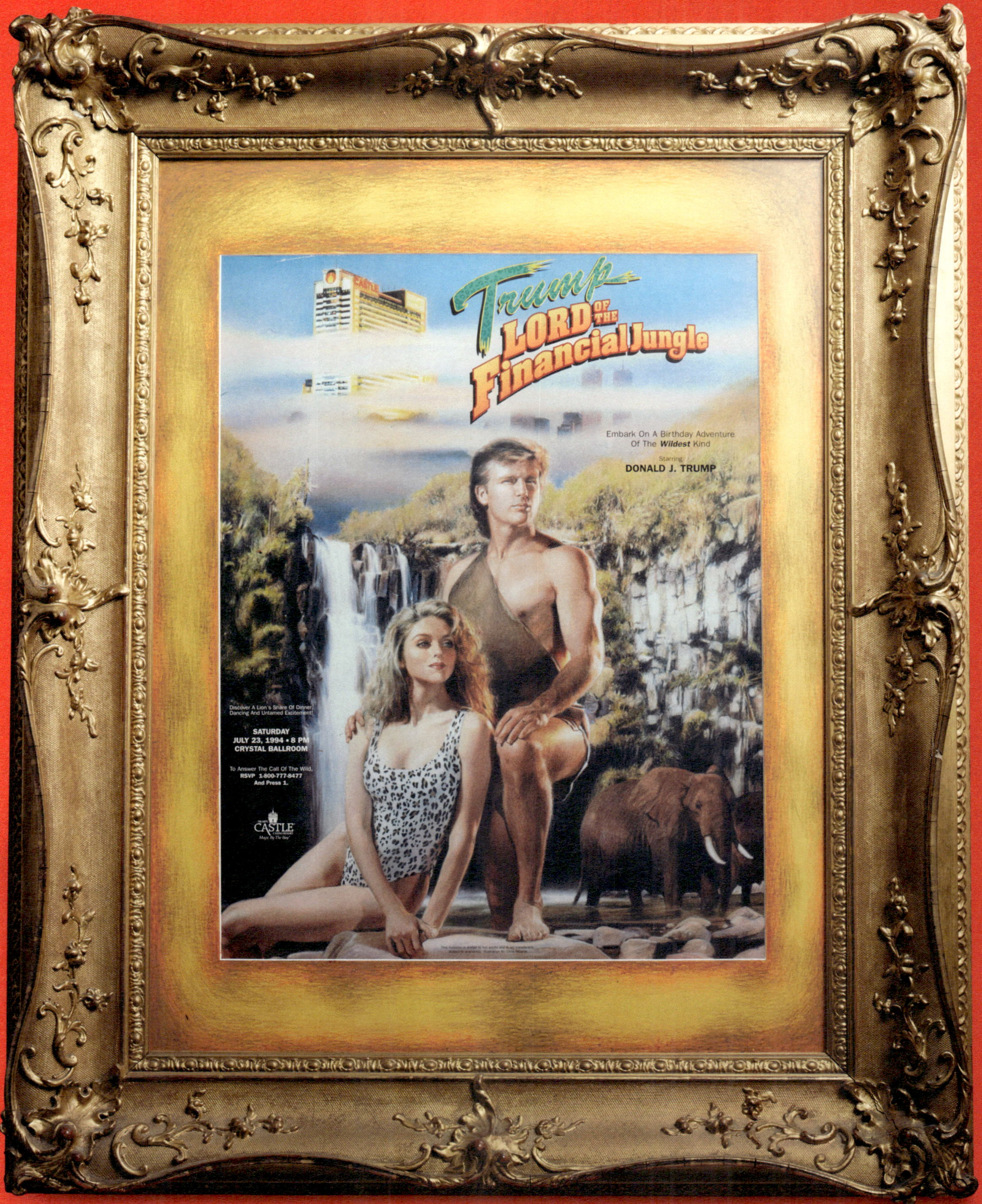

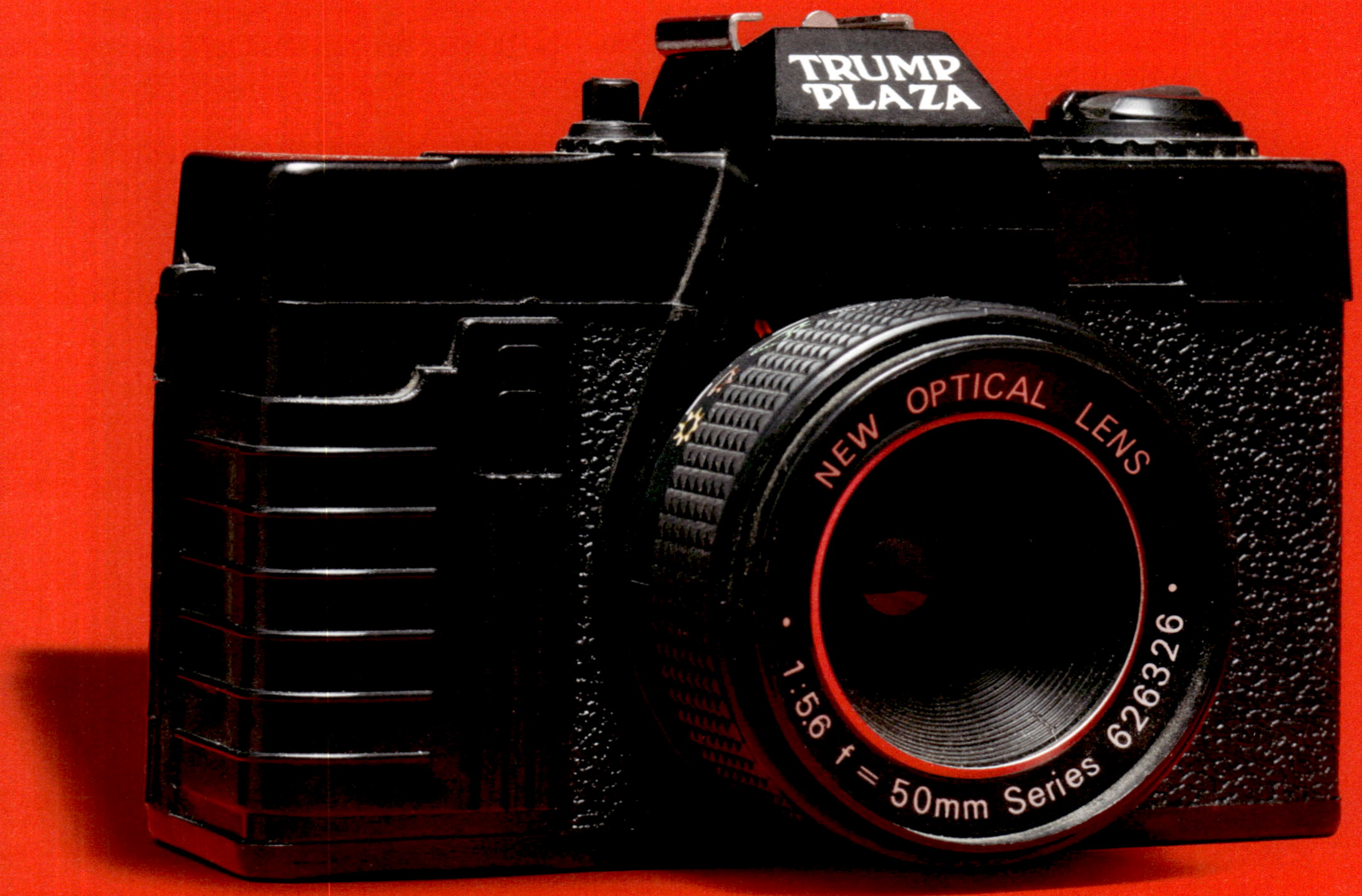
TRUMP
PLAZA
NEW OPTICAL LENS
1:5.6 f = 50mm Series 626326

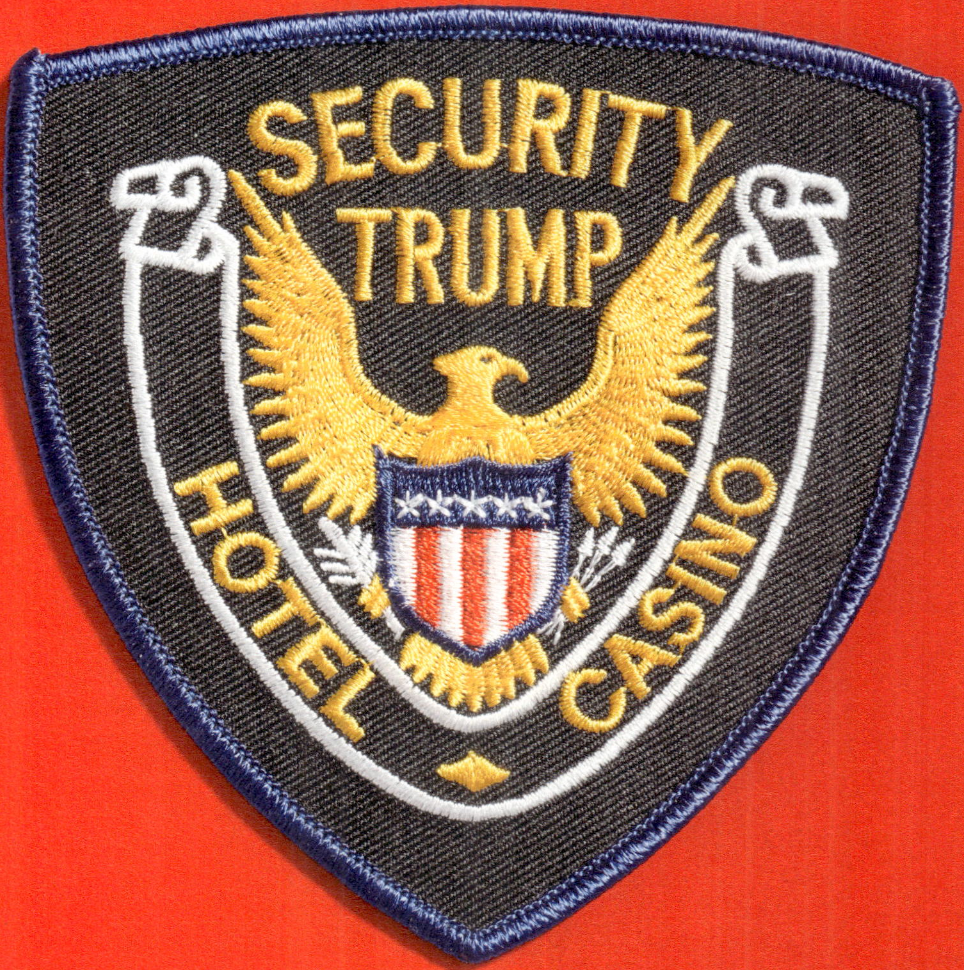
SECURITY
TRUMP
HOTEL
CASINO

DONALD TRUMP'S REAL ESTATE TYCOON VIDEO GAME FOR PC, 2002

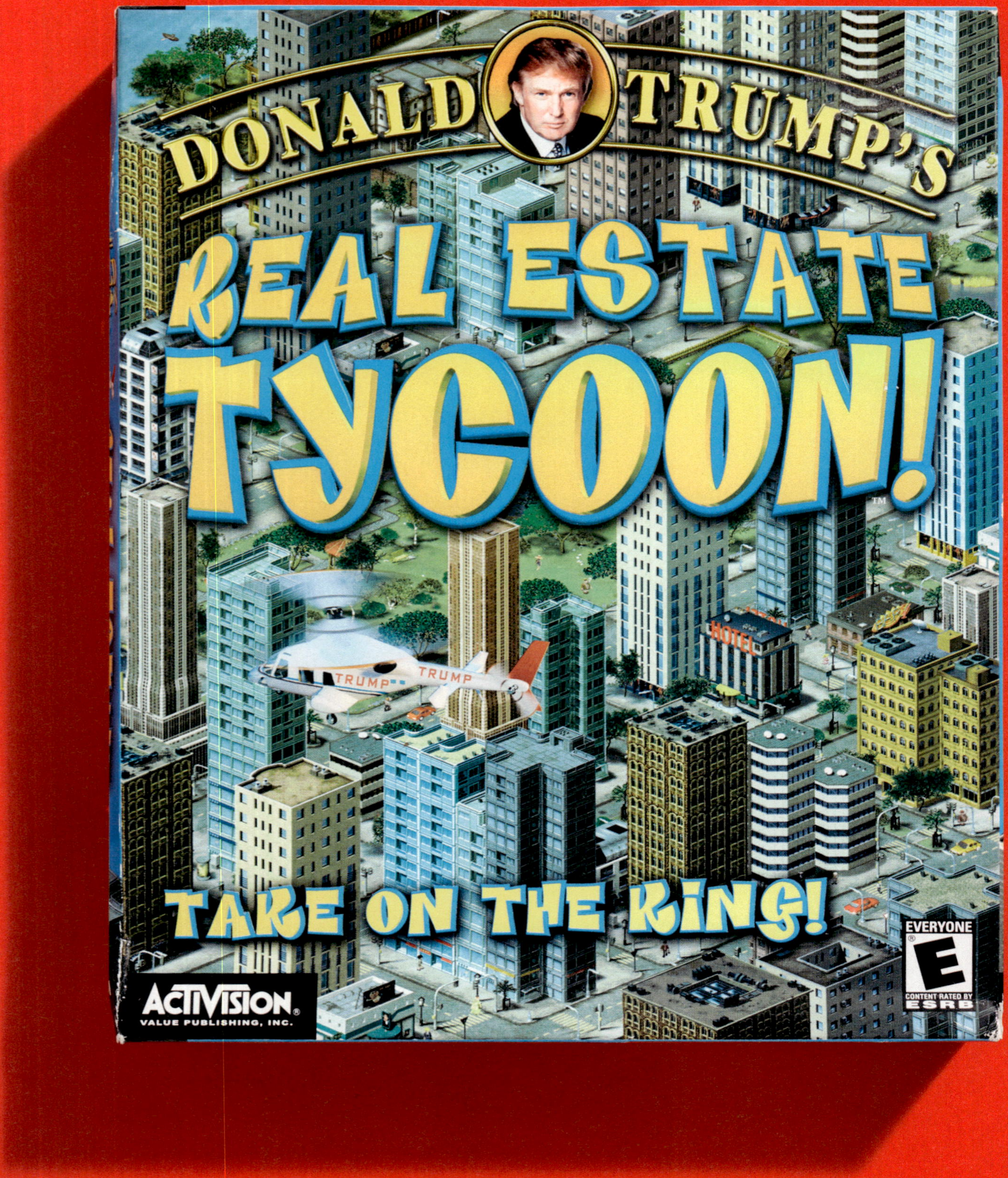

NEWSWEEK MAGAZINE, SEPTEMBER 28, 1987
SIGNED DONALD TRUMP

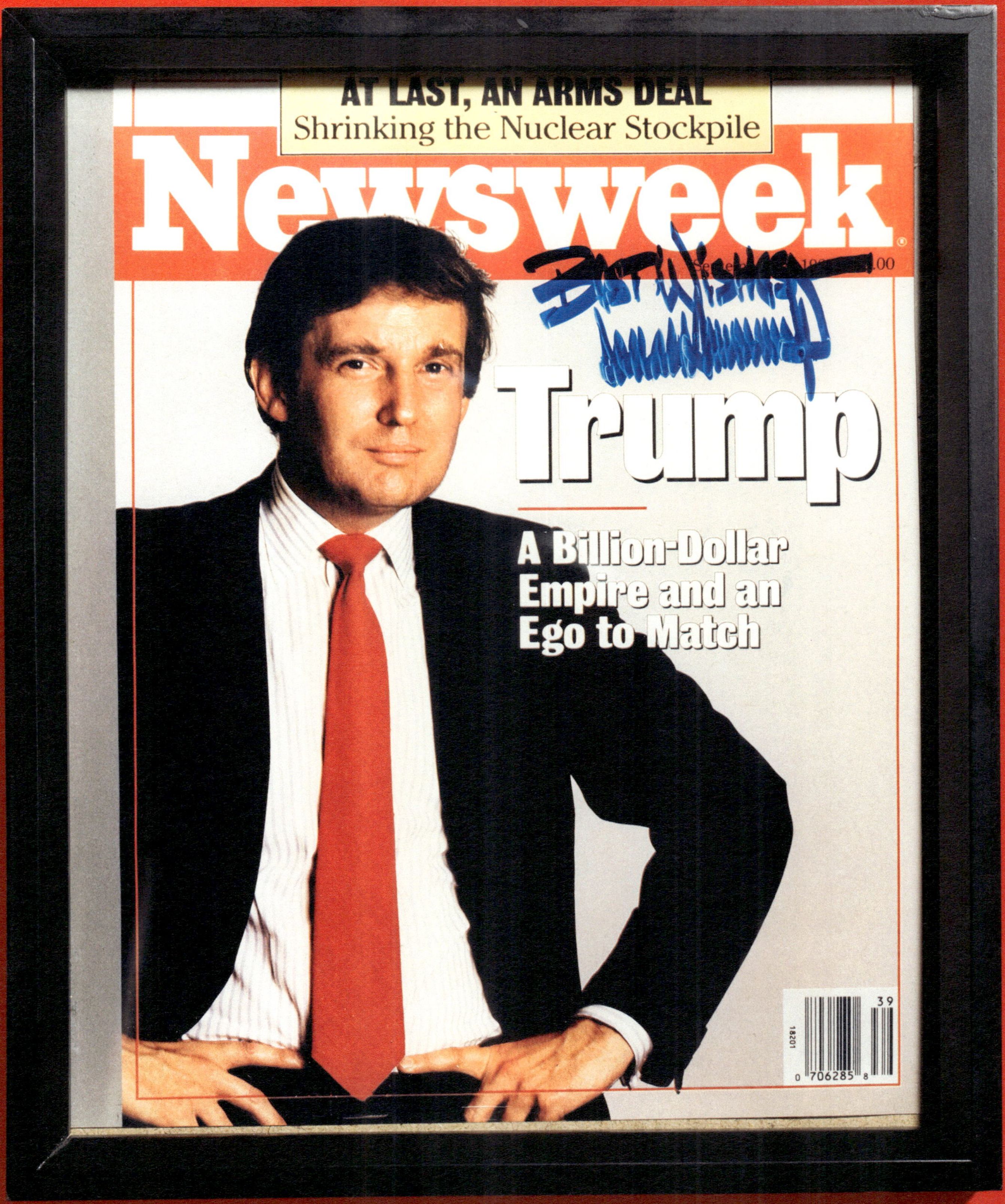

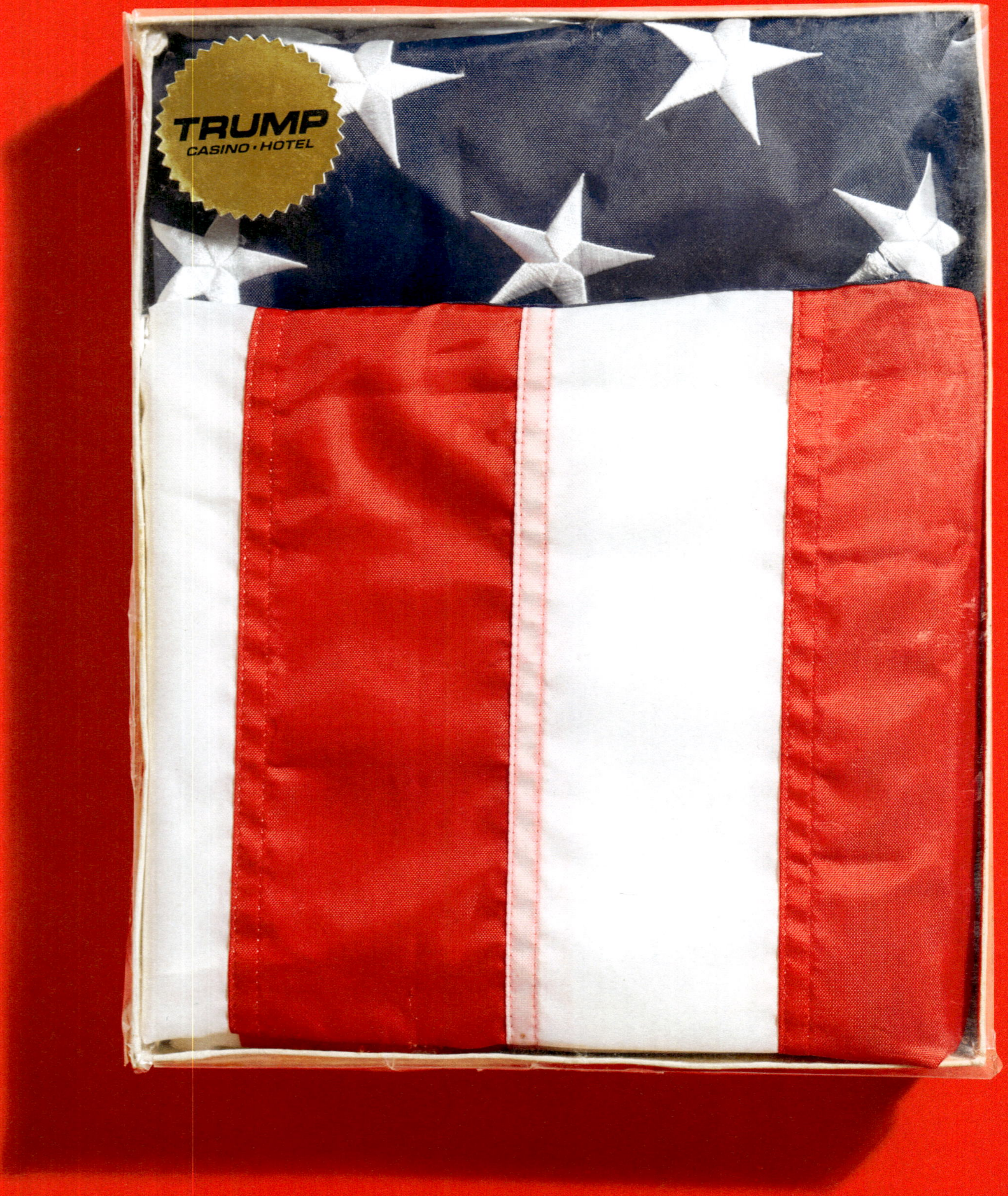
TRUMP
CASINO · HOTEL

DONALD J. TRUMP 12-INCH TALKING DOLL
PHRASES INCLUDE: "THINK BIG AND LIVE LARGE;
THAT WAS A TOUGH ONE;
NEVER GIVE UP....UNDER ANY CIRCUMSTANCES, NEVER GIVE UP"

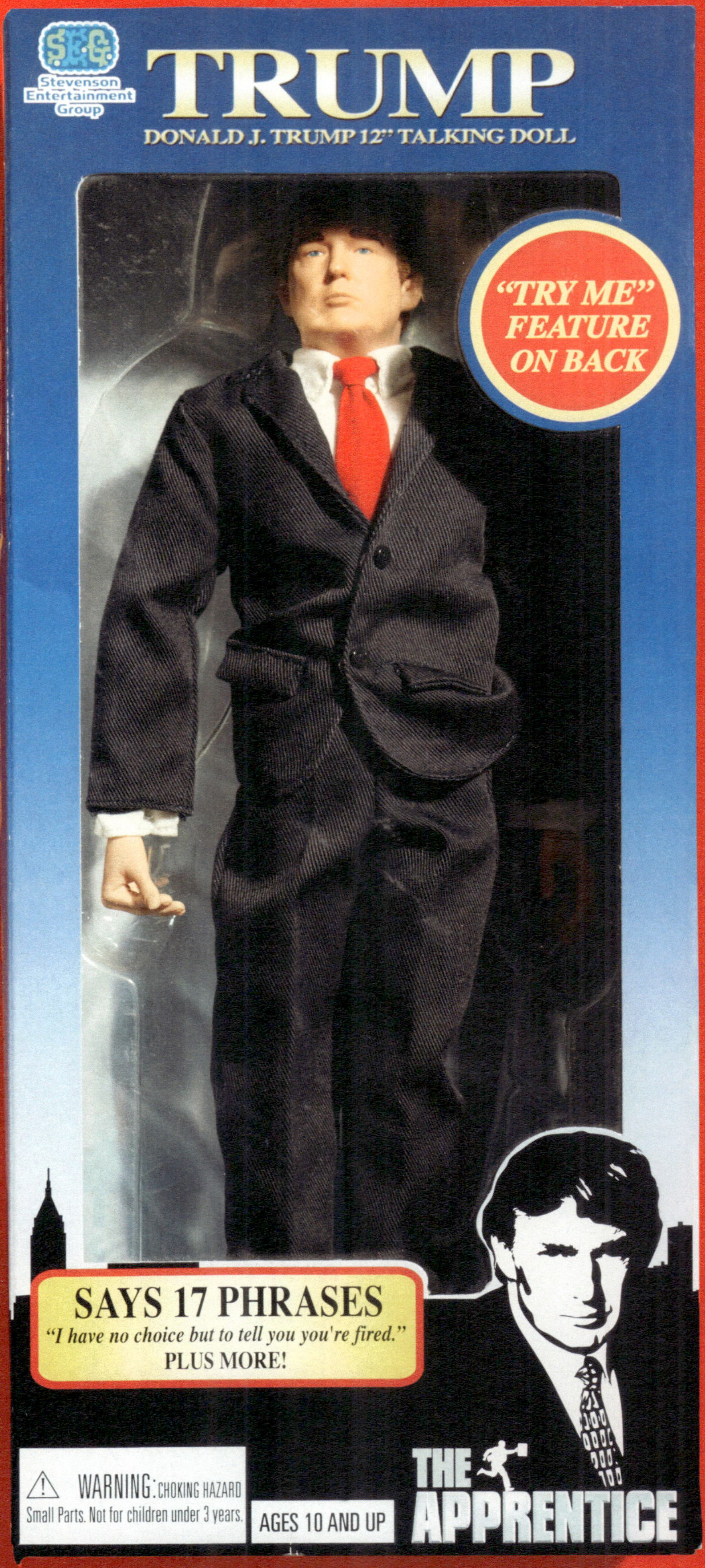

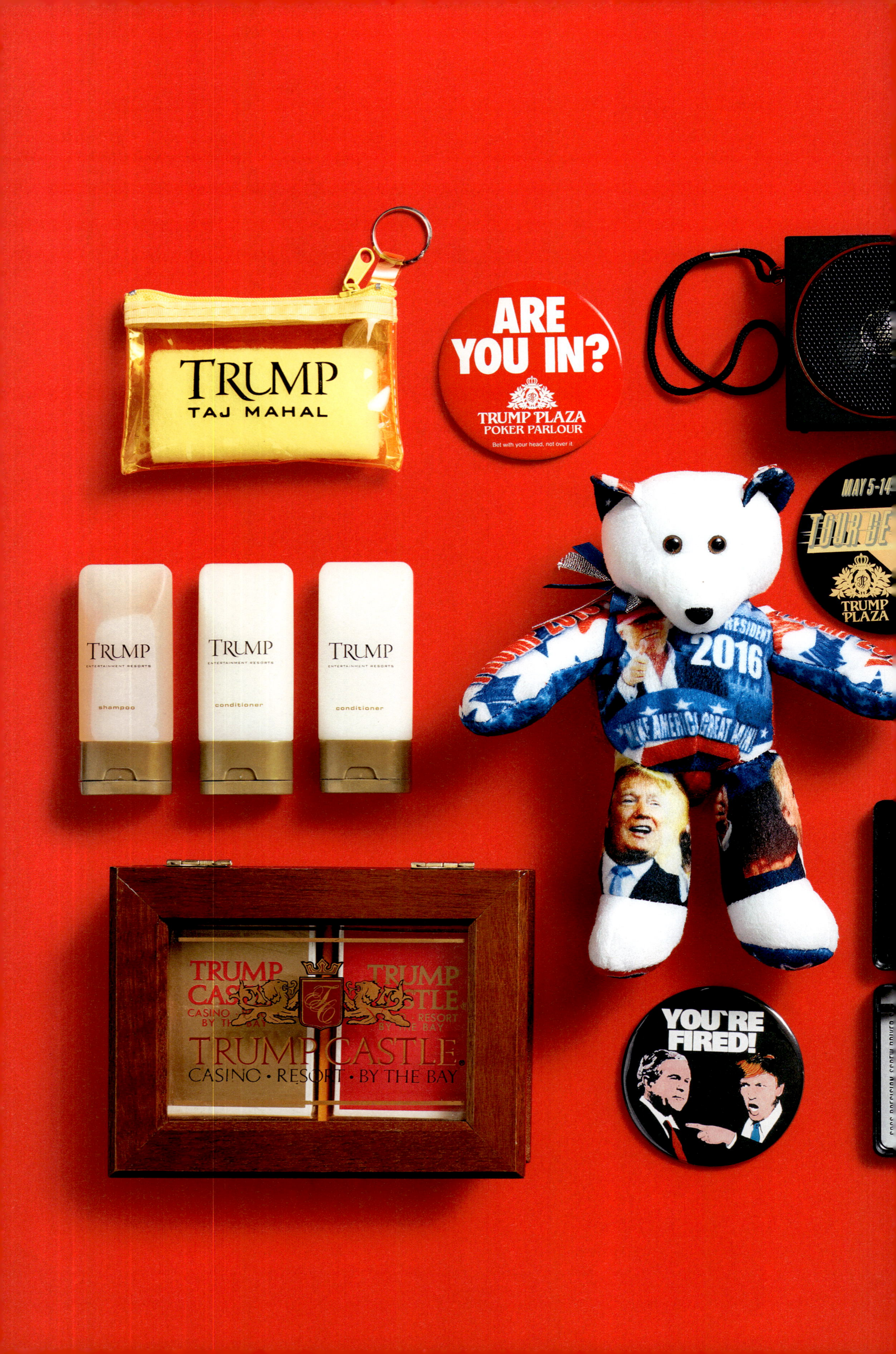
TRUMP
TAJ MAHAL
ARE YOU IN?
TRUMP PLAZA
POKER PARLOUR
Bet with your head, not over it
TRUMP
shampoo
TRUMP
conditioner
TRUMP
conditioner
2016
MAY 5-14
TRUMP PLAZA
TRUMP CASTLE
CASINO • RESORT • BY THE BAY
YOU'RE FIRED!

SELECTION OF TRUMP-BRANDED OBJECTS

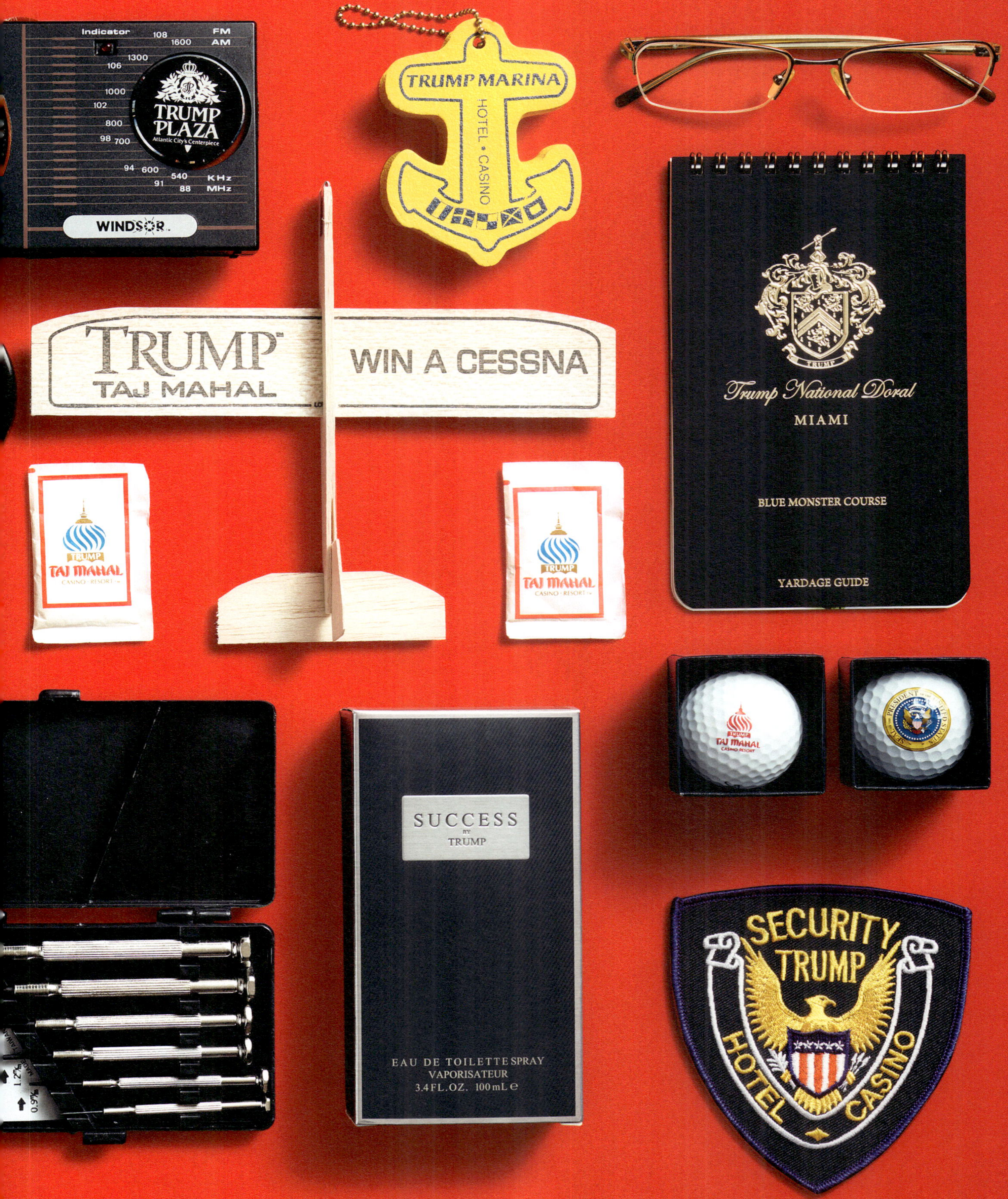

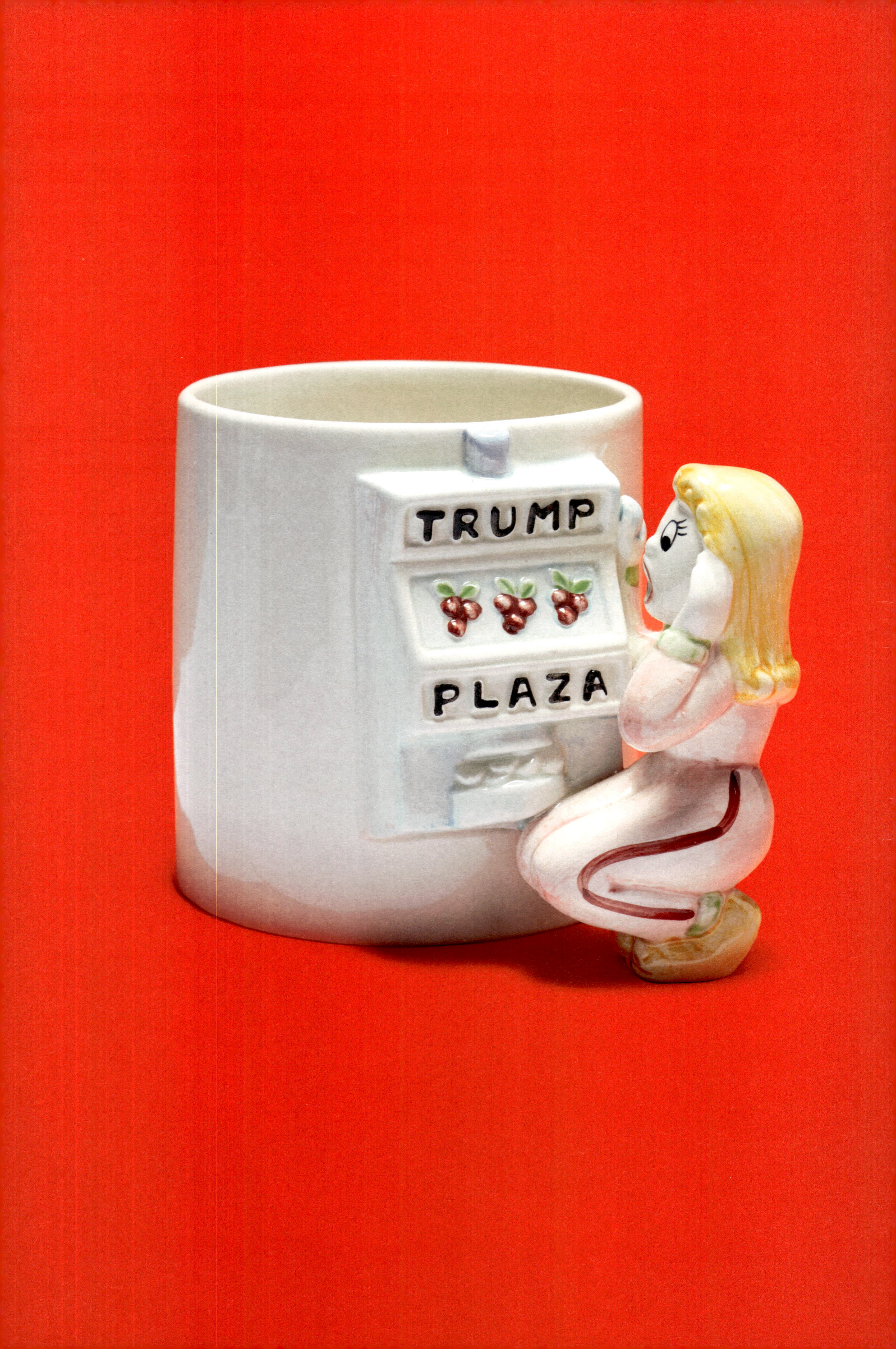
TRUMP
PLAZA

VINTAGE TRUMP PLAZA FITZ AND FLOYD
SLOT MACHINE PORCELAIN MUGS

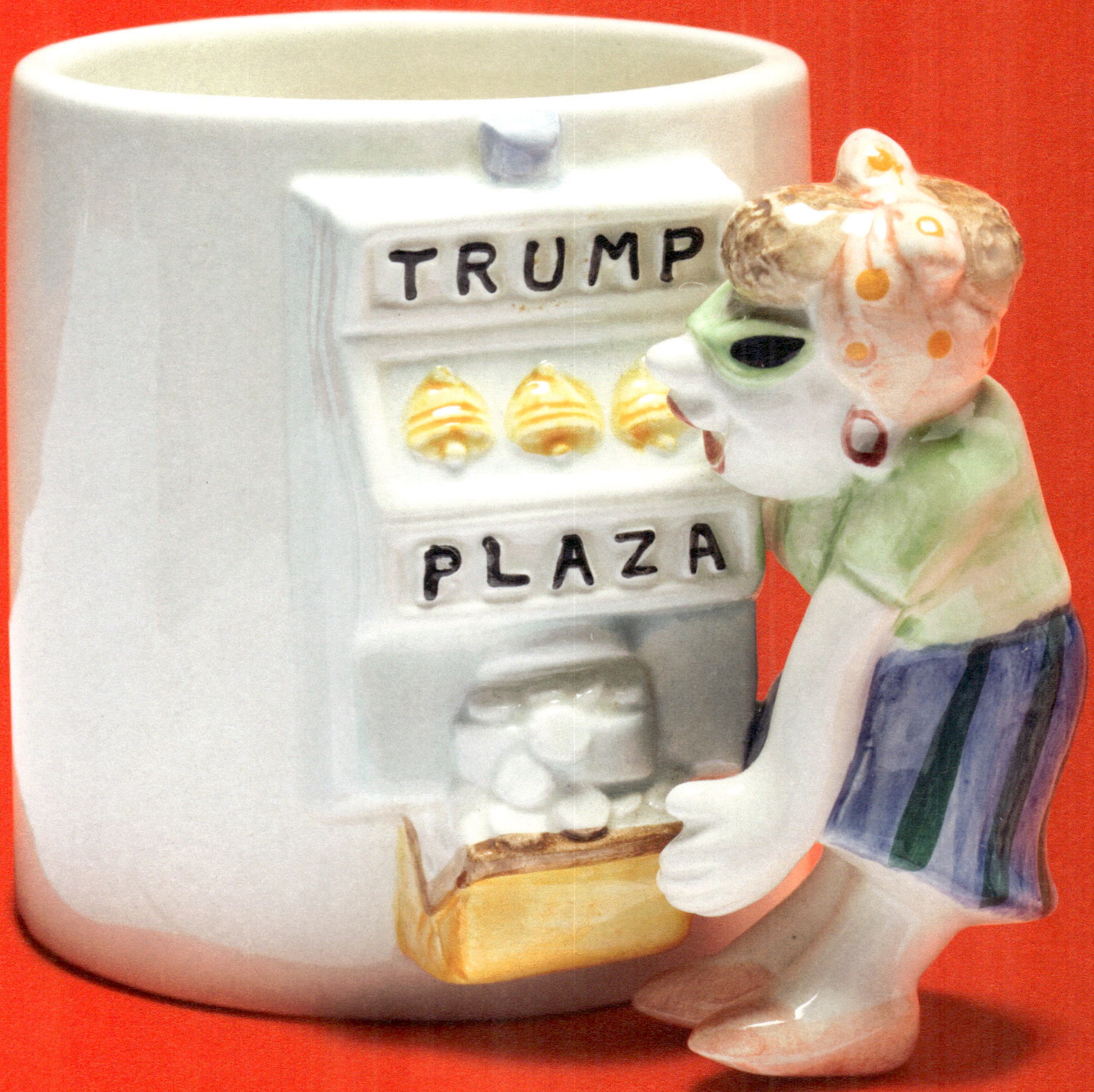

TRUMP TAJ MAHAL SLOT MACHINE PIGGYBANK SOUVENIR

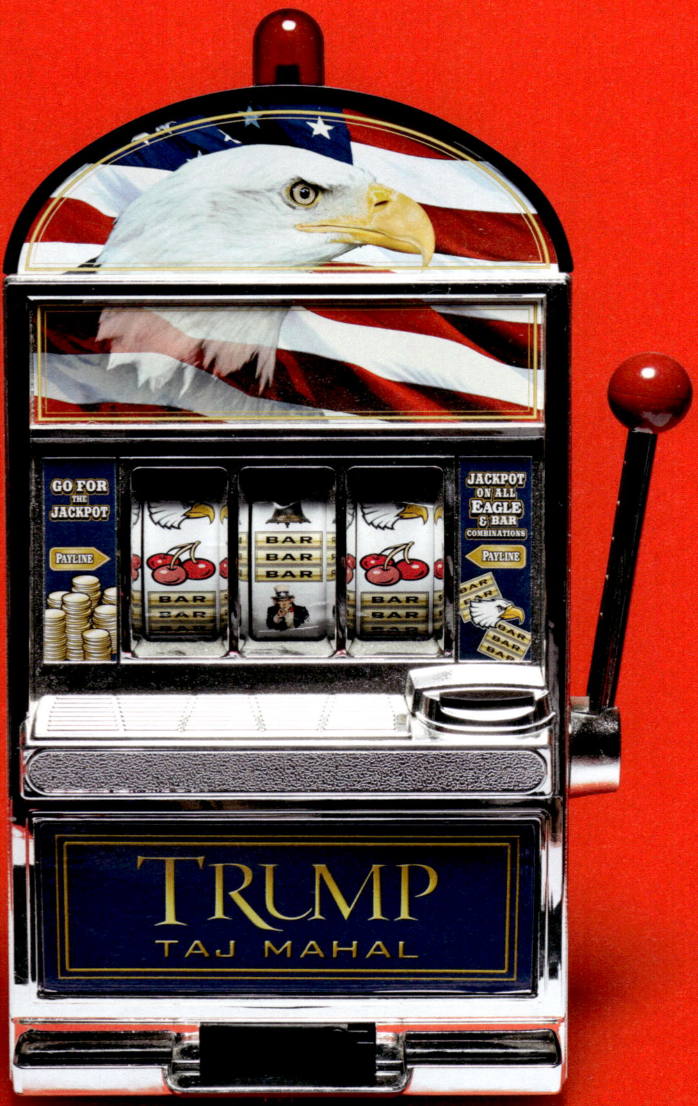

TRUMP PLAZA 25TH ANNIVERSARY CASINO SLOT MACHINE

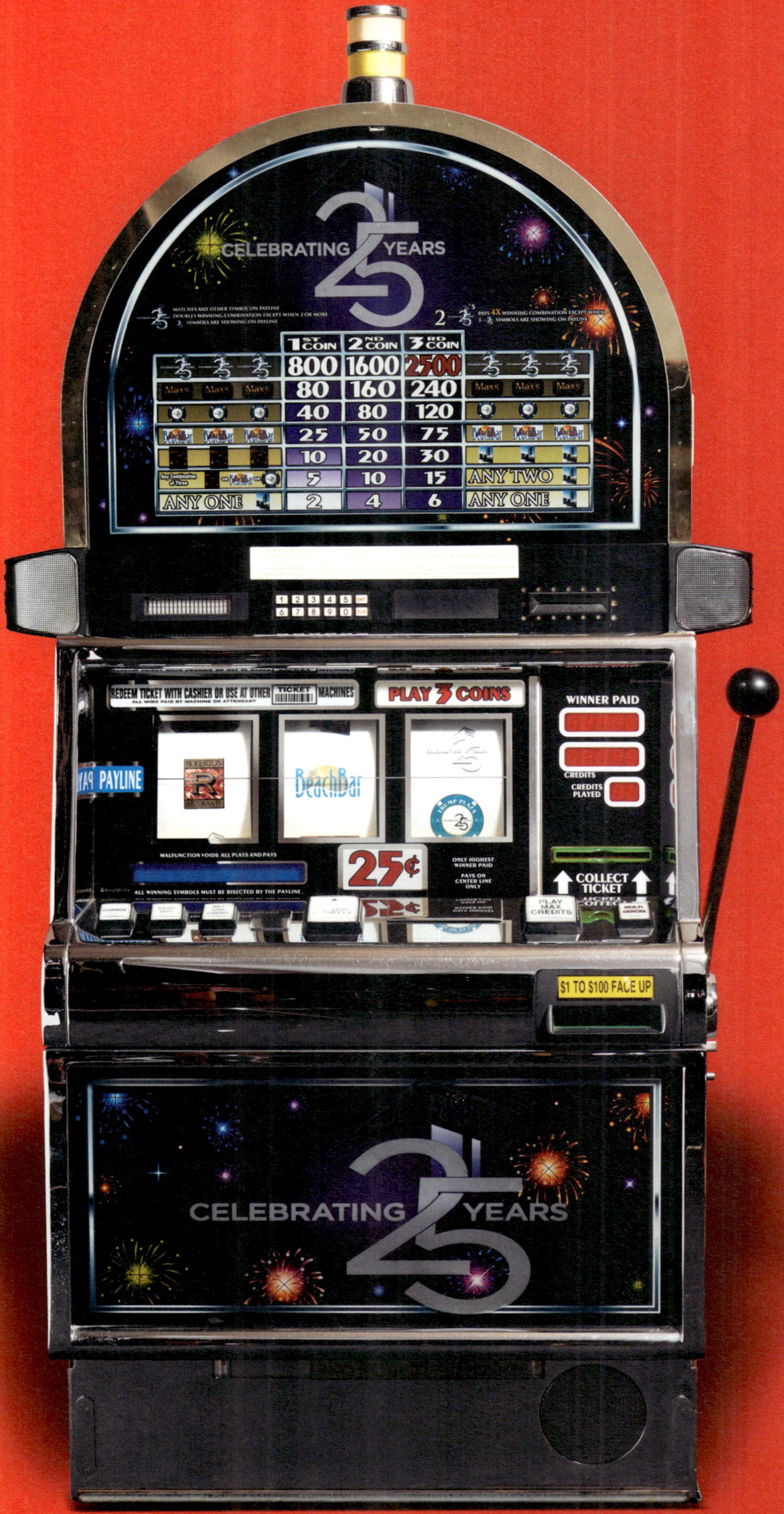

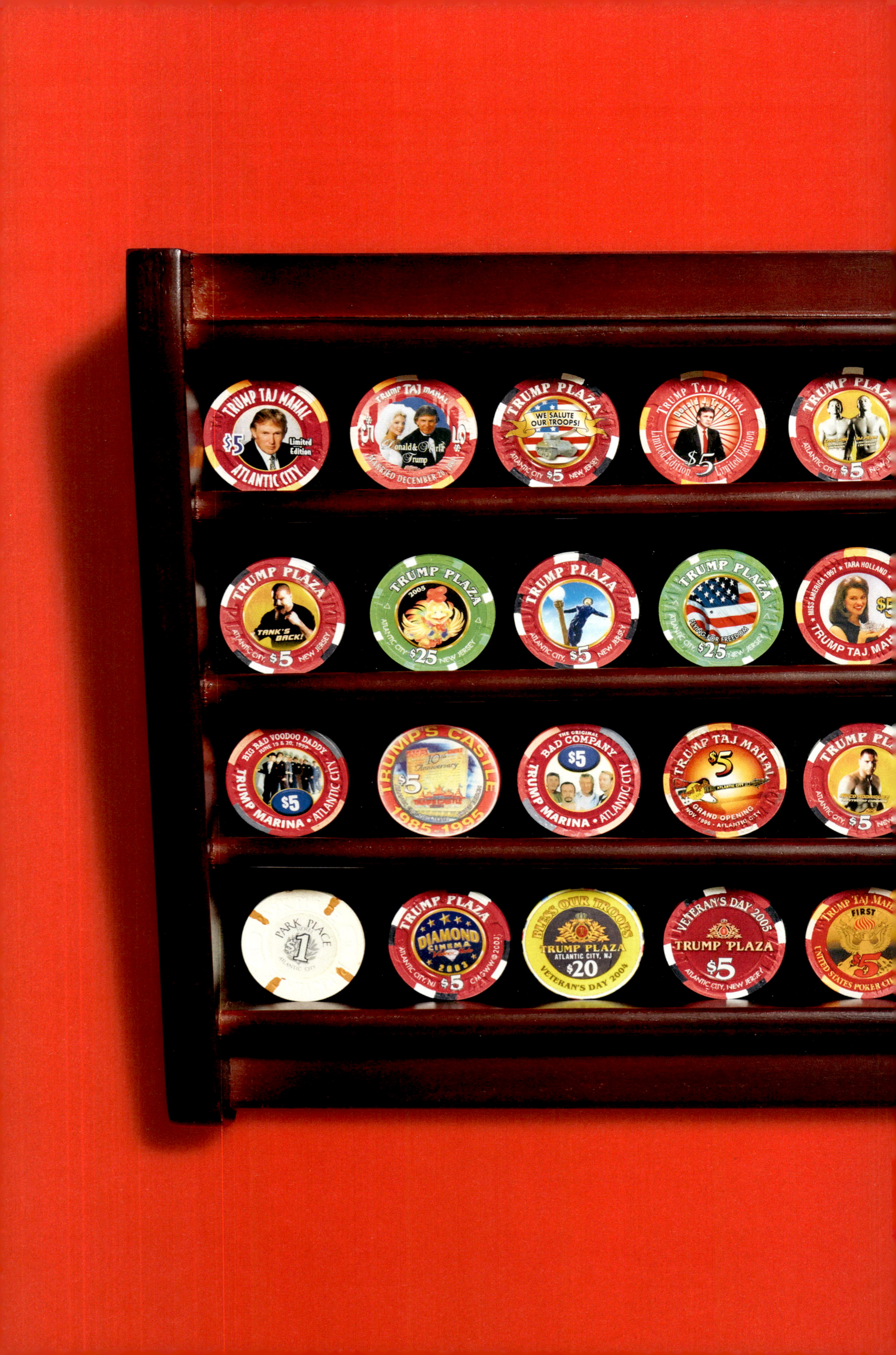

TRUMP TAJ MAHAL
$5
Limited Edition
ATLANTIC CITY
Donald & Marla Trump
TRUMP PLAZA
WE SALUTE OUR TROOPS!
ATLANTIC CITY $5 NEW JERSEY
TRUMP TAJ MAHAL
Donald J. Trump
Limited Edition $5 Limited Edition
TRUMP PLAZA
TANK'S BACK!
ATLANTIC CITY $5 NEW JERSEY
TRUMP PLAZA
2005
ATLANTIC CITY $25 NEW JERSEY
TRUMP PLAZA
ATLANTIC CITY $5 NEW JERSEY
TRUMP PLAZA
FLYING FOR FREEDOM
ATLANTIC CITY $25 NEW JERSEY
MISS AMERICA 1957 ★ TARA HOLLAND
BIG BAD VOODOO DADDY
TRUMP MARINA • ATLANTIC CITY
$5
TRUMP'S CASTLE
10th Anniversary
$5
1985-1995
THE ORIGINAL BAD COMPANY
$5
TRUMP MARINA • ATLANTIC CITY
TRUMP TAJ MAHAL
$5
GRAND OPENING
PARK PLACE
$1
TRUMP PLAZA
DIAMOND CINEMA
2003
ATLANTIC CITY, NJ $5
BLESS OUR TROOPS
TRUMP PLAZA
ATLANTIC CITY, NJ
$20
VETERAN'S DAY 2004
VETERAN'S DAY 2005
TRUMP PLAZA
$5
ATLANTIC CITY, NEW JERSEY
FIRST

SELECTION OF TRUMP MARINA, TRUMP TAJ MAHAL AND TRUMP PLAZA CASINO CHIPS

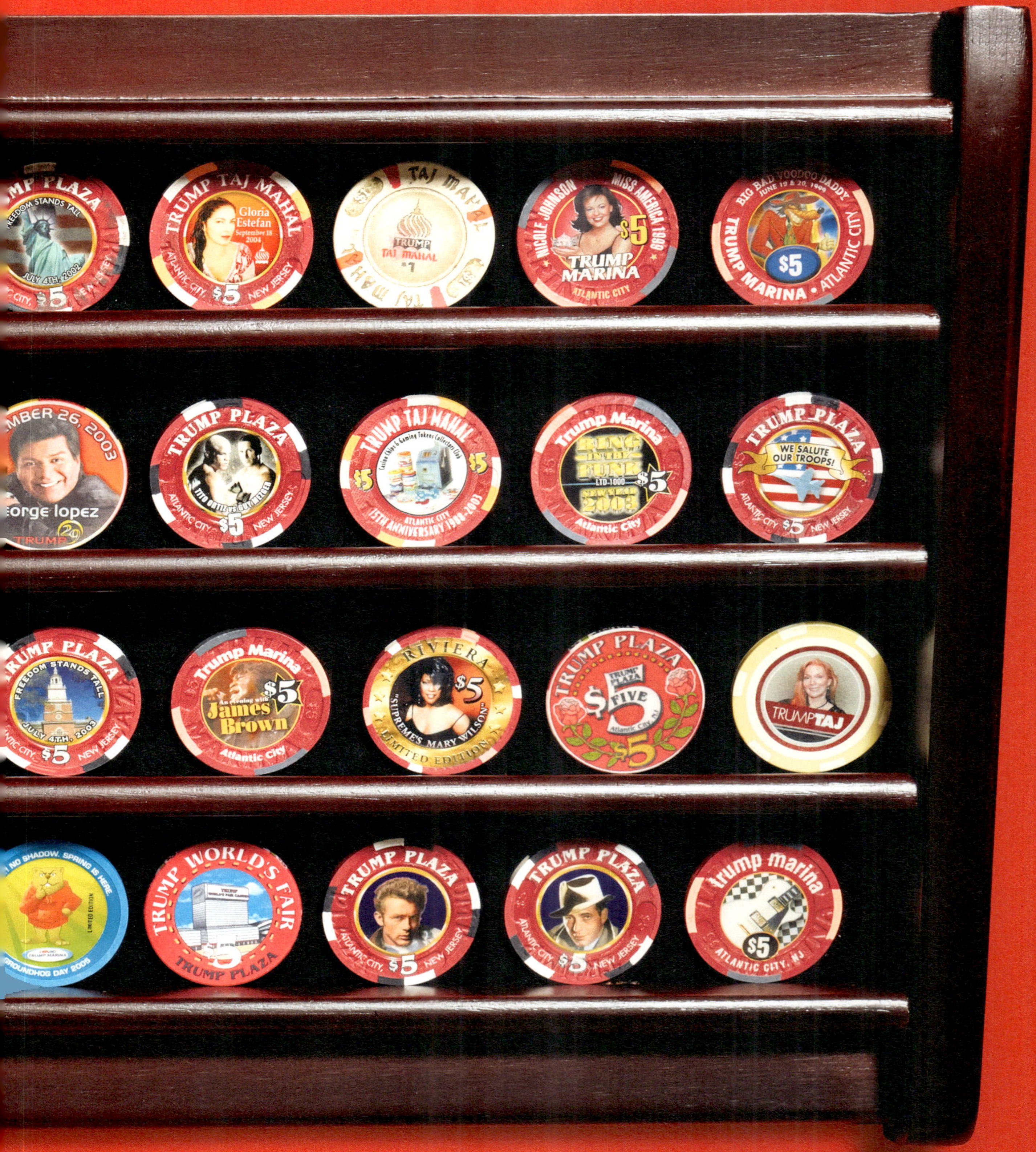

SIGNED PHOTOGRAPH OF DONALD TRUMP

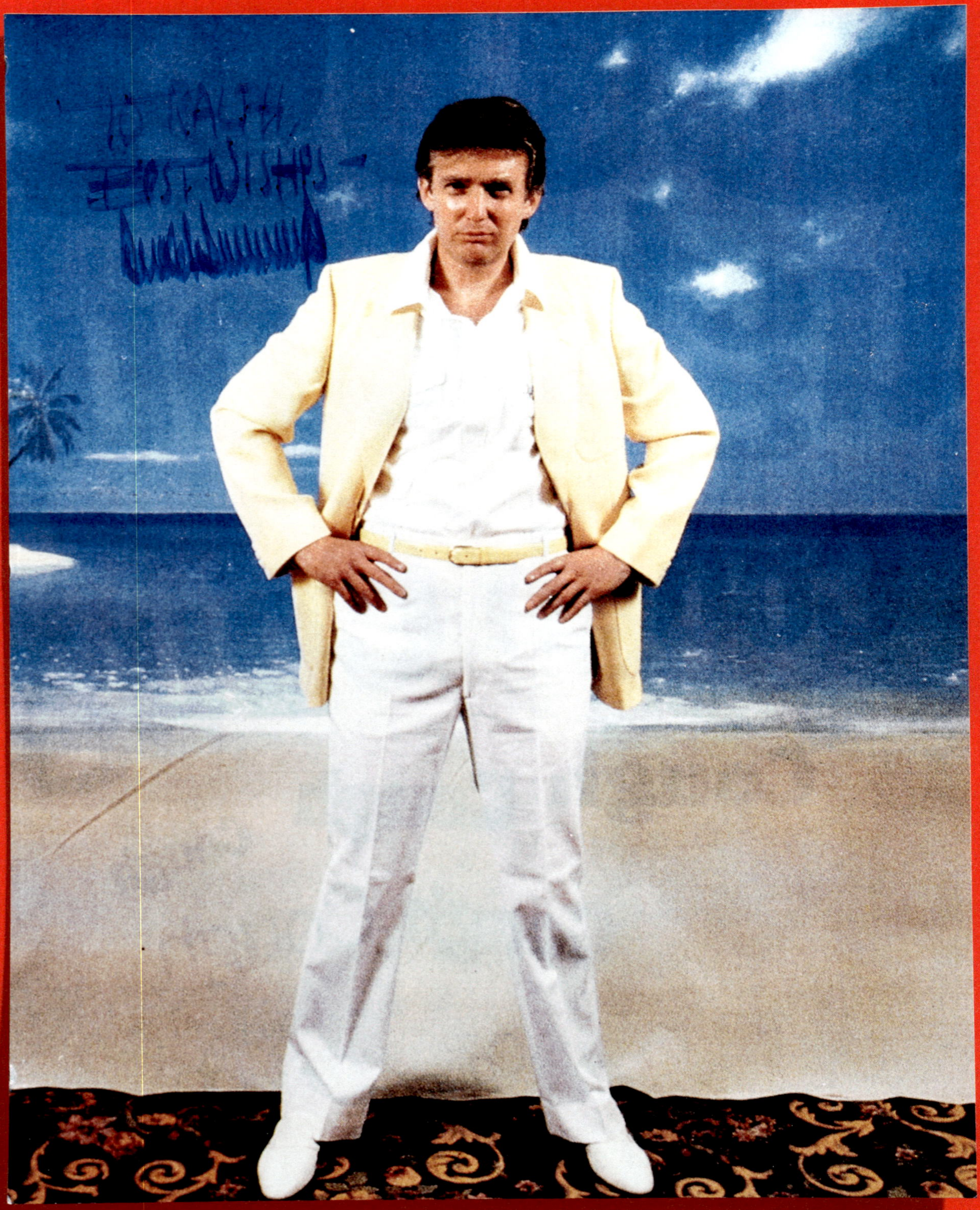

SIGNED PHOTOGRAPH OF MARLA MAPLES, 2008

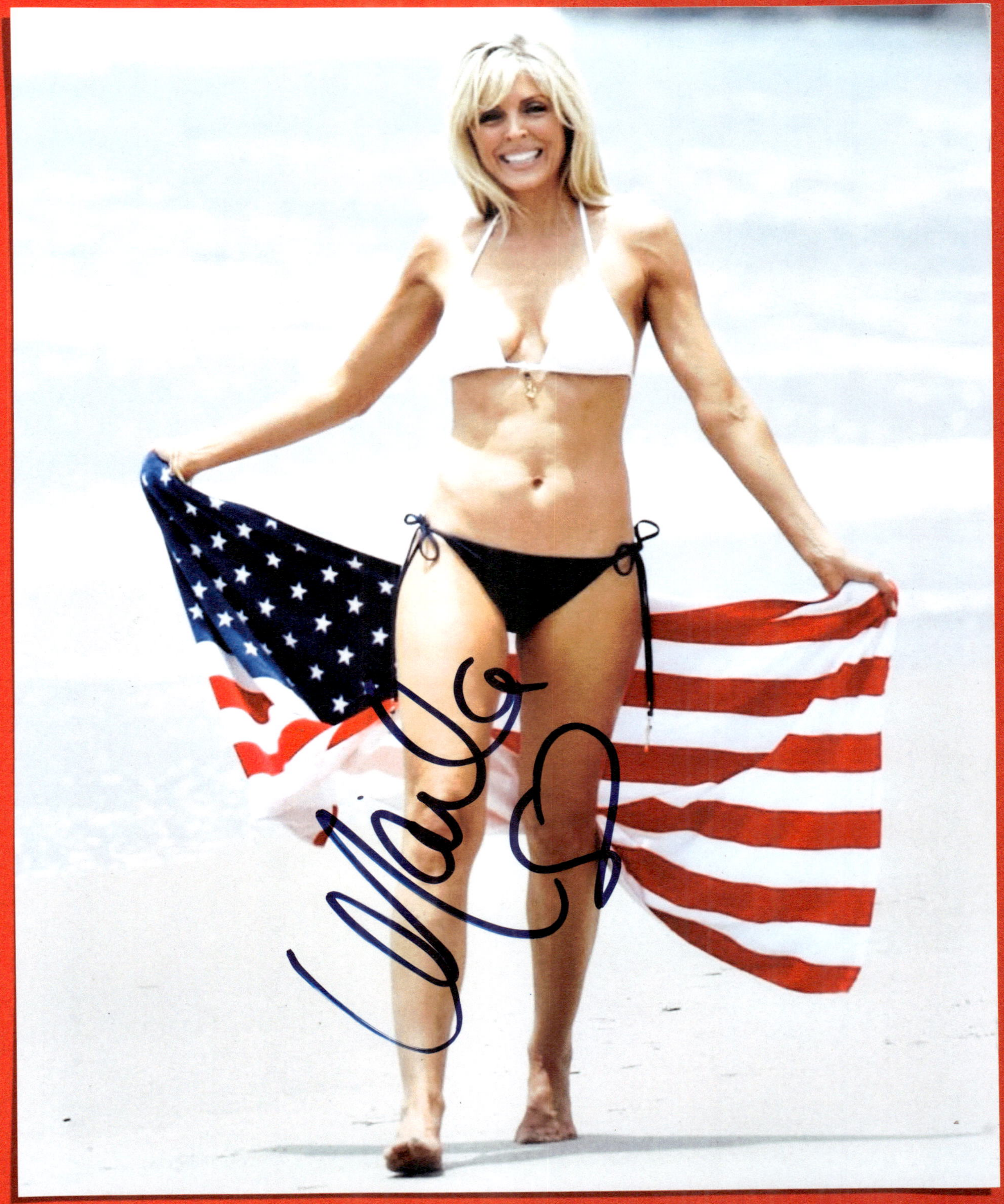

SIGNED PHOTOGRAPH OF IVANKA TRUMP, 2007
COMMISSIONED FOR MAXIM MAGAZINE

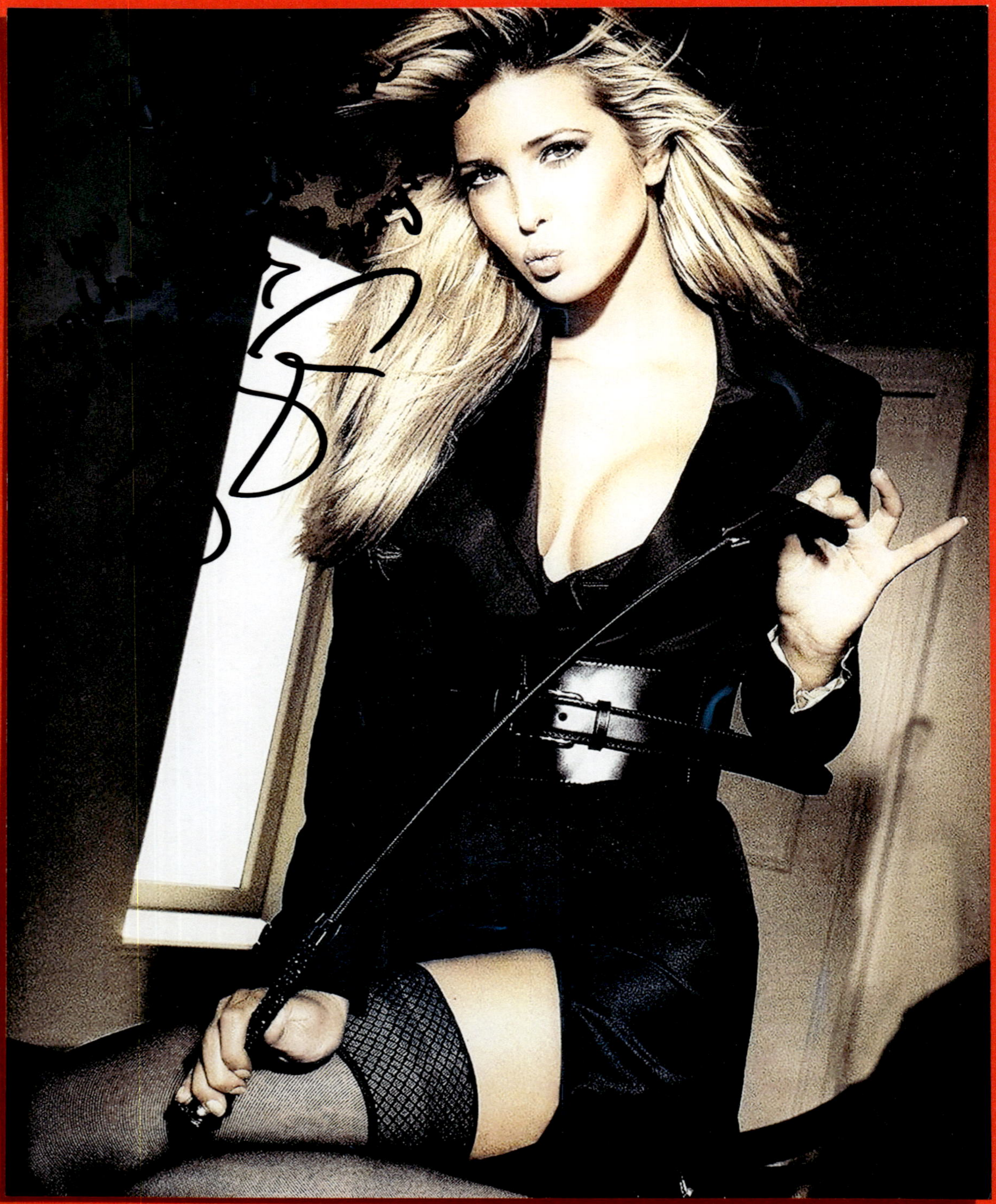

SIGNED PHOTOGRAPH OF DONALD TRUMP, 2004
COMMISSIONED FOR ESQUIRE MAGAZINE

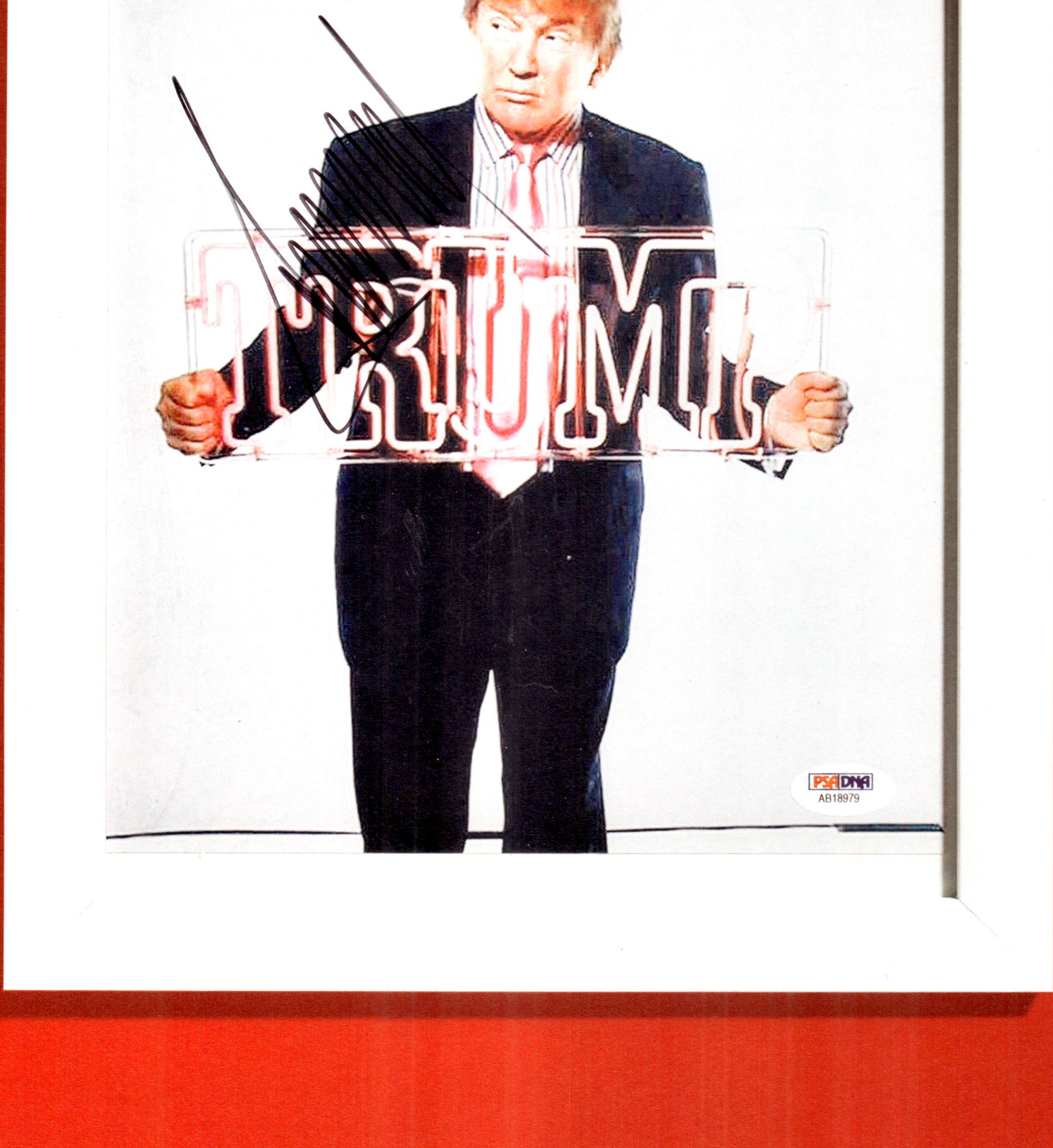

TRUMP PLAZA BRANDED JOHN F. KENNEDY
COMMEMORATIVE COIN FROM 1964

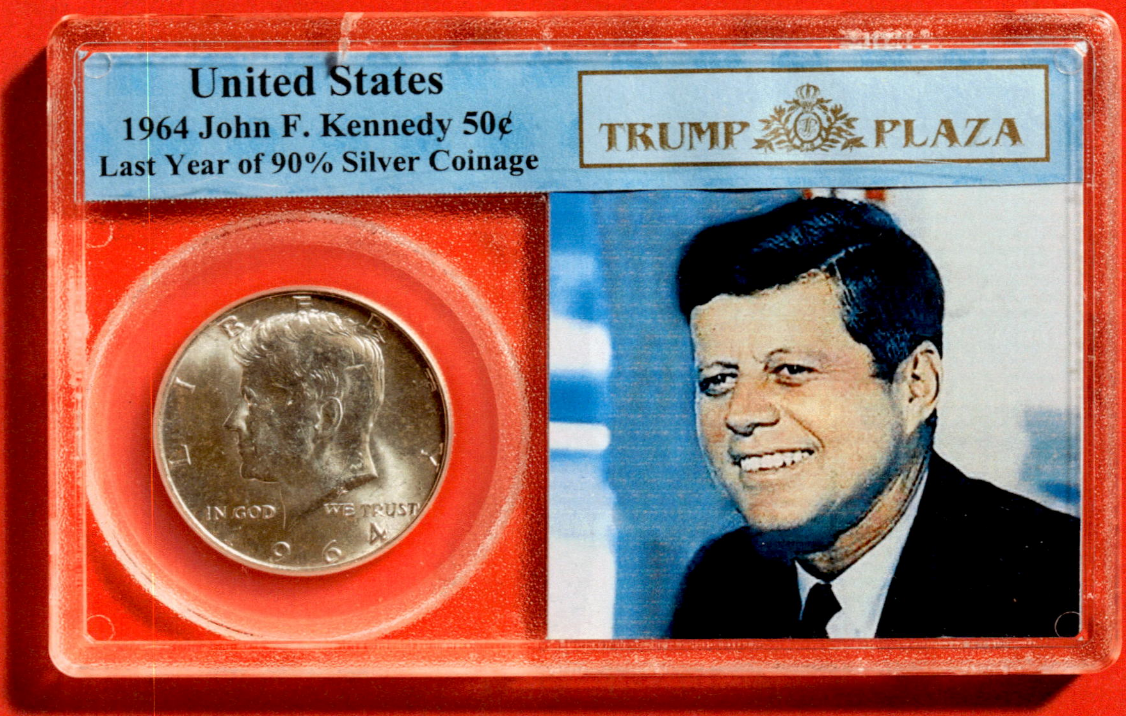

SIGNED PHOTOGRAPH OF DONALD TRUMP
AS HOST OF SATURDAY NIGHT LIVE, 2004

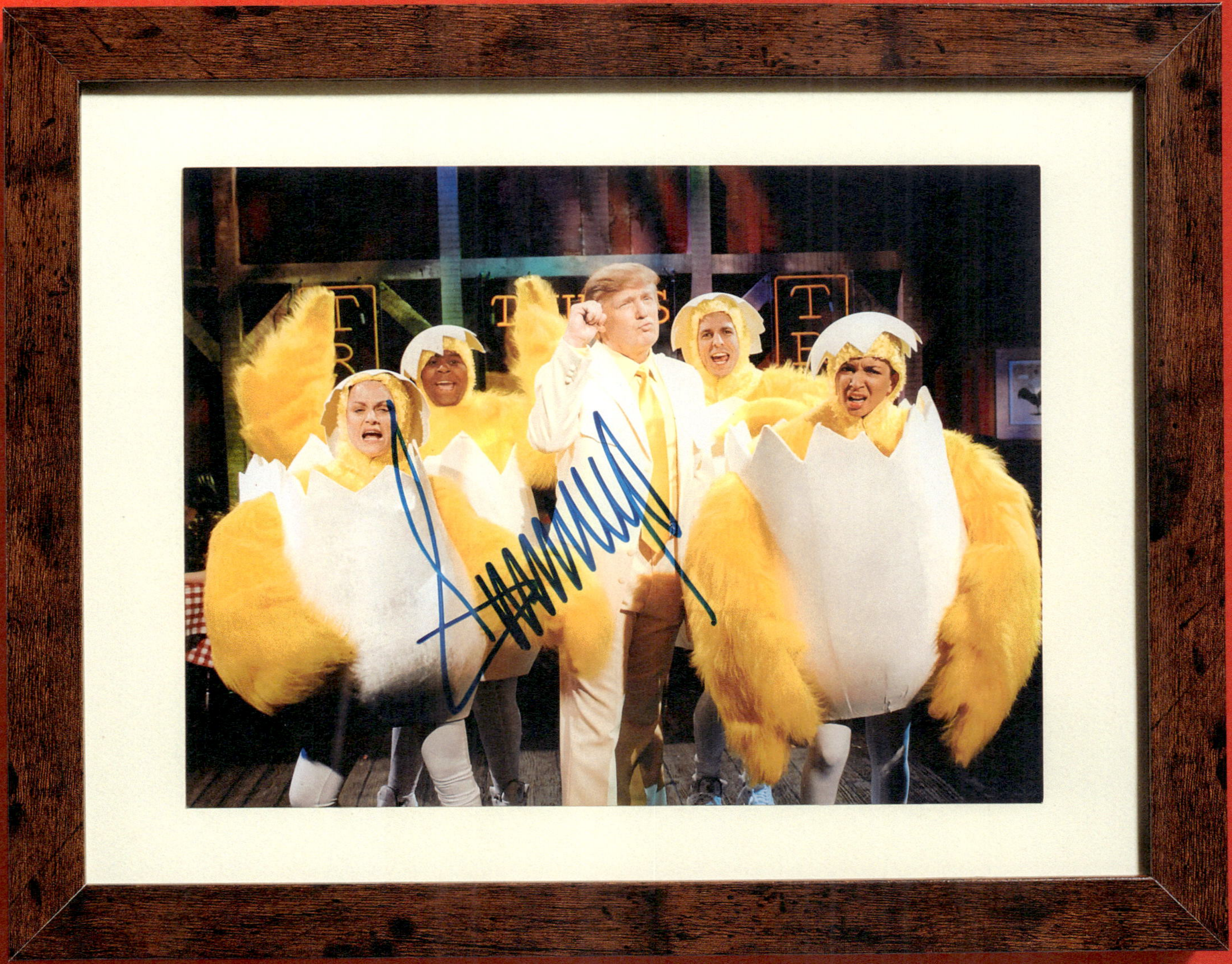

PHOTOGRAPH OF DONALD, IVANA, IVANKA AND ERIC TRUMP FRAMED WITH TITLE PAGE FROM IVANA TRUMP'S ROMANTIC NOVEL "FREE TO LOVE"

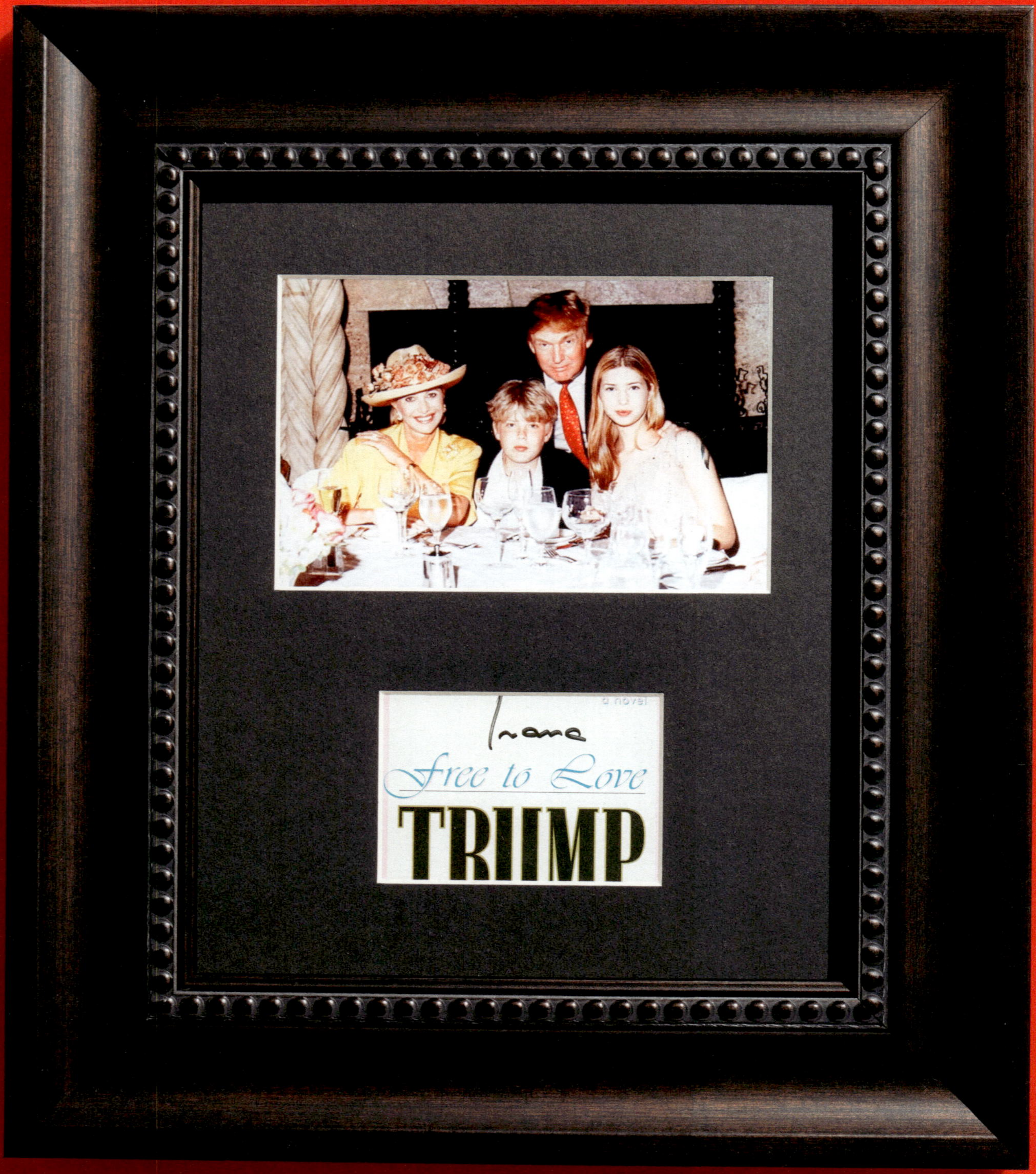

LIMITED EDITION DONALD & MARLA TRUMP
$5 TRUMP TAJ MAHAL CASINO CHIP

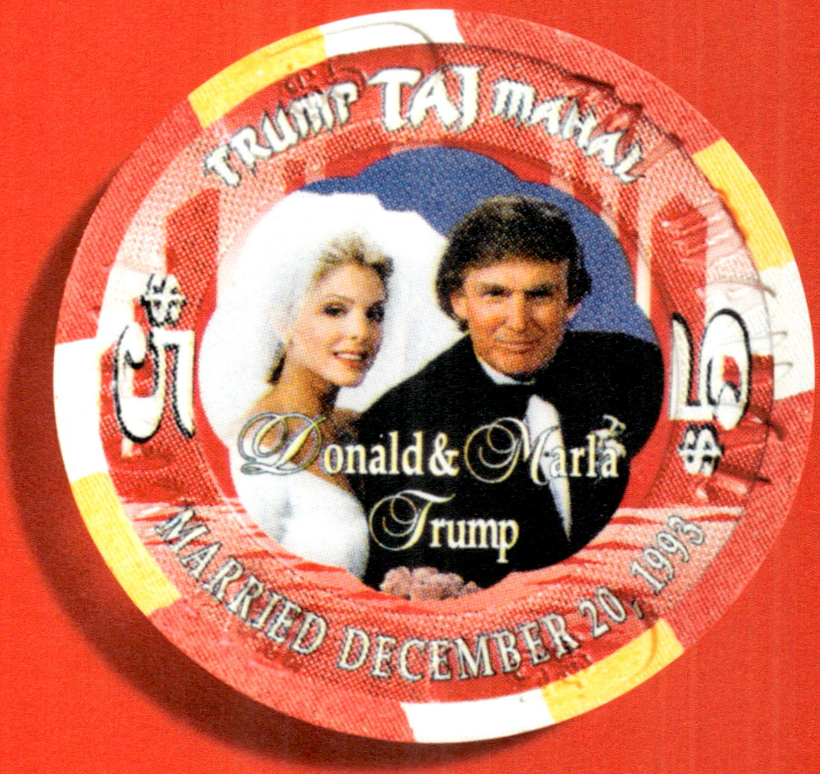

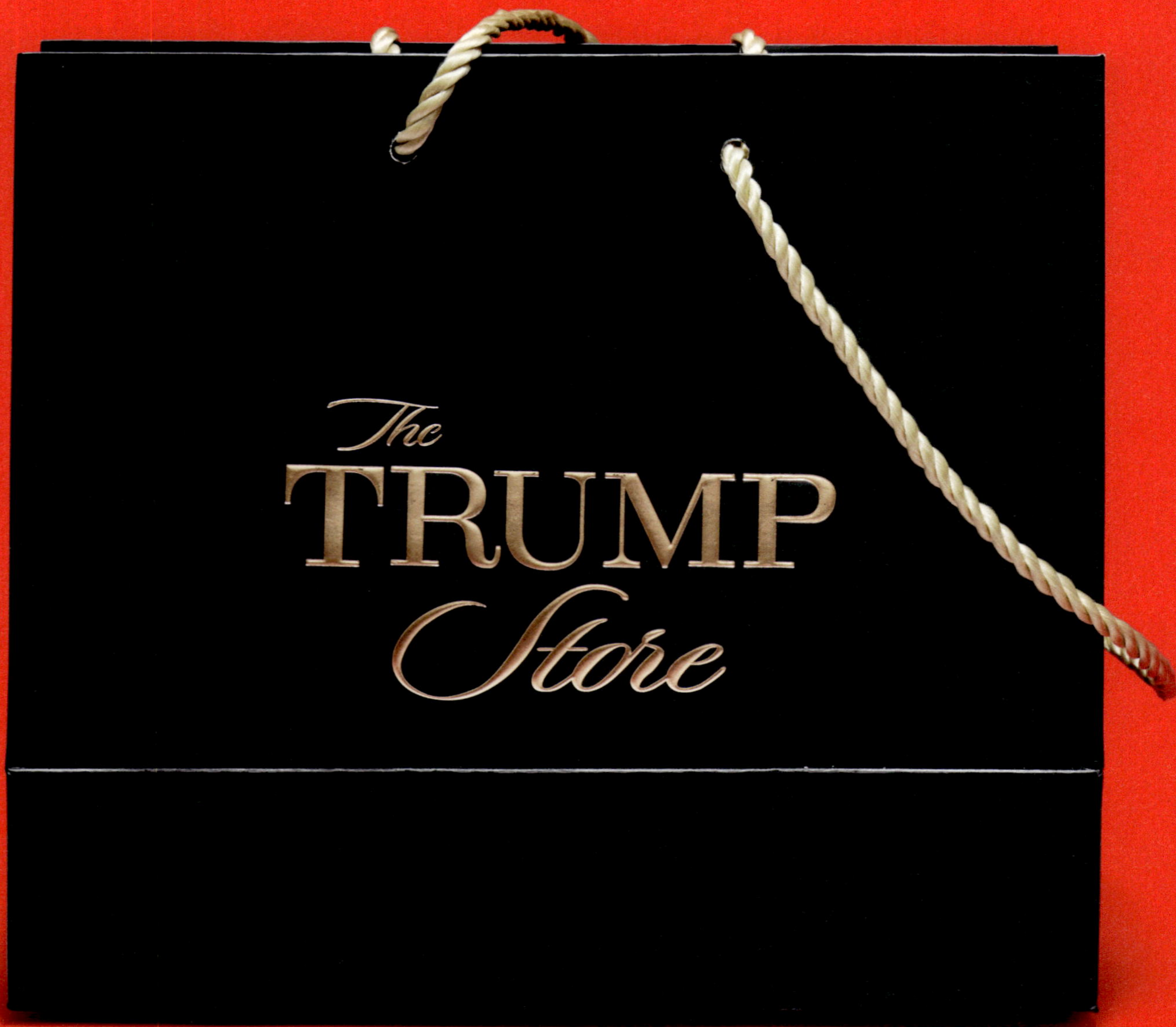
The
TRUMP
Store

TRUMP UNIVERSITY WORKBOOKS, 2008

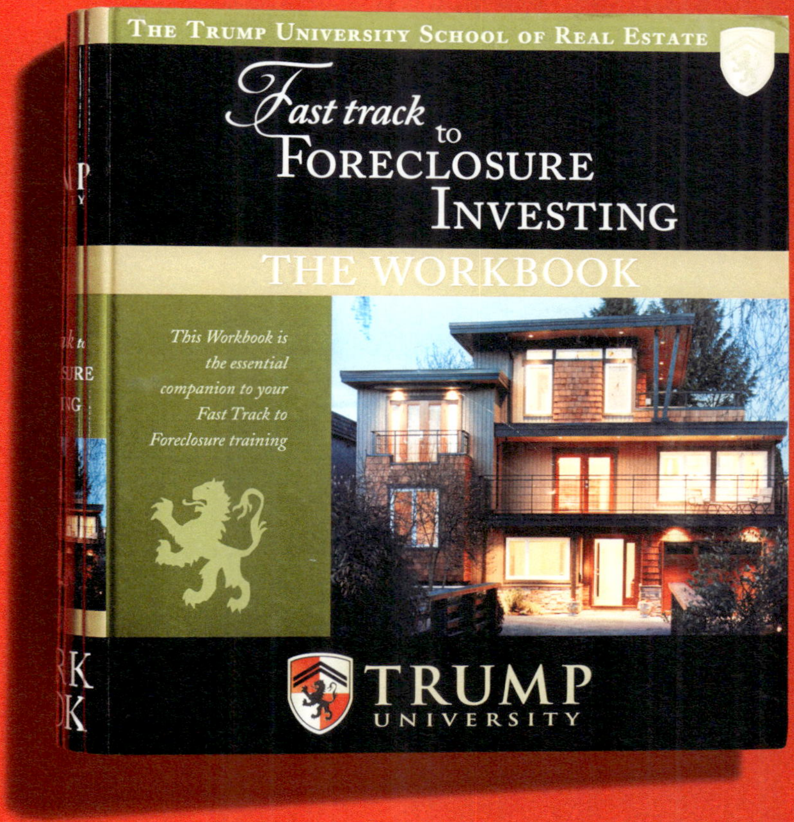

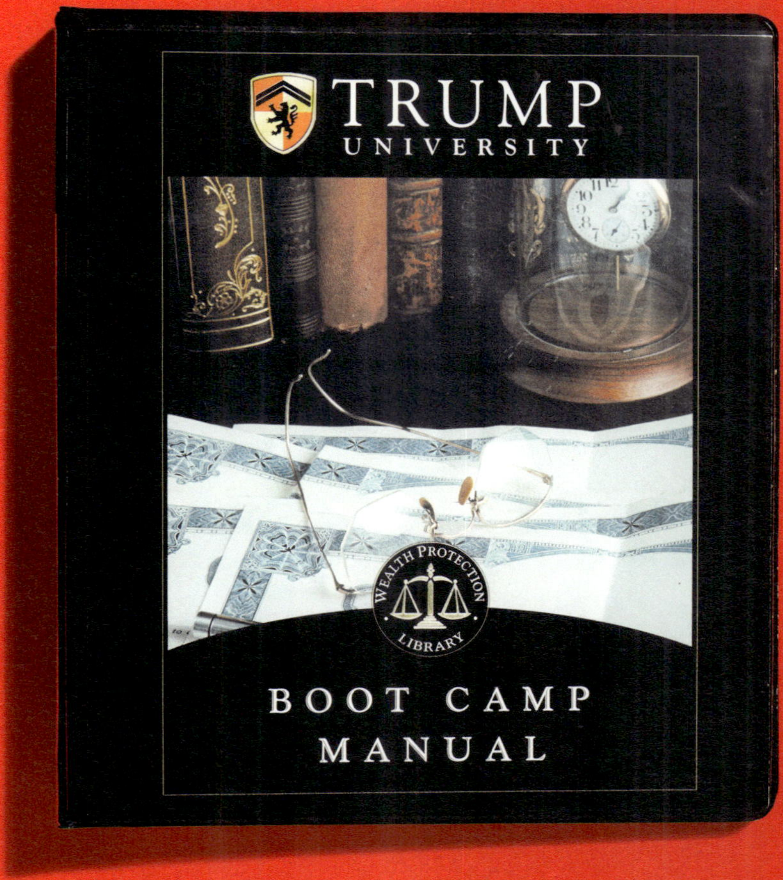

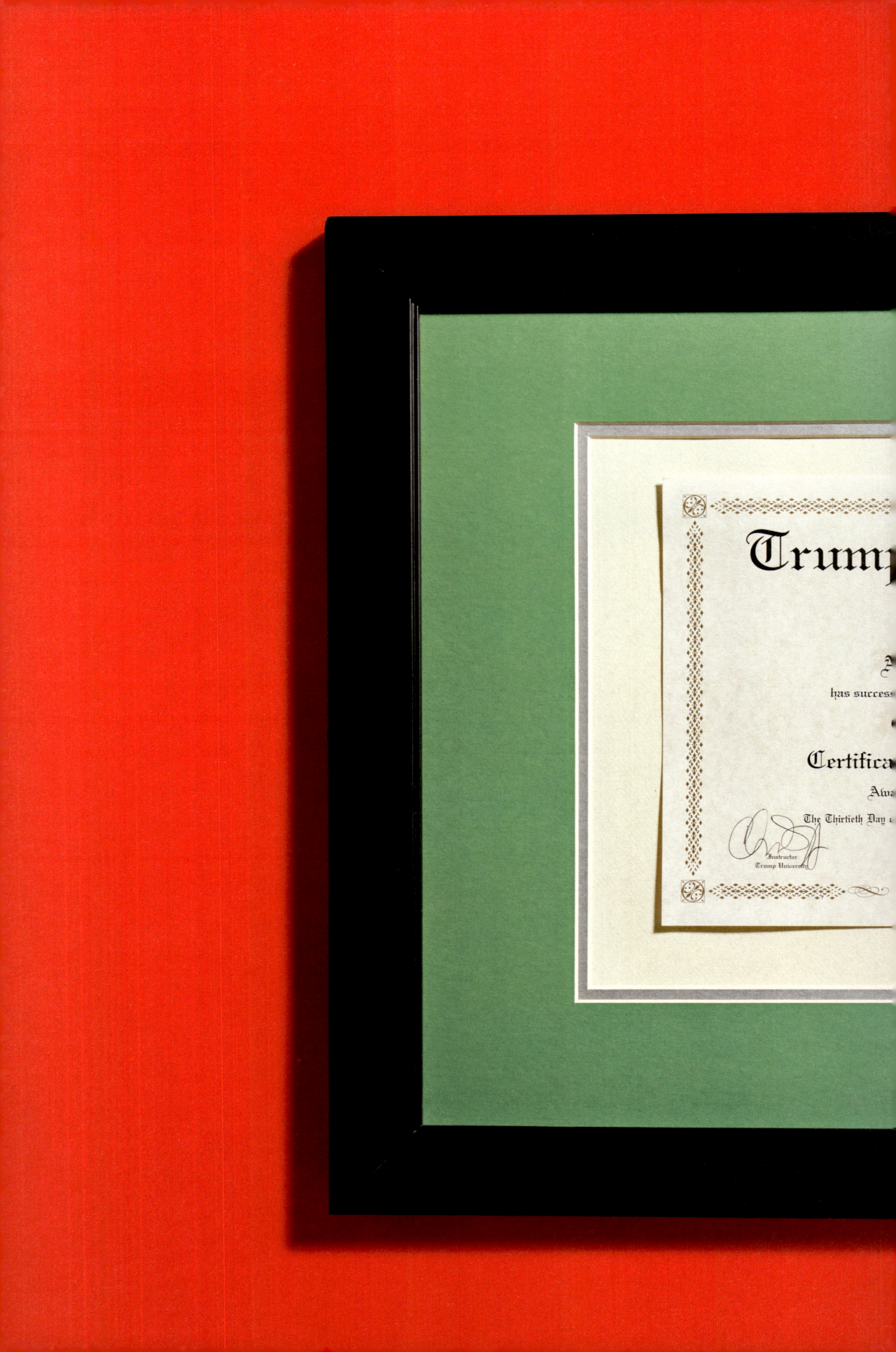
The Thirtieth Day
Instructor

TRUMP UNIVERSITY DIPLOMA, 2009
TRUMP UNIVERSITY WAS A REAL ESTATE TRAINING PROGRAM FROM 2005 TO 2010. IN 2016, FOLLOWING AN OFFICIAL INQUIRY AND PUBLIC SCANDAL, TRUMP SETTLED MULTIPLE LAWSUITS FOR A TOTAL OF $25 MILLION

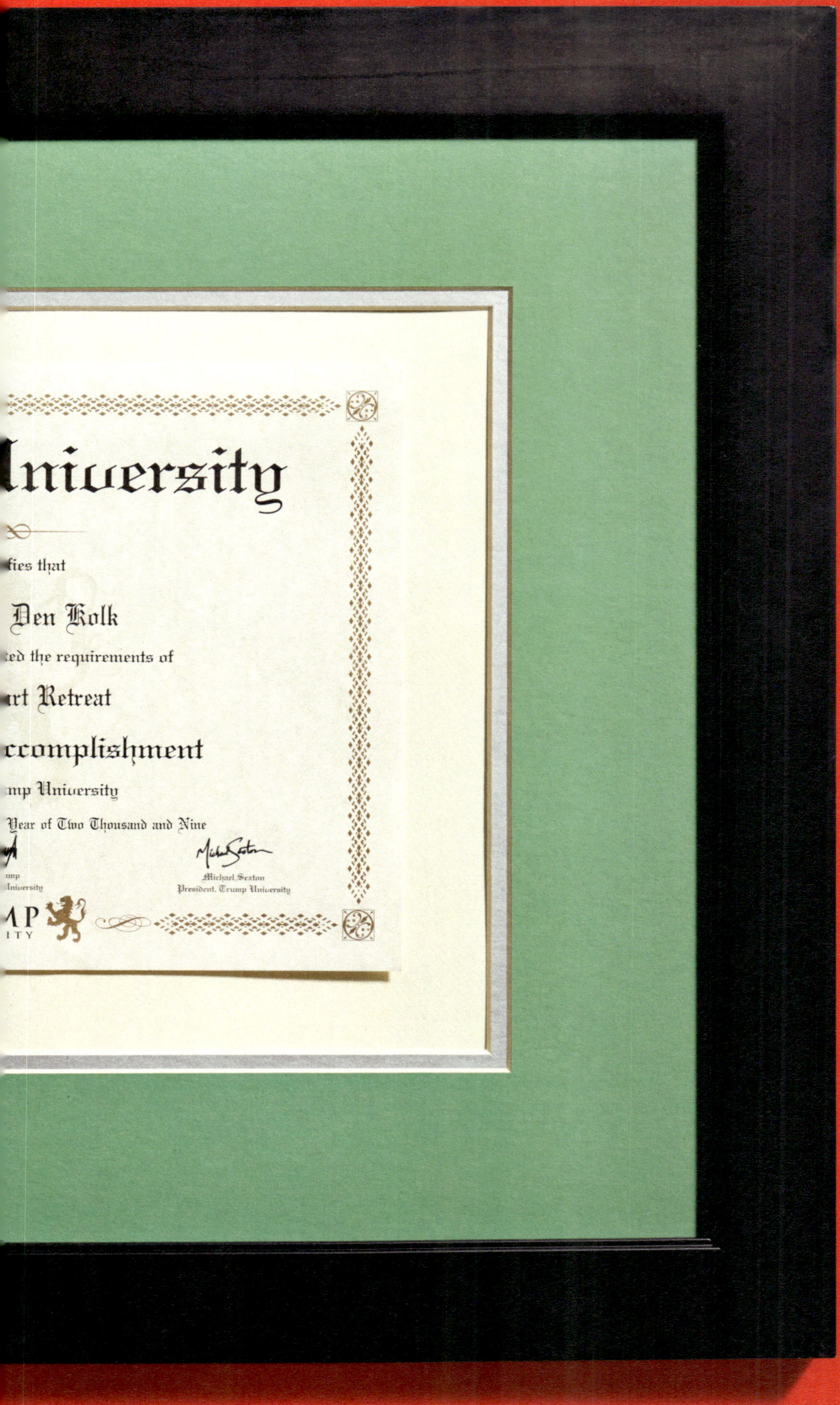

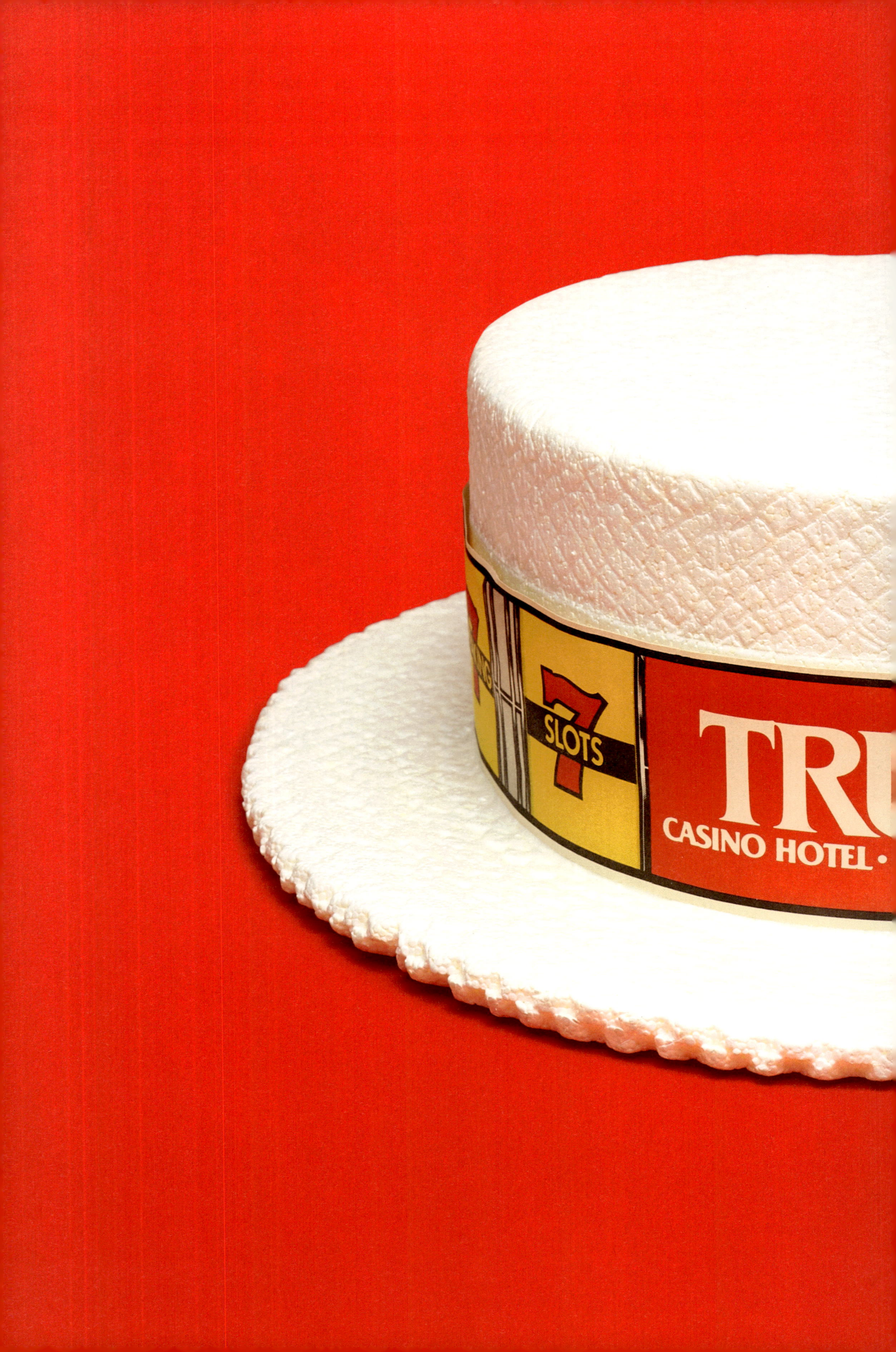
SLOTS
CASINO HOTEL •

TRUMP CASINO HOTEL ON THE BROADWALK SKIMMER HAT
WITH LUCKY 7 BAND

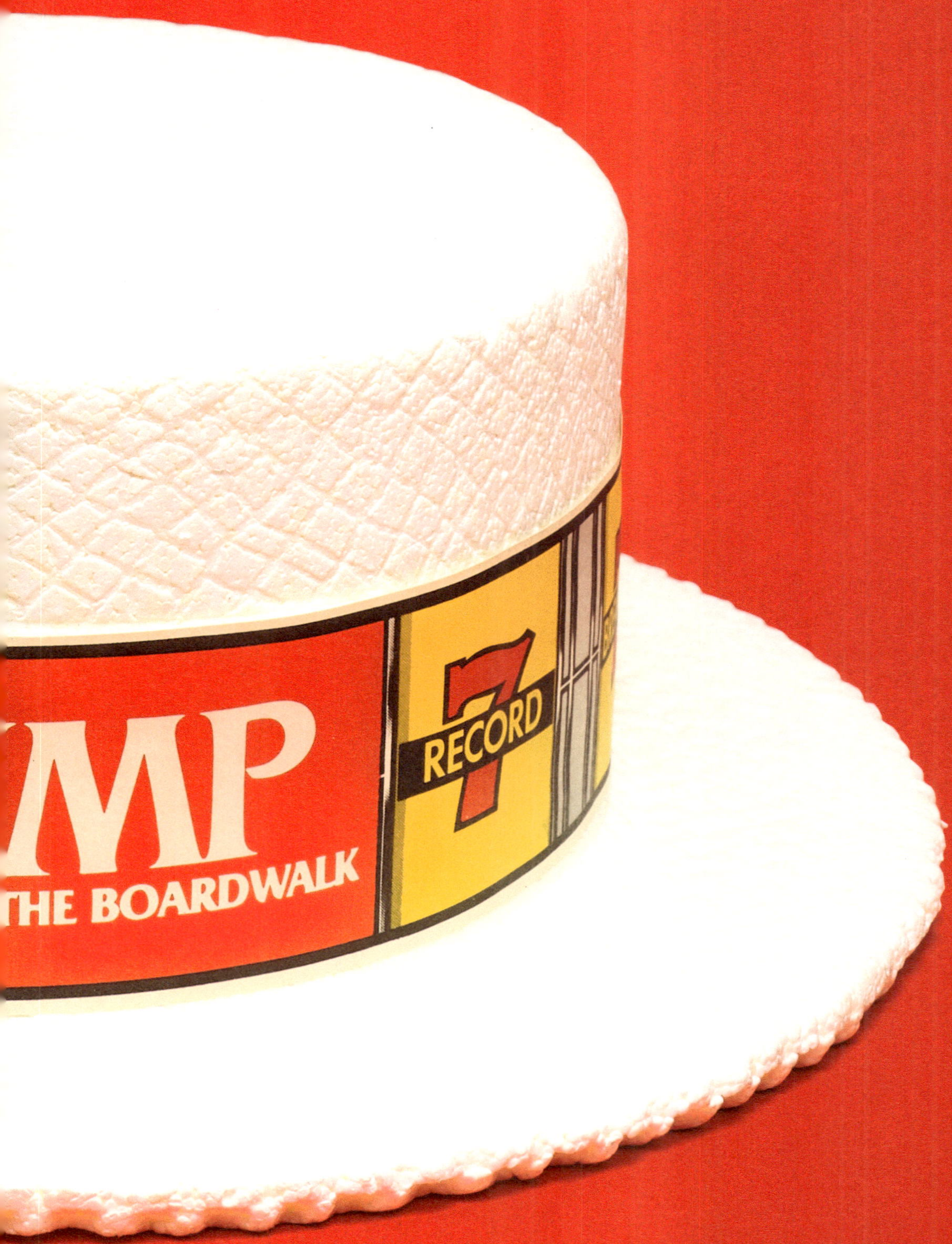

TRUMP PLAZA CASH MONEY TUXEDO TEDDY BEAR, 1999

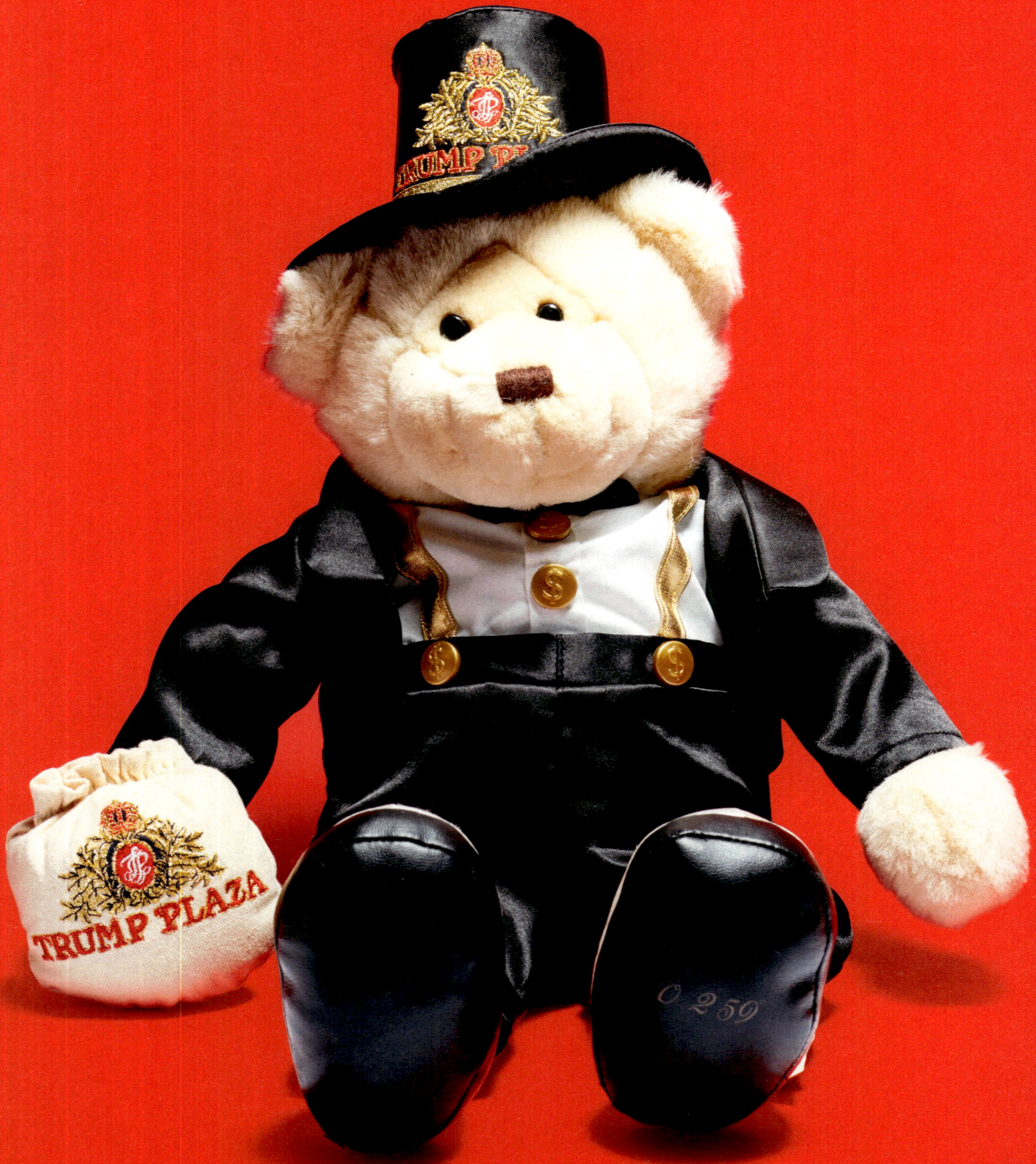

SIGNED PHOTOGRAPH OF DONALD TRUMP

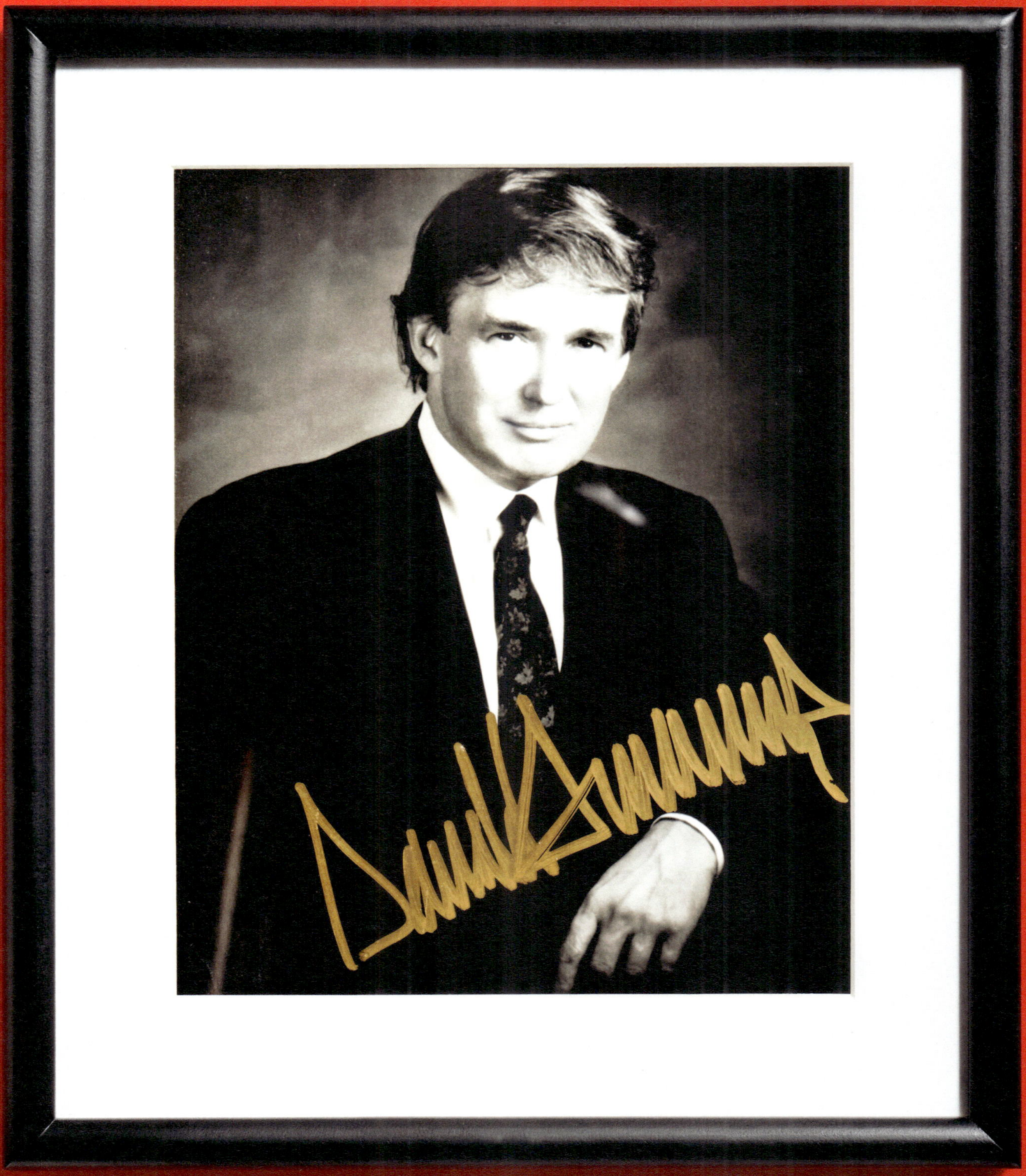

OFFICIAL VETERANS FOR TRUMP 2016 CAMPAIGN SIGN
SIGNED DONALD TRUMP

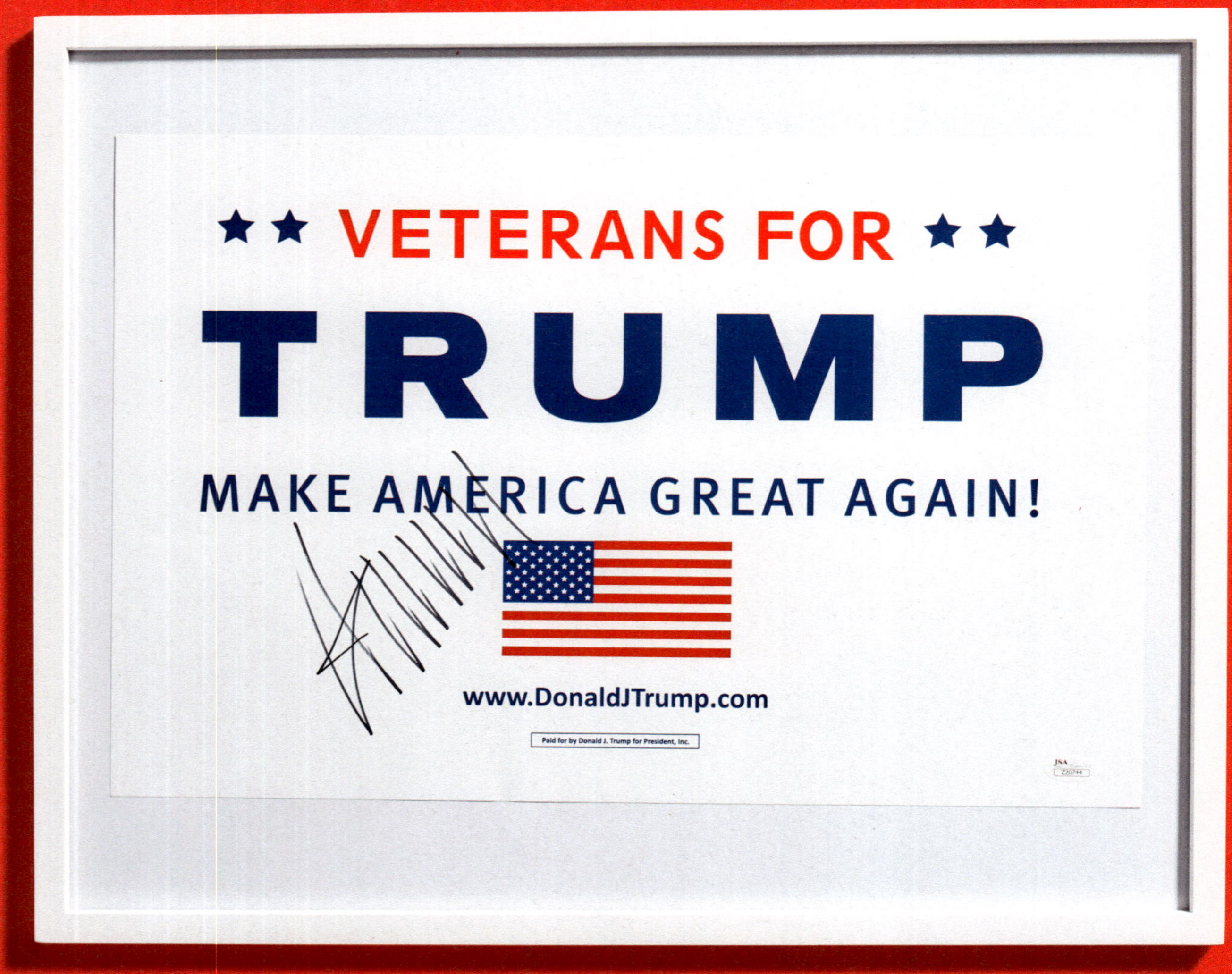

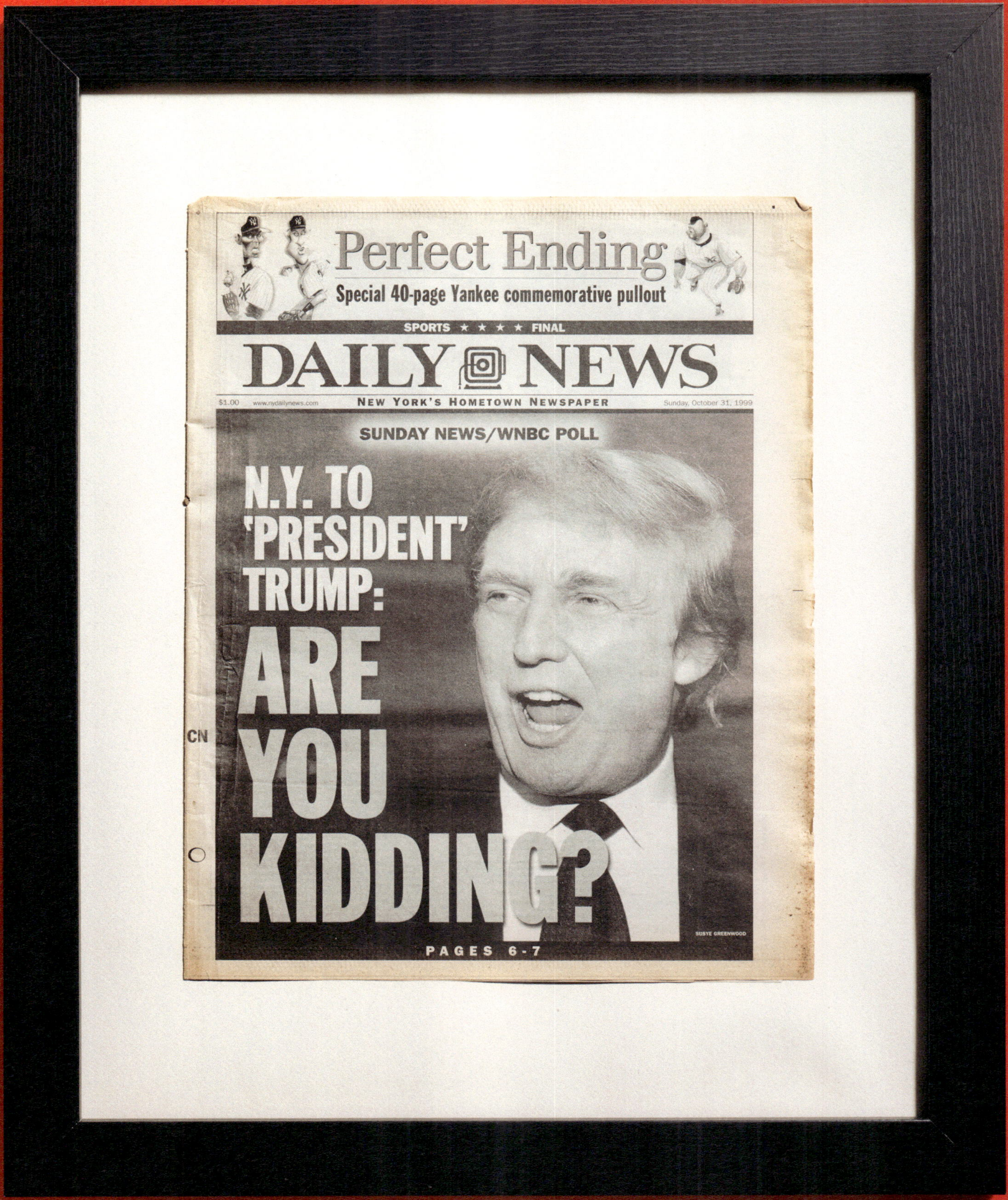
Perfect Ending
Special 40-page Yankee commemorative pullout
SPORTS ★ ★ ★ ★ FINAL
DAILY NEWS
$1.00
www.nydailynews.com
NEW YORK'S HOMETOWN NEWSPAPER
Sunday, October 31, 1999
SUNDAY NEWS/WNBC POLL
N.Y. TO 'PRESIDENT' TRUMP:
ARE YOU KIDDING?
PAGES 6-7

TRUMP 2016 CAMPAIGN BADGE

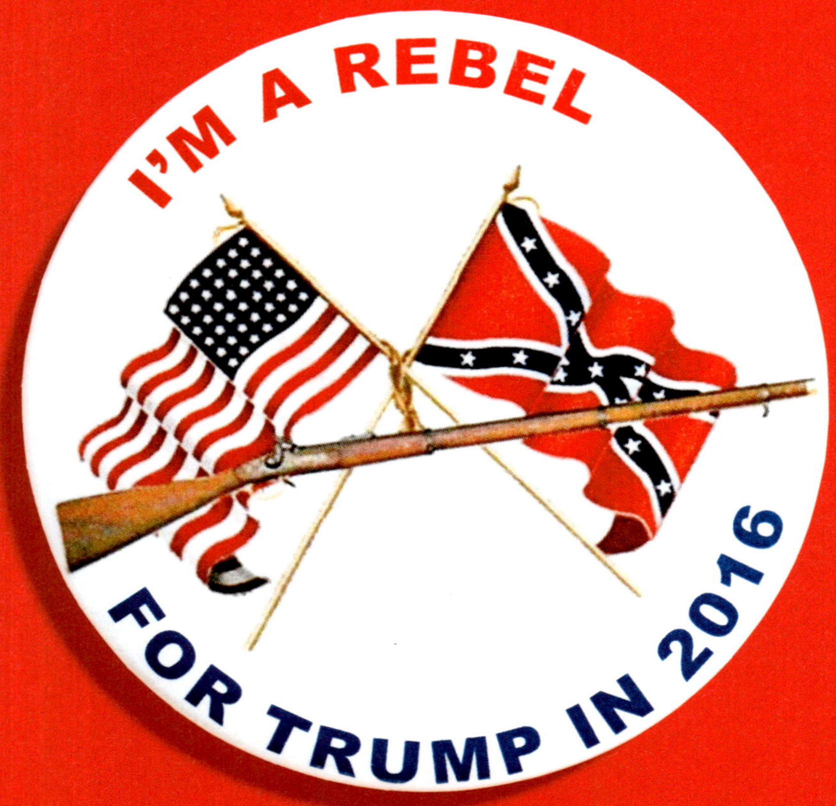

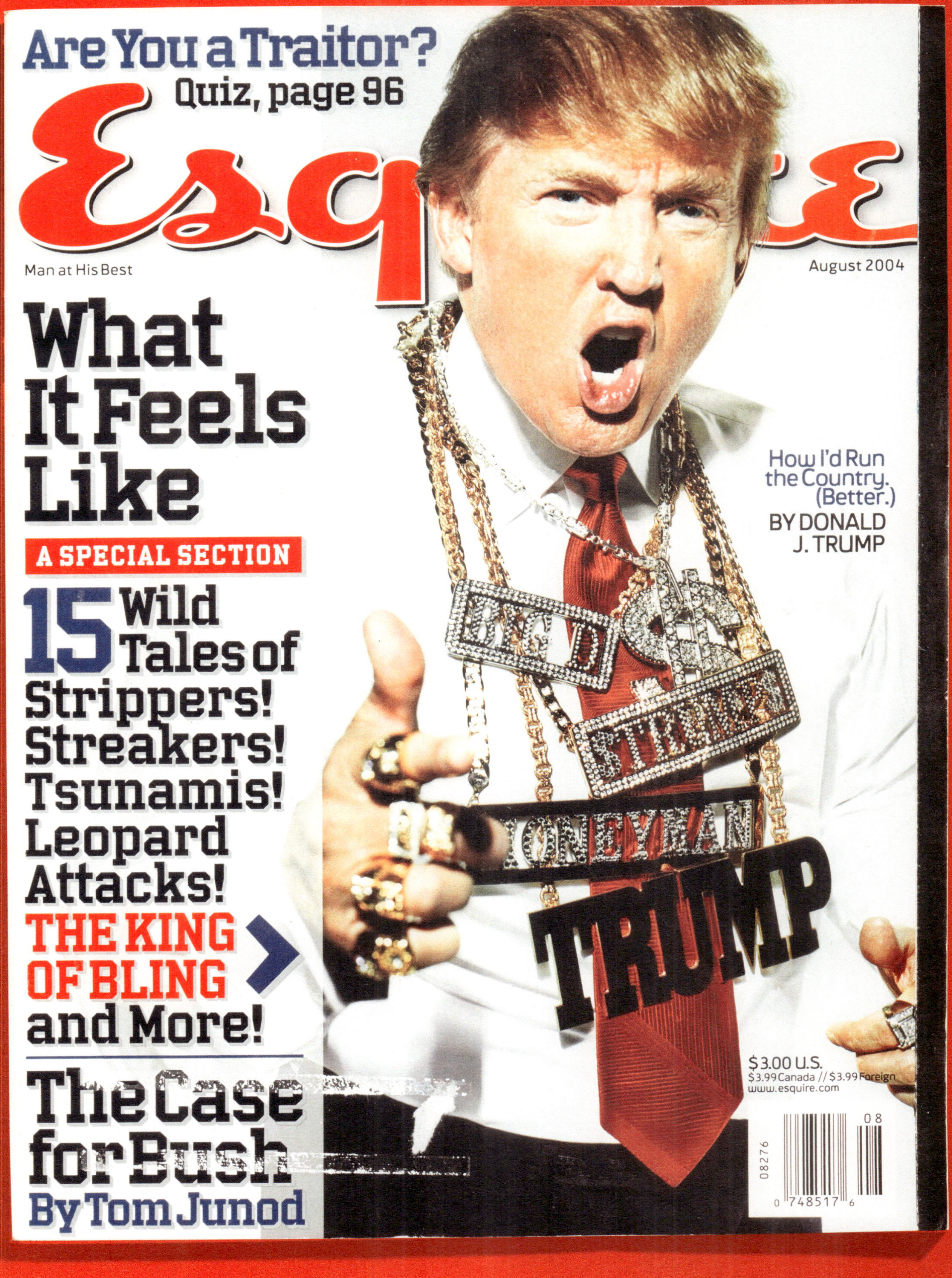
Are You a Traitor?
Quiz, page 96
Esquire
Man at His Best
August 2004
What It Feels Like
A SPECIAL SECTION
15 Wild Tales of Strippers! Streakers! Tsunamis! Leopard Attacks!
THE KING OF BLING
and More!
The Case for Bush
By Tom Junod
How I'd Run the Country. (Better.)
BY DONALD J. TRUMP
TRUMP
$3.00 U.S.
$3.99 Canada // $3.99 Foreign
www.esquire.com

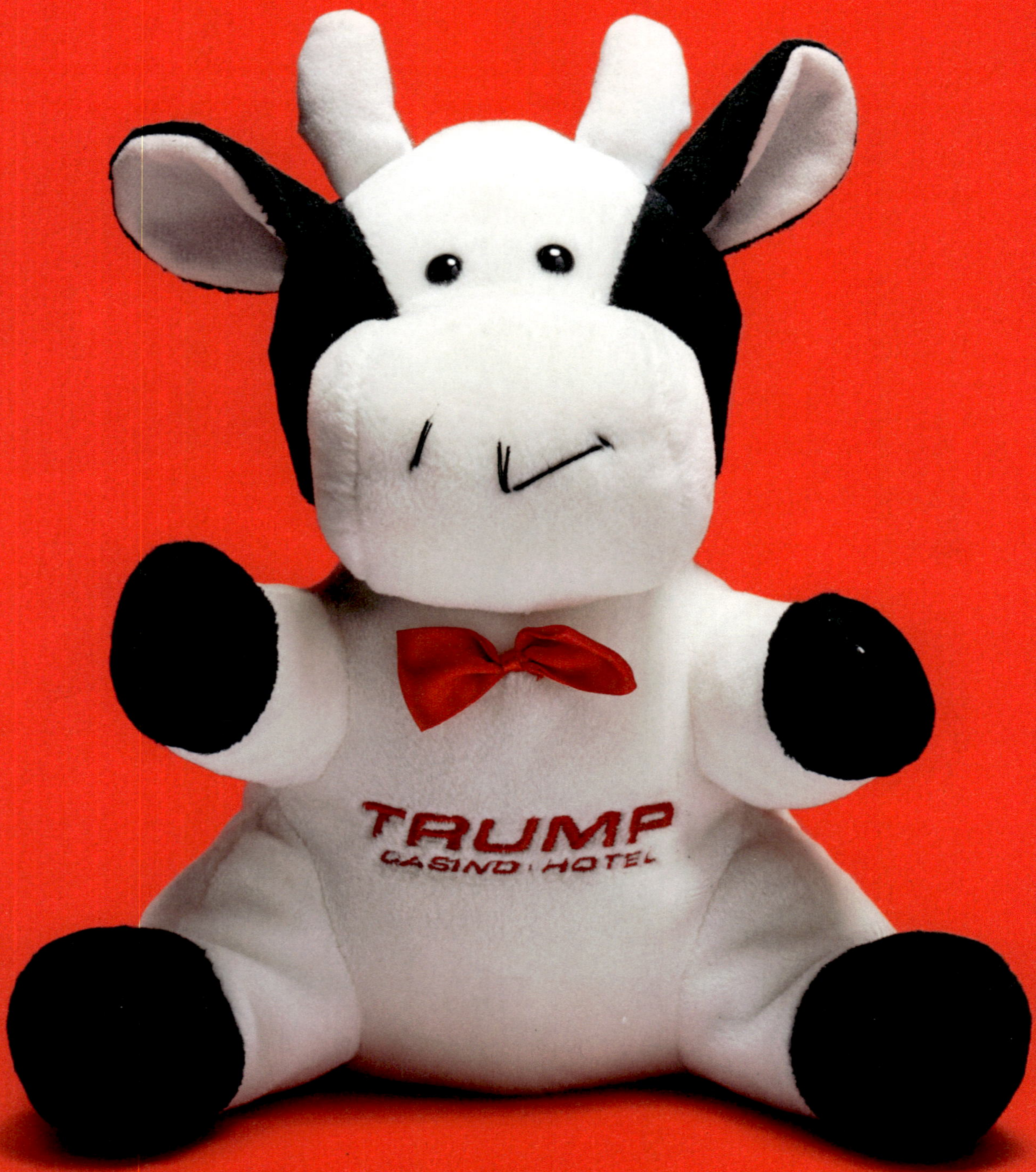
TRUMP
CASINO HOTEL

SIGNED PHOTOGRAPH OF DONALD TRUMP, 1989

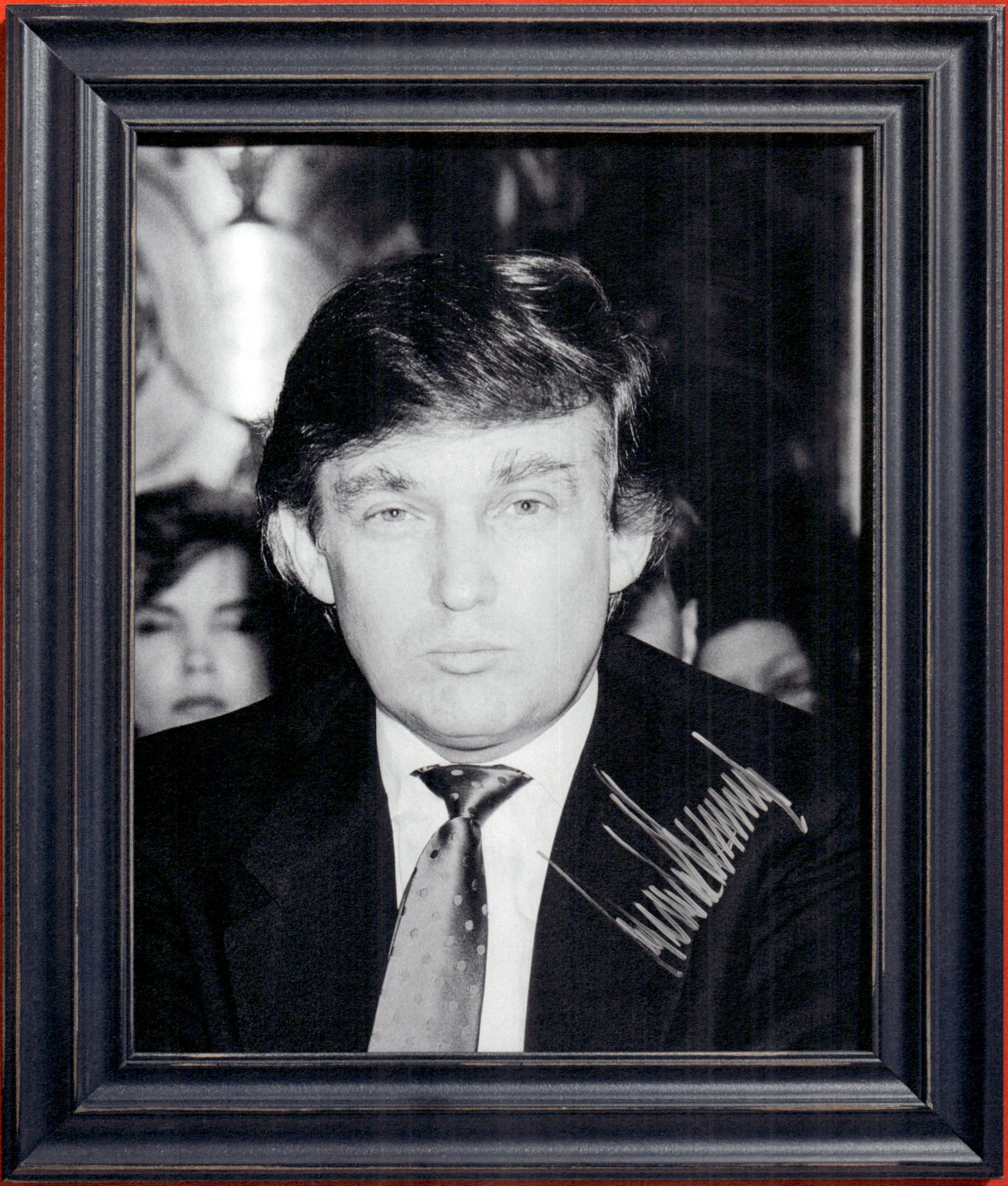

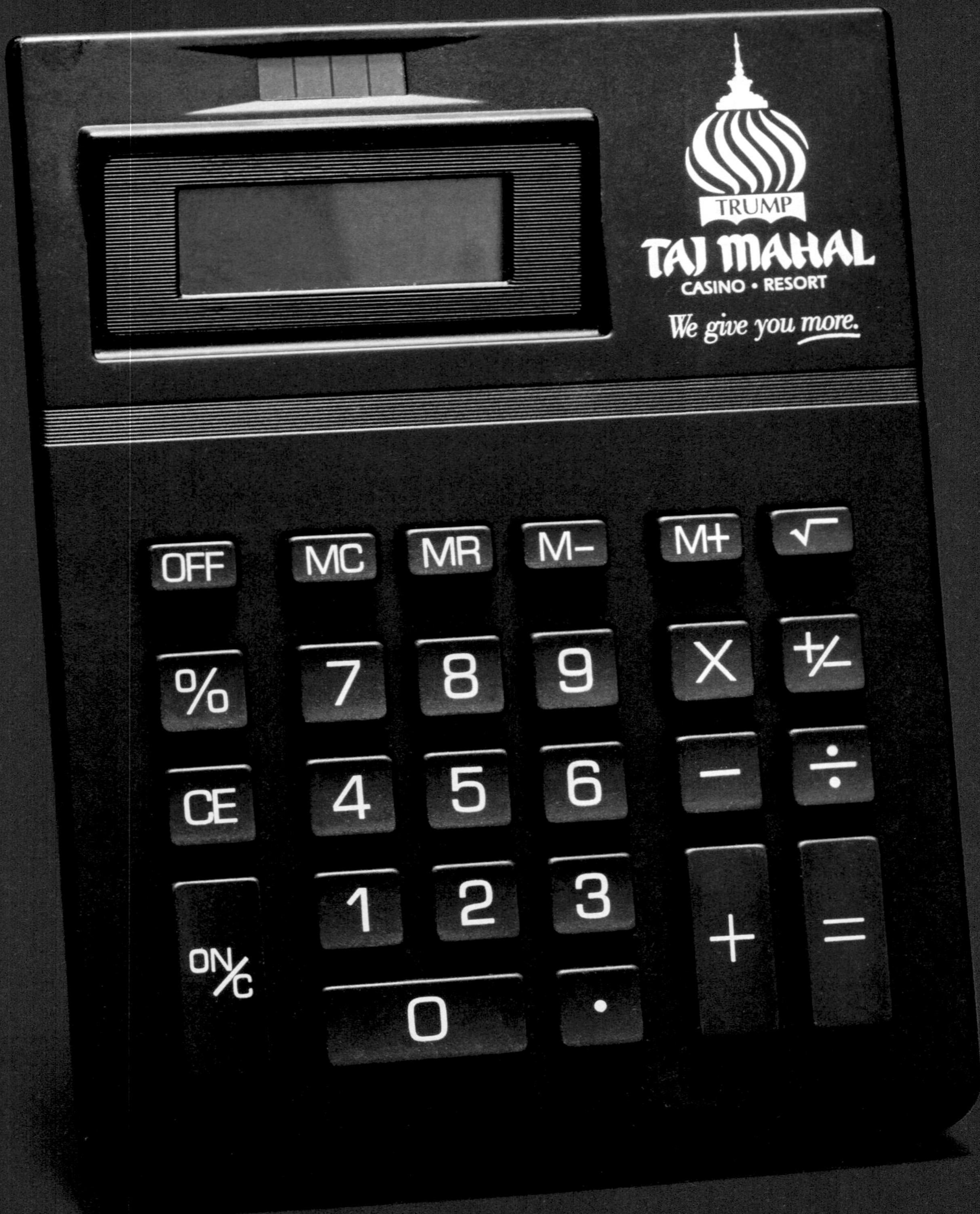
TRUMP
TAJ MAHAL
CASINO • RESORT
We give you more.
OFF
MC
MR
M-
M+
√
%
7
8
9
X
+/-
CE
4
5
6
−
÷
ON/C
1
2
3
+
=
0
•

OFFICIAL TRUMP 2016 CAMPAIGN BUMPER STICKER
SIGNED DONALD TRUMP

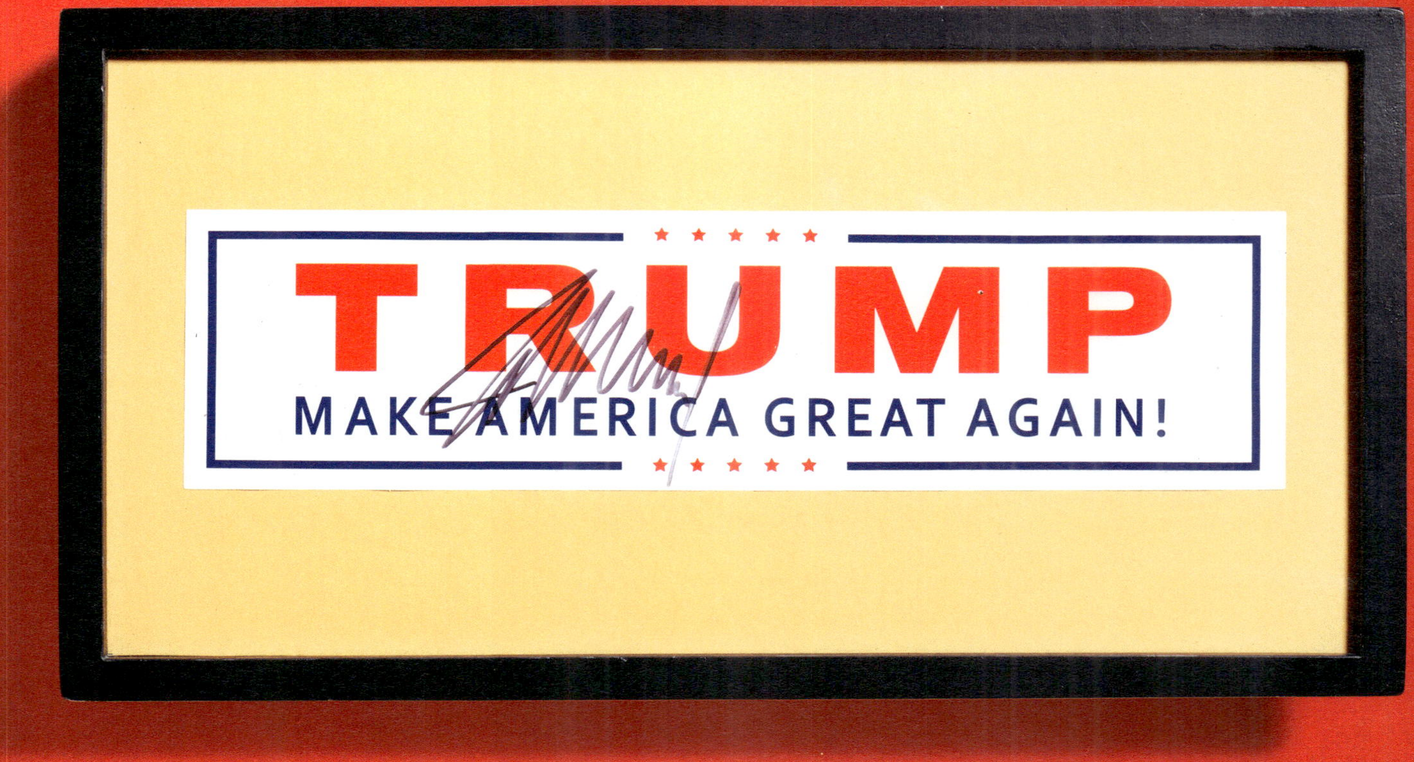

TIME MAGAZINE, MARCH 14, 2016
SIGNED DONALD TRUMP

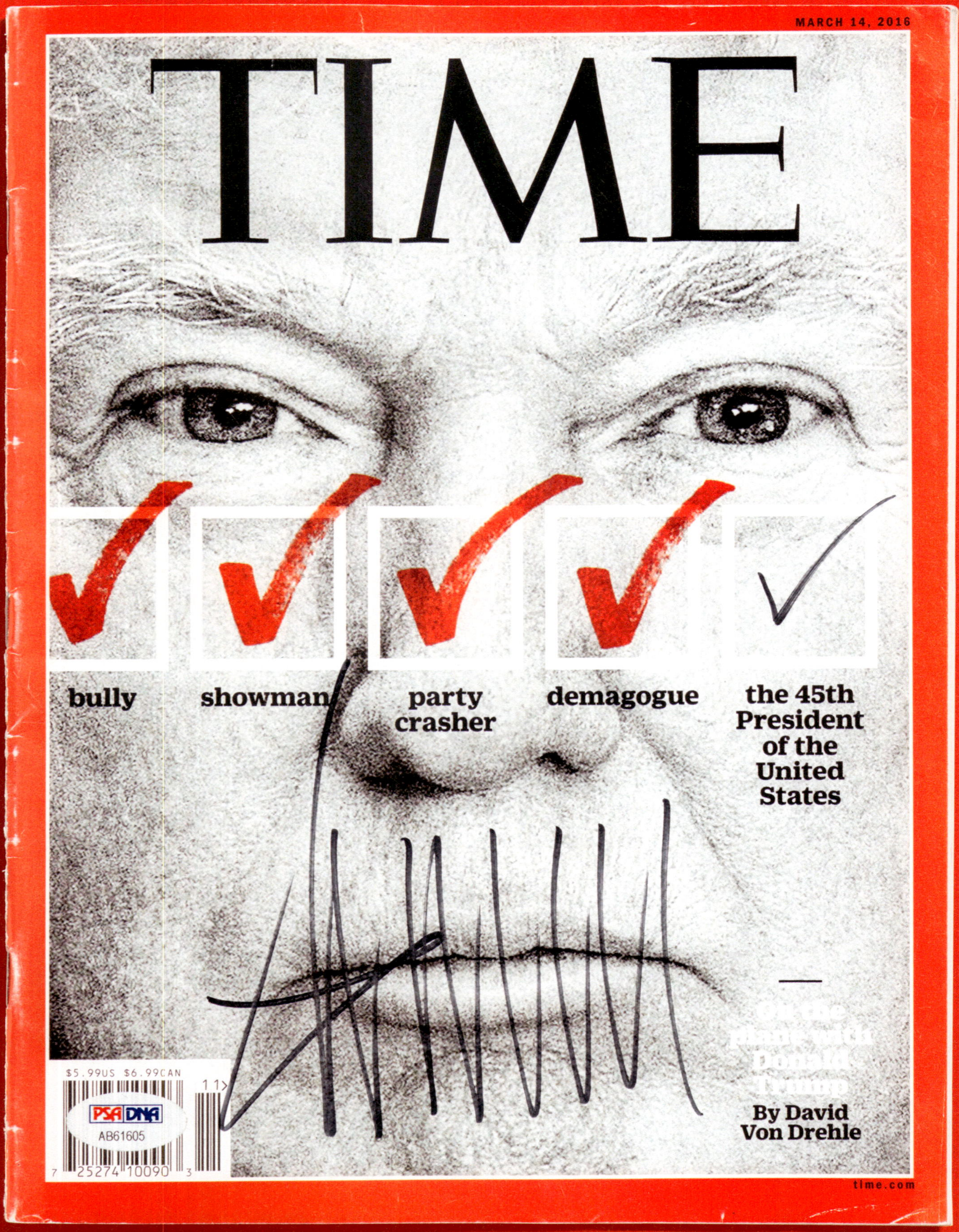

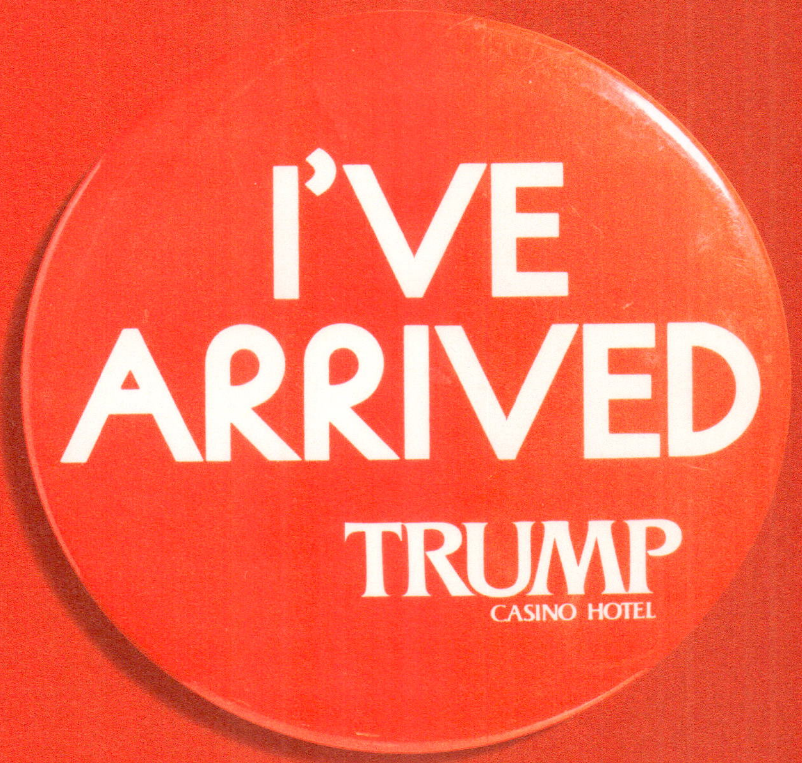
I'VE
ARRIVED
TRUMP
CASINO HOTEL

DONALD TRUMP'S 50TH BIRTHDAY INVITATION, JUNE 13, 1996
THE PARTY FEATURED A CAKE DEPICTING TRUMP AS SUPERMAN STANDING AMONG HIS PROPERTY EMPIRE. AS A FINALE, EARTHA KITT SANG "HAPPY BIRTHDAY," AS 600 GOLD BALLOONS DESCENDED FROM THE CEILING

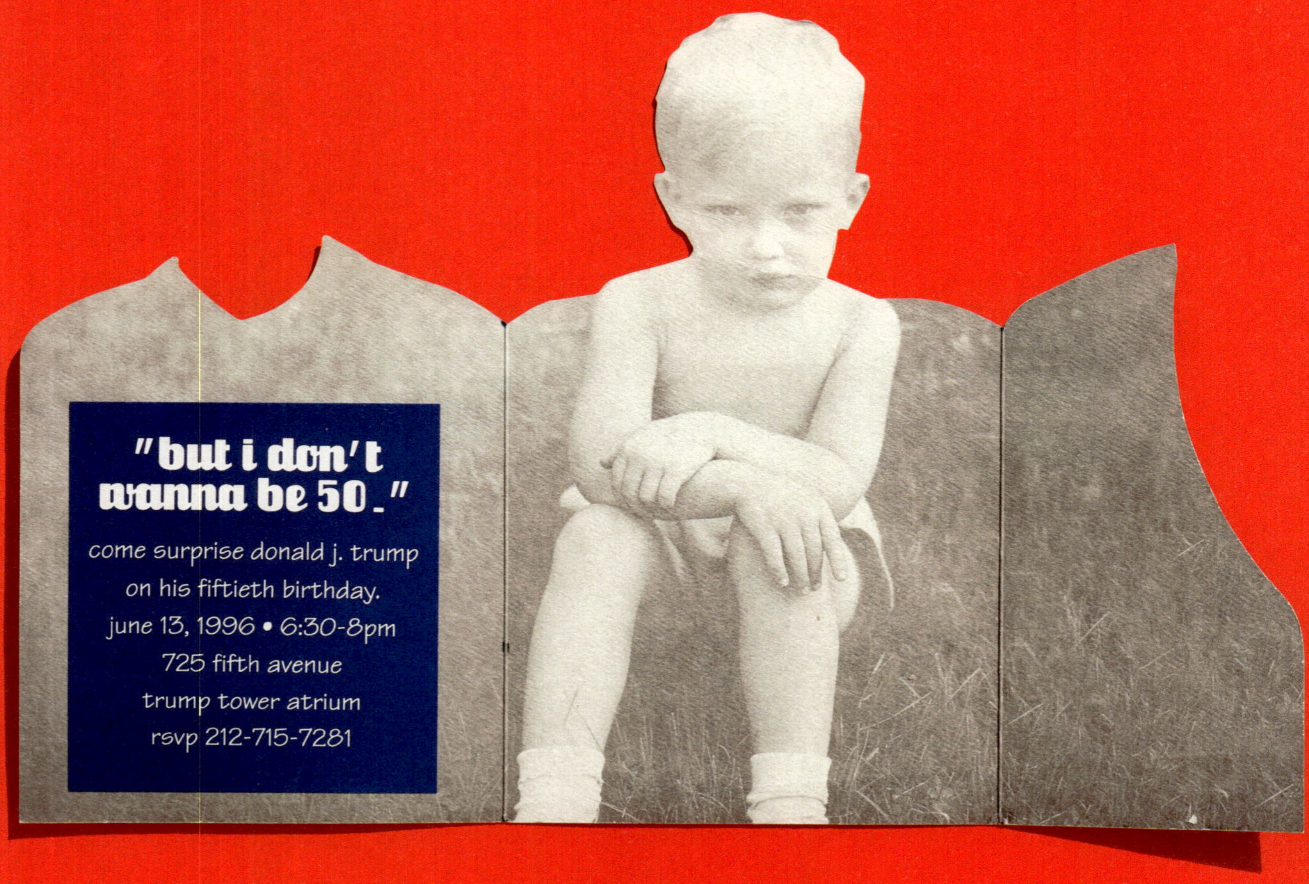

TIME MAGAZINE, JULY 2, 2018
SIGNED AND INSCRIBED "MAKE AMERICA GREAT AGAIN!"
BY DONALD TRUMP

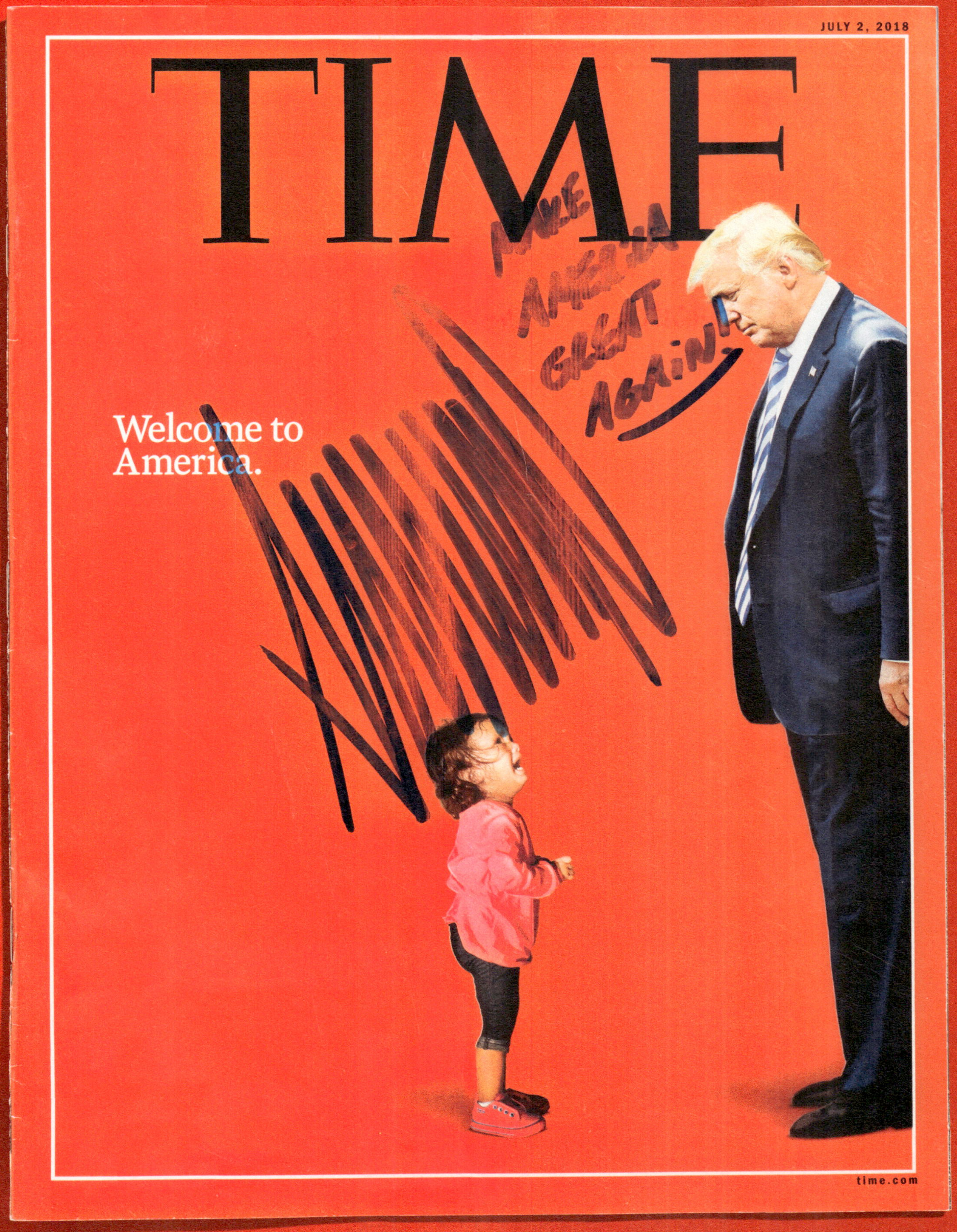

MAD MAGAZINE, AUGUST 2016
SIGNED DONALD TRUMP

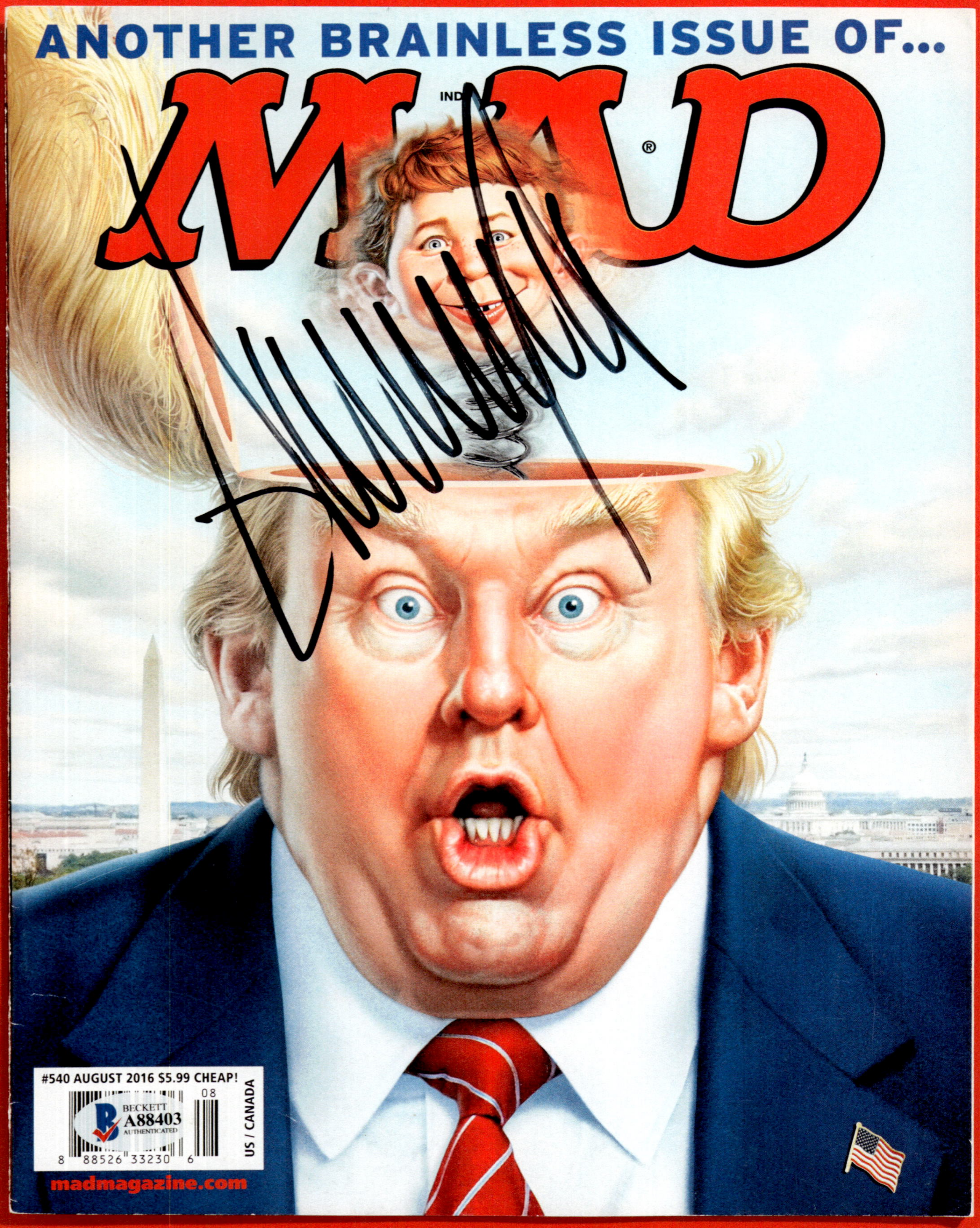

DONALD TRUMP RUBBER MASK
SIGNED DONALD TRUMP

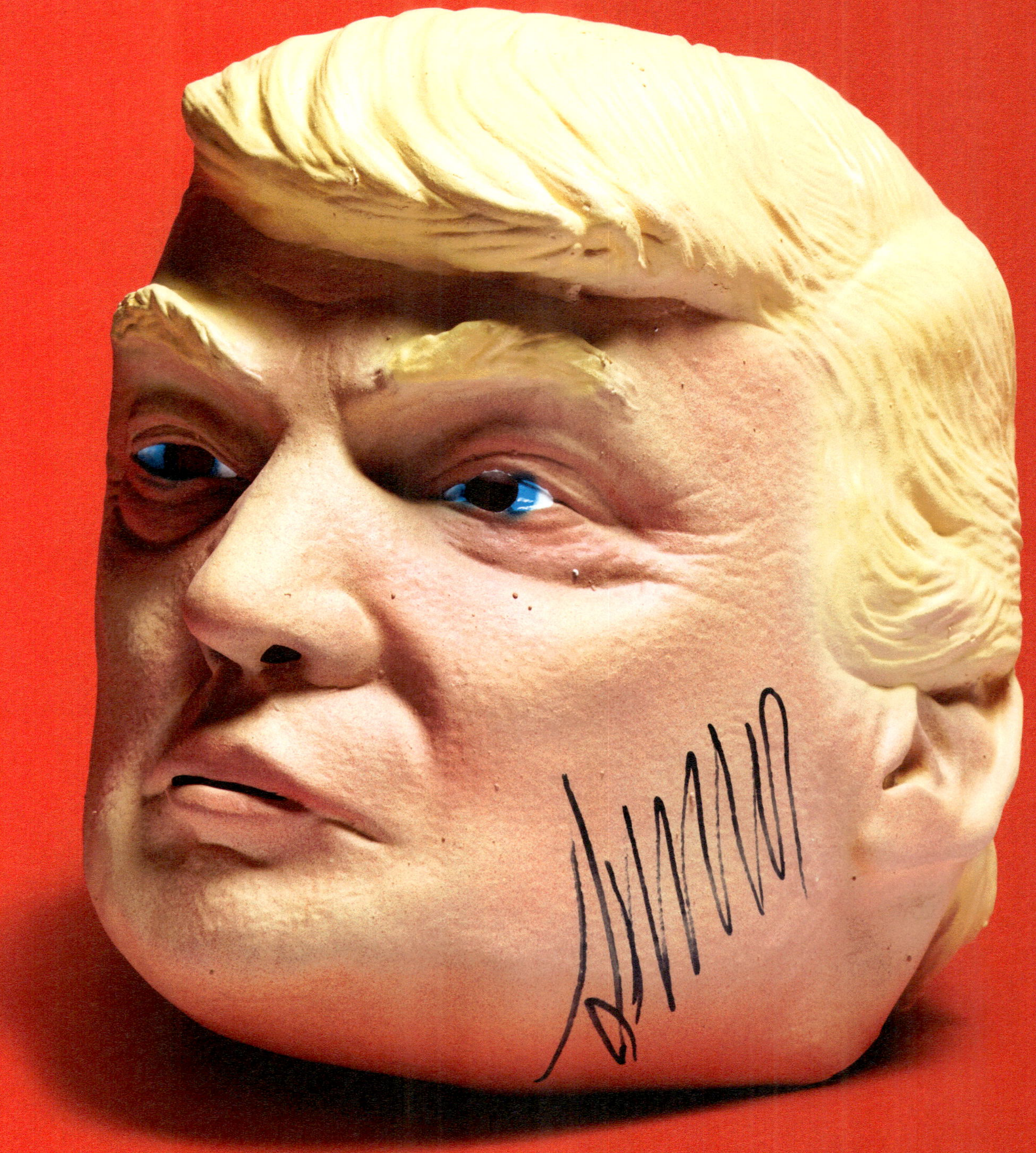

SIGNED PHOTOGRAPH OF DONALD TRUMP
AS HOST OF SATURDAY NIGHT LIVE, 2015

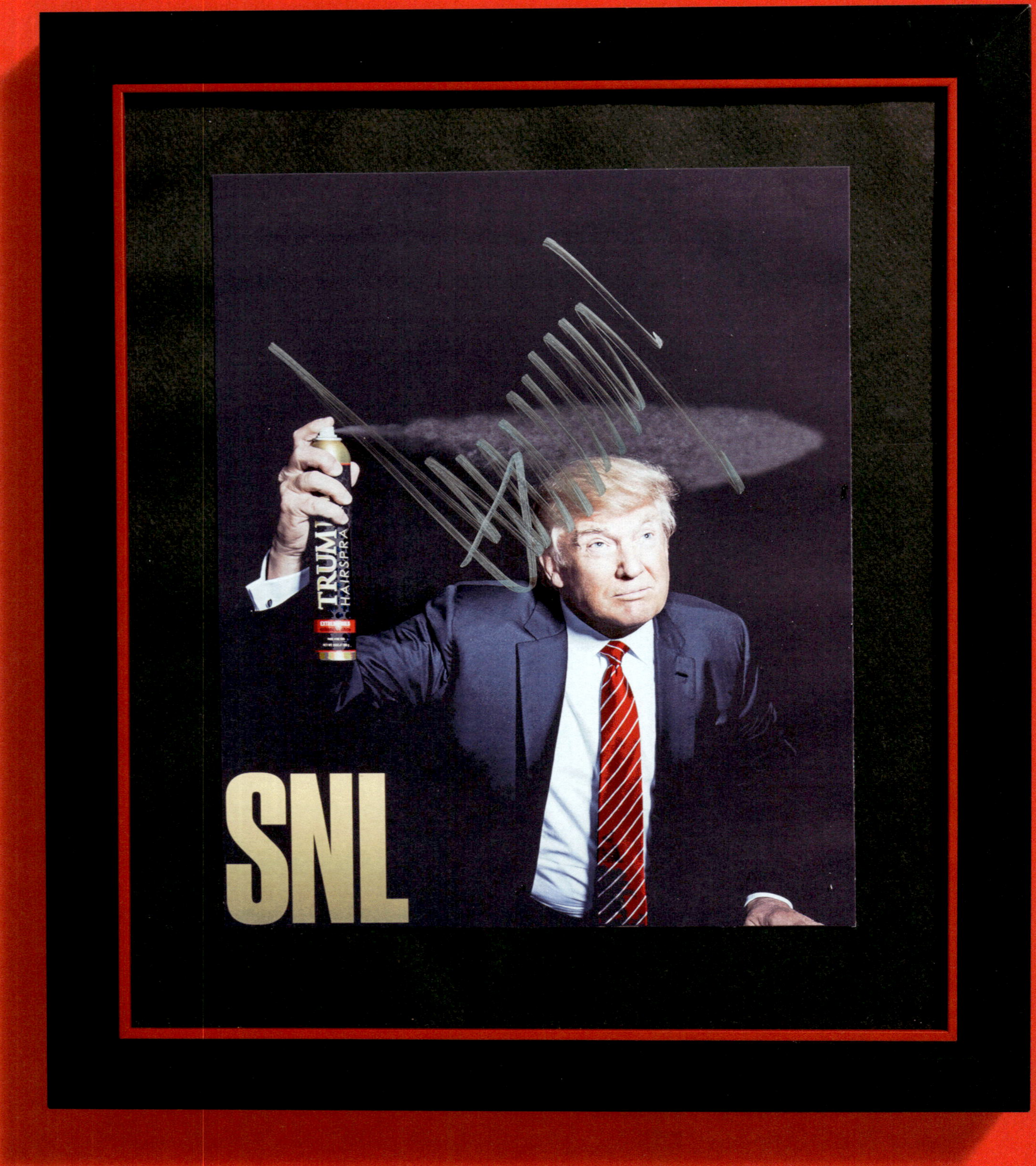

THE TRUMP SUPERMAN COLORING BOOK, 2015
SIGNED DONALD TRUMP

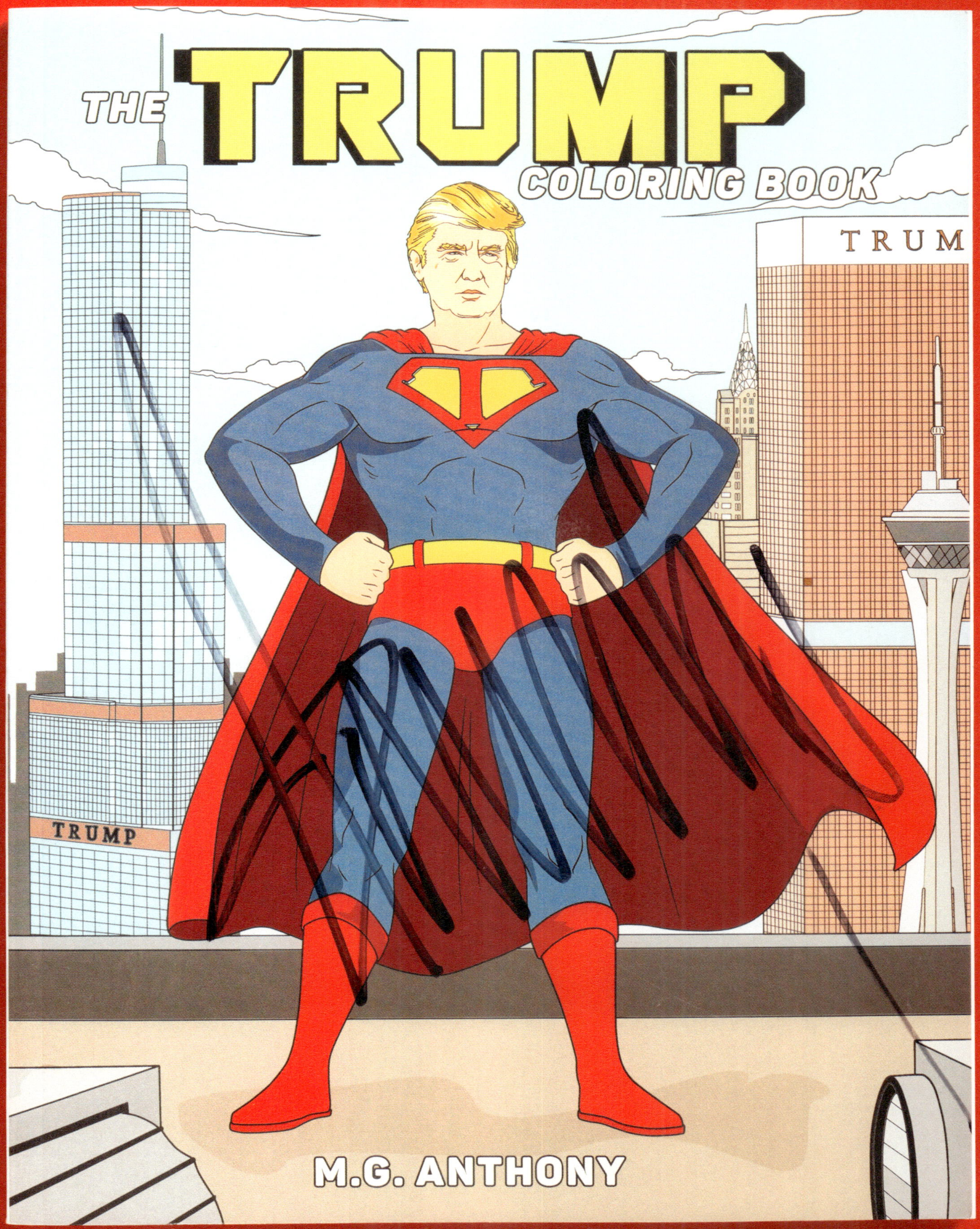

TRUMP TAJ MAHAL GOLF BALLS AND BASEBALL
SIGNED DONALD TRUMP

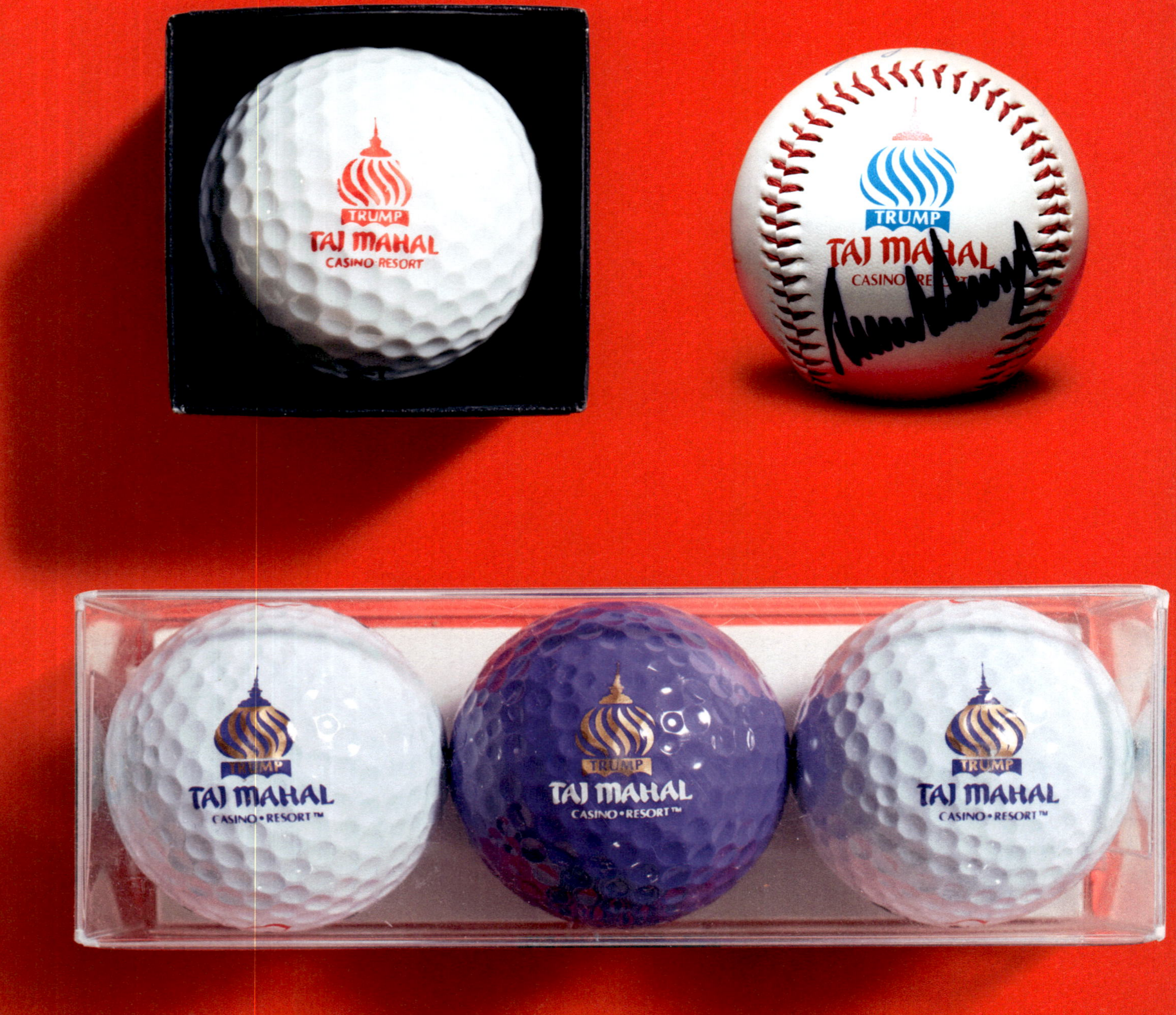

TRUMP TAJ MAHAL SPECIAL EDITION GOLF BAG AND CLUBS COMMEMORATING THE RESORT'S GRAND OPENING, APRIL 1990

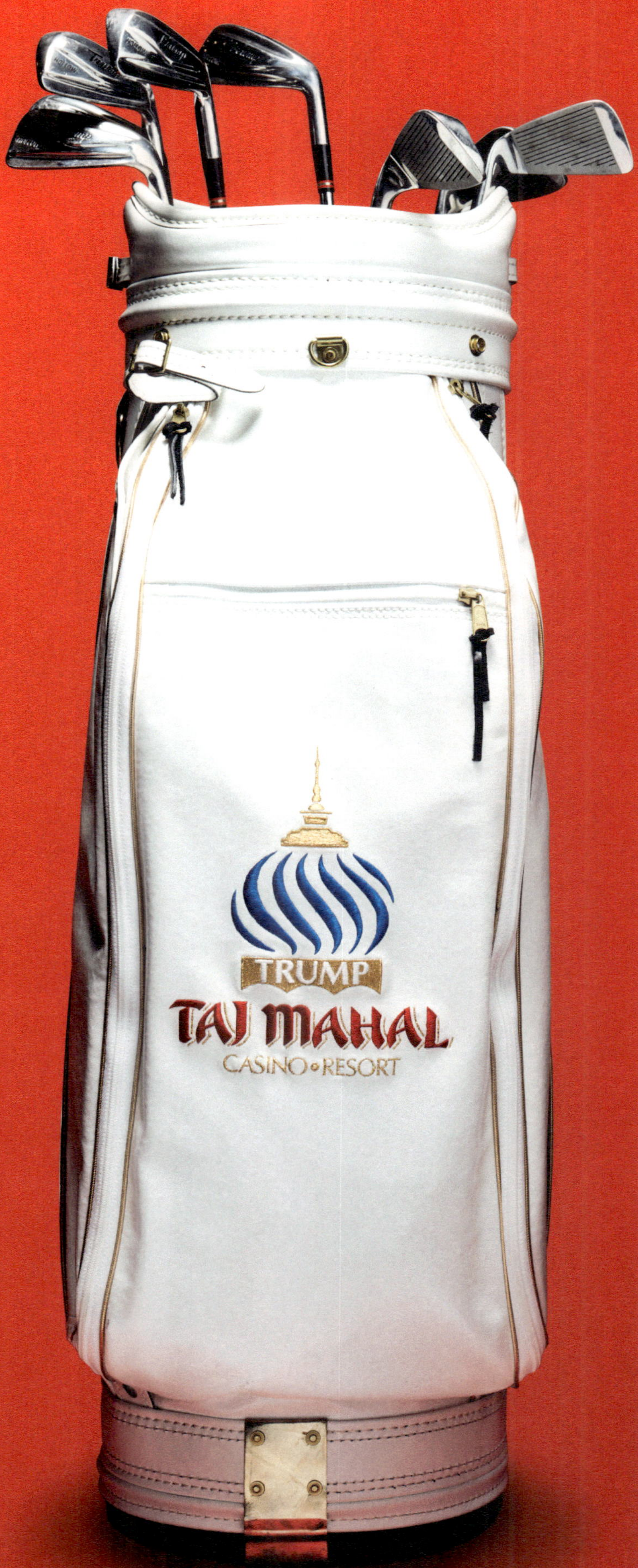

TRUMP CASINO HOTEL GOLD PLASTIC KAZOOS

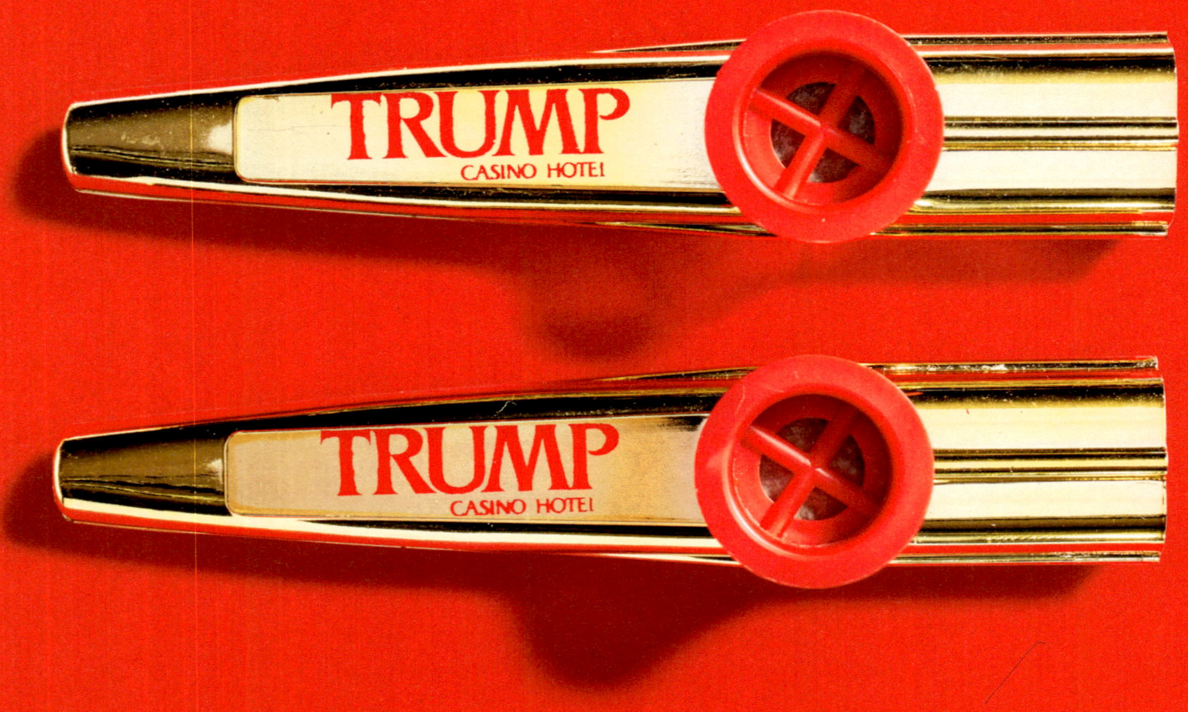

AMERICAN FLAG ELECTRIC GUITAR
SIGNED DONALD TRUMP

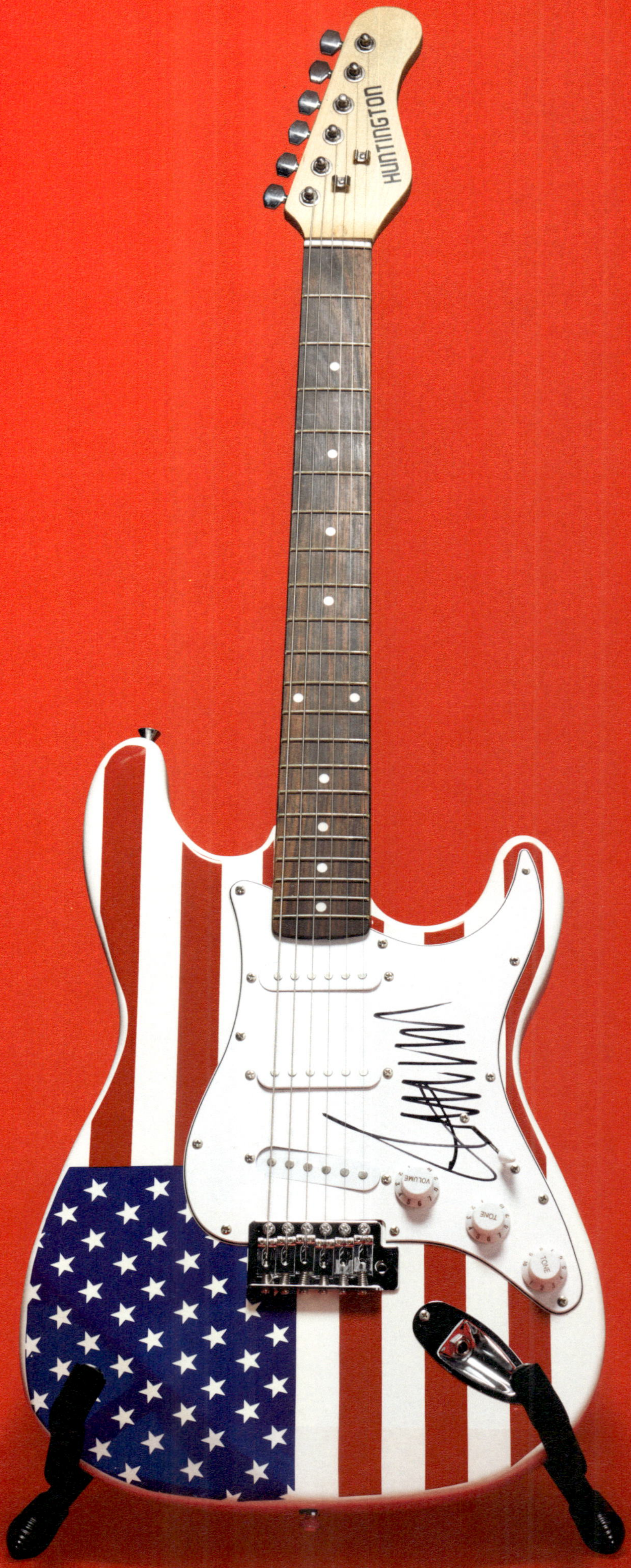

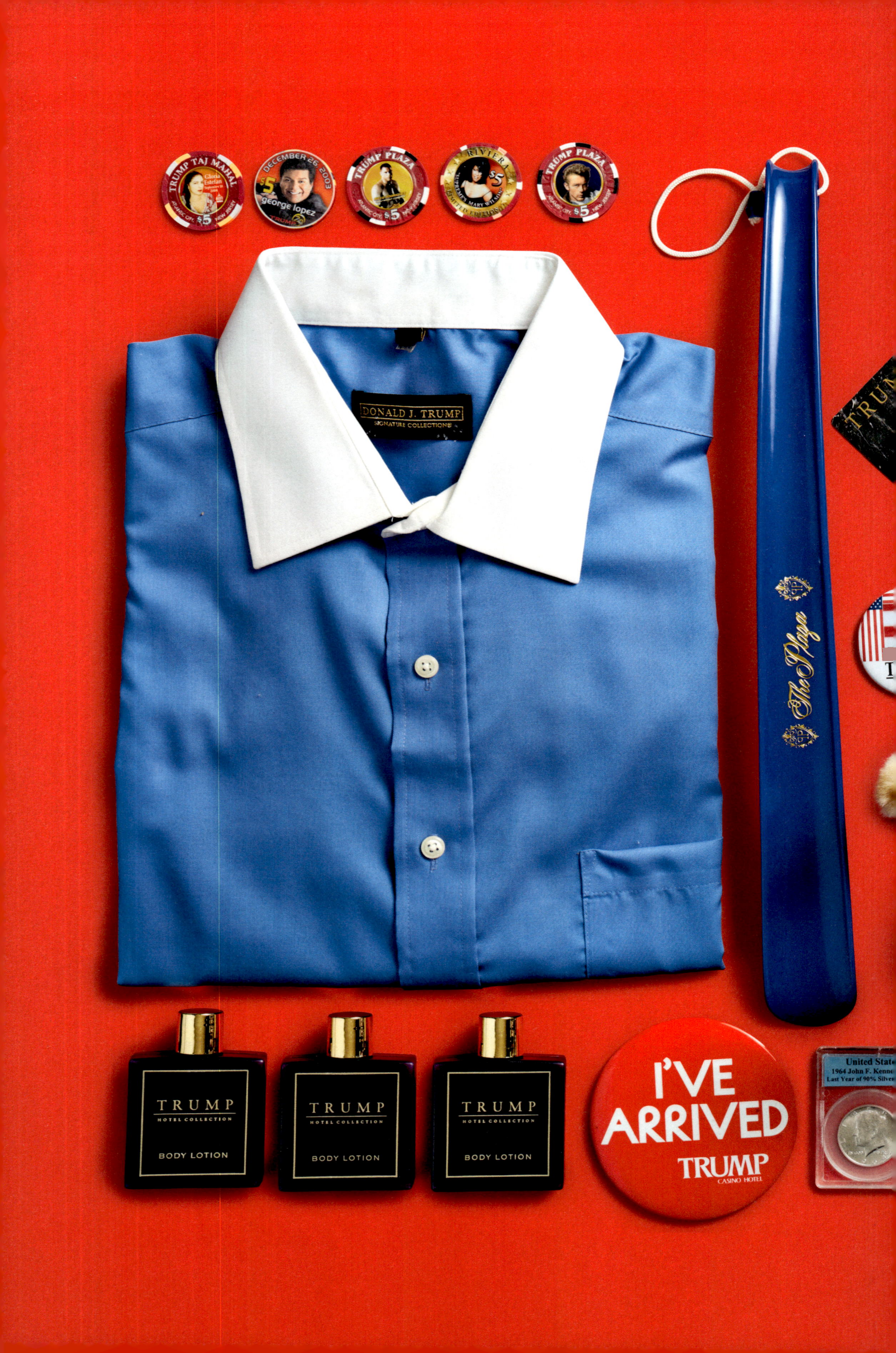

TRUMP TAJ MAHAL
DECEMBER 26 2003
george lopez
TRUMP PLAZA
RIVIERA
TRUMP PLAZA
DONALD J. TRUMP
SIGNATURE COLLECTION
The Plaza
TRUMP
HOTEL COLLECTION
BODY LOTION
TRUMP
HOTEL COLLECTION
BODY LOTION
TRUMP
HOTEL COLLECTION
BODY LOTION
I'VE ARRIVED
TRUMP
CASINO HOTEL

SELECTION OF TRUMP-BRANDED OBJECTS

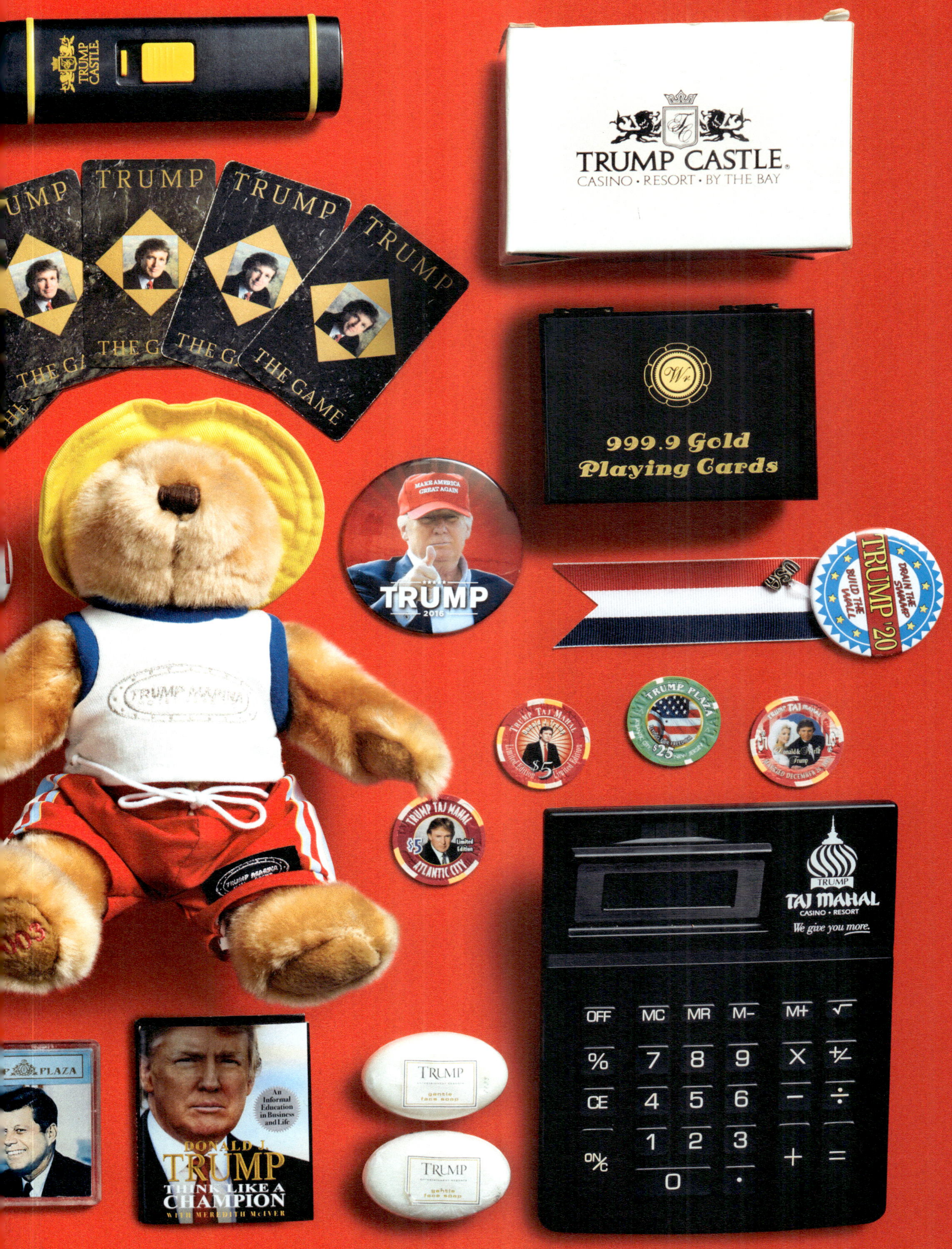

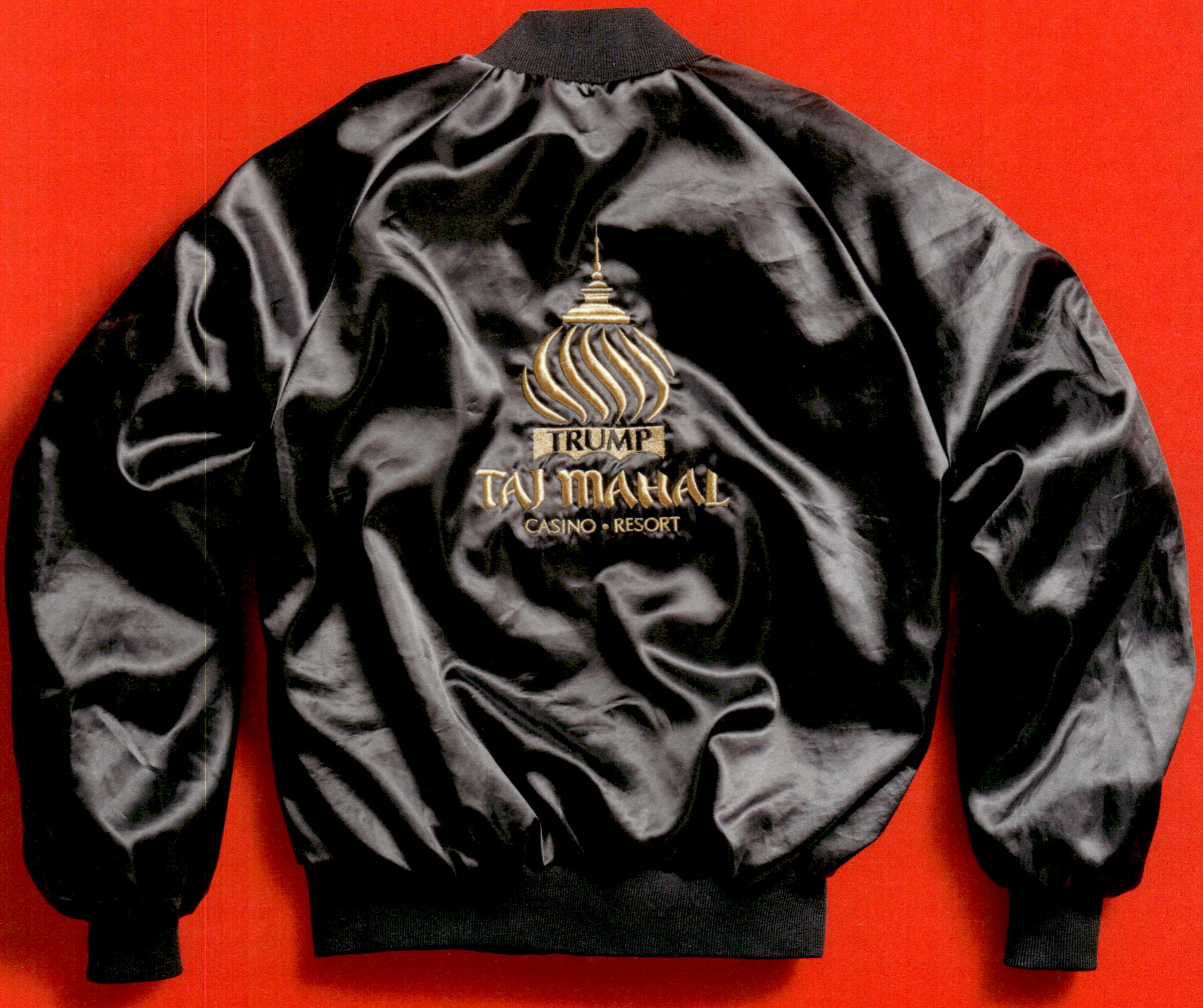
TRUMP
TAJ MAHAL
CASINO • RESORT

TRUMP TAJ MAHAL LIMITED EDITION LEATHER JACKET
GIVEN TO VIPS AT THE CASINO OPENING, 1990

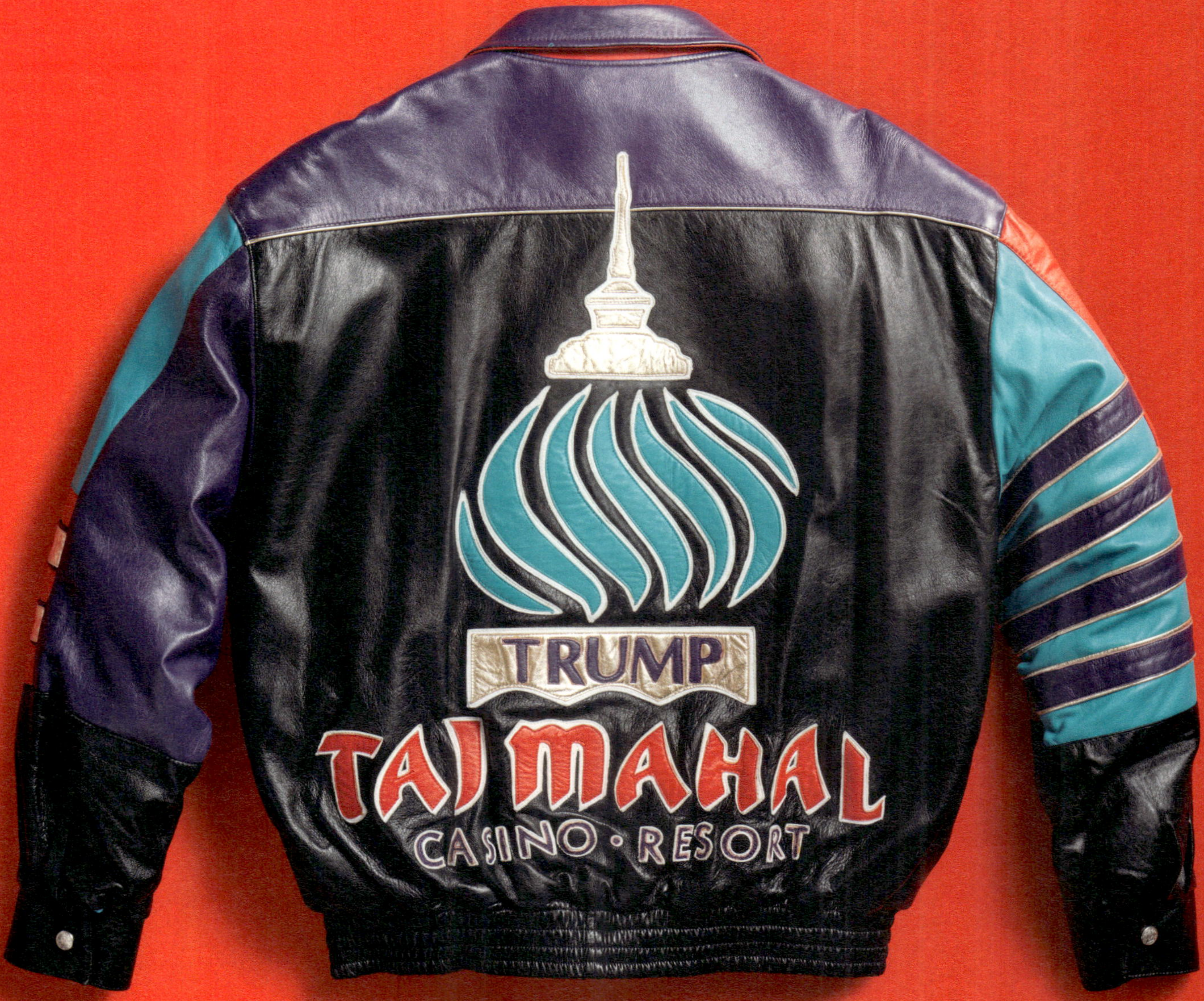

FRANKFURTER ALLGEMEINE WOCHE MAGAZINE, JULY 20, 2018

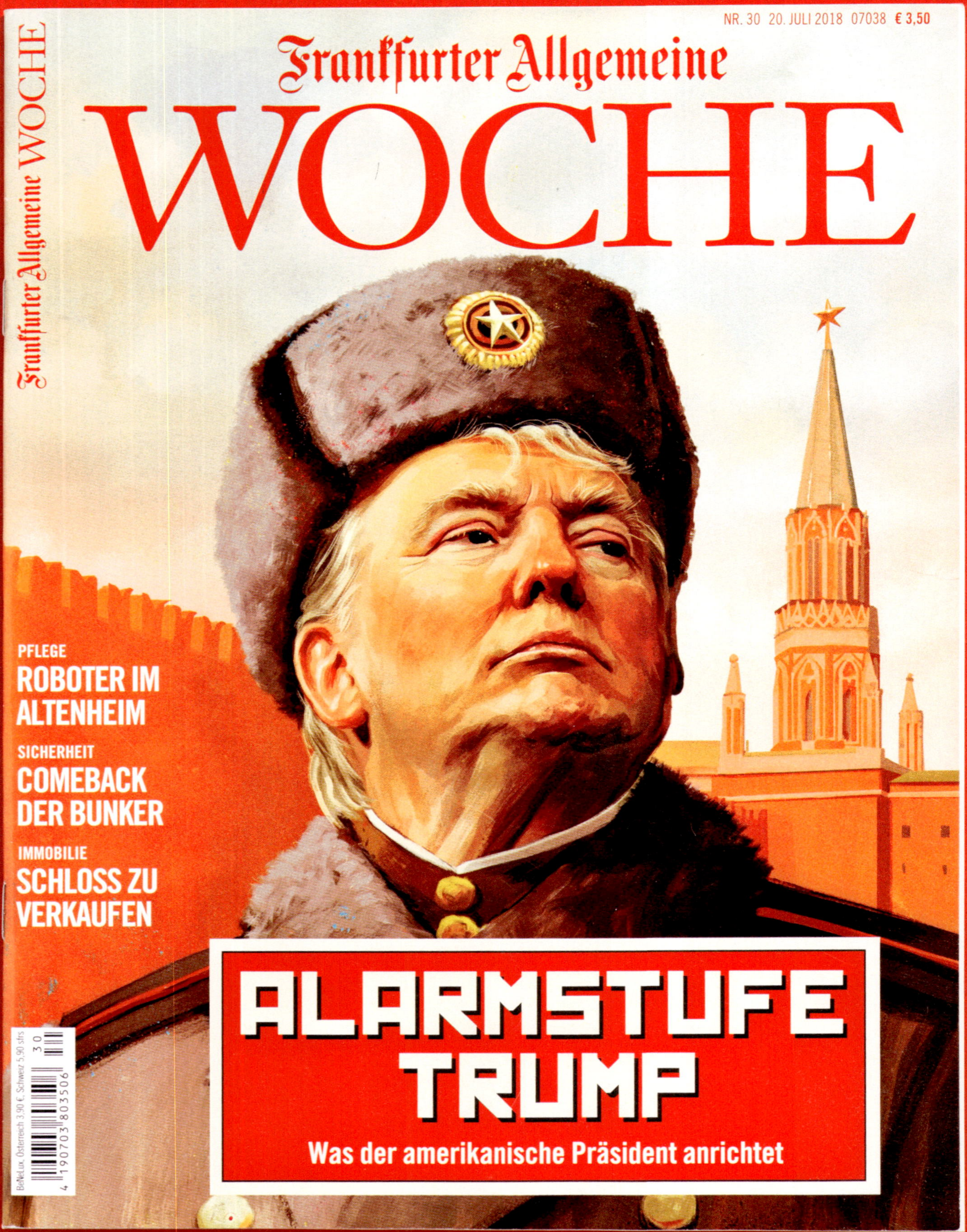

TRUMP VODKA "SUCCESS DISTILLED" 24K GOLD-LEAF LABEL, 2006

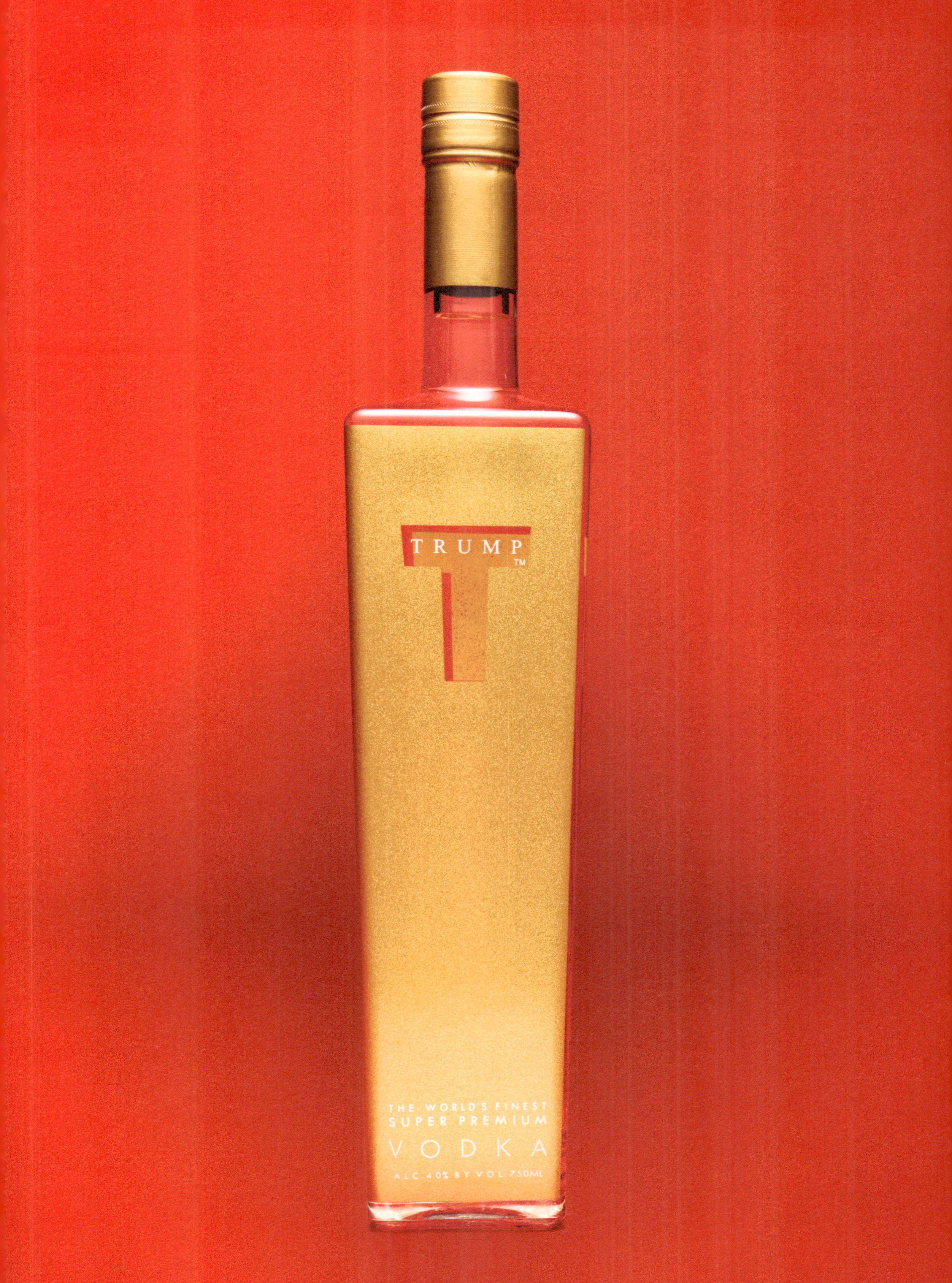

SELECTION OF TRUMP-BRANDED CAMPAIGN BADGES AND PLAYING CARDS

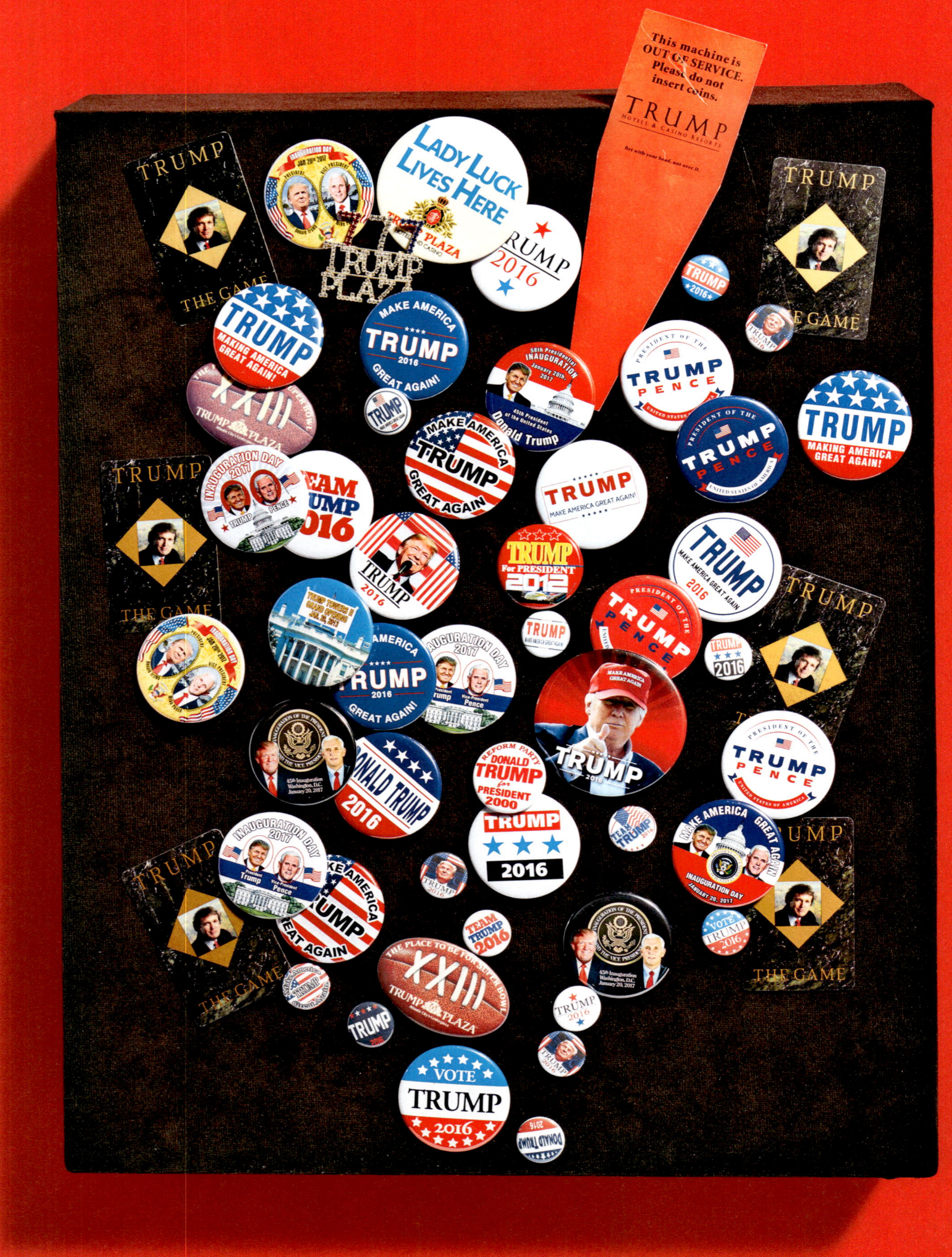

TRUMP FOR PRESIDENT 2016 CAMPAIGN BADGE
SIGNED DONALD TRUMP

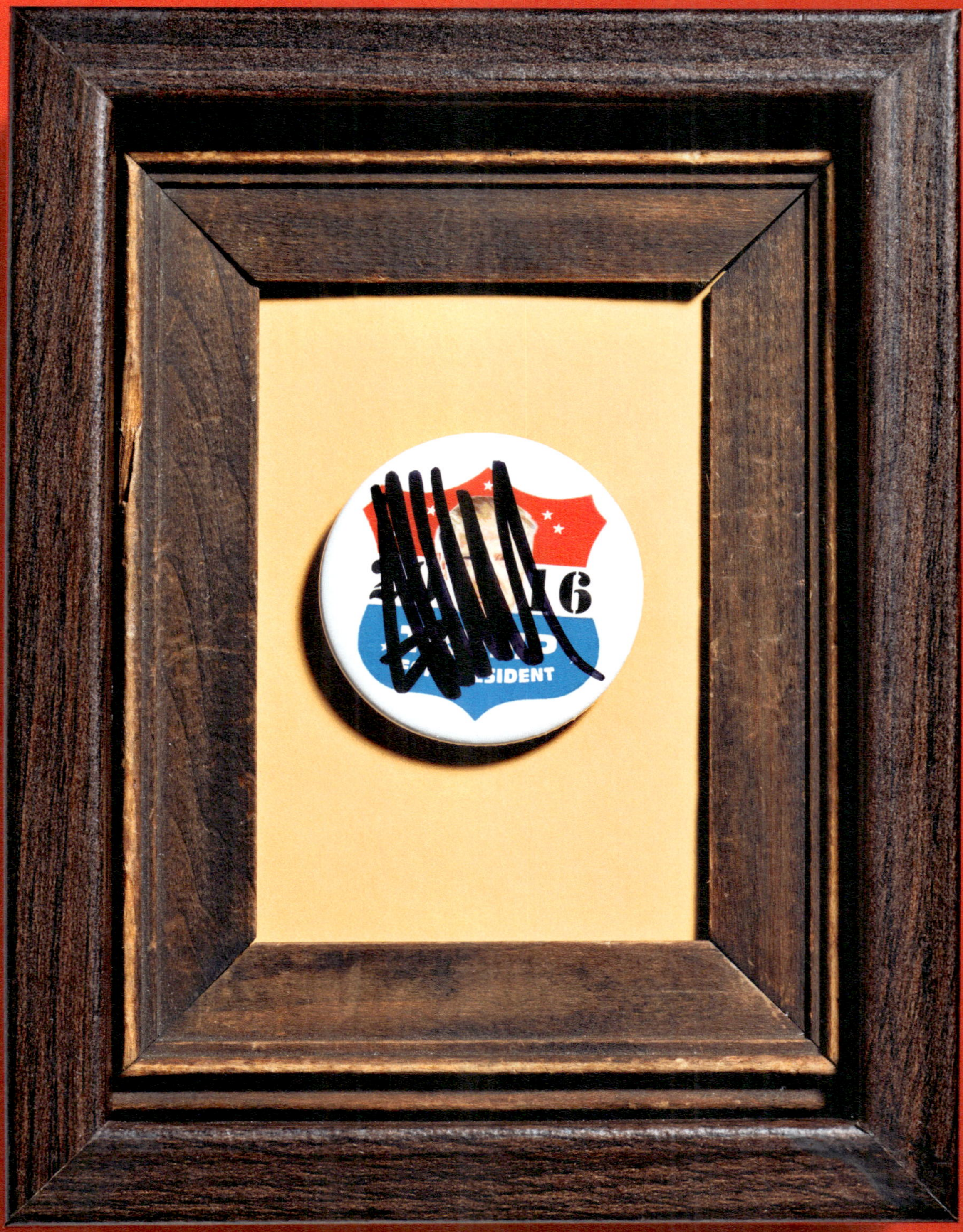

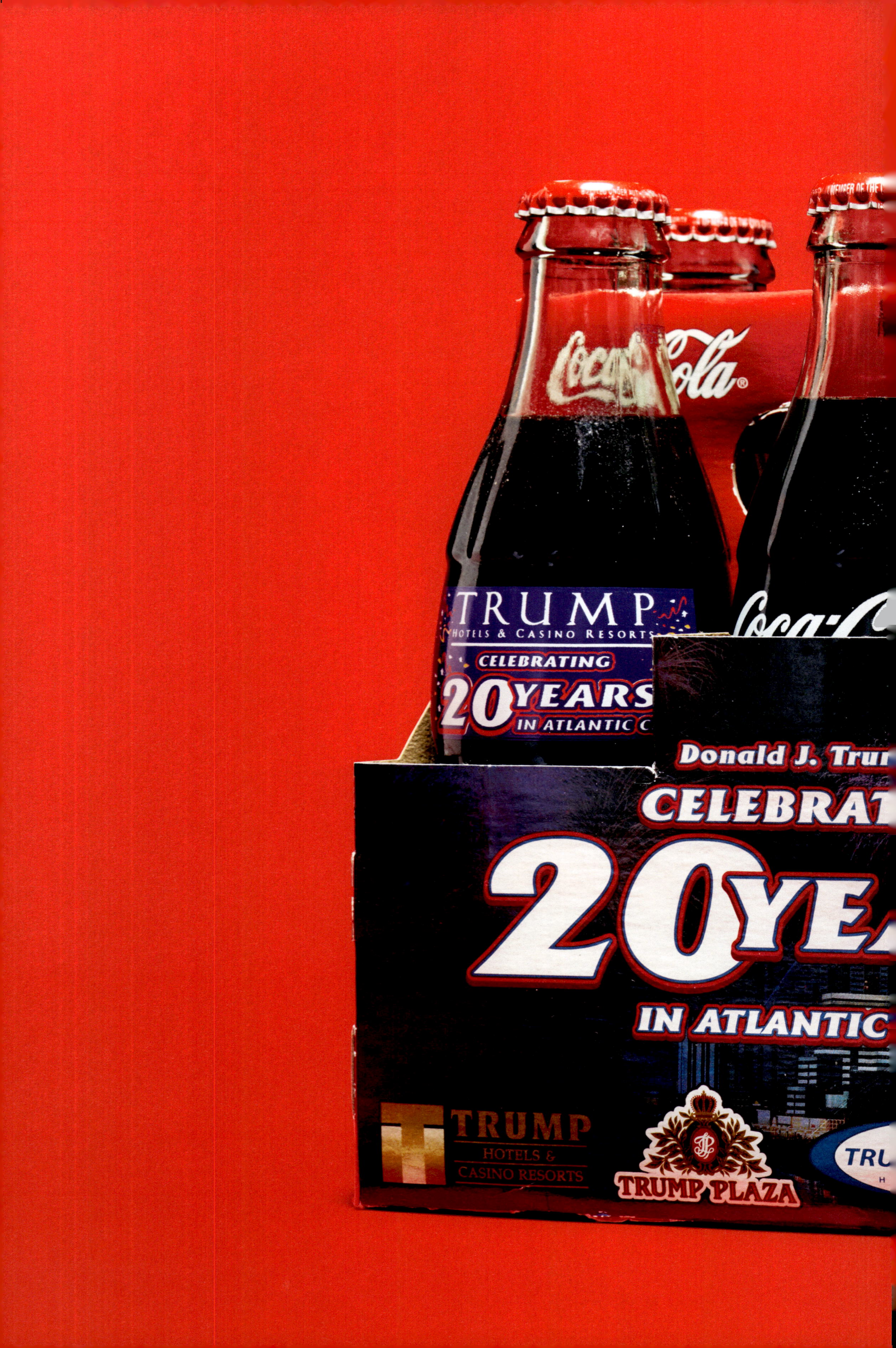

Coca-Cola
TRUMP
HOTELS & CASINO RESORTS
CELEBRATING
20 YEARS
20
TRUMP
HOTELS &
CASINO RESORTS
TRUMP PLAZA

DONALD J. TRUMP COCA-COLA 6-PACK
CELEBRATING 20 YEARS IN ATLANTIC CITY, 2003

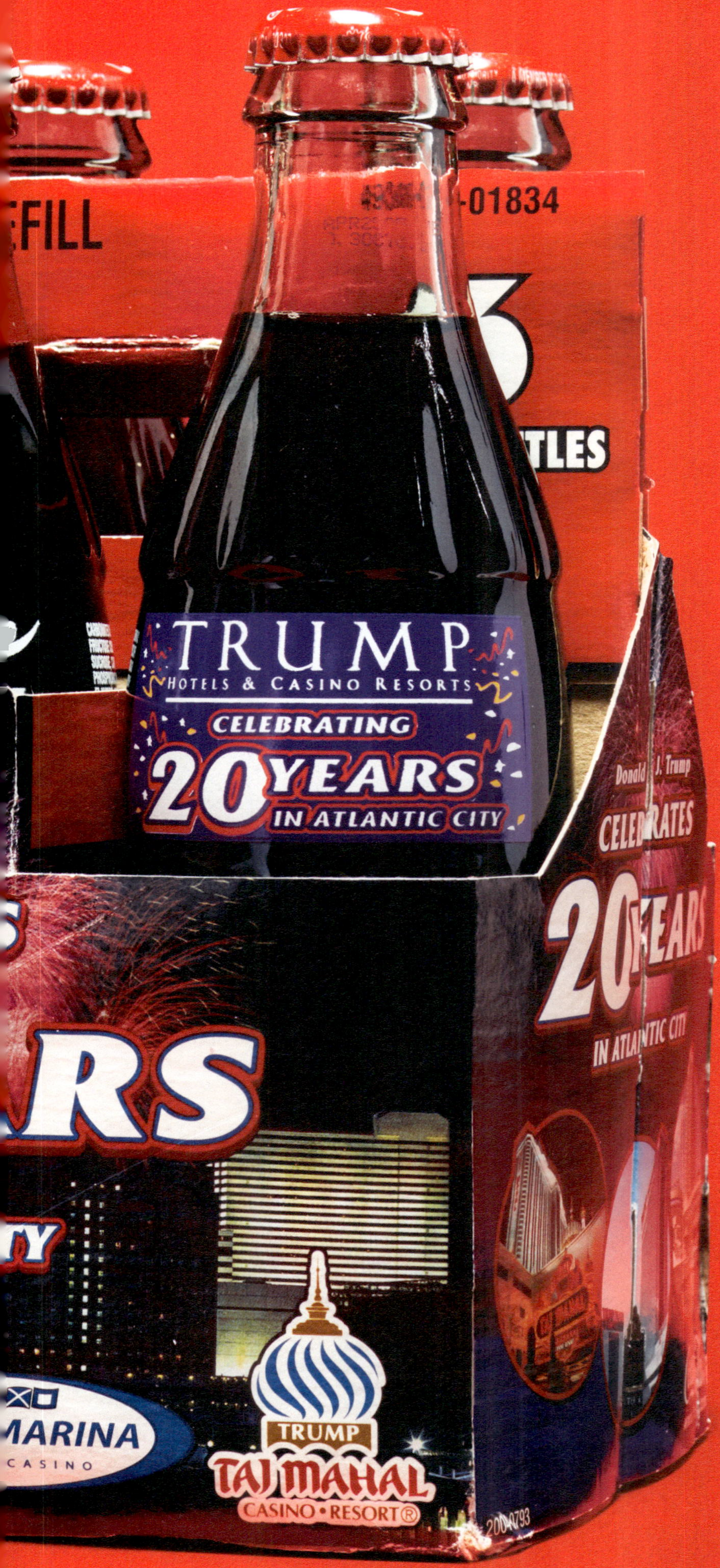

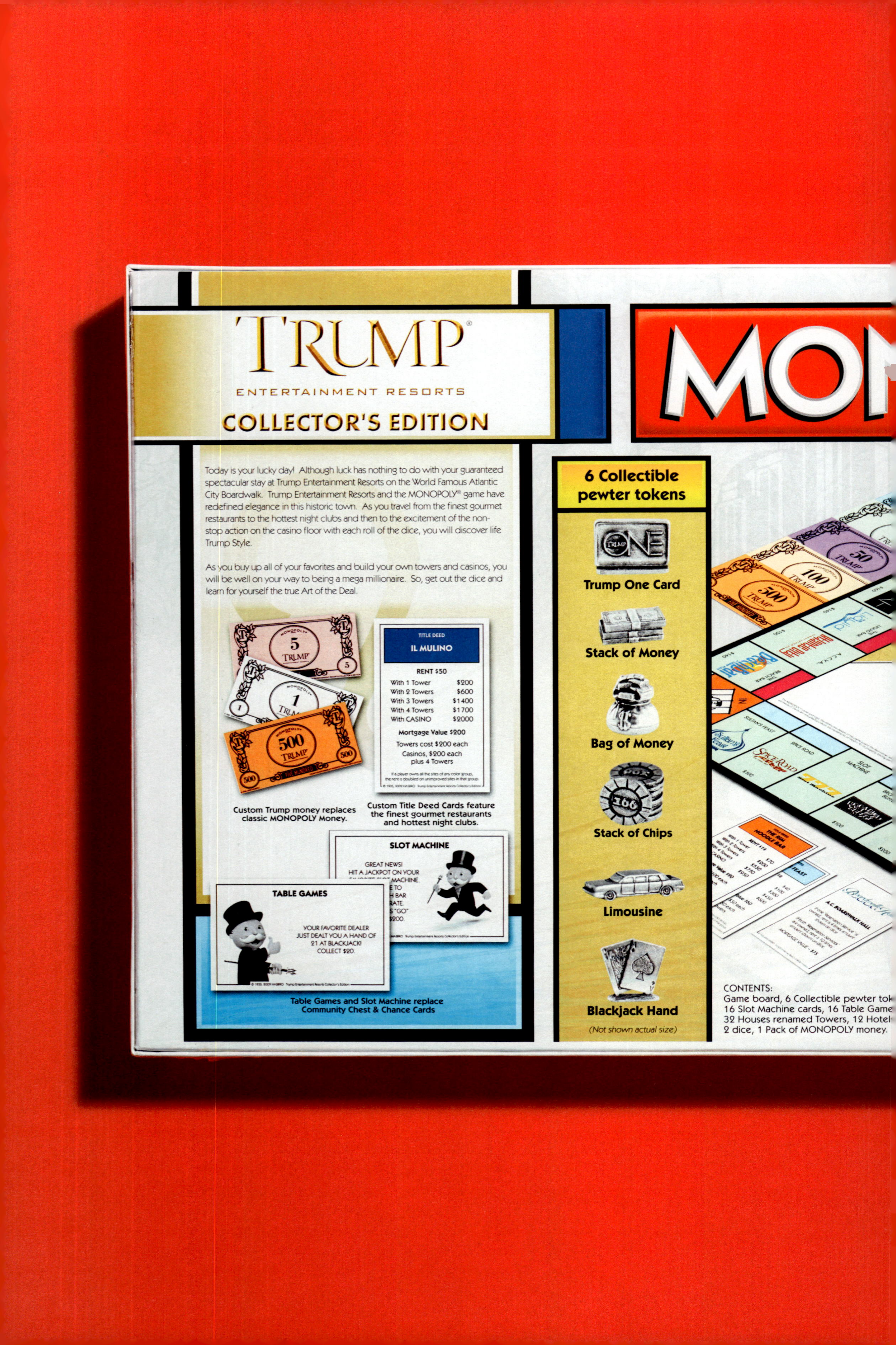
TRUMP®
ENTERTAINMENT RESORTS
COLLECTOR'S EDITION
MON
Today is your lucky day! Although luck has nothing to do with your guaranteed spectacular stay at Trump Entertainment Resorts on the World Famous Atlantic City Boardwalk. Trump Entertainment Resorts and the MONOPOLY® game have redefined elegance in this historic town. As you travel from the finest gourmet restaurants to the hottest night clubs and then to the excitement of the non-stop action on the casino floor with each roll of the dice, you will discover life Trump Style.
As you buy up all of your favorites and build your own towers and casinos, you will be well on your way to being a mega millionaire. So, get out the dice and learn for yourself the true Art of the Deal.
TITLE DEED
IL MULINO
RENT $50
With 1 Tower $200
With 2 Towers $600
With 3 Towers $1400
With 4 Towers $1700
With CASINO $2000
Mortgage Value $200
Towers cost $200 each
Casinos, $200 each plus 4 Towers
Custom Trump money replaces classic MONOPOLY Money.
Custom Title Deed Cards feature the finest gourmet restaurants and hottest night clubs.
SLOT MACHINE
TABLE GAMES
YOUR FAVORITE DEALER JUST DEALT YOU A HAND OF 21 AT BLACKJACK! COLLECT $20.
Table Games and Slot Machine replace Community Chest & Chance Cards
6 Collectible pewter tokens
Trump One Card
Stack of Money
Bag of Money
Stack of Chips
Limousine
Blackjack Hand
(Not shown actual size)
CONTENTS:
Game board, 6 Collectible pewter tok
16 Slot Machine cards, 16 Table Game
32 Houses renamed Towers, 12 Hotel
2 dice, 1 Pack of MONOPOLY money.

MONOPOLY BOARD GAME: TRUMP COLLECTOR'S EDITION, 2009

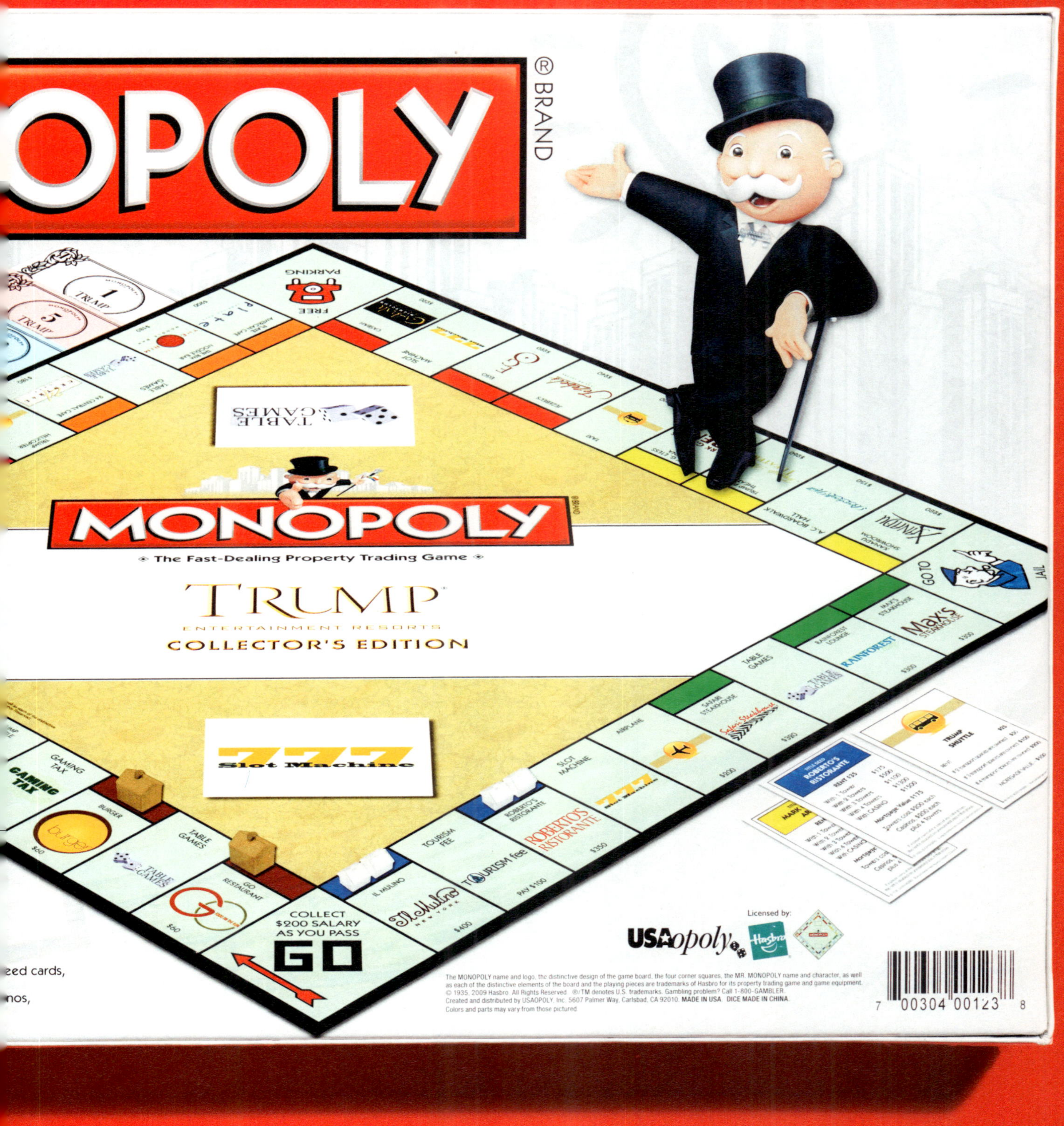

TRUMP MARINA DONALD J. TRUMP BOBBLEHEAD, 2004

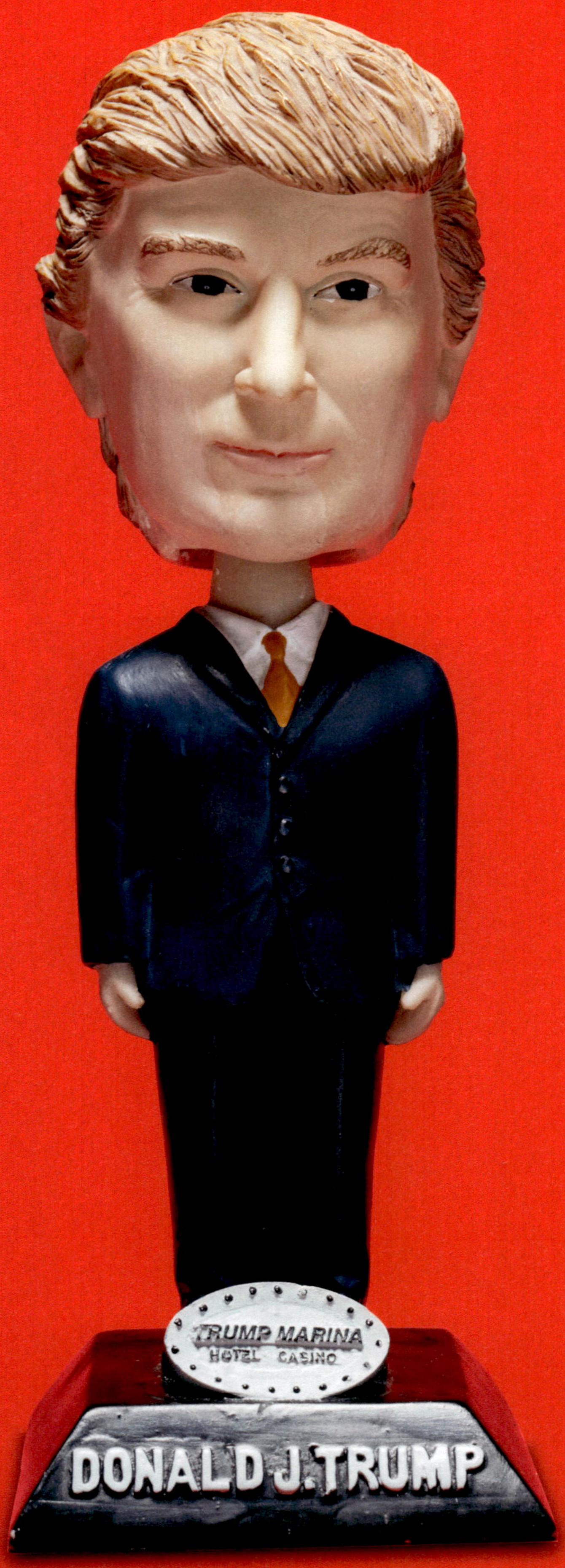

PRESIDENT DONALD J. TRUMP HISTORICAL BUST

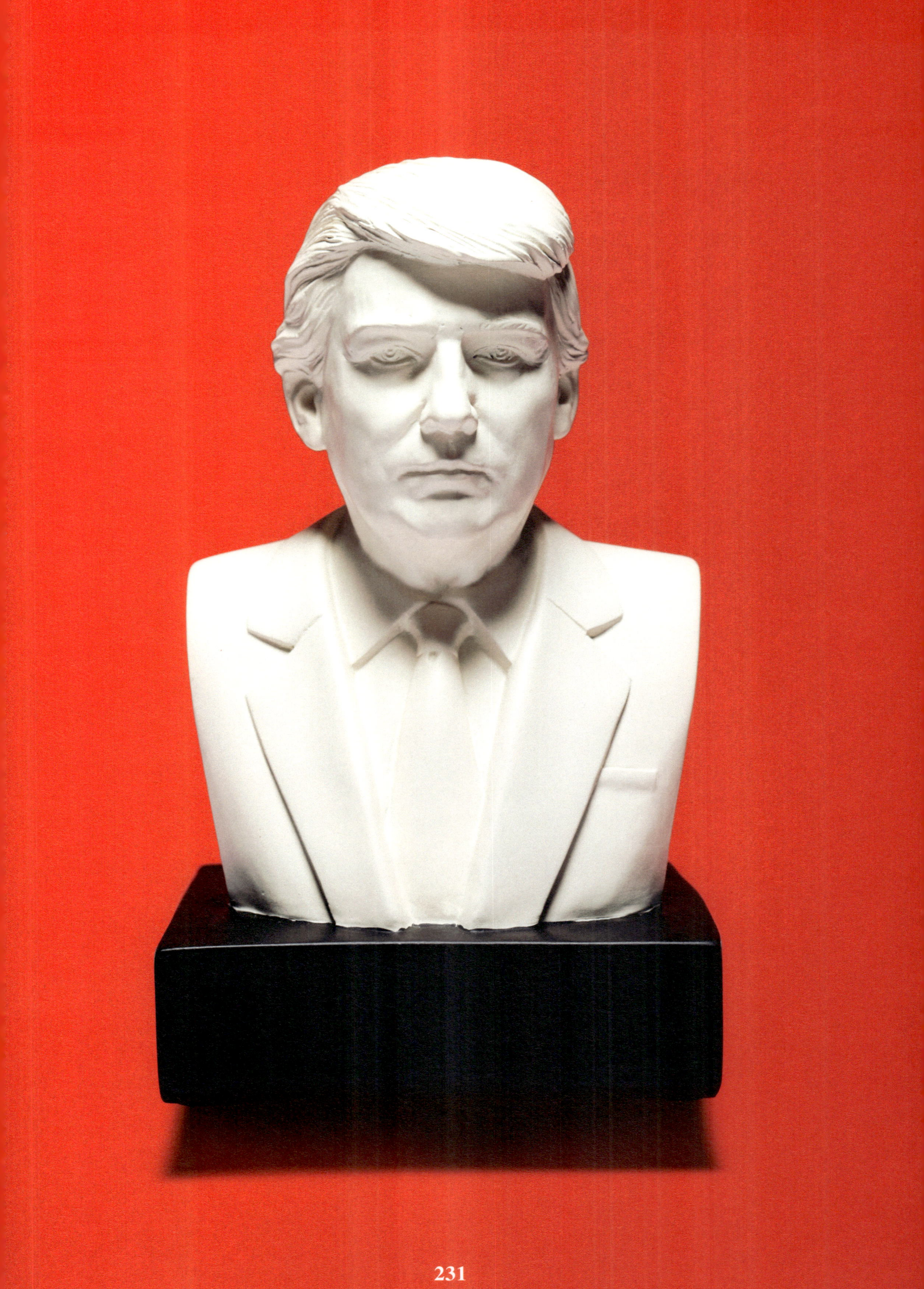

NEW JERSEY MAGAZINE, NOVEMBER 1987

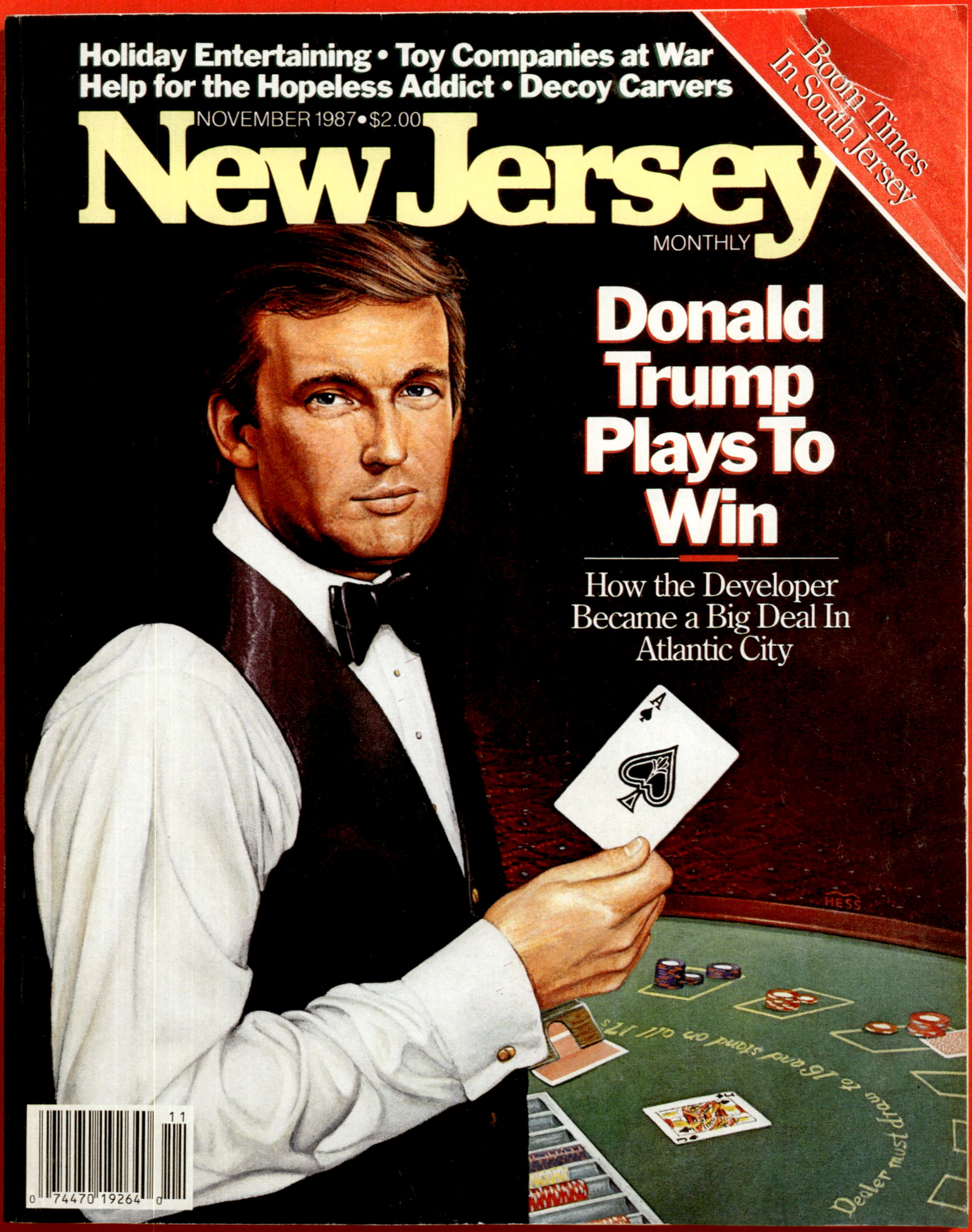

TIME MAGAZINE, NOVEMBER 18, 2019

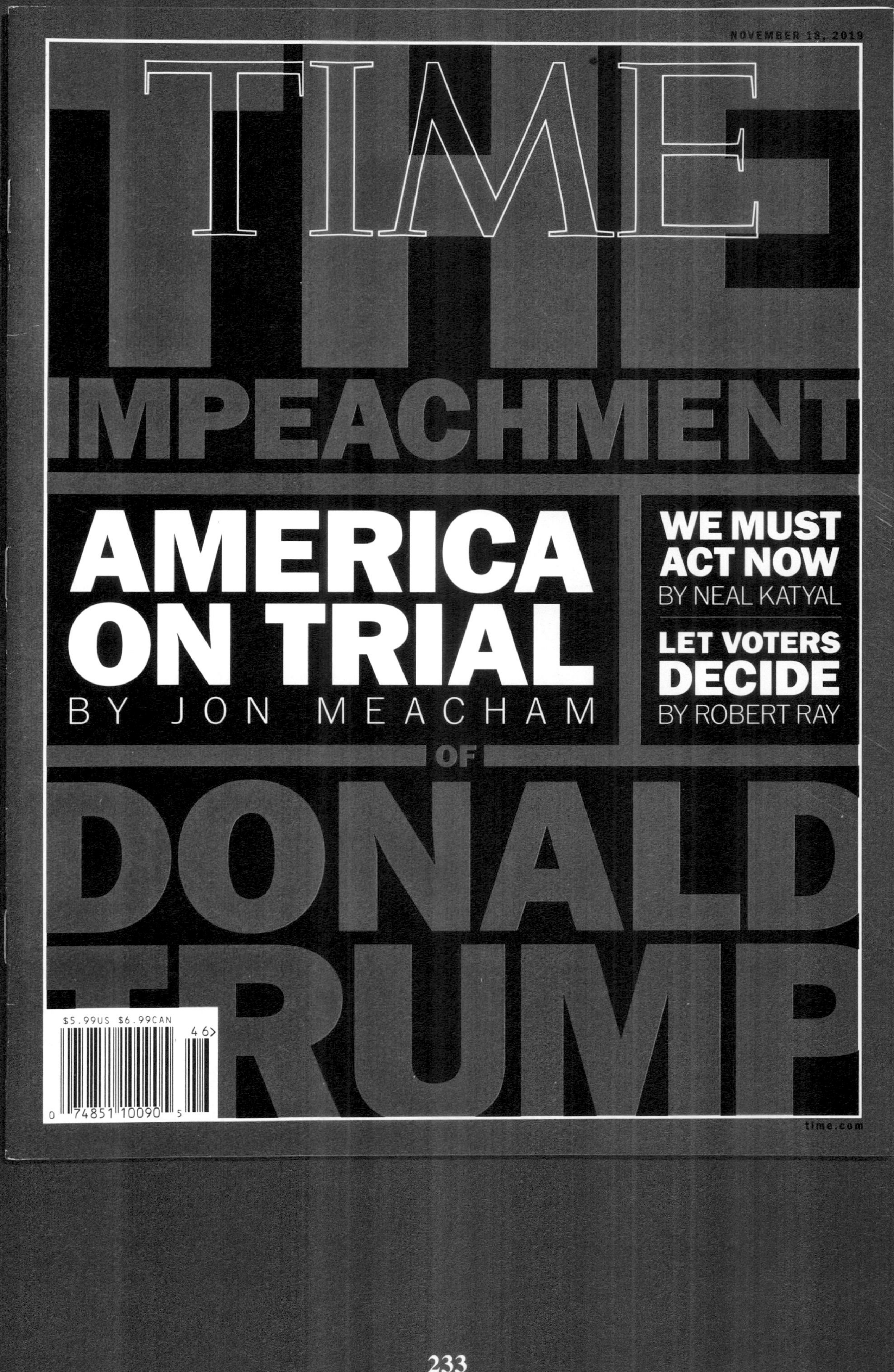

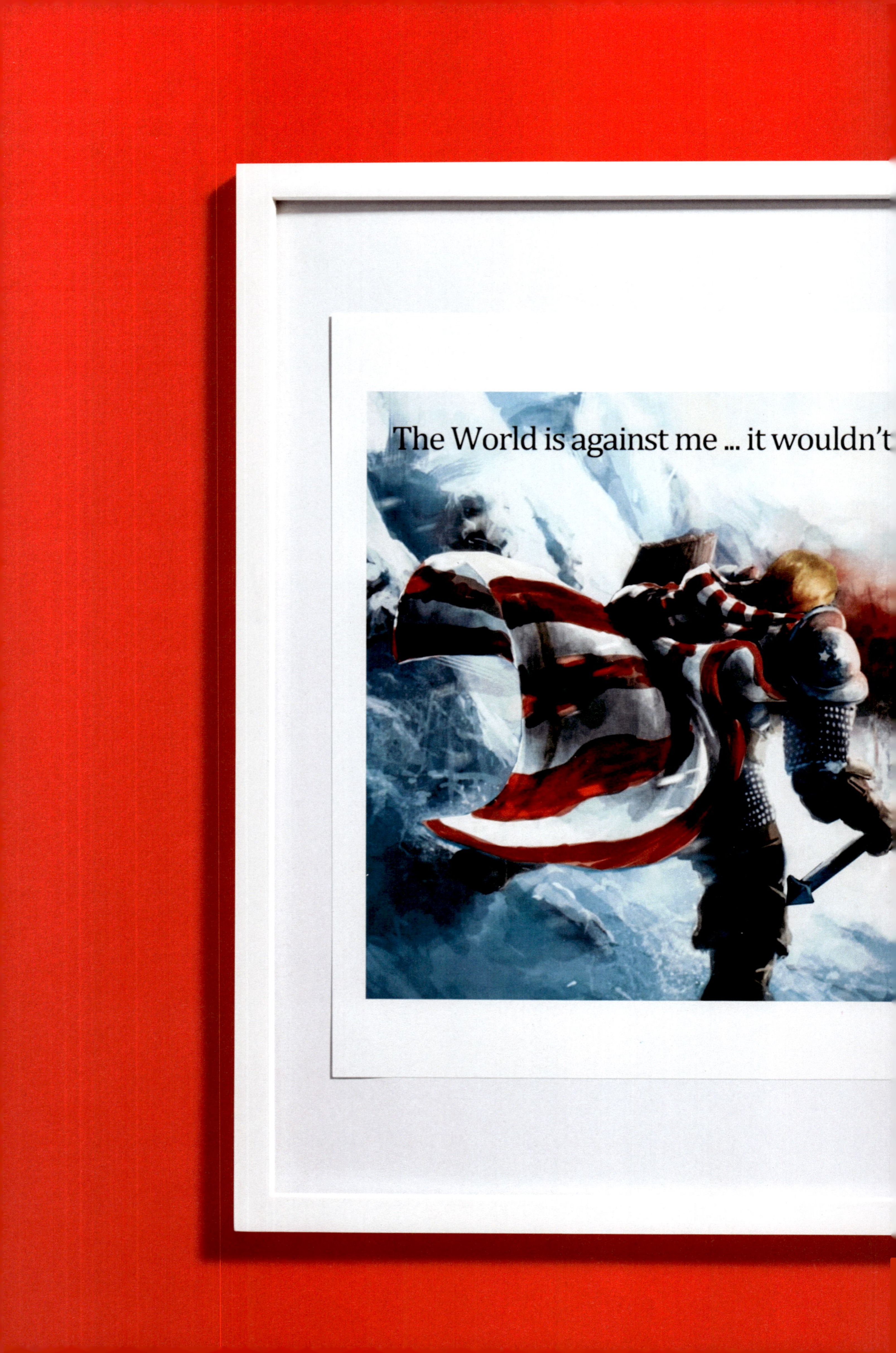
The World is against me ... it wouldn't

UNOFFICIAL TRUMP 2016 CAMPAIGN POSTER
SIGNED DONALD TRUMP

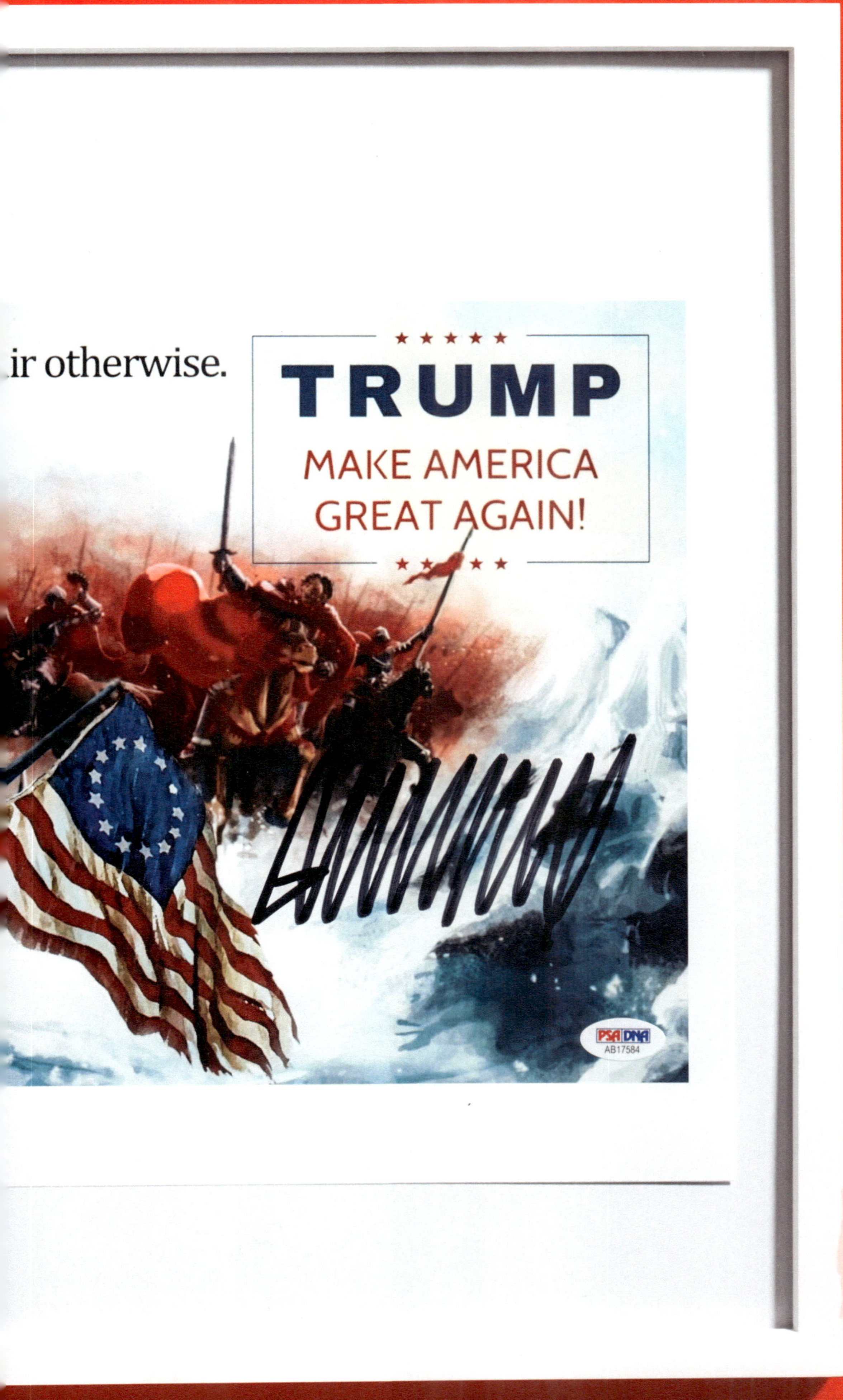

NEW YORK POST, JULY 28, 2017

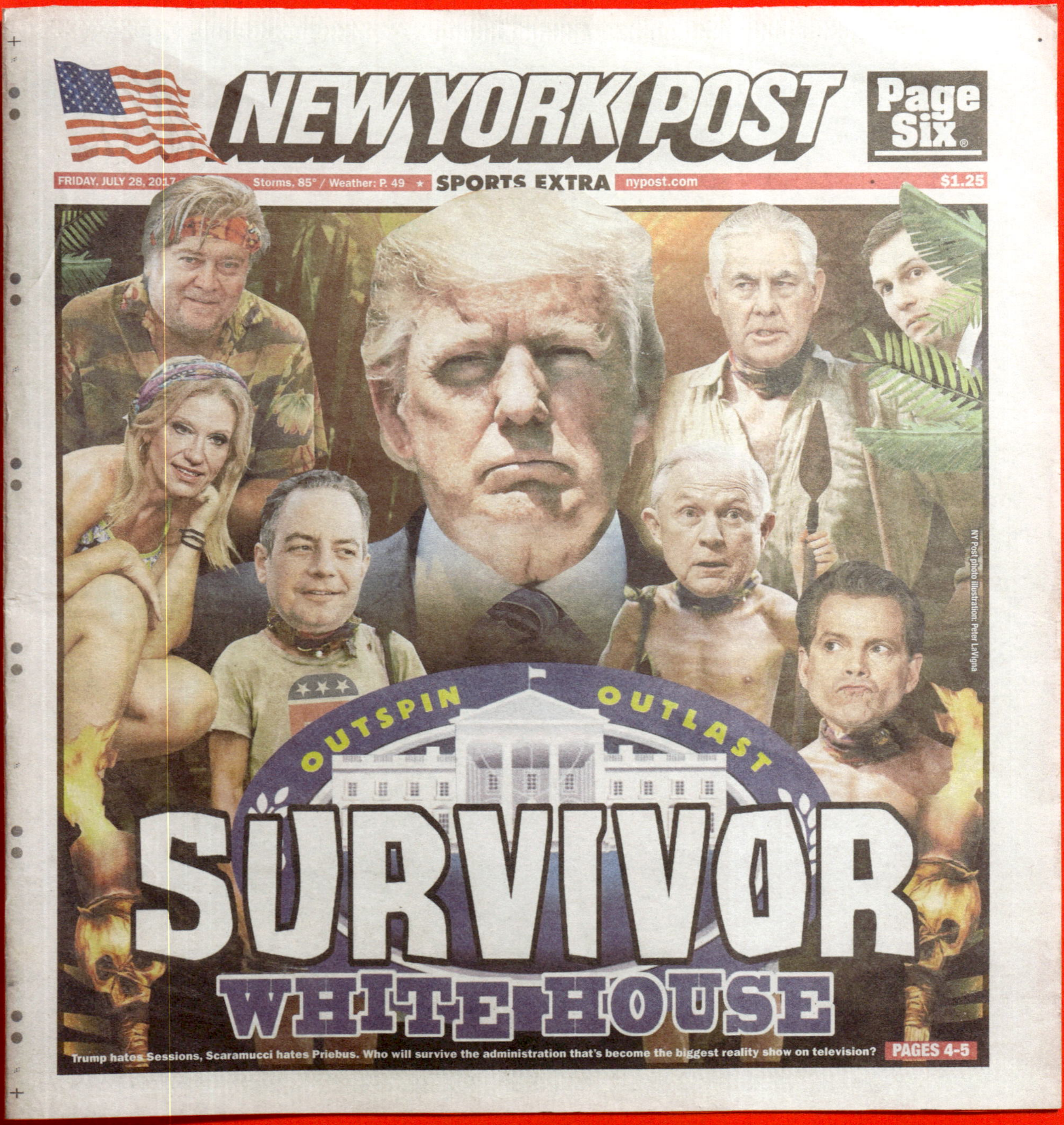

NEW YORK POST

Page Six

FRIDAY, JULY 28, 2017 | Storms, 85° / Weather: P. 49 | SPORTS EXTRA | nypost.com | $1.25

OUTSPIN OUTLAST

SURVIVOR

WHITE HOUSE

Trump hates Sessions, Scaramucci hates Priebus. Who will survive the administration that's become the biggest reality show on television? PAGES 4-5

NY Post photo illustration: Peter LaVigna

NEW YORK POST, JULY 6, 2018

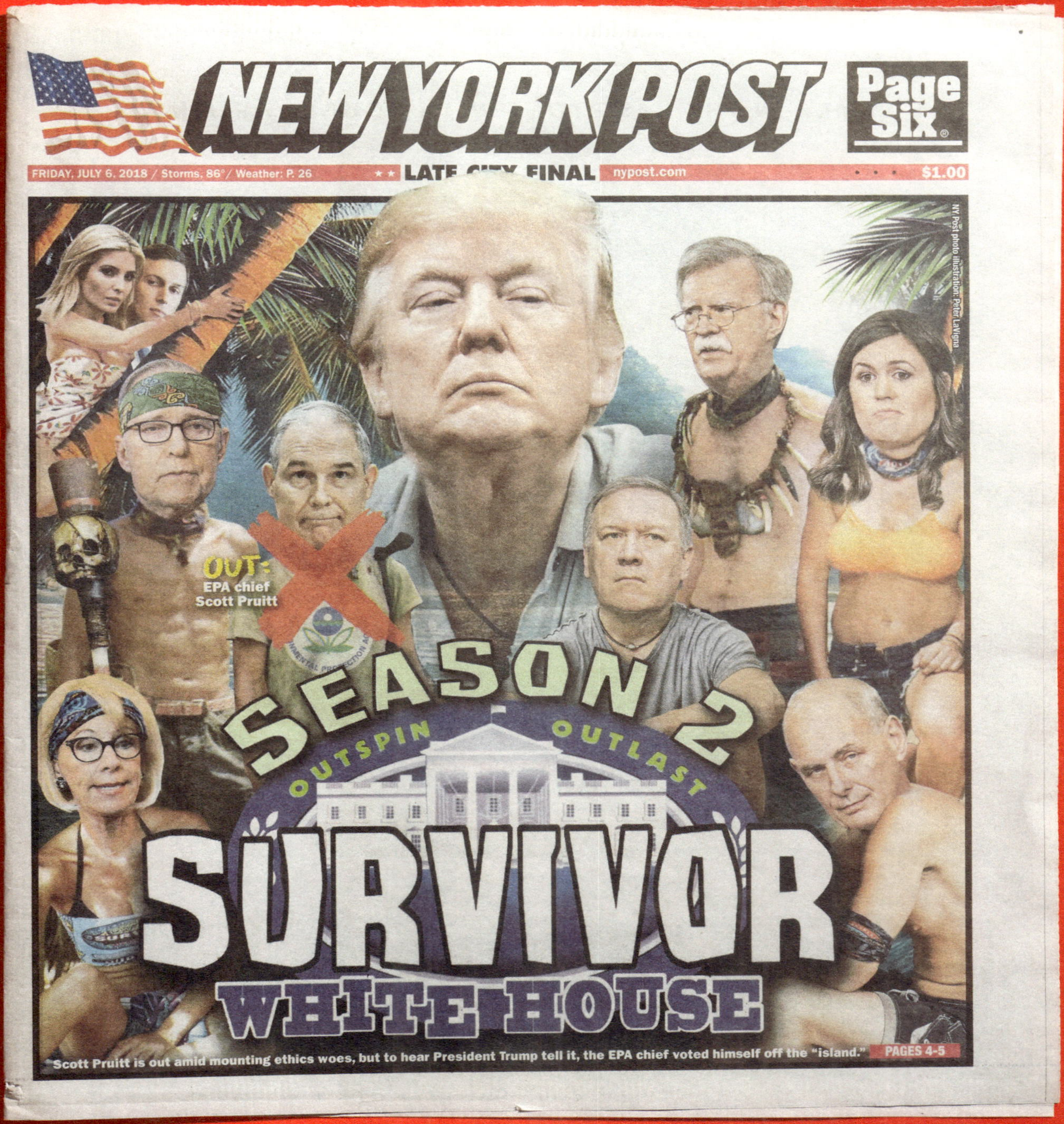
NEW YORK POST

Page Six

FRIDAY, JULY 6, 2018 / Storms, 86° / Weather: P. 26 ★★ LATE CITY FINAL nypost.com $1.00

NY Post photo illustration: Peter LaVigna

OUT: EPA chief Scott Pruitt

SEASON 2

OUTSPIN OUTLAST

SURVIVOR

WHITE HOUSE

Scott Pruitt is out amid mounting ethics woes, but to hear President Trump tell it, the EPA chief voted himself off the "island." PAGES 4-5

THE WHITE HOUSE

WASHINGTON

NOTICE DATE: May 6, 2020
NOTICE NUMBER: 1444 (EN-SP)

Your Economic Impact Payment Has Arrived

My Fellow American:

Our great country is experiencing an unprecedented public health and economic challenge as a result of the global coronavirus pandemic. Our top priority is your health and safety. As we wage total war on this invisible enemy, we are also working around the clock to protect hardworking Americans like you from the consequences of the economic shutdown. We are fully committed to ensuring that you and your family have the support you need to get through this time.

On March 27, 2020, Congress passed with overwhelming bipartisan support the Coronavirus Aid, Relief, and Economic Security Act (CARES Act), which I proudly signed into law. I want to thank the United States House of Representatives and the United States Senate for working so quickly with my Administration to fast-track this $2.2 trillion in much-needed economic relief to the American people.

This includes fast and direct economic assistance to you.

I am pleased to notify you that as provided by the CARES Act, you are receiving an Economic Impact Payment of $ 1,200.00 by direct deposit . We hope this payment provides meaningful support to you during this period.

Every citizen should take tremendous pride in the selflessness, courage and compassion of our people. America's drive, determination, innovation and sheer willpower have conquered every previous challenge---and they will conquer this one too. Just as we have before, America will triumph yet again---and rise to new heights of greatness.

We will do it together, as one nation, stronger than ever before.

President Donald J. Trump

For more information on your Economic Impact Payment, please visit IRS.gov/coronavirus or call 800-919-9835.

WHITE HOUSE COVID-19 STIMULUS LETTER IN ENGLISH AND SPANISH IN 2020, THE INTERNAL REVENUE SERVICE MADE ECONOMIC IMPACT PAYMENTS TO LOW- AND MIDDLE-INCOME AMERICAN CITIZENS IN RESPONSE TO THE CORONAVIRUS PANDEMIC

THE WHITE HOUSE

WASHINGTON

FECHA DEL AVISO: 6 de mayo de 2020
NÚMERO DEL AVISO: 1444 (EN-SP)

Su Pago de alivio por el impacto económico ha llegado

Mi compatriota estadounidense:

Nuestro gran país experimenta un desafío económico y de salud pública sin precedentes, como resultado de la pandemia mundial del coronavirus. Nuestra prioridad principal es su salud y seguridad. A medida que libramos una guerra total contra este enemigo invisible, también estamos trabajando las 24 horas del día para proteger a los estadounidenses trabajadores como usted, de las consecuencias del cierre económico. Estamos totalmente comprometidos a asegurar que usted y su familia tengan el apoyo que necesitan para sobrepasar este tiempo.

El 27 de marzo de 2020, el Congreso aprobó con un abrumador apoyo bipartidista, la Ley de Asistencia, Alivio y Seguridad Económica por el Coronavirus (CARES, por sus siglas en inglés), que yo orgullosamente firmé convirtiéndola en ley. Deseo agradecer al Senado de los Estados Unidos y a la Cámara de Representantes de los Estados Unidos por trabajar tan rápidamente con mi Administración para acelerar este alivio económico de $2.2 billones de dólares muy necesario para el pueblo estadounidense.

Esto incluye la asistencia económica rápida y directa para usted.

Me complace notificarle que según lo dispuesto en la Ley CARES, usted recibe un Pago de alivio por el impacto económico de $ 1,200.00 por depósito directo. Esperamos que este pago le proporcione un apoyo significativo durante este período.

Cada ciudadano debe enorgullecerse enormemente de la abnegación, el coraje y la compasión de nuestro pueblo. El impulso, la determinación, la innovación, y la pura fuerza de voluntad de los Estados Unidos han conquistado todos los desafíos anteriores---y conquistarán éste también. Como lo hemos hecho antes, los Estados Unidos triunfará una vez más---y se elevará a nuevas alturas de grandeza.

Lo haremos juntos, como una nación, más fuerte que nunca.

Presidente Donald J. Trump

Para obtener más información sobre su Pago de alivio por el impacto económico, por favor, visite IRS.gov/coronavirus, o llame al 800-919-9835.

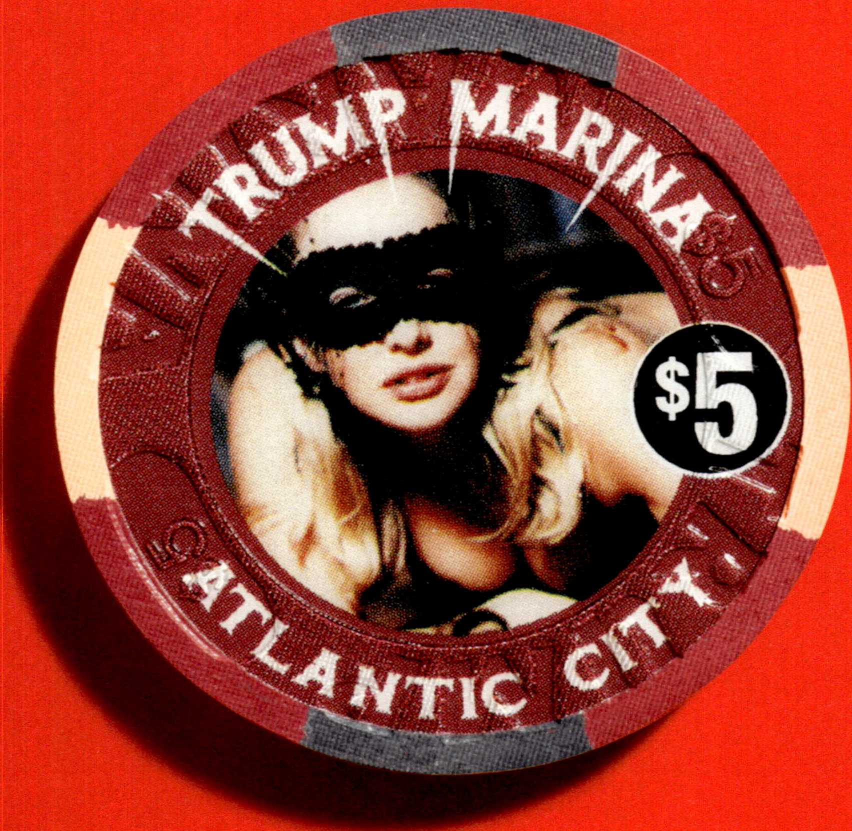
TRUMP MARINA
$5
ATLANTIC CITY

OFFICIAL DONALD J. TRUMP 24K GOLD INAUGURATION MEDALLION PRODUCED BY THE REVOLUTIONARY MINT, A COMPANY ESTABLISHED TO COMMEMORATE THE 2016 PRESIDENTIAL ELECTION

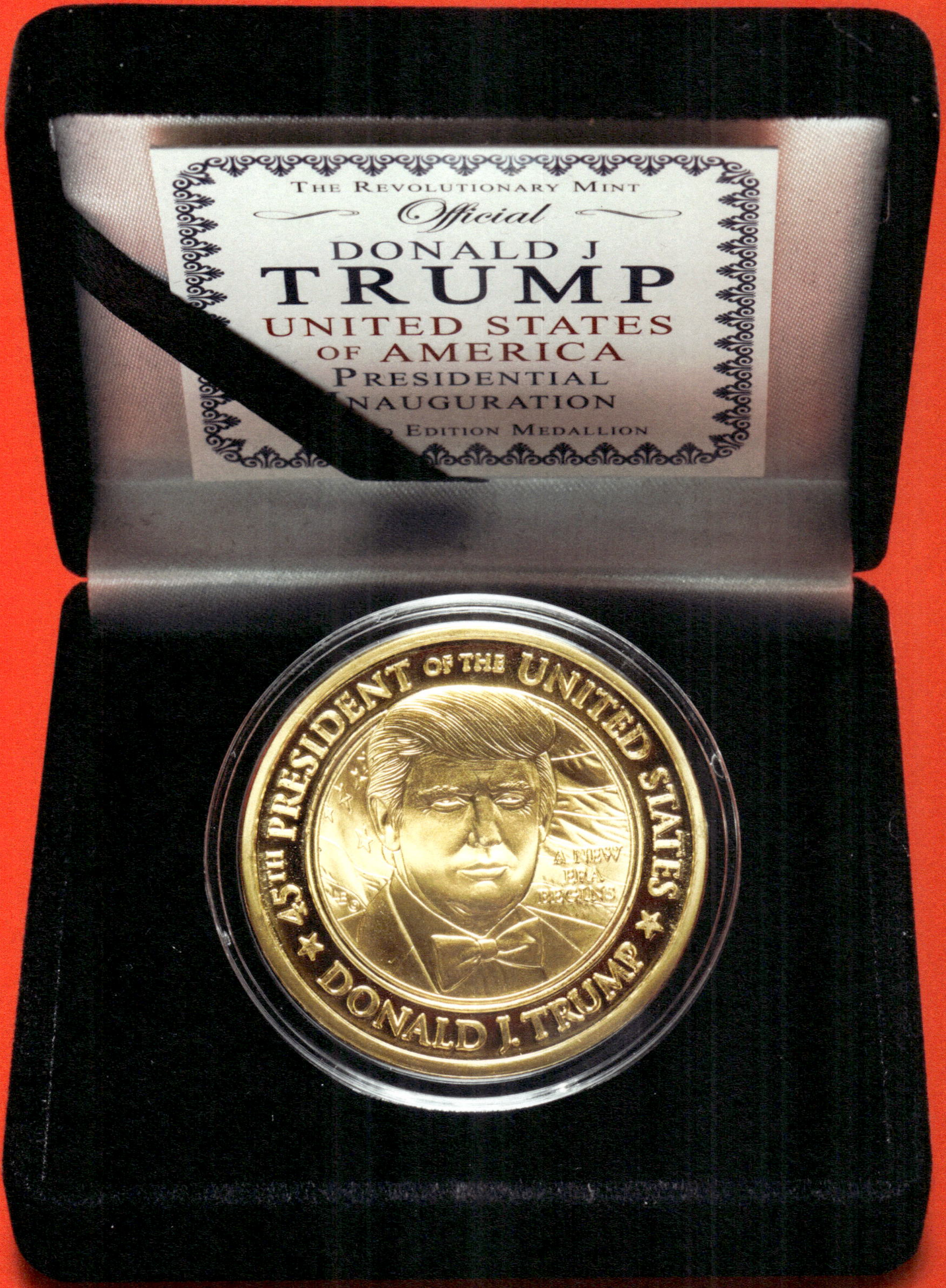

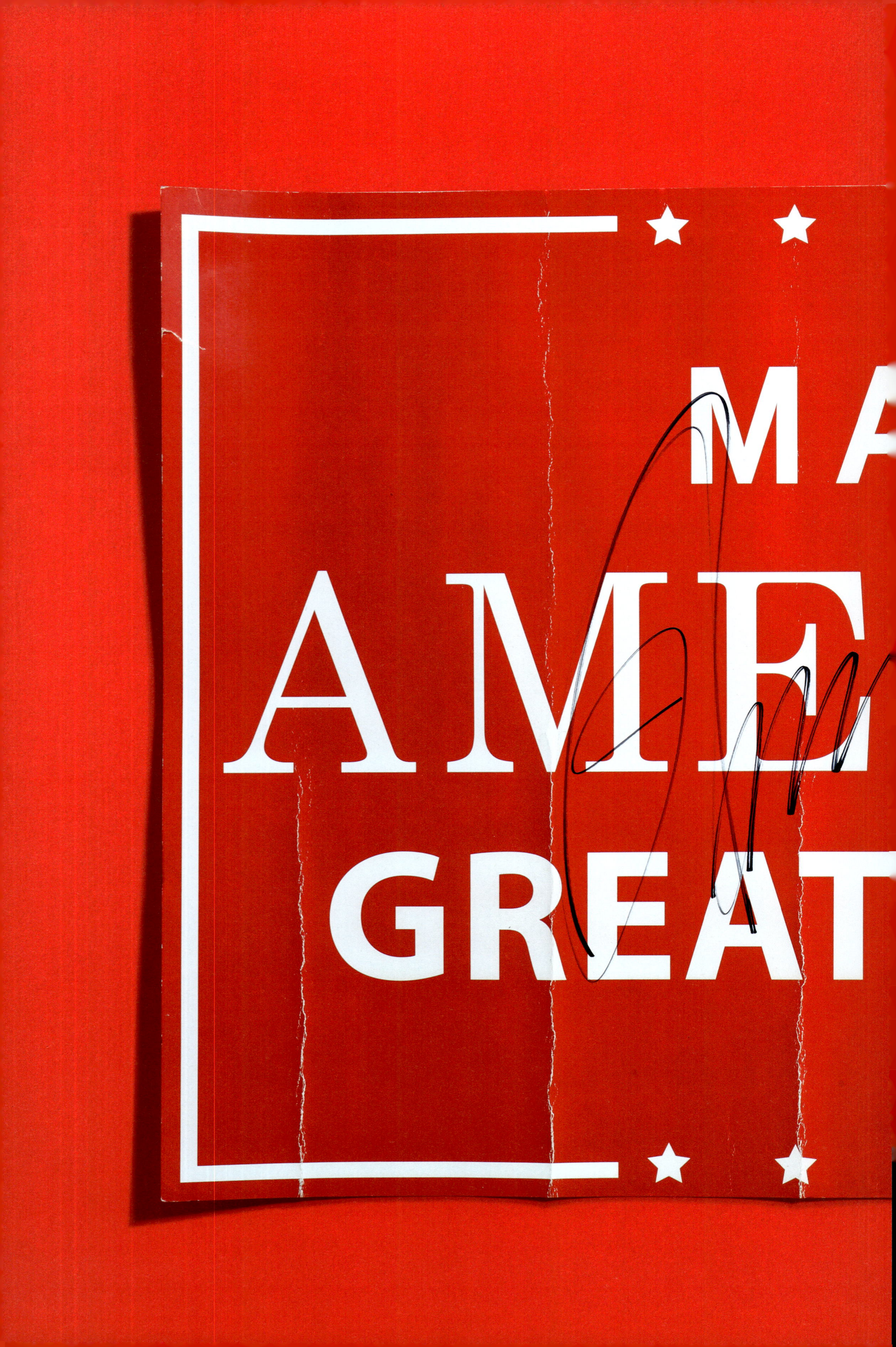
MA
AME
GREAT

OFFICIAL TRUMP 2016 CAMPAIGN SIGN
SIGNED DONALD TRUMP

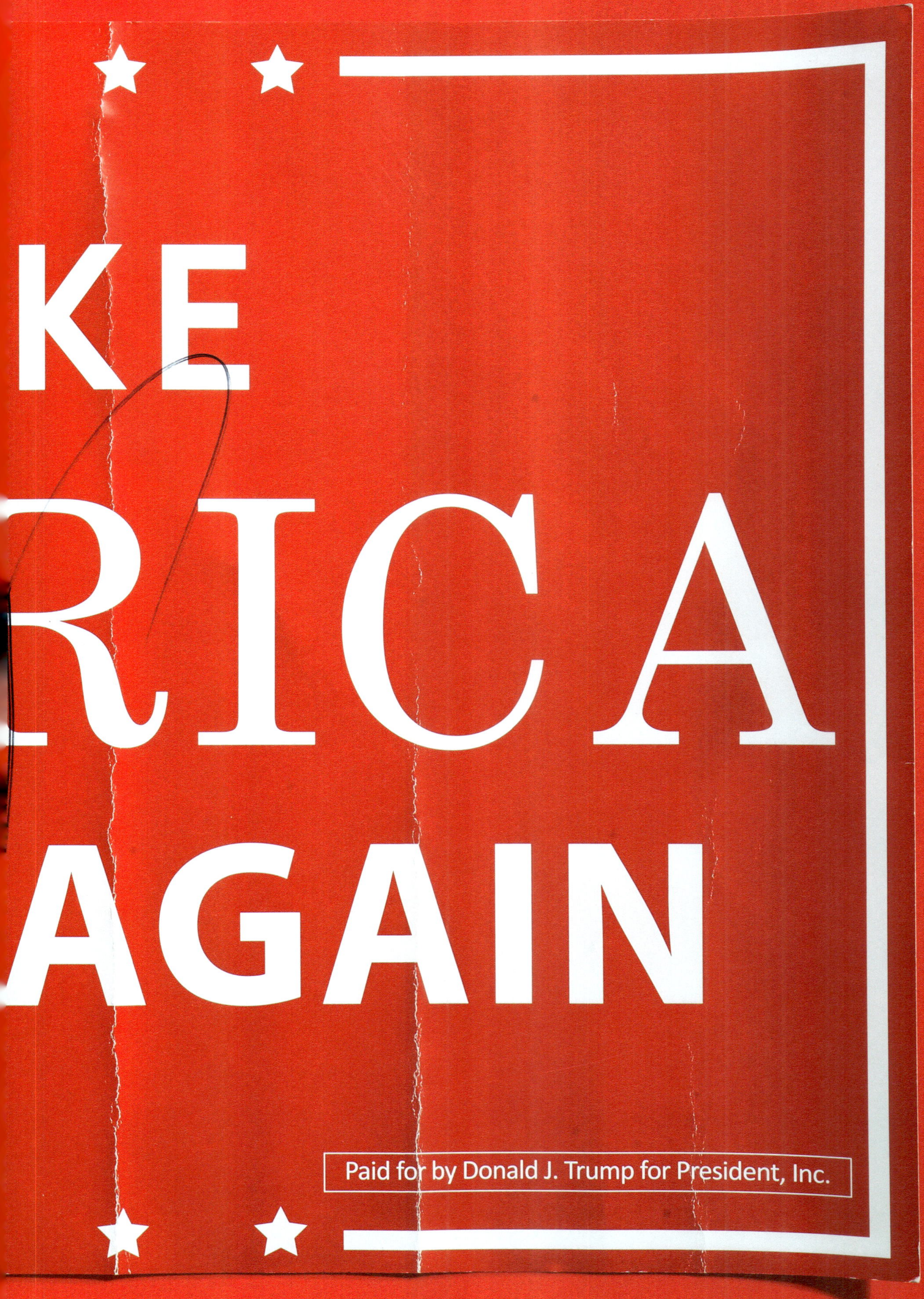

PHOTOGRAPH OF MELANIA KNAUSS COMMISSIONED BY FHM, 2000
SIGNED MELANIA TRUMP

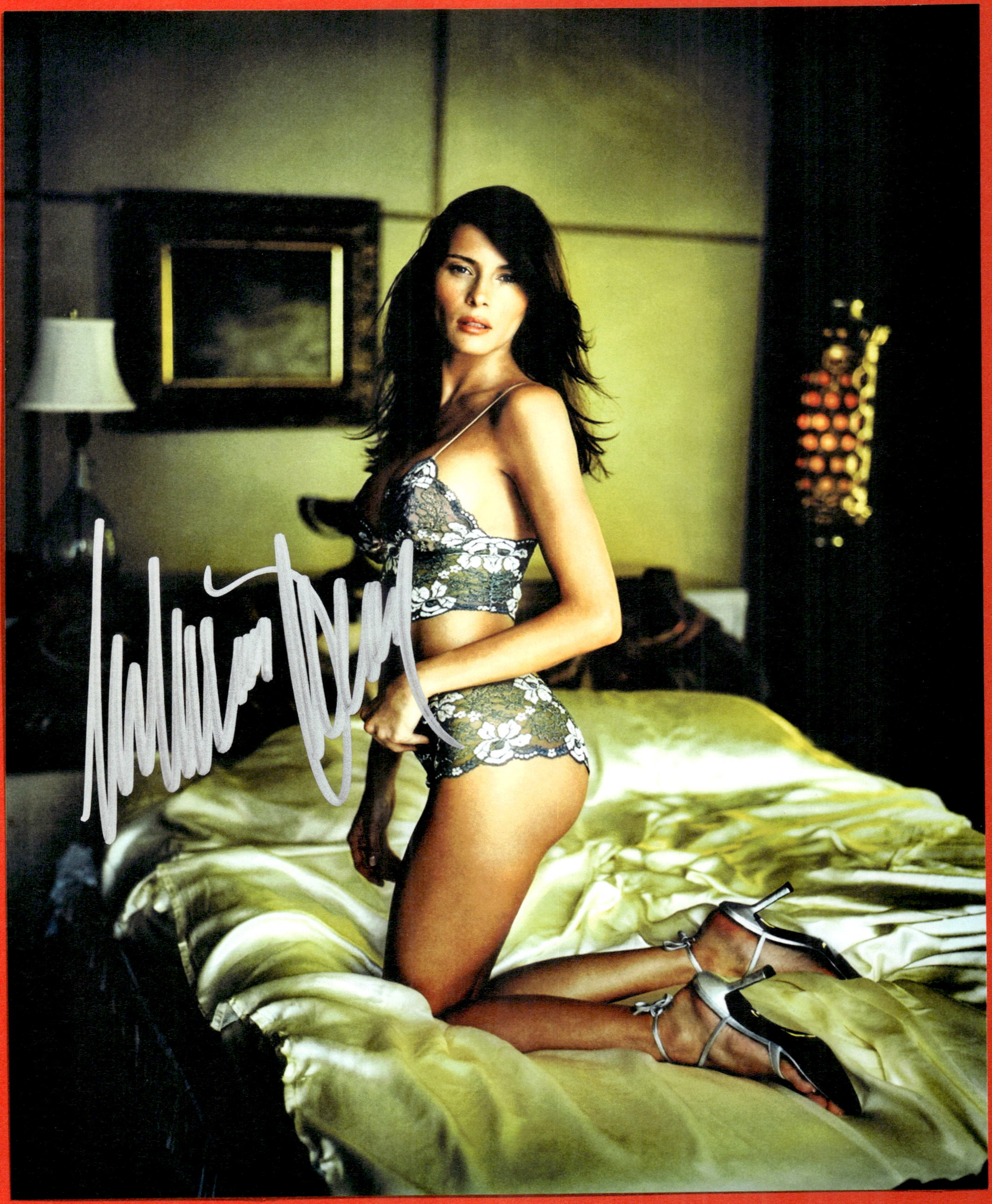

THE GAME: ALL THINGS TRUMP

AN INSTALLATION BY ANDRES SERRANO

ELEANOR HEARTNEY

HAS THERE EVER BEEN A POLITICAL FIGURE AS INESCAPABLE AS DONALD TRUMP?

ANDRES SERRANO'S FIRST MULTIMEDIA INSTALLATION BLASTS THROUGH THE WEB OF WORDS AND IMAGES THAT HAVE BLANKETED AMERICA OVER THE LAST SEVERAL DECADES TO PRESENT A PORTRAIT OF THE MAN AS THE SUM OF THE OBJECTS THAT GLORIFY HIS NAME. THE GAME: ALL THINGS TRUMP

IS A COLLECTION OF OVER 1,000 OBJECTS RELATED TO DONALD TRUMP. AMASSED FROM AUCTIONS, EBAY AND WORD OF MOUTH, IT INCLUDES TRUMP HOTEL AND CASINO SOUVENIRS, TRUMP-BRANDED MERCHANDISE, SPORTS MEMORABILIA, SLOT MACHINES, POSTERS AND SIGNED MAGAZINE COVERS AND PHOTOGRAPHS. IT ALSO DOCUMENTS SOME OF HIS LESS SUCCESSFUL VENTURES, AMONG THEM TRUMP VODKA, TRUMP STEAKS AND TRUMP SHUTTLE. THERE IS EVEN A TRUMP UNIVERSITY DIPLOMA. THE ARTIFACTS ARE INSTALLED IN A MUSEOLOGICAL SETTING, AND AS CAREFULLY CATALOGUED AND LABELED AS THE ITEMS IN ANY NATURAL HISTORY MUSEUM. AS IS SO OFTEN THE CASE IN OUR INFORMATION ERA, THE MASS OF ALL THIS DATA ULTIMATELY

OVERWHELMS ANY SINGLE INTERPRETATION. WE ARE LEFT WITH A FIGURE WHO IS AS SLIPPERY AS HE IS UBIQUITOUS.

TRUMP HAS BEEN HAILED AS THE QUINTESSENTIAL POSTMODERN PRESIDENT. HIS BLITHE DISMISSAL OF COMMONLY ACCEPTED TRUTHS, HIS EMBRACE OF ALTERNATIVE FACTS, HIS OBSESSIVE CULTIVATION OF HIS IMAGE, HIS TRANSFORMATION OF POLITICS INTO THEATER AND HIS CONFIDENCE IN THE MALLEABILITY OF REALITY SEEM TO CONFIRM JEAN BAUDRILLARD'S OBSERVATION THAT "THE SIMULACRUM IS NEVER THAT WHICH CONCEALS THE TRUTH – IT IS THE TRUTH WHICH CONCEALS THAT THERE IS NONE." AS SUCH HE BECOMES THE PERFECT SUBJECT FOR A

DISSECTION OF CONSEQUENCES OF OUR INCREASINGLY FRAUGHT RELATIONSHIP WITH MEANING AND AUTHENTICITY. AND A MATERIAL PORTRAIT CREATED FROM THE BUILDING BLOCKS HE HAS USED TO CONSTRUCT HIS OWN IDENTITY SEEMS AN APPROPRIATE WAY TO EXPRESS THE VOID WITHIN.

THE GERM OF THIS PROJECT LIES IN SERRANO'S 2004 PHOTO ESSAY, "AMERICA." THAT WORK CONJURED THE DIVERSITY OF THE UNITED STATES THROUGH PHOTOGRAPHS OF ITS EDUCATORS, SHOWGIRLS, HEROIN ADDICTS, PUBLIC SERVANTS, MIGRANT WORKERS, AND SOCIALITES. INCLUDED WAS A PHOTOGRAPH OF A CERTAIN YELLOW-HAIRED ENTREPRENEUR WHO PEERS QUIZZICALLY AT THE VIEWER SURROUNDED BY AN AURA

OF GOLDEN LIGHT. IN THE GAME: ALL THINGS TRUMP, THIS PORTRAIT OF TRUMP HAS PRIDE OF PLACE, ALONG WITH A THREE DIMENSIONAL, ELEVEN-FOOT SIGN FROM TRUMP'S TAJ MAHAL CASINO LOUNGE THAT IS COMPOSED OF THE WORD "EGO."

THIS IS SERRANO'S FIRST NON-PHOTOGRAPHIC PROJECT. HOWEVER, ALTHOUGH IT DIFFERS IN FORMAT FROM PREVIOUS UNDERTAKINGS, IT EXHIBITS THE INDEXICAL IMPULSE FOUND IN ALL HIS WORK. SERRANO'S PREVIOUS PHOTOGRAPHIC SERIES HAVE EXPLORED SUCH THEMES AS THE DEAD ("THE MORGUE"), BODY FLUIDS AND INSTRUMENTS OF TORTURE AND HAVE PRESENTED PORTRAITS OF SUCH DIVERSE GROUPS AS KLANSMEN, HOMELESS PEOPLE AND THE CATHOLIC CLERGY.

IN ALL THESE BODIES OF WORK, INDIVIDUAL IMAGES ARE PIECES OF A LARGER MOSAIC THAT BUILDS TO A MEDITATION ON ETERNAL THEMES. SERRANO'S WORK HAS ALWAYS GRAPPLED WITH THE COMPLEXITIES OF SEX, POWER, RELIGION AND MYTHOLOGY AND THE WAY THAT THESE INTERSECT. WITH THE GAME: ALL THINGS TRUMP, ALL OF THESE MOTIFS COME TOGETHER IN THE FIGURE OF DONALD TRUMP.

THE GAME: ALL THINGS TRUMP SHARES THE ARCHIVAL IMPULSE THAT CHARACTERIZES SUCH MASSIVE PROJECTS AS GERHARD RICHTER'S "ATLAS", HANNE DARBOVEN'S "CULTURAL HISTORY 1880–1983" AND THOMAS HIRSCHHORN'S MONUMENTS TO HIS FAVORITE PHILOSOPHERS.

IT ALSO REFLECTS THE CURATORIAL TENDENCY TO MINGLE ART AND ARTIFACT THAT INCREASINGLY DOMINATES SUCH MEGA-SHOWS AS DOCUMENTA AND THE VENICE BIENNALE. LIKE SUCH COMPENDIUMS OF DIVERSE MATERIALS, THE GAME: ALL THINGS TRUMP PRESENTS AN OPEN-ENDED COLLECTION WHOSE MEANINGS WILL BE AS VARIOUS AS THE VISITORS WHO ENCOUNTER IT.

AN EVEN MORE CLOSELY RELATED ART PROJECT IS CATHERINE OPIE'S "700 NIMES ROAD." THAT WORK IS A PHOTOGRAPHIC ESSAY DOCUMENTING THE HOME AND BELONGINGS OF SCREEN LEGEND ELIZABETH TAYLOR. TAKEN WITH TAYLOR'S PERMISSION DURING HER LAST YEAR OF LIFE, THIS COLLECTION OF IMAGES ALSO BUILDS A PORTRAIT THROUGH THINGS. ALTHOUGH

SERRANO'S PORTRAYAL OF DONALD TRUMP IS NOT OFFICIALLY SANCTIONED, IT SHARES WITH OPIE'S PROJECT AN ACKNOWLEDGEMENT OF THE EXTENT TO WHICH A MEDIA SAVVY PUBLIC INTERPRETS PEOPLE THROUGH THEIR POSSESSIONS. PERSONAL BELONGINGS ARE CLUES THAT TANTALIZE WITH THE PROMISE OF SECRET KNOWLEDGE. FROM ANOTHER PERSPECTIVE, SUCH OBJECTS ALSO TAKE ON THE AURA OF SACRED RELICS. BECAUSE THEY ARE IMBUED WITH THE SPIRIT OF THE ABSENT OWNER, THEY GAIN A VALUE VASTLY OUT OF PROPORTION TO THEIR MATERIAL IDENTITY. TO SEE THEM, OR EVEN BETTER, TO OWN THEM, IS TO COMMUNE WITH THE GODS. COLLECTIONS LIKE THESE REMIND US THAT CELEBRITY WORSHIP HAS BECOME ONE OF THE RELIGIONS OF OUR TIME.

ON THE SIMPLEST LEVEL, THE GAME: ALL THINGS TRUMP IS A MULTIFACETED PORTRAIT OF DONALD TRUMP. AMONG THE OLDEST ITEMS IS A YEARBOOK PHOTO FROM TRUMP'S YEARS AS A FRESH-FACED CADET IN THE NEW YORK MILITARY ACADEMY. OTHER OBJECTS ATTEST TO THE CAREFUL CONSTRUCTION OF HIS PERSONAS AS MASTER BUILDER, TABLOID SEX SYMBOL, BUSINESSMAN EXTRAORDINAIRE, REALITY TV STAR, AND NOW, "LEADER OF THE FREE WORLD." A ROCK AND ROLL SOUNDTRACK GROUNDS THE COLLECTION IN THE BABY BOOMER ERA THAT PRODUCED THE MAN. WITH OBJECTS THAT GO BACK TO THE 1960S, THE GAME: ALL THINGS TRUMP UNDERSCORES HOW LONG TRUMP HAS BEEN EMBEDDED IN OUR CONSCIOUSNESS AS AN

EMBODIMENT OF A PARTICULAR INTERPRETATION OF THE AMERICAN DREAM.

THE OBJECTS HERE ALSO REMIND US THAT TRUMP REPRESENTS THE TRIUMPH OF SPECTACLE OVER SUBSTANCE IN OUR POLITICAL WORLD. THOUGH BY NO MEANS THE FIRST AMERICAN POLITICIAN TO EXPLOIT THE MECHANISMS OF MARKETING AND THE PSYCHOLOGY OF RESENTMENT, HE IS BY FAR THE MOST ACCOMPLISHED AT MANIPULATING THE SUBLIMINAL MESSAGES THAT ALLOW HIS SUPPORTERS TO SEE ONLY WHAT THEY WANT TO SEE. THE PORTRAIT OF THE MAN WHO EMERGES FROM THE ARTIFACTS COLLECTED HERE IS AN HEROIC OUTSIDER WHOSE BRILLIANCE AND BUSINESS ACUMEN HAVE ALLOWED HIM TO TROUNCE THE SMALL-MINDED ESTABLISHMENT

THAT KEEPS TRYING TO TRIP HIM UP. HE IS A MAN WHOSE MOTTO, DECLARED IN A SIGNED POSTER, IS "THE WORLD IS AGAINST ME, IT WOULDN'T BE FAIR OTHERWISE."

IF THE GAME: ALL THINGS TRUMP PROVIDES A COMPOSITE PORTRAIT OF THE MAN WHO IS NOW PRESIDENT OF THE UNITED STATES, IT IS ALSO A RORSCHACH TEST THAT TELLS US ABOUT OURSELVES. IN HIS OBSESSION WITH HIS OWN IMAGE, TRUMP PROVIDES A MIRROR FOR AMERICA'S FASCINATION WITH WEALTH, SUCCESS, GLAMOUR, POWER AND CELEBRITY. BY REFERRING IN HIS TITLE TO THE GAME, SERRANO GIVES A NOD TO ONE OF THE VARIOUS BOARD GAMES INSPIRED BY THE TRUMP PERSONA. BUT THE INSTALLATION'S NAME ALSO UNDERSCORES THE ROLE PLAYED BY COMPETITION IN

ALL ASPECTS OF AMERICAN LIFE. ECONOMICS, ENTERTAINMENT, SPORTS, AND POLITICS ARE ALL CONSTRUED AS CONTESTS IN WHICH, AS THE MOTTO OF ONE TRUMP GAME HAS IT, "IT'S NOT WHETHER YOU WIN OR LOSE, IT'S WHETHER YOU WIN."

THE SAME MIGHT BE SAID OF ART. AS A LONG-TIME PARTICIPANT IN THE CONTEMPORARY ART SCENE, SERRANO HAS HIMSELF EXPERIENCED THE FICKLENESS OF THE GATEKEEPERS OF TODAY'S ART WORLD. AND HE HAS PUNCHED BACK WITH PROVOCATIONS THAT FORCE THEM TO PAY ATTENTION. THUS, THE GAME: ALL THINGS TRUMP ALSO ACTS AS A SUBTLE CRITIQUE OF THE ART WORLD. AFTER ALL, ART IS ALSO A KIND OF SPORT. FOR ARTISTS, IT INVOLVES THE STRUGGLE TO FIND AND KEEP A PLACE IN THE RING.

FOR GALLERIES, IT IS A BATTLE TO SECURE CONTROL OVER CELEBRATED ARTISTS AND COMMITTED BUYERS. FOR COLLECTORS AND ART ADVISORS, IT IS AN ECONOMIC COMPETITION IN WHICH BETS ARE HEDGED, TRENDS ARE ANALYZED, FUTURES ARE PREDICTED AND AUCTION PRICES ARE INVOKED AS THE STANDARD BY WHICH AN ARTWORK'S MEANING AND VALUE IS JUDGED. DESPITE HIGH-MINDED RHETORIC ABOUT ART AS A REFUGE FROM THE CRASSNESS OF DAILY LIFE, THE ART WORLD IS LITTERED WITH WINNERS AND LOSERS. THE REPUTATIONS OF ARTISTS, GALLERIES AND COLLECTIONS THEMSELVES WAX AND WANE ACCORDING TO THE INSCRUTABLE WORKINGS OF ELITE TASTE.

IN A FURTHER PARALLEL, ONE CAN SEE CONNECTIONS BETWEEN DONALD TRUMP'S IDENTIFICATION WITH THE MATERIAL EMBODIMENTS OF HIS SUCCESS AND ART COLLECTORS WHO CAREFULLY CURATE THEIR IMAGES THROUGH THE CHOICE OF THE WORKS IN THEIR COLLECTIONS. TRUMP IS WIDELY REGARDED AS A PHILISTINE BY CULTURAL LEADERS WHO DISDAIN HIS PREFERENCE FOR BURGERS OVER STEAK TARTARE, TED NUGENT OVER LUCIANO PAVAROTTI OR ROCKY OVER THE SEVENTH SEAL. HOWEVER, THOUGH TRUMP MAY PREFER TO COLLECT BRANDED POKER CHIPS AND GOLD-PLATED VODKA BOTTLES RATHER THAN BLUE CHIP PAINTINGS AND SCULPTURES, THE DIFFERENCE MAY BE MORE ONE OF DEGREE THAN OF KIND. COLLECTABLES ARE COLLECTABLES. ONE OF THE

LESSONS OF THE CAREER OF ARTIST JEFF KOONS, WHO IS CELEBRATED FOR HIS MULTI-MILLION DOLLAR RECREATIONS OF DIME STORE TCHOTCHKAS, IS THAT THE ONLY REAL DIFFERENCE BETWEEN HIGH AND LOW TASTE IS THE PRICE TAG. IN THIS SENSE, THE ART WORLD IS MERELY A MICROCOSM OF THE LARGER WORLD THAT GAVE BIRTH TO THE PHENOMENA OF TRUMP.

DESPITE THE PROTESTATIONS OF ITS DETRACTORS, TRUMP'S AMERICA IS NOT AN ABERRATION OR A MISTAKE. RATHER, IT IS THE NAKED FACE OF A WORLD THAT HAS BEEN A LONG TIME IN THE MAKING. THE GAME: ALL THINGS TRUMP SUGGESTS THAT, WILLINGLY OR NOT, THE GAME IS ON AND WE ARE ALL CAUGHT UP IN ITS PLAY.

OFFICIAL TRUMP 2020 CAMPAIGN STRAWS
SOLD UNDER THE SLOGAN “LIBERAL PAPER STRAWS DON’T WORK”,
THE LASER-ENGRAVED PLASTIC STRAWS RAISED OVER $500,000
FOR TRUMP’S RE-ELECTION CAMPAIGN

PLAYLIST OF THE GAME: ALL THINGS TRUMP EXHIBITION

1. “ONCE IN A LIFETIME.” TALKING HEADS. 4:20
2. “LONDON CALLING.” THE CLASH. 3:20
3. “UP AROUND THE BEND.” CREEDENCE CLEARWATER REVIVAL. 2:41
4. “(I CAN’T GET NO) SATISFACTION.” THE ROLLING STONES. 3:45
5. “WATCHING THE RIVER FLOW.” BOB DYLAN. 3:34
6. “FORTUNATE SON.” CREEDENCE CLEARWATER REVIVAL. 2:19
7. “SOMEBODY TO LOVE.” JEFFERSON AIRPLANE. 2:55
8. “TAKING CARE OF BUSINESS.” BACHMAN-TURNER OVERDRIVE. 4:59
9. “WE GOTTA GET OUT OF THIS PLACE.” THE ANIMALS. 3:14
10. “GIMME SHELTER.” THE ROLLING STONES. 4:31
11. “HOUND DOG.” ELVIS PRESLEY. 2:13
12. “BLUE SUEDE SHOES.” ELVIS PRESLEY. 2:01
13. “LOVE ME TWO TIMES.” THE DOORS. 3:16
14. “YOU’RE SO VAIN.” CARLY SIMON. 4:18
15. “SUBTERRANEAN HOMESICK BLUES.” BOB DYLAN. 2:17
16. “PIECE OF MY HEART.” JANIS JOPLIN. 4:13
17. “ROCK AROUND THE CLOCK.” BILL HALEY & HIS COMETS. 2:10
18. “ROLL OVER BEETHOVEN.” CHUCK BERRY. 2:22
19. “OH, PRETTY WOMAN.” ROY ORBISON. 2:57
20. “TWIST AND SHOUT.” THE BEATLES. 2:33
21. “DO WAH DIDDY DIDDY.” MANFRED MANN. 2:33
22. “BACK TO BLACK.” AMY WINEHOUSE. 4:01
23. “PURPLE HAZE.” JIMI HENDRIX. 2:51
24. “LA BAMBA.” RITCHIE VALENS. 2:06
25. “DO YOU LOVE ME.” THE CONTOURS. 2:52
26. “PATA PATA.” MIRIAM MAKEBA. 3:02
27. “BAILA ME.” GIPSY KINGS. 3:44
28. “BACK IN MY ARMS AGAIN.” THE SUPREMES. 2:53
29. “WHERE DID OUR LOVE GO.” THE SUPREMES. 2:40
30. “PUMP IT UP.” ELVIS COSTELLO & THE ATTRACTIONS. 3:18
31. “RADIO RADIO.” ELVIS COSTELLO & THE ATTRACTIONS. 3:06
32. “WE WILL ROCK YOU.” QUEEN. 2:02
33 “JAILHOUSE ROCK.” ELVIS PRESLEY. 2:28
34. “RESPECT.” ARETHA FRANKLIN. 2:26
35. “WILD NIGHT.” VAN MORRISON. 3:34
36. “THE TIMES THEY ARE A-CHANGIN’.” BOB DYLAN. 3:11
37. “YOUNG AMERICANS.” DAVID BOWIE. 3:15
38. “A HAZY SHADE OF WINTER.” SIMON & GARFUNKEL. 2:17
39. “IF YOU WANT ME TO STAY.” SLY & THE FAMILY STONE. 3:01
40. “HELP.” THE BEATLES. 2:19
41. “WAR.” EDWIN STARR. 3:50
42. “HE GOT GAME.” PUBLIC ENEMY. 4:46
43. “STUCK IN THE MIDDLE WITH YOU.” STEALER’S WHEEL. 3:24
44. “GLAD ALL OVER.” THE DAVE CLARK FIVE. 2:42
45. “DON’T LET ME BE MISUNDERSTOOD.” THE ANIMALS. 2:28
46. “SWEET DREAMS (ARE MADE OF THIS.)” EURYTHMICS. 3:37
47. “A HARD DAY’S NIGHT.” THE BEATLES. 2:33
48. “WOULDN’T IT BE NICE.” THE BEACH BOYS. 2:33
49. “ROCK BOX.” RUN-DMC. 5:30
50. “CRY ME A RIVER.” JOE COCKER. 3:58

51. "NO PARTICULAR PLACE TO GO." CHUCK BERRY. 2:41
52. " I WANT TO HOLD YOUR HAND." THE BEATLES. 2:26
53. "MO MONEY MO PROBLEMS." THE NOTORIOUS B.I.G. 4:17
54. "I GOT YOU BABE." SONNY AND CHER. 3:12
55. "SUNSHINE OF YOUR LOVE." CREAM. 4:11
56. "SHATTERED." THE ROLLING STONES. 3:47
57. "GET UP OFFA THAT THING." JAMES BROWN. 4:10
58. "JESSIE'S GIRL." RICK SPRINGFIELD. 3:13
59. "(LOVE IS LIKE A) HEAT WAVE." MARTHA REEVES & THE VANDELLAS. 2:44
60. "THE NEXT EPISODE." DR. DRE & SNOOP DOGG. 2:42
61. "SHE WAS HOT." THE ROLLING STONES. 4:41
62. "I WANNA BE YOUR LOVER." PRINCE. 3:00
63. "LA GRANGE." ZZ TOP. 3:53
64. "LET'S WORK TOGETHER." CANNED HEAT. 3:14.
65. "BAD MOON RISING." CREEDENCE CLEARWATER REVIVAL. 2:19
66. "HANGING ON THE TELEPHONE." BLONDIE. 2:33
67. "THE PASSENGER." IGGY POP. 4:43
68. "BIG PIMPIN'." JAY-Z & UGK. 4:44
69. "19TH NERVOUS BREAKDOWN." THE ROLLING STONES. 3:58
70. "BORN TO RUN." BRUCE SPRINGSTEEN. 4:30
71. "LOSING MY RELIGION." R.E.M. 4:28
72. "THE BOYS ARE BACK IN TOWN." THIN LIZZY. 4:30
73. "YOU REALLY GOT ME." THE KINKS. 2:15
74. "I FOUGHT THE LAW." THE CLASH. 2:43
75. "MAGGIE MAY." ROD STEWART. 3:42
76. "OOH LA LA." ROD STEWART. 3:35
77. "LIVIN' THING." ELECTRIC LIGHT ORCHESTRA. 3:32
78. "ON THE ROAD AGAIN." WILLIE NELSON. 2:32
79. "GO YOUR OWN WAY." FLEETWOOD MAC. 3:40
80. "SHE WORKS HARD FOR THE MONEY." DONNA SUMMER. 4:34
81. "CALIFORNIA GIRLS." THE BEACH BOYS. 2:48
82. "I WANNA BE SEDATED." RAMONES. 2:30
83. "GOING UP THE COUNTRY." CANNED HEAT. 2:51
84. "JUST WHAT I NEEDED." THE CARS. 3:44
85. "TUTTI-FRUTTI." LITTLE RICHARD. 2:21
86. "HEY YA!" OUTKAST. 3:55
87. "DELTA LADY." JOE COCKER. 2:51
88. "BACK ON THE CHAIN GANG." PRETENDERS. 3:53
89. "COME SEE ABOUT ME." THE SUPREMES. 2:44
90. "I THINK WE'RE ALONE NOW." TOMMY JAMES & THE SHONDELLS. 2:12
91. "AIN'T TOO PROUD TO BEG." THE TEMPTATIONS. 2:33
92. "ROLLING IN THE DEEP." ADELE. 3:48
93. "LIKE A PRAYER." MADONNA. 5:41
94. "RUNAROUND SUE." DION & THE BELMONTS. 2:40
95. "ROCKING ROBIN." BOBBY DAY. 2:35
96. "I CAN'T HELP MYSELF (SUGAR PIE, HONEY BUNCH.)" THE FOUR TOPS. 2:46
97. "SHE'S NOT THERE." THE ZOMBIES. 2:25
98. "OYE COMO VA." SANTANA. 4:18
99. "ROXANNE." THE POLICE. 3:11
100. "(YOUR LOVE KEEPS LIFTING ME) HIGHER AND HIGHER." JACKIE WILSON. 3:01

5 HOURS, 26 MINUTES

THE A/POLITICAL TEAM CONSISTS OF BECKY HAGHPANAH-SHIRWAN, SYLWIA SERAFINOWICZ, GEORGE CHETWODE, AND ANTHONY MARTIN.

SPECIAL THANKS GO TO THE FOUNDER OF A/POLITICAL ANDREI TRETYAKOV, STEPHEN STAPLETON, PHOENIX & DOUG EISENBERG, AND IRINA SERRANO, WITHOUT WHOM THIS WOULD NOT HAVE BEEN POSSIBLE. FURTHER THANKS GO TO JERRY SALTZ, ELEANOR HEARTNEY, NADINE JOHNSON, JOSEPH LATIMORE, DAMIEN ANGER, NATHAN BENNETT, LEERFORM, FRANCOIS BERNADI, ANDREI MOLODKIN, ZOE HUI, AND JOHN MIRELES.

FIRST PUBLISHED IN 2020 BY BOOTH-CLIBBORN EDITIONS

DESIGN: JONATHAN BARNBROOK AND ANIL AYKAN AT BARNBROOK
EDITORS: STEPHEN STAPLETON AND BECKY HAGHPANAH-SHIRWAN
EDITOR FOR BOOTH-CLIBBORN EDITIONS: MARK SUTCLIFFE
EDITORIAL ASSISTANCE: GEORGE CHETWODE
OBJECT PHOTOGRAPHER: SEAN MCCORMICK
EXHIBITION PHOTOGRAPHER: GLEB KOSORUKOV
EXHIBITION LEAD: SYLWIA SERAFINOWICZ

FRONT COVER IMAGE: RED HAT AND CROPPED TIME MAGAZINE COVER "DEAL WITH IT" AUGUST 31, 2015, SIGNED DONALD TRUMP
BACK COVER IMAGE: TRUMP JOKER PLAYING CARD

 A CATALOGUING-IN- PUBLICATION RECORD FOR THIS BOOK IS AVAILABLE FROM THE PUBLISHER.

PRINTED IN ITALY

ISBN 978-1-86154-386-8

BOOTH-CLIBBORN EDITIONS
EMAIL: INFO@BOOTH-CLIBBORN.COM
WWW.BOOTH-CLIBBORN.COM